PHILOSOPHY OF HUMAN NATURE

BY

CHU HSI

AMS PRESS
NEW YORK

THE PHILOSOPHY OF HUMAN NATURE

BY

CHU HSI

TRANSLATED FROM THE CHINESE, WITH NOTES

BY

J. PERCY BRUCE, M.A. (LOND.)

AUTHOR OF "AN INTRODUCTION TO THE PHILOSOPHY OF
CHU HSI AND THE SUNG SCHOOL"

PROBSTHAIN & CO.,
41 GREAT RUSSELL ST., LONDON, W.C.
1922

Library of Congress Cataloging in Publication Data

Chu, Hsi, 1130-1200.
    The philosophy of human nature.

    Original ed. issued as v. 10 of the Probsthain's
oriental series.
    "The work here translated forms a part of the
imperial edition of Chu Hsi's complete works...
published in ... 1713 ... The title of the present work,
which is complete in itself, is Hsing li."
    I. Title.
B128.C53H7413   1973   128'.3   73-38057
ISBN 0-404-569-13-7

Reprinted from an original copy in the collection of the
Library of the University Museum, University of Pennsylvania,
Philadelphia, Pennsylvania

From the edition of 1922, London
First AMS edition published in 1973
Manufactured in the United States of America

AMS PRESS INC.
NEW YORK, N. Y. 10003

CONTENTS

LIST OF ABBREVIATIONS USED IN THIS VOLUME

Analects   = the translation of *The Analects of Confucius* by Legge, Soothill, or by Ku Hung Ming. The figures in brackets refer to Legge's translation, vol. i of his series of *Chinese Classics*.

G.L.   = "The Great Learning", in vol. i of Legge's *Chinese Classics*.

D.M.   = "The Doctrine of the Mean", in the same volume as above.

Mencius   = vol. ii of the same series as above.

Shu Ching   = vol. iii   „   „

Odes   = vol. iv   „   „

Yi Ching   = vol. xvi of the *Sacred Books of the East*. The references to the Chinese Edition (Ch. Ed.) are to the 易 經 體 註 會 解. In the Imperial Edition the order of the text is the same as in Legge's translation.

Li Chi   = vols. xxvii and xxviii of the *Sacred Books of the East*.

Complete Works = "The Complete Works of Chu Hsi, Imperial Edition" (御 纂 朱 子 全 書).

語 類   朱 子 語 類 大 全

大 全   御 製 性 理 大 全

精 義   御 纂 性 理 精 義

學 案   宋 元 學 案

宗 傳   理 學 宗 傳

遺 書   河 南 程 氏 遺 書

外 書   河 南 程 氏 外 書

粹 言   河 南 程 氏 粹 言

PREFACE

THE work here translated forms a part of the Imperial Edition of *Chu Hsi's Complete Works* (御 纂 朱 子 全 書), compiled under the direction of the Manchu Emperor K'ang Hsi, and published in the year A.D. 1713. It is composed of selections from two earlier compilations, entitled *Chu Hsi's Conversations* (朱 子 語 類) and *Chu Hsi's Collected Writings* (朱 子 文 集). The former, as the title indicates, consists of verbatim reports of the Philosopher's lectures, which, like the discussions of the Greek Academy, assumed the form of conversations between the lecturer and his pupils. They were recorded by the more intimate of those pupils, and collated by them in various collections, some during the Philosopher's lifetime, and others soon after his death (A.D. 1230). From these the work entitled *Chu Hsi's Conversations* was later compiled, and published in A.D. 1270. The compilation entitled *Chu Hsi's Collected Writings* does not include Chu Hsi's larger works, such as his *Commentaries*, *Modern Thought*, *The Object of Learning*, etc., but only his miscellaneous writings. It consists mainly of letters to correspondents, most of them pupils, but some of them opponents, of the Philosopher. The edition now extant under this title—based upon a much earlier edition not now obtainable—was published about the year A.D. 1700, in the reign of K'ang Hsi.

The title of the present work, which is complete in itself,

is *Hsing Li* (性 理). As has been pointed out elsewhere,[1] the expression has a double application. It is used for philosophy in its broadest sense, including the investigation of all things physical and metaphysical ; and it is also used in the narrower and more specialized sense of Mental and Moral Philosophy, or the study of the constitution of man's nature. Here, as is indicated in our translation of the title, it is in the latter sense that it must be understood.

The work is arranged according to subject in seven books— Books xlii to xlviii of the *Complete Works*—and in groups of sections, these groups being chosen alternately from the two compilations above named. Each section, both from the *Conversations* and from the *Collected Writings*, stands by itself and has no connexion with those that follow or precede, except in the similarity of subject.

The companion volume referred to above includes an account of the life and works of Chu Hsi, and it is not necessary to repeat here what is there said, nor to discuss the Philosopher's system of philosophy, which is there treated at considerable length. A few words, however, are needed concerning the nature of the task here attempted, and the object in view.

With regard to the latter, it is a matter for some surprise that, while translations of the Chinese Classics into English have long been before the public, and translations of the works of other Chinese philosophers have appeared from time to time, no serious effort has hitherto been made to present to the English reader the works of Chu Hsi, the philosopher whose teachings have done more than almost any other to

---

[1] *An Introduction to the Philosophy of Chu Hsi and the Sung School*, by J. P. Bruce.

mould the thought of the Chinese race. The omission is the more noteworthy inasmuch as the Western student, in his efforts to understand the mentality of the Chinese people, finds that the Classics, valuable as they are from the point of view of their high ethical standard, are, nevertheless, somewhat heterogeneous in their contents ; and, while it is obvious that the study of those writings is one indispensable means to the attainment of his end, it must be confessed that not infrequently he sighs for some presentation of Chinese thought more systematized and compendious in its nature. Such a presentation is contained in the work of which this is a translation. On almost every page the reader will find modes of thought and expression which may be observed among all classes of the people, from peasants to literati ; and will have abundant evidence that, however unconsciously to themselves, their mental outlook has been formed in the matrix of this philosophy.

What has just been said has reference more particularly to the student of Oriental thought and the Western resident in China. My aim, however, goes further. In my *Introduction to the Philosophy of Chu Hsi and the Sung School*, I have endeavoured to show that Chu Hsi ranks, not only as one of China's master minds, but also as one of the world's great thinkers. If that be the case, his lectures and writings on such a theme as the Philosophy of Human Nature have a claim to be rendered accessible to students of philosophy and religion in general, if only with a view to comparative study ; and even apart from the subject matter, it may not be without interest to some to examine the workings of the Philosopher's mind and the method of his dialectic as they are revealed in the numerous arguments and philosophic statements contained in this work.

With regard to the nature of the translator's task, the first impression made upon the reader of the original text is the simplicity of its style, when compared with that of the Classics, or even with that of the earlier philosophers of the Sung School. This is particularly the case in the sections selected from the *Conversations*, in which we have the *ipsissima verba* of the Master as he taught and conversed with his pupils. But, while the phraseology is thus simple, it by no means follows that the thought is easy to grasp. On the contrary, the work is so full of allusions to, and quotations from, the works of other philosophers, and consists so largely of answers to arguments of which not more than isolated sentences are quoted, and to letters the tenor of which must be inferred from the answers themselves, that to follow the drift of the argument is often extremely difficult. Moreover, the Philosopher in his lectures not unnaturally assumed a knowlege in his hearers which they indeed possessed, but which to readers of a later generation is often inaccessible.

When the effort is made to transfer the thought of the writer or speaker into the English language there emerges a new set of difficulties. In works of history or poetry the translator may with perfect propriety claim a measure of freedom from strict literalness and mechanical consistency ; but in an argumentative work such as this is, if he would be faithful to his author's purpose, he must adhere closely to the text, no matter how much his literary sense may be offended ; otherwise the very point of the argument will be lost. The difficulty thus created is enhanced by the fact that the quotations from the works of other philosophers, to which reference has just been made, are in many cases repeated in different connexions, and arguments built upon them which would be confusing and bewildering unless there were exactness of expression and consistency in the rendering. And the difficulty is still further accentuated when, as is frequently the case, one part of a given passage is cited in one instance, and another in another, while in a third instance the two parts overlap, or possibly the quotation ends in the very middle of a sentence. To obtain consistency of rendering in such circumstances is almost the despair of the translator.

What is true of arguments and quotations as a whole is in large part also true of individual words. Needless to say, the content of the Chinese word in many cases does not wholly coincide with that of any one English word, and yet arguments frequently turn upon a single word ; arguments which would become unintelligible if the rendering of that word were changed with every change of aspect from which it is regarded. An obvious and easy escape from the difficulty would be to reproduce the original word, and in some exceptional instances this must of necessity be done. For example, in Chu Hsi's controversy with the Taoists the word *Tao* as used by the latter manifestly has a different connotation from that which it has as used by Chu Hsi. In other words the dispute is as to the meaning of the word itself. In such arguments to adopt, say, the rendering " Moral Law " to accord with Chu Hsi's interpretation would be to beg the question for Chu Hsi, while to adopt the rendering " Reason " to accord with the Taoist interpretation would make Chu Hsi's argument meaningless. But, apart from such exceptional

instances, unless an English equivalent is found which will
fit all connexions, the English reader will often be very much
at a loss to know what the argument is about, and might
even plead that algebraic signs would be preferable.

Subject to the limitations and restrictions indicated in
the preceding paragraphs, I have allowed myself a large
measure of liberty in the mode of expression ; and the aim,
kept steadily in view, has been, not only to represent the
thought of the original truly, but to do so in clear and readable
English.   In particular I may mention that I have fully availed
myself of this liberty in the matter of connecting particles.
In the *Conversations* especially, these particles abound with
what in English would seem monotonous redundancy.   So
long, therefore, as the sentence as a whole reproduces the
complete thought of the writer or speaker, the particles have
been translated freely, or, in some cases, not translated at all.

The reader is further reminded that the construction of
the Chinese and English languages is so different that many
words not actually occurring in the original need to be supplied
in the translation if the thought is to be completely expressed.
It has not been considered desirable to disfigure the page and
confuse the reader by indicating in all cases words so supplied.
Where words or phrases are needed, not merely to complete
the sense, but to indicate some fact implied but not expressed
in the original, the necessary supplied words are printed in
italics, or, in a few instances inserted in square brackets.
Words inserted in curved brackets are in all cases interpolations by the Chinese compiler.

It will be noted that for the adjective derived from the
noun " ether " the spelling adopted—" etherial "—is that

used by Sir Oliver Lodge in his writings in order to distinguish this word, with its somewhat technical meaning, from the more common word " ethereal ".

For my justification for the rendering of certain key-words, such as the names of the five cardinal virtues and the words *tao* (道), *li* (理), *Ch'i* (氣), etc., the reader is again referred to my *Introduction to the Philosophy of Chu Hsi and the Sung School*. The reader is also begged to suspend judgment on any rendering which may appear to be unusual until he has followed the development of the Philosopher's arguments in the body of the work itself.

In the foot-notes the source of the quotation or allusion on which any particular argument is based has been indicated wherever possible, so that the reader with a knowledge of Chinese will be in a position to acquaint himself with the statement quoted in its original setting. I have also, within the limits afforded by foot-notes, given such biographical information as is available concerning those correspondents and participators in the dialogue who are mentioned by name. Some there are whose names recur so frequently that they become familiar friends.

In the citations from the Classics I have freely availed myself of the translations of Legge, Soothill, Ku Hung Ming, and others. I have not, however, refrained from adopting my own variations of their renderings in cases where it has seemed desirable, particularly when a more literal rendering than that adopted by them is required in order to make clear the Philosopher's argument.

I cannot allow this opportunity to pass without expressing my sense of obligation to the Rev. Sun P'êng Hsiang and other

Chinese scholars for their help, given always with the utmost readiness, in the elucidation of the text and of literary historical problems related thereto.

I desire also gratefully to acknowledge my deep indebtedness to my former tutor, Professor S. W. Green, M.A., of Regent's Park College, University of London, and to my colleague, the Rev. J. C. Keyte, M.A., of the Shantung Christian University, China, for valuable criticisms and suggestions; and to express my gratitude to the latter for unstinted help in the arduous task of correcting the proofs.

Owing to difficulties entailed by war and post-war conditions there has been considerable delay in the publication of this work. That the delay has not been longer extended is largely due to generous assistance in seeing the work through the press rendered by the Rev. C. E. Wilson, B.A., of the Baptist Missionary Society, and by Mr. W. E. Cule, of the Carey Press, to whom my sincere thanks are here accorded. I take this opportunity also to express my appreciation of the courtesy and patience of the publishers through all the difficulties mentioned above—difficulties greatly enhanced by the fact of the translator's residence in China.

J. PERCY BRUCE.

TSINGCHOWFU,
SHANTUNG, CHINA.
March, 1921.

THE PHILOSOPHY OF HUMAN NATURE

BOOK I

BEING BOOK XLII OF
THE COMPLETE WORKS OF CHU HSI

―――――

THE NATURE AND THE DECREE

THE NATURE

THE NATURE IN MAN AND OTHER CREATURES

BOOK I
THE NATURE AND THE DECREE

(ELEVEN SECTIONS FROM THE "CONVERSATIONS".)

1. *Question.* In distinguishing between the four terms HEAVEN and the DECREE, the NATURE and LAW, would it be correct to say that in the term Heaven the reference is to its attribute of self-existence, that in the term Decree the reference is to its all-pervading activity and immanence in the universe, that in the term Nature the reference is to that complete substance by which all things have their life, and that in the term Law the reference is to the fact that every event and thing has each its own rule of existence ;[1] but that taking them together, HEAVEN is LAW, the DECREE is the NATURE, and the NATURE is LAW ?

Answer. Yes, but in the present day it is maintained that the term Heaven has no reference to the EMPYREAN,[2] whereas, in my view, this cannot be left out of account.

[1] There is an allusion here to a passage in the Odes ; see Legge's *Chinese Classics*, vol. iii, pt. ii, p. 541. See also p. 54 of this volume, where the passage is quoted in full.

[2] The reference is to the use of this expression in the Classics, where it frequently occurs in the title of the Supreme Ruler. It literally means " azure azure ". See *Introduction to Chu Hsi and the Sung School*, chap. xii.

2.   Law is Heaven's substance, the Decree is Law in operation, the Nature is what is received by man, and the Feelings are the Nature in operation.

3.   The Decree is like letters patent appointing a man to office, the Nature is the duty pertaining to such office, the Feelings[1] are the performance of that duty, and the Mind is the man himself.[2]

4.   The Philosopher remarked to Hou Chih : Yesterday evening it was said that the Nature consists of the processes of creation and transformation. This is not correct; creation and transformation are material processes, while Law, by which creation and transformation proceed, is immaterial.

Fei Ch'ing[3] asked : When it is said, " Perfection also is undying,"[4] is it Law or the Ether that is referred to ?

---

[1] There are two groups of feelings to which this term is applied ; the one set are known as the 七 情 (Seven Feelings), named joy, anger, sorrow, fear, love, hatred, and desire (see Giles' Dictionary).   The other set are the 四 端 (Four Terminals), occurring in Mencius, viz. solicitude, conscientiousness, courtesy (sometimes given as respectfulness), and moral insight.   The reference in this paragraph, and generally throughout the work, is to the latter group of Four Terminals, answering to the four cardinal virtues which constitute the Nature.   See Legge's *Chinese Classics*, vol. ii, pp. 78–9.

[2] That is, the Mind corresponds to the man who in the illustration is appointed to office.

[3] Surnamed Chu (朱).

[4] See *Doctrine of the Mean*, p. 285.   Legge translates this sentence, " Singleness likewise is unceasing " ; Ku Hung Ming translates it, " Moral perfection also never dies."   Legge, in his note, gives the meaning of 純 as " fine and pure ", " unmixed".   The latter word " unmixed," represents the particular kind of purity represented by 純, and, as applied to character, may be expressed by such words as " perfection " and

Answer. It is Law that is referred to, as also in the dictum, "The Decree of Heaven is what is termed the Nature."[1] The Decree of Heaven is like the command of a sovereign ; the Nature is the receiving of office from the sovereign ; and in the Ether lies, as it were, the difference between those who can, and those who cannot, discharge the duties of their office.[2]

K'o Hsüeh[3] asked : Even if you interpret the dictum, "The Decree of Heaven is what is termed the Nature," as referring only to Law, is it not the case that the moment you speak of the Decree the Ether also is implied ? For if there were no Ether how could there be men and things ? Moreover, what would there be to receive Law ?

"integrity ". Cf. *The Conduct of Life*, by Ku Hung Ming, p. 49. Note : The word *yi* (—), rightly translated " singleness " or " sincerity ", also occurs in the *Doctrine of the Mean* ; see D.M., pp. 271, 275.

[1] The first sentence in the *Doctrine of the Mean*. In Legge's translation the significance of 命 is in part lost. It is not simply that the Nature is conferred by Heaven ; it is the all-pervading immanent Will of God individuated in Man. See Legge's *Chinese Classics*, vol. i, p. 247 ; cf. Ku Hung Ming's *Conduct of Life*, p. 14.

[2] That is : the difference in the good and evil of men is due, not to differences in the Decree, or the Nature, or Law, but to differences in the material element in their constitution.

[3] Chêng K'o Hsüeh (鄭 可 學), *style* Tzǔ Shang (子 上), was left an orphan while still young. After taking his degree of Chü Jên (M.A.), he made two ineffectual attempts to obtain that of Chin Shih (D.Lit.). He first met Chu Hsi at a place called Wu I, and thenceforth became one of his most devoted disciples. With a deep sense of his own limited abilities K'o Hsüeh applied himself to hard study, and in the end surpassed the majority of his fellow-pupils in his power to assimilate the Master's teaching. While Chu Hsi was at Chang Chou, K'o Hsüeh was tutor in his family, but treated as an honoured guest rather than as a dependant. In later years the Philosopher entrusted to him some of his most important literary work. After his Master's death K'o Hsüeh became a teacher in a college at Chung Chou (忠 州). He was the author of a work entitled 春 秋 博 議.

Answer. Just so, just so ; the fact is, Tzŭ Ssŭ [1] spoke
in a comprehensive sense. The passage is specially worthy
of study.

5.   Heaven may be likened to the Emperor ; [2] the Decree
is like his handing to me letters patent ; the Nature is the
duty attached to the office which I thus receive, just as the
duty attached to the office of district police is to arrest
robbers, and the duty of the Comptroller of the Archives
is the custody of documents ; the Feelings are like the
personal attention given to these duties ; and Capacity [3]
is like the various forms of effort and achievement.   Shao
K'ang Chieh, in his preface to the *Chi Jang Chi*,[4] says :
"The Nature is the concrete expression of Moral Order ;
the Mind is the enceinte of the Nature ; the body is the
habitation of the Mind ; and the external world is the
vehicle of the body."

6.   Liu asked : Mencius says, "These things are the
Nature, but there is Heaven's Decree concerning them,"
and "These things are the Decree, but there is also the
Nature",[5] thus making the Nature and the Decree two

[1] Tzŭ Ssŭ, the grandson of Confucius, was the reputed author of the
Doctrine of the Mean ; cf. Legge's *Chinese Classics*, vol. i, Prolegomena,
pp. 36 ff.

[2] Lit. the Son of Heaven.

[3] For a detailed exposition of the word 才 see the concluding section of
Book II, pp. 152 ff.

[4] See *Introduction to Chu Hsi and the Sung School*, chap. ii.   For an
interpretation of the sentence quoted see p. 48 of this volume.

[5] See Mencius, p. 365, for the whole passage from which these quotations
are taken.   Legge's note, with a quotation from Chu Hsi, is specially
interesting.   Mencius shows that, though the appetites are the offspring
of the Nature, they must be regulated in accordance with the Decree ; and
though the cardinal virtues are the Decree, the noble man will develop his

different entities; while Tzŭ Ssŭ says, "The Decree of Heaven is what is termed the Nature," thus making the Nature and the Decree one. How do you explain this?

Answer. You must take the words in the sense in which they are used by the respective writers. What Mencius here calls the Decree includes the etherial endowment, while Tzŭ Ssŭ is speaking only of that which is imparted by Heaven.

7. I Ch'uan says: "That which Heaven imparts is the Decree; that which the creature receives is the Nature."[1] Law is one: as imparted by Heaven to the universe it is called the Decree, as received by the creature from Heaven it is called the Nature. It is the point of view from which the terms are used that differs.

8. Yung Chih asked: The other day, sir, referring to the passage, "If Virtue fails to overcome the Ether the Nature and the Decree follow the Ether; but if Virtue succeeds in overcoming the Ether, the

Nature, and not rest idly content with the thought that they are decreed. The passage is quoted here simply to show that for Mencius " the Nature " and " the Decree " were not synonymous terms, but represented distinct entities, set in antithesis to each other, and so were inconsistent with the teaching of the *Doctrine of the Mean,* which says that they are identical (D.M., p. 247; Ku Hung Ming's *Conduct of Life,* p. 14). Chu Hsi reconciles the two passages by pointing out that both terms, *hsing* and *ming,* are used in two different senses; in one case, they both refer to the essential nature as imparted by Heaven apart from the material element; in the other case, the term " Nature " refers to the whole nature of man, including both the ethical and physical elements, and the term " Decree " to the Divine appointment respecting his whole life.

[1] Cf. 二 程 遺 書 (*Literary Remains of the Brothers Ch'êng*), pt. vi, f. 9.

Nature and the Decree follow Virtue," [1] you said that the
word "Decree" is to be interpreted as "to obey
a command"; but, at that very time, I happened to read
your former reply to P'an Kung Shu, in which you argue
that the words "Decree" and "Nature" are two terms
for the same thing, reading the phrase as "the Nature and
the Decree"; [2] and that it is because of this that the

---

[1] Quoted from Chang Tsai's work, the *Chêng Mêng* (正 蒙), part vi,
entitled 誠 明, "True Intelligence"; see 大 全, book v; also 學 案,
pt. xvii, p. 39. The Ethe (氣) is the physical and psychical element
in man's nature, as distinguished from Law (理), or the ethical
principle. The question raised by Yung Chih is as to the meaning of
the word 命 (Decree) in the passage quoted. Is it a noun meaning "the
Decree" as generally used? Or is it a verb meaning "to be decreed or
determined by", i.e. "to obey"? In either case the construction is
forced. In the former case the particle 於 acquires the force of a verb, "to
follow"; in the latter case the use of *ming* as a passive verb is not common.
In the former case, however, the meaning and the use of the two words
"Nature" and "Decree" are more in accord with general usage so far as
this School, and especially Chang Tsai, are concerned. This is the interpretation adopted by Chu Hsi, and therefore in this translation. On the
other interpretation the passage would read, "If Virtue fails to overcome the Ether, the Nature is subject to the Ether; but if Virtue
succeeds in overcoming the Ether, the Nature is ruled by Virtue."
Chu Hsi, however, seems to have been inconsistent in his interpretation at different times (cf. p. 11). But, as Hsien shows (p. 9),
the meaning is not essentially different in either case. There are two
roads open to us. Either the lower nature may be made subject to the
higher, perfectly serving its uses, in which case it is, as it were, absorbed
into it, and the Nature and the Decree, or endowment of Heaven, are
wholly Virtue. Or, per contra, the higher is brought into subjection to
the lower and absorbed by it; there is no more than a capacity to
receive a material endowment imparted by Heaven. Cf. pp. 121-2 of this
volume.

[2] And so interpreting "Decree" as a noun, whereas on the other interpretation it would have the force of a passive verb, "to be decreed,"
i.e. compelled to obey.

philosopher Chang later on distinguishes the two—the Nature as Heaven's Virtue, and the Decree as Heaven's Law.[1]

Answer. And it is so, but the word "Decree" is somewhat slighter.

Hsien asked : If you regard the words "Nature" and "Decree" as two substantive words, how do you explain the particle which is combined with the terms "Ether" and "Virtue"? You will surely have to interpret it as meaning that the Nature and the Decree both "follow" the Ether, or both "follow" Virtue, as the case may be.

Answer. That is just what Hêng Ch'ü's[2] text says.

9. On being asked a question with regard to the chapter on Virtue failing to overcome the Ether, the Philosopher replied : What Chang Tzŭ says is that the Nature and the Ether both flow down from above. If, however, the Virtue in me is not adequate to overcome the etherial element, then there is no more than a capacity to receive the Ether which Heaven[3] imparts to me. But if this Virtue is adequate to overcome the etherial element, then what I receive of Heaven's endowment is wholly Virtue. If, therefore, there is "the exhaustive investigation of principles" with "the complete develop-

---

[1] The whole passage in Chang Tsai's text reads : "If Virtue fails to overcome the Ether, the Nature and the Decree follow the Ether ; but if Virtue succeeds in overcoming the Ether, the Nature and the Decree follow Virtue. If there is the exhaustive investigation of principles and the complete development of the Nature, then the Nature is Heaven's Virtue and the Decree is Heaven's Law."

[2] That is, Chang Tsai. The text referred to is the passage under discussion.

[3] Lit. "He".

ment of the Nature ",[1] what I receive [2] is wholly Heaven's Virtue, and what He bestows[3] upon me is wholly Heaven's Law. Of the etherial element the only things which cannot be changed are life and death, longevity and brevity of life ; for life and death, longevity and brevity of life, with poverty and wealth, these return to Him as the etherial element.[4]   On the other hand, the things spoken of by Mencius when he says, " Righteousness as between sovereign and minister, and Love as between father and son, these things are the Decree, but there is also the Nature ; the noble man does not say with reference to them ' They are decreed '," [5] these must all proceed from myself and not from Him.[6]

10. *Question*. In the statement, "If there is the exhaustive investigation of principles with the complete development of the Nature, then the Nature is Heaven's Virtue and the Decree is Heaven's Law,"[7] how are the words " Nature " and " Decree " to be distinguished ?

Answer. The word " Nature " refers to what is individualized, the word " Decree " to that which is all-pervading. The Decree is like water flowing, as in this

[1] These expressions are quoted by Chang Tsai from the *Yi Ching* ; see *Sacred Books of the East*, vol. xvi, p. 422.   See also Legge's *Chinese Classics*, vol. i, pp. 229, 280.

[2] That is, the Nature.

[3] That is, the Decree.

[4] That is, they return to Him as the Ether with which I was endowed, and for which I have no responsibility.

[5] Mencius, pp. 365–6.

[6] These virtues in contrast to life and death, etc., which cannot be changed by anything that we can do, are all possible of attainment and depend upon our own personal effort.

[7] Quoted from the *Chêng Mêng*, by Chang Tsai ; see above.

stream ;[1] the Nature is as if you took a bowl and filled it from the stream. A big bowl contains more ; a small bowl contains less. The water in a clean bowl will be clear, while that in a dirty bowl will be muddy.[2]

11. Hêng Ch'ü said: " Form implies the Physical Nature. He who succeeds in reversing his Physical Nature will preserve the Nature of Heaven and Earth."[3] He also said, "If Virtue fails to overcome the Ether, the Nature and the Decree follow the Ether ; but if Virtue succeeds in overcoming the Ether, the Nature and the Decree follow Virtue."[4] Again, "The Nature is Heaven's Virtue, the Decree is Heaven's Law" ;[5] for the etherial endowment of men necessarily differs in different individuals, and this not because Heaven differs, but because men themselves are differently endowed. By education the Nature and Decree may be made to follow Virtue ; without such education, the Nature and Decree remain an etherial endowment only.

Question. Formerly you interpreted the sentence, "the Nature and the Decree follow Virtue," as if it read, "The Nature follows that which is decreed by Virtue"; now, however, you would interpret it as meaning that the Nature and the Decree both are Virtue. Is it not so ?

Answer. Yes.

---

[1] Lit. " water flowing thus". The Philosopher probably was standing by a stream and pointing to it as he spoke.

[2] The " bowl " represents the physical element in man's constitution, the differences in which account for the moral differences between men.

[3] Quoted from the *Chêng Mêng*, chap. vi, " True Intelligence " ; see 大 全, book v, f. 27; or 精 義, pt. ii, f. 21 ; or 學 案, pt. xvii, f. 39. Cf. p. 88 of this volume.

[4] See p. 8, n. 1.   [5] See p. 9, n. 1.

(FOUR SECTIONS FROM THE "COLLECTED WRITINGS".)

1. The statement, "Truth in the creature is what is termed Heaven," I have already discussed in detail in my former communication. As to the contention in your letter that what I said is still not the real meaning : I may say that when I wrote I was following the idea of the passage, "To everything is given its Nature free from anything false" ; [1] and showed from this that the Decree of Heaven is diffused throughout the whole universe, and is thus the Heaven of each individual creature. But although this is what I meant, I am bound to confess that, owing to the poverty and restriction of language, the idea was not very happily expressed. (Reply to Lin Tsê Chih.)[2]

2. *Question.* Would it be correct to say : The Decree is that which Heaven imparts to the creature, and the Nature is that which is received by the creature from Heaven ; [3] but the Nature and the Decree have each two applications : from the point of view of Law, Heaven decrees it to inhere in the creature, and therefore it is called the Decree, while the creature receives it from Heaven, and so it is called the Nature ; from the point of view of the Ether, Heaven decrees it to inhere in the creature, and therefore this too is called the Decree, and, as the creature receives the Ether from Heaven, it is also called the Nature ?

[1] *Yi Ching*, p. 299.
[2] Lin Yung Chung (林 用 中), *style* Tsê Chih, was a native of Ku T'ien (古 田). He became one of Chu Hsi's pupils at Chien An, and was singled out for special commendation by his Master as clever, careful, tireless in study, and worthy of highest esteem as a friend.
[3] Compare I Ch'uan's statement, p. 7.

Answer. The Ether cannot be called the Nature or the Decree; all you can say is that [1] the Nature and Decree exist by reason of it. Therefore, when the Nature of Heaven and Earth is spoken of, it is Law only that is referred to; when the Physical Nature is spoken of, Law and Ether are referred to in combination. But the Ether alone can never be regarded either as the Nature or the Decree. (Reply to Chêng Tzŭ Shang.)[2]

3. "Heaven in giving birth to the multitudes of the people so ordained it that inherent in every single thing there is its rule of existence."[3] This means that at the very time when a particular man[4] is born, Heaven has already decreed for him this Nature. The Nature is simply Law; it is as received by man that it is called the Nature. It is not a separate entity, without beginning and without end, which can be made into the Nature by the Decree; for, to use the illustration I have already given, the Decree is like the appointment to office by the Throne, and the Nature is like the office received by the officer, so that I Ch'uan makes it very clear when he says, "That which Heaven imparts is the Decree, and that which the creature receives is the Nature."[5] Therefore the saints and sages of old time, when they spoke of the Nature and the Decree, spoke of them in their relation to the realities of life. For example, when they tell us "to give full development to

---

[1] 但 = "it is only that".
[2] See p. 5, n. 3.
[3] See p. 52 and note.
[4] 此 民 = "this man".
[5] 學 案, pl. xv, f. 42.

our Nature ",[1] they mean that we should without any
omission perfect the principles embodied in the Three Bonds
and Five Constants,[2] such as the relationship between
sovereign and minister, father and son ; and when they bid
us "nourish our Nature ",[3] they would have us so nourish
these same ethical principles as to preserve them from
injury, and thus unite together in one unity the most subtle
principles and the most overt deeds without the slightest
omission or defect. These are not empty words. (Reply
to Ch'ên Wei Tao.)

4. The Su school say, " The sages held that *to be
conscious of* the Nature as still remaining in my Mind,
means that I still possess this Mind ; and they regarded the
possession of this Mind as the initial cause of error.[4] From
this they traced the Nature to its ultimate *source*, and,
borrowing a name, called it the Decree. Now ' Decree '
means command : the decree of a sovereign is termed a
command, the command of Heaven is termed a decree. But
the ultimate *source* of the Nature is not the Decree ; it was
simply that there was no other name to give to it, and
therefore they borrowed this." [5] I maintain that when Su

[1] Mencius, p. 348.

[2] The " Three Bonds " are those between sovereign and minister,
father and son, and husband and wife. The " Five Constants " are the
five cardinal virtues, Love, Righteousness, Reverence, Wisdom, and
Sincerity.

[3] Mencius, p. 325.

[4] Buddhism maintains that there is the one universal mind ; that what we
call mind is an illusion, the cause of sorrow and sin ; and that it is only
when we *lose this mind* that we attain to the true mind.

[5] The Su School was founded by " The Three Su's ", viz. Su Hsün,
Su Shih, and Su Chè. See *Introduction to Chu Hsi and the Sung School*,
chap. iv. This passage is quoted from Su Hsün's *Exposition of the Yi Ching*.

says that *the consciousness of* the Nature as remaining in my mind is the beginning of error, he has not grasped the truth of the Nature ; and when he says that the ultimate *source* of the Nature is not the Decree, but that the name is simply borrowed, he does not see that the Decree is a reality. It is as much as to say that without any apparent cause men inherit this root of gross error, and the sages deliberately concealed it, using a fictitious name to cover it up. What sort of reasoning is this ? The fact is : there has not been, *on the part of the Su school*, the thorough examination of the teaching of the "Great Appendix ",[1] the " Book of History ", the " Odes ", the " Doctrine of the Mean", and " Mencius ", necessary to a clear understanding of this chapter ; and so they have fallen into the erroneous teachings of the Buddhists that, before ever heaven and earth came to be, this Nature was in existence. Trying to prove that the Nature was antecedent to heaven and earth and all life, and realizing that then the term Decree would be inapplicable, they invented this explanation to avoid self-contradiction. If they really knew the true meaning of the Nature and the Decree, and still wished to maintain that the Nature was before heaven and earth and all life, they surely would have some regard to reason, and not indulge in such irrelevant talk. (From the " Criticism of the Su School Exposition of the Yi ".)[2]

[1] That is, of the *Yi Ching.*
[2] See 學 案, pt. xcix, f. 14 ff.

THE NATURE

(Eighteen Sections from the "Conversations".)

1. Moral Law is the Nature, and the Nature is Moral Law. It is true, these two are one and the same thing; but we need to understand why the term Nature is used, and why the term Moral Law is used.

2. "The Nature is Law." [1] Subjectively it is the Nature, objectively it is Law.

3. The principle of life is termed the Nature. [2]

4. The Nature consists of innumerable principles produced by Heaven.

5. The Nature consists of substantive principles; Love, Righteousness, Reverence, and Wisdom are all included in it.

6. The differences which appear in the Confucian school in their discussion of the Nature are not because the writers were not clear as to whether it is good or evil, but because the meaning of the term Nature itself was not definitely settled.

7. The sages understood the meaning of the term

[1] A dictum by Ch'eng I; see 遺 書, pt. xviii, f. 24; cf. also 學 案, pt. xv, f. 27. In the latter work the complete statement is: "The Nature is Law, what we term the moral nature" (性 即 理 也。所 謂 理 性 是 也。).

[2] This statement must not be confused with the statement of Kao Tzŭ, "Life is what is termed the Nature." The apparent agreement of Ch'êng Tzŭ with Kao Tzŭ is fully discussed in the *Introduction to Chu Hsi and the Sung School*, chap. viii. On the Nature as the law of life, compare Sir Oliver Lodge's remarks on the soul in his *Man and the Universe*, pp. 164–7.

Nature ; the divisions in the later schools[1] were simply because the word itself was not understood. The philosopher Yang[2] flounders, while the philosopher Hsün[3] is like the proverbial man who tries to scratch his leg through his boot.

8. After reading some essays by Yün and others on the Nature, the Philosopher said : In discussing the Nature it is important first of all to know what kind of entity the Nature is. (Pi Ta's record[4] adds the words : The Nature as a matter of fact is formless ; it consists of principles implanted in man's mind.) Ch'êng Tzŭ put it well when he said, " The Nature is Law."[5] Now if we regard it as Law, then surely it is without form or similitude. It is nothing but this single principle. In man Love, Righteousness, Reverence, and Wisdom are the Nature, but what form or shape have they ? They are principles only. It is because of such principles that men's manifold deeds are done. It is because of them that we are capable of solicitude, that we can be ashamed of wrong-doing, that

[1] Lit. " the hundred schools ".

[2] A philosopher whose opinions were in vogue in the time of Mencius. He was an egoist. See Legge's *Chinese Classics*, vol. ii, Prolegomena, pp. 95–102.

[3] A philosopher who maintained that the nature of man is essentially evil, in opposition to the teachings of Mencius. See Legge's *Chinese Classics*, vol. ii, Prolegomena, pp. 82–91.

[4] Pi Ta in the first instance studied under Chang Ch'ih and Lü Tsu Ch'ien, but subsequently attached himself to Chu Hsi. His surname was Wu (吳), and *style* Po Fêng (伯 豐). Through the influence of his father he was appointed to office as Magistrate at a place called Chi Shui (吉 水), but retired when Chu Hsi was disgraced. See 學 案, pt. lxix, f. 53.

[5] See 遺 書, pt. xviii, f. 24 ; cf. also 學 案, pt. xv, f. 27.

we can be courteous, and can distinguish between right
and wrong.[1] Take as an illustration the nature of drugs,
some have cooling and some heating properties. But in
the drug itself you cannot see the shape of these properties :
it is only by the result which follows upon taking the drug
that you know what its property is ; and this constitutes
its nature. It is so with Love, Righteousness, Reverence,
and Wisdom. According to Mencius these four principles
have their root in the Mind. When, for example, he speaks
of a solicitous mind, he attributes feeling to the Mind.

The Philosopher said further : Shao Yao Fu said, " The
Nature is the concrete expression of Moral Order, and the
Mind is the enceinte of the Nature." [2] This is well said,
for Moral Order in itself is without concrete expression ;
it finds it in the Nature. But if there were no Mind where
could the Nature be ? There must be Mind to receive the
Nature and carry it into operation ; for the principles
contained in the Nature are Love, Righteousness, Reverence,
and Wisdom, and they are real principles. We of the
Confucian cult regard the Nature as real. Buddhists
regard it as unreal. To define the Nature as the Mind,
as is done so frequently in these days, is incorrect. It is
essential first to understand our terms and then proceed
to definition. (Pi Ta's[3] record adds : If we point to that

---

[1] The allusion is to Mencius' doctrine of the Four Terminals ; see Legge's
Chinese Classics, vol. ii, p. 78. These are solicitude, conscientiousness,
courtesy, and moral insight—four feelings which are the outflow of the four
principles, Love, Righteousness, Reverence, and Wisdom, and by means
of which these four principles can be discerned. The whole subject is
discussed in the *Introduction to Chu Hsi and the Sung School*, chap. xi.

[2] Quoted from Shao's preface to the " Chi Jang Chi " ; see p. 6.

[3] See p. 17, n. 4.

which possesses consciousness as the Nature, we are speaking
of what is really the Mind.)   For example, there is the
Nature as implanted by the Decree of Heaven, and there is
the physical element.   If we regard the Nature, as it is
implanted by the Decree of Heaven, as having its origin
in the Mind, where will you place the Physical Nature ?
When, for example, it is said, "The natural mind is unstable, the spiritual mind is but a spark," [1] the word 'mind'
is used in both cases, but we do not say that the 'spiritual
mind' is Mind, while 'the natural mind' is not Mind.

9.   Just as in the case of the body : within are the five

---

[1] Quoted from the speech of Shun, the sage-emperor, to Yŭ, his successor,
as recorded in the "Shu Ching".   See Legge's *Chinese Classics*, vol. iii,
pt. i, p. 61.   Legge translates the passage : " The mind of man is restless,
prone to err; its affinity for the right way is small."   But this fails to bring
out the play on the word "mind" (心).   The expression 人 心 (natural
mind) is contrasted with 道 心 (spiritual mind).   Although 道 心, as
Legge says, is not a different entity from 人 心, it represents a different
condition.   Legge objects to Medhurst's translation of 人 心 as " carnal
mind ", and he is right in so far as the word " carnal " is too one-sided
in its generally accepted meaning.   The mind of man as ordained by the
Divine will is the 道 心, i.e. the mind which is in accord with and wholly
subject to 道 (Tao), Moral Law ; it is the ethically pure mind.   The
人 心 is the mind of man as affected by the physical element.   Chu Hsi
says elsewhere when consciousness is in accord with right ethical principle
we have the 道 心, and that the 人 心 easily falls into error, while the
道 心 is manifested with difficulty.   To the word 微 (*wei*), which I have
translated by the phrase " is but a spark ", he gives more than one meaning :
it is " minute ", it is also " obscure " (知 覺 從 義 理 上 去 便
是 道 心。人 心 則 危 而 易 陷。道 心 則 微 而 難 著。
. . . 道 心 惟 微 妙 亦 是 微 昧 . . . 亦 是 微 暗。);
see Chu Hsi's *Conversations* (語 類), pt. 78, ff. 31-6.

organs and six viscera,[1] and without are the four senses
of hearing, sight, taste, and smell, with the four limbs,
and all men possess them alike ; *so with the moral nature:*
within are Love, Righteousness, Reverence, and Wisdom,
and these are manifested in solicitude, conscientiousness,
respectfulness, and moral insight, and all men possess them;
so that in all relationships, such as those of father and son,
elder and younger brother, husband and wife, friend and
friend, sovereign and minister, the same moral sentiments
exist. Even in inferior creatures it is the same, except that
in their case these principles are restricted by the rigidity
of form and matter. Nevertheless, if you study their habits
you find that in some particular direction they too manifest
the same principles : they, as well as we, have the affection
of parent and child ; in their male and female there is the
relationship of husband and wife, in their differing ages
that of elder and younger brothers, in the flocking together
of those of a class that of friends, and in their leadership
that of sovereign and minister. It is because all things
are produced by Heaven and Earth, and together proceed
from the One Source, that there is this prevailing
uniformity. When the holy and wise men of the past
subjugated the inferior creatures, their treatment of each
was in accordance with its nature. In the animal and
vegetable world, for example, they invariably acted on this
principle. In their appropriation and use of nature's wealth
they recognized seasons and exercised moderation. In the
birth season of spring they refrained from killing young

---

[1] Giles gives the Five Organs (五 臟) as heart, liver, stomach, lungs,
and kidneys; and the Six Viscera (六 腑) as stomach, intestines, bladder,
gall bladder, and the two functional passages.

animals, they did not overturn nests, nor kill those that
were with young. It was not till the plants and trees had
begun to drop their leaves that the woodman entered the
hill forests with the axe. It was not till the otter had
sacrificed its fish that the forester entered the meres and
dams. It was not till the wolf had offered its prey in
sacrifice that the hunter commenced his hunting.[1] The
reason why they were able to give all things their appropriate spheres was because they first understood the original
purpose of Heaven and Earth in the production of things.

10. I Ch'uan's four words, " The Nature is Law," [2] are
not to be gainsaid ; they are really the outcome of subjective investigation. Later teachers only repeat what they
have heard from others, without examining into the constitution of their own being, and therefore err in many
directions.

11. *Question.* Ming Tao says [3] that most modern
philosophers in their discussion of the Nature maintain
that the sentence, " The law of their succession is goodness," [4] refers to the same thing as the dictum of Mencius,
" The Nature is good." [5] Does not Ming Tao here imply

[1] The whole passage is quoted, though in different order of the sentences
from the *Li Chi* ; see *Sacred Books of the East*, vol. xxvii, p. 221. The wild
beast having caught his prey has more than he can devour at once, and
therefore spreads it out on the ground all round him, watching it until he is
able to eat it. The appearance is as if it were laid out for sacrifice; hence
the expressions used.

[2] See p. 16, n. 1.

[3] See 學 案, pt. xiii, f. 29 ; 遺 書, pt. i, f. 10.

[4] A sentence in the *Yi Ching*, pp. 355–6. The two paragraphs, 24 and
25, are frequently quoted by the writers of this school, and are very
important. See p. 56 of this volume, n. 1.

[5] Mencius, p. 110.

that the original substance of the Nature cannot be defined, and that all those who expound the Nature do no more than describe its outflow; as, for example, when Mencius says, " If we look at the Feelings which flow from the Nature, we may know that they are constituted for the practice of what is good ? "

The philosopher nodded assent.

Subsequently, a scholar of Kiangsi² asked about the above statement by Ming Tao, and the Master replied in a letter that the saying in the "Great Appendix of the Yi", " The law of their succession is goodness," refers to the time before birth, while Mencius, in saying that the Nature is good, refers to the time after birth.

That very evening he again referred to this subject in conversation with Wên Wei,³ and said : It seems to me that what I wrote to-day was not right.

Wên Wei said : Is it not that, when the " Yi " speaks of their succession being goodness, it speaks of the flowing movement of Heaven's Moral Order, and that Mencius, in

¹ Mencius, p. 278. The " Feelings " are the Four Terminals, referred to on p. 18 (see note), which flow from the four principles constituting the Nature, and therefore furnish the ground on which is based the doctrine that the Nature is good. The nature of the source is inferred from the nature of the stream. The questioner here quotes the passage simply as describing the outflow of the Nature, and so explaining the point of similarity between the two sayings quoted by Ming Tao. Note, Legge takes the subject of the last clause to be " the Nature ", Chu Hsi takes it to be " the Feelings ", see p. 234 ; the meaning is the same in both cases.

² A man named Ch'ên Yüan from Kiangsi studied under Chu Hsi (see 學 案, pt. xciii, f. 1).

³ A pupil of Chu Hsi at Shao Hsing. His full name was Hsü Wên Wei. He held office at T'ung Chou, but owing to false accusations made against him he went into retirement. After about six years, however, the Throne recognizing his integrity appointed him to a secretariat.

saying that the Nature is good, speaks of the outflow of man's Nature. The "Yi" and Mencius each speak of a "flow", the one referring to Heaven, the other referring to man, and Ming Tao uses the one to illustrate the other. Thus it is not, as you, sir, said, the distinction between the time before and the time after birth.

The Philosopher replied : You are quite right.

12. The Nature of man is universally good. Even Chieh and Chou,[1] who exhausted the possibilities of violence and went to the utmost extreme of wickedness, still knew that their actions were evil. But, *though my Nature is good*, when I would act in accordance with it I fail, and find that it has been made captive by human desire.

13. The Master asked the question : How does the Nature come to be "the concrete expression of Moral Order ? "

Ch'un [2] replied : Moral Order is a principle inherent in the Nature.

The Master said : The term Moral Order is used in a universal sense, the term Nature is used in the individual sense. How do we know that Moral Order exists in the external world ? Simply by our experience of it here.[3] (Ti-Lu reads : By seeking it in our own persons.) Where-ever the Nature is, there is Moral Order. The Moral Order

---

[1] Chieh was Chieh Kuei (桀 癸), the last Emperor of the Hsia dynasty, and Chou was Chou Hsin (紂 辛), the last Emperor of the Yin dynasty. Both were notorious for their almost inconceivable tyranny and lust. The one was overthrown by T'ang and the other by Wu.

[2] Probably Ch'ên An Ch'ing ; see p. 195, n. 2.

[3] Here the Philosopher pointed to his breast.

is Law as we find it in the external world ; the Nature is Law as we find it in ourselves. But the laws which we find in the external world are all comprehended in this Law which is in myself. The Nature is the framework of the Moral Order.

14. Chi Sui, following the teaching of his school,[1] said: You cannot speak of the Nature as being good in the moral sense, for ultimate goodness has no opposite, whereas the moment you say that a thing is good you are contrasting it with evil, and when you speak of it as being good or evil you are speaking of what is not the original Nature. The original Nature is from above, so honourable as to be above comparison. Good as the correlative of evil is from beneath. The moment you say it is good you contrast it with evil, and then you are speaking of what is not the original Nature. When Mencius said, " The Nature is good," he was not speaking of moral goodness, but simply using the language of admiration, as if to say, " What an excellent thing the Nature is ! " just as Buddha exclaimed " Excellent ! " with reference to " the Path ". (This is the theory of Wên Ting.)[2]

---

[1] Chi Sui was the third son of Hu Wu Fêng (see p. 25), and grandson of Hu An Kuo, the founder of the Hu School of Philosophy (see *Introduction to Chu Hsi and the Sung School*). Hu Chi Sui was Chu Hsi's contemporary and the chief representative of the Hu school in his day. He studied under Chang Ch'ih (*style* Nan Hsien), whose daughter he married, and who had himself studied under Hu Wu Fêng, the father of Chi Sui. See 學 案, pt. xlii, f. 21 ; pt. lxxi, f. 1.

[2] Hu An Kuo (胡 安 國), canonized as Wên Ting, was the founder of the Hu School, and grandfather of Hu Chi Sui. His teachings are recorded in two important works 胡 氏 遺 書 and 胡 氏 文 集. See 學 案, pt. xxxiv, f. 12 ; 宗 傳, pt. xvi, f. 15.

In criticizing this statement I said: The original Nature, it is true, is the all-comprehensive perfect goodness apart from any comparison with evil. This is what is imparted to me by Heaven. But the practice of it rests with man, and then it is that you have evil in addition to good. Conduct in accord with this original Nature is good. Conduct out of accord with it is evil. How can it be said that the good is not the original Nature? It is in man's conduct that the distinction arises, but the good conduct is the outcome of the original Nature. If, as Wên Ting says, there is both an absolute and a relative goodness, then there are two natures. Now the Nature which is received from Heaven, and the Nature from which good conduct proceeds, are essentially one; but the moment the good appears, there immediately appears with it the not-good, so that necessarily you speak of good and evil in contrast. It is not that there is an antecedent evil waiting for the goodness to appear with which it is to be contrasted, but that by wrong actions we fall into evil. The doctrine taught by Wên Ting was adopted by his descendants; and from the time of Chih T'ang [1] and Wu Fêng [2] it diverged still further from the truth, and ended in the development of the doctrine

[1] Hu Yin (胡 寅), *style* Chih T'ang, was a nephew of Hu An Kuo. Chih T'ang studied under Yang Kuei Shan, and held high office in the state. He died when Chu Hsi was 21 years old.

[2] Hu Hung (胡 宏), *style* Wu Fêng, was cousin to the above, being the son of Hu An Kuo. He also studied under Yang Kuei Shan, and in turn was the teacher of Chang Nan Hsien, a friend of Chu Hsi's. He was the author of the *Words of Wisdom* (知 言, see p. 28, n. 3), so often quoted and criticized in this work. Like his cousin Chih T'ang, Wu Fêng stood high in the confidence of the Emperor and filled prominent positions at the Court.

of two natures, the original Nature and that in which good
and evil are contrasted. They only speak, however, of
one, the original Nature, contending that that in which
good is contrasted with evil is not the Nature. How can
such a theory hold? Wên Ting obtained his idea in the
first instance from Kuei Shan,[1] and Kuei Shan obtained it
from Ch'ang Tsung of Tung Lin.[2] Tsung had formerly
been a neighbour of Kuei Shan's, and thus they had had
friendly intercourse together. Subsequently Tsung went
to live at Tung Lin in the Lu Mountains, where Kuei Shan
visited him on his way to the capital. Tsung was an able
man and deeply read in Buddhist literature, besides being
a man of high moral principle. Kuei Shan asked him
whether Mencius' doctrine, "The Nature is good," was
correct. Tsung answered that it was. Again, Kuei Shan
asked, "How can the Nature be defined in terms of good
and evil?" Tsung replied, "The original Nature is not
contrasted with evil." The saying which was thus
originated by him was handed down from one to another.
But Tsung's statement in itself was not incorrect, because
it is true that originally the Nature was without evil. The
error began with Wên Ting, who asserted that the dictum,

---

[1] Yang Shih (楊 時), *style* Kuei Shan, was a philosopher of Fuhkien,
and born five years after the birth of Chu Hsi. He studied under both
Ch'êng Hao and Ch'êng I. Most of his life was spent in Honan, their
native province. See *Introduction to Chu Hsi and the Sung School*,
chap. iv.

[2] Tung Lin (Eastern Forest), in the Lu Mountains, is in Kiang Si. Yang
Kuei Shan established a school at Ch'ang Chou (常 州) in Fuhkien, which
was called the Tung Lin College (東 林 書 院). The School in
Ch'ang Chou was rebuilt by Ku Hsien Ch'êng (顧 憲 成) in the reign of
Wan Li (Ming dynasty).

" The Nature is good," was the language of admiration. Later, Chih T'ang and Wu Fêng followed by making a distinction between the two " goods ", maintaining that that of which good is predicated is not the Nature. But if that of which good is predicated is not the original Nature, where will you get your " good " from ? Since, as is admitted, the words in the dictum are used in admiration of the Nature, it follows that it is the Nature. (Hsien's record reads : it follows that the Nature is good.) [1] If the Nature were not good, how could it inspire admiration— just as Buddha, when in admiration he exclaims " Excellent ! Excellent ! " implies that the Path is good and so calls forth his admiration. The two Sus [2] in their discussion of the Nature fall into the same error as the Hus. Their contention is that Mencius' assertion that the Nature is good is as if he said fire can cook, while Hsün Ch'ing's [3] assertion that the Nature is evil is as if he said fire burns. Kuei Shan turns this statement, and criticizes it by saying : " The reason why fire can cook is because it burns. If otherwise, how could there be any cooking ? " The Sus in their discussions concerning the Nature say : " From the times of the ancient sages until Confucius, the only way in which the Nature was interpreted was as ' Singleness ', [4]

[1] Hsien's record is probably the correct one ; the sense of the text is otherwise not complete.

[2] Su Shih (or Su Tung P'o) and Su Chè. See *Introduction to Chu Hsi and the Sung School*, chap. iv ; also p. 14 of this volume.

[3] Hsün Ch'ing (the Minister Hsün) was the famous philosopher who asserted that the Nature is evil in direct opposition to Mencius. He lived in the third century B.C.

[4] See D.M., pp. 271, 275. The word — literally means " one ", and is translated by Legge as " singleness ". In his note on p. 271 Legge quotes

and then the idea of the 'Mean'[1] was introduced; but
the question whether it was good or evil had not as yet
been raised. When Mencius, however, said, 'The Nature
is good', the ideas of 'Singleness' and the 'Mean' sank
into the background." All this is beside the mark. The
authors of such arguments simply content themselves with
plausible statements, without regard to underlying
principles. The Hus, too, represented at the present time
by Chi Sui,[2] show the same tendency.

15. On the occasion of a remark in praise of the " Chih
Yen ",[3] made by one who was discussing the Hu Hsiang
School,[4] the Philosopher said : The " Chih Yen "
admittedly has its good points, but it also contains serious
errors. For example, it says that the distinction between
good and evil, or between right and wrong, has no real

Ying Ta's translation of the passage in which the word occurs, in which he
translates ━ as " one ", meaning one method of practising the five duties
referred to. Legge, however, is not satisfied with this, and adopts
Chu Hsi's interpretation of the word ━ as meaning " sincerity ", which is
doubtless the meaning here. I have retained Legge's rendering of " singleness " to distinguish from 誠 , the regular word for " sincerity ", which
occurs so often in this work.

[1] Lit. " middle ", interpreted by Legge as meaning " equilibrium "
(see D.M., p. 248); and by Ku Hung Ming as " right, true, fair and square "
(*Conduct of Life*, p. 7).

[2] See p. 24 and note.

[3] The " Chih Yen " (*Words of Wisdom*) is a treatise by Hu Wu Fêng (see
p. 25, n. 2). It is still extant, and can be referred to in the 學 案,
pt. xlii, ff. 2–12.

[4] Hu Hsiang (湖 湘) was a name by which the Hu (胡) School was
known (see 學 案, pt. lxxi, f. 2), probably taken from a district named
Hsiang T'an (湘 潭), in Hunan (湖 南), or from a river in the same
region called the Hsiang River (湘 水).

existence in the Nature. But thus to obliterate all moral distinctions is simply to fall into the " Whirling Water" heresy of Kao Tzŭ.[1] Again, it says, " The Nature consists of the faculty of liking and disliking : the noble man in his liking and disliking is actuated by Moral Law and the ignoble man by selfishness."[2] The Nature being thus defined as liking and disliking, Moral Law comes to be a thing outside the Nature. Where such principles come from I cannot understand.

Question. Does not the statement, that by investigating the continuity of the functions of sight, hearing, speech, and activity we may understand the Feelings,[3] express the same idea as that of Kao Tzŭ's assertion that " Life is what is termed the Nature "?[4]

Answer. Yes, this statement also is at fault. Again, later on it is said, " Moral Law and Righteousness are clearly manifested, but who can say that they constitute the Mind ? The seductions of the world betray us, but who can say that they are men's desires ? " Thus Moral Law and Righteousness are contrasted with the seductions of the

[1] See Mencius, p. 271. Kao Tzŭ maintained that man's nature in relation to good and evil is like whirling water ; it will take the line of least resistance, flowing east or west in whichever direction a passage may be opened for it.

[2] See 學 案, pt. xlii, f. 6.

[3] I cannot find this statement in my copy of the *Chih Yen*, but it is undoubtedly quoted from that work. The same thing is true of some others of the statements criticized. The word " Feelings " here is equivalent to the word " Nature ", and the text maintains that, the functions enumerated being the functions of life, the statement is in effect the same as Kao Tzŭ's famous dictum.

[4] Mencius, p. 272.

world ; and yet, according to this school, there is
no Moral Law or Righteousness in the Nature originally,
but the two opposites, good and evil, are subsequently
implanted in it, and thus it is possible to define the
Nature also as " not good ".   Finally it is said :
" The Nature is the mystery of the universe and of
the spirit-world : the word ' goodness ' is inadequate to
describe it, how much more the word ' evil ' ! When
Mencius says, ' The Nature is good,' he is using the
language of admiration, and not contrasting good with
evil." To say that the Nature is the mystery of the universe
and of the spirit-world is to use highflown and exaggerated
language, whereas, as I have said before, it is characteristic
of the saints and sages that they expressed themselves in
simple language. Although Mencius sometimes breaks out
in vehement terms, Confucius is always even and exact.
The theory that "good" in the dictum, "The Nature is
good," is not moral good, originated in an interview which
Kuei Shan had with the venerable Tsung, when the teaching
of Mencius on the Nature of man was discussed, and this
statement made.[1] Wên Ting [2] frequently heard Kuei Shan
quote Tsung's remark, and based his theory upon it.
But what the venerable Tsung said at that time seems to
have been that the all-comprehensive transcendent goodness is not contrasted with evil, which does not look as if he
had altogether abandoned the position that the Nature is
good.   To-day, disregarding what he said as to the all-
comprehensive transcendent goodness, they insist that his
statement that it is not contrasted with evil implies that he

[1] See pp. 25–7.   [2] See p. 24 and n. 2.

meant that Mencius' dictum is the language of admiration, and, as a result, have fallen into very serious error.

16. Mencius shows the goodness of the Nature from its manifested operations, and thus supports his statement that the Nature is good. Ch'êng Tzŭ calls it the Original and Essential Nature,[1] but also shows the original ethical principle by its manifested operations.

17. *Question.* What is meant by Hêng Ch'ü when he says " The Nature is that by reason of which we cannot but be acted upon by the external world' ? "[2]

Answer. The possession of the Nature in itself means that we are acted upon by the external world. For example, when we recognize the daily obligations of the relationship between sovereign and minister, and father and son, our minds are being acted upon externally. The same thought is expressed in the *Yi Ching* in the words, " When acted upon, it penetrates forthwith to all phenomena."[3] This sentence of Hêng Ch'ü's is parallel to his other statement : " The Decree is that by reason of which Heaven cannot but be unceasing."[4] For Law in the nature of things is

---

[1] The saying is by I Ch'uan ; see 遺 書, pt. iii, f. 4.

[2] Quoted from the *Chêng Mêng* (正 蒙). This passage is not in the 性 理 精 義. It may be found, however, in the 性 理 大 全, or in the 宋 元 學 案, pt. xviii, f. 33. Hêng Ch'ü (Chang Tsai) is alluding to a passage in the *Li Chi* ; see *Sacred Books of the East*, vol. xxviii, p. 96, also p. 38 of this volume.

[3] *Yi Ching*, p. 370.

[4] See *Chêng Mêng* (學 案, pt. xvii, f. 33), in which this sentence appears immediately preceding that quoted by the questioner. Heng Ch'ü alludes to a sentence in the *Doctrine of the Mean*, which reads : " The Decree of Heaven, how profound it is and unceasing ! " In the statement quoted by the questioner there are two ideas : the first is that the Nature is the

without cessation ; day and night, winter and summer, it
goes on without pause. Hence the saying of Confucius,
referring to the Nature : " It passes on just like this " ; [1]
and that of Ch'êng Tzŭ: " It is one with the Moral Order."
This principle, both now and from all eternity, never ceases
for a single moment day or night ; therefore it is said,
" It cannot cease."

18. Again, referring to the saying of Shao Tzŭ, " The
Nature is the concrete expression of Moral Order," [2] the
Philosopher said : Though Moral Order is present everywhere, how are we to find it ? The answer is : simply by
turning and looking within. It is wholly found within
our Nature. From the fact that we ourselves possess the
principles of Love, Righteousness, Reverence, and Wisdom,
we infer that others possess them also ; that, indeed, of the
thousands and tens of thousands of human beings, and of
all things in the universe, there are none without these
principles. Extend our investigations as far as we will,
we still find that there is nothing which does not possess
them. Shao Tzŭ states it well when he defines the Nature
as the concrete expression of Moral Order.

(Twenty-two Sections from the " Collected Writings ".)

1. *Question.* The Master I Ch'uan said: " The Nature
is Law." [3] My definition of the term Law is that it consists

seat of consciousness, and the second is the continuity of consciousness
expressed in the words " cannot but be affected ". It is in virtue of the
second idea that the sentence is said to be parallel to the one here quoted.

[1] Analects, IX, xvi (p. 86).

[2] See p. 6.

[3] See p. 16, n. 1.

of Love, Righteousness, Reverence, and Wisdom. I[1] am not sure whether I am correct or not.

Answer. These four most certainly are the fundamental principles of the Nature, but what they include is boundless. You need to think into this more closely. (Reply to Liu T'ao Chung.)[2]

2. It is said, " The word ' good ' in the expression ' The Nature is good ' is not moral good." I hold, on the contrary, that the original and essential good, and the good which in its issue is contrasted with evil are identical. But though from the point of view of the time before and the time after its emanation there is a difference—for goodness before its emanation stands alone as absolute goodness —yet the good which emanates as the relative good is still the same good. After its emanation there is intermingled with it the not-good, but that which is termed good is none the less the emanation of the original essential good. The thought is made clear in the expressions, " Before there was any action," and " After the Nature became active ", which occur in the " Ts'ung Shu ".[3] To say, in spite of these considerations, that good in the expression, "The Nature is good " is not moral good, is in my judgment self-contradictory, and can only raise doubt in the mind of the student. (Reply to Kuo Ch'ung Hui.)

[1] 炳 refers to the questioner Liu Ping.

[2] Liu Ping (*style* T'ao Chung) and his elder brother Liu Yo (劉 燿) were natives of Chien Yang (建 陽), and pupils of Chu Hsi; see 學 案, pt. lxix, ff. 5, 6.

[3] Ts'ung Shu are collections of works on a particular subject or of a particular period. There are many such collections in existence (see Appendix to Wylie's *Notes on Chinese Literature*), and it is difficult to tell which of them it is to which reference is here made.

3. " The Decree of Heaven is what is termed the Nature "[1] The possession of this Nature implies numerous principles included in it. Thus, when it is said, " The Nature is the seat of the assemblage of principles," [2] it is not meant that there is a pre-existent Nature without such principles, waiting for them to assemble within it. If we consider it in the light of I Ch'uan's dictum, " The Nature is Law," [3] we shall readily apprehend the idea. In the sentence, " The Mind moulds the virtues of the Nature and Feelings," the word " moulds " [4] means to direct their activities. Further, as to the saying quoted that filial piety is the root of virtue, I grant that, though in my opinion filial piety cannot be characterized in terms of either root or fruit, it is nevertheless one among the virtues. But suppose it to be as you say, and the virtue of filial piety to be the root, do the other virtues then become the fruit ? You say that the Nature is the root of Law, can you then say that the Nature is simply one instance of Law ? Again, you say, " The laws of the universe all have their origin and root in the Nature," in which case the laws of the universe spring from the Nature, and at the same time are outside the Nature. Hence there are two entities, the Nature and Law, not to speak of Law being the greater of the two. (Reply to Ho Shu Ching.)

---

[1] D. M., p. 247.   [2] A statement by I Ch'uan.   [3] See p. 16 and note.
[4] *Miao* (妙) originally means "wonderful' or "mysterious". Here it is used as a verb—a very rare use of the word. It must be interpreted as stated in the text, but as including the meaning of excellence and wonderfulness as to method. The passage quoted occurs in *The Sayings of Wu Fêng* (五峯先生語). See 學案, pt. xlii, f. 12. Cf. p. 176 of this volume.

4. In your letter you say, "We do not know whence comes this human desire." The question thus raised is of great importance. In my opinion what is called "human desire" is exactly the opposite of "Divine Law". You can say that human desire exists because of Divine Law, but to say that it is Divine Law is wrong. For originally there is no human desire in Divine Law. It is from the deviation in the latter's flow that human desire originates. When Ch'êng Tzŭ says, "Good and evil are both Divine Law (this statement seems very startling),[1] what he calls evil is not evil originally (as thus explained the statement is considerably altered), but it comes to be such by excess or shortcoming"[2] (this statement is an answer to the question "Whence comes human desire?"). The sentence which you quote, "Evil also must be called the Nature," is to be interpreted in this sense. (Reply to Ho Shu Ching.)

5. Sung Ch'ing[3] says, "Law is the Nature. The Nature is not to be defined as the root."[4] This is well said. (Ch'êng Tzŭ also says, "The Nature is Law," see "The Remains", Pt. 22, a.) When, however, he proceeds to draw a distinction between subjective and objective influences, then he is at fault. Tso Hsü[5] denies this, and rightly. Tso Hsü also says, "The Nature is spontaneous,

[1] The sentences in parentheses are interpolations of the Chinese compiler

[2] See 遺 書, pt. iia, f. 2.

[3] Lien Sung Ch'ing (連 嵩 卿), a pupil of Chu Hsi.

[4] The statement refers back to section 3 on p. 34.

[5] Fêng Tso Hsü (馮 作 蕭), a native of Shao Wu Hsien, and pupil of Chu Hsi, who praised his lectures to students as specially worthy of commendation. The master named his pupil's home "The Seat of Intelligence" (見 齋). See 學 案, pt. lxix, p. 41.

while Law is necessary and cannot be disobeyed or confused." This is fairly correct (there is error here also), but he goes on to say, " It is not that the existence of Law is subsequent to the Nature, but its manifestation as resulting from the Nature is necessarily subsequent to it." Now this is very erroneous, for it makes the Nature and Law two distinct entities. Again, he is right when he says, " The Nature is the assemblage of principles," but he is wrong when he defines Law as the unification of the Nature. For Law consists of the principles inherent in the Nature, and the Nature is the seat of the assemblage of those principles. Sung Ch'ing errs in making no distinction at all, while Tso Hsü errs in distinguishing overmuch, so that both are one-sided in their statements. (Reply to Fêng Tso Hsü.)

6. The doctrine that goodness as predicated of the Nature is not contrasted with evil was originally learned by Kuei Shan from the Buddhist priest Ch'ang Tsung,[1] and it must be confessed that, on the face of it, it appears to be not incorrect. While, however, you may say in reference to the goodness of the Nature that as yet there is no evil which can be affirmed as its opposite, to say that it never can have an opposite is a mistake. For the Nature is one. Since we say that it is universally good, then of course there can be no evil to be opposed to the good. That is a truism. The reason why it is termed good, however, is its opposition to evil. By the statement that the Nature is good, Divine Law is distinguished from human desire. Although these are not synchronous entities, nevertheless, whenever you

See pp. 25-7 and notes.

describe them in terms of before and after *birth*, or of altruism and selfishness, or of ethical perfection and moral obliquity, you cannot avoid their correlation as opposites. This is the reason why I cannot accept the theory that there is another good which is not contrasted with evil.[1] (Reply to Hu Kuang Chung.[2])

7.   The Master I Ch'uan said :[3] " When Heaven and Earth stored up the subtle essences, it was man who received the choicest excellence of the Five Agents. In its origin the Nature is true[4] and in repose.[5] Before its manifestation it is possessed of the five nature-principles, Love, Righteousness, Reverence, Wisdom, and Sincerity.   When bodily form is brought into existence it is acted upon by the external world and the mind[6] becomes active ; the

[1] That is : There was a time when there was no human desire, and when Divine Law alone existed, and yet that fact does not prevent our contrasting them as in the text. So with good and evil : the fact that at first good alone existed does not make it a different good from the good which later is contrasted with evil.

[2] A second cousin of Hu Wu Fêng. At the age of fifteen Kuang Chung sought the advice of Wu Fêng and became his pupil. He declined office in order to devote himself to teaching his doctrines. He had considerable controversy with Chu Hsi and also with Chang Nan Hsien. He died at the early age of 38. Selections from his writings are given in the 學 案, pt. xlii, p. 20.

[3] See 學 案, pt. xvi, f. 5.

[4] True, i.e. without intermixture of human falsity. See 近 思 錄 (*Modern Thought*), by Chu Hsi, pt. ii, f. 2.

[5] Repose, i.e. not yet affected by the external world, and therefore still.

[6] Note : the word 中, not 心, is here used. The fact that this word is used for the viscera 五 中 (cf. Giles' Dictionary, No. 2875) suggests the mind in its lower and more passionate aspect, giving rise to the seven passionate emotions (七 情, see p. 4, n. 1), by which the Nature is wounded. Contrast these with the Four Feelings (also 情) solicitude,

mind being active there issue the seven emotions, pleasure, anger, sorrow, joy, love, hate, and desire. The emotions blazing up and increasing in intensity, the Nature is wounded." [1]

I have thought over these words carefully, and their meaning seems to me not different from the teaching of the "Yo Chi". [2] The word "repose", too, refers to the time previous to the Nature's being acted upon from without, when the Mind is wholly filled by Heaven's Law, with as yet none of the deceitfulness of human desire ; from which we get the phrase, "The Nature as imparted by Heaven." [3] When it is acted upon by the external world and so becomes active, there arises the distinction between right and wrong, truth and error. But if there were no conscientiousness, respectfulness, and moral insight, which proceed from the Nature.

[1] Or " pierced ". Chu Hsi on one occasion was asked how the Nature could be " pierced ". His answer was : " The Nature, of course, cannot literally be ' pierced ', but when men do not obey its principles and give reign to their own desires, then it receives injury." See 近 思 錄, pt. ii, f. 2 ; cf. quotation from the *Li Chi* below.

[2] The " Yo Chi " or " Record of Music " is Book XVII of the " Li Chi " (*Sacred Books of the East*, vol. xxvii), of which sec. 1, par. 11, reads : 人 生 而 靜。天 之 性 也。感 於 物 而 動。性 之 欲 也。物 至 知 知。然 後 好 惡 焉。好 惡 無 節 於 內。知 誘 於 外。不 能 反 躬。天 理 滅 矣。 "At man's birth there is repose, and we have the Nature as imparted by Heaven. Acted upon by the external world activity ensues, and we have the desires incident to the Nature. As external things are presented to us knowledge is developed, and liking and disliking assume definite form. When liking and disliking are not regulated within, knowledge is led astray by external things, and thus there cannot be a proper examination of self, and Divine Law perishes ! "

[3] The phrase " The Nature as imparted by Heaven ", and those which follow, refer to the passage from the " Yo Chi " given above.

Nature, there would be nothing from which desire could spring forth, and thus we have the phrase, " Desires incident to the Nature." The expression "activity ensues" does not differ in meaning from "to spring forth" in "The Doctrine of the Mean"; [1] for right and wrong, truth and falsity of actions, depend upon whether there is "regulation" or not, whether such actions strike the due Mean or not.[2] This is the same idea as you express when you say, "It is at this very point we must distinguish between the true and the false." But in our daily affairs there needs to be ethical nurture, so that when the time comes for action we may act intelligently. If we act hastily and without self-control, delaying preparation until it is too late, then by sheer neglect we fail to keep pace with events. As to your remark, with reference to the word "repose", that "This is the word which represents the mystery of the Nature as imparted by Heaven, and not the contrasted expressions, activity and repose, truth and falsity", I am doubtful; for the Nature is all-inclusive: the laws both of activity and of repose are contained in it. If we use only the word "repose" to represent the Nature, then the definition of the term becomes one-sided and defective. When in the "Yo Chi"[3] repose is predicated of the Nature as imparted by Heaven, it simply means that before it is acted upon by the external world, and before selfish desires have sprung forth, it is wholly Heaven's Law: it is not necessary to use the word "repose" to represent the mystery of the Nature. The words "true" and "false" on the other hand are different

[1] D.M., p. 248.
[2] See the passage referred to above in the *Doctrine of the Mean.*
[3] See above.

from the words " activity " and " repose ". The Nature as
such is possessed by everything in the universe, but there
is nothing false in it. The attempt is now made to include
truth also in this negative assertion, just as Mr. Han
says, "Moral Law is neither true nor false," for which he
is ridiculed by Ming Tao. In the statement of I Ch'uan,
" In its origin it is true and in repose," there is a
fundamental difference between the words " true " and
" repose ", for the word " true " refers to the original
substance, while the word " repose " refers only to the fact
that in the beginning it has not yet been acted upon by
the external world. The Master Ming Tao says : " The
time preceding man's birth and the repose which then exists
needs no discussion. The moment you apply the term
' Nature ', what you are speaking of has already ceased to
be the Nature." [2] For the moment of repose at man's
birth is the time when the emotions have not yet sprung
forth ; but this merely shows the perfection of the Nature
as imparted by Heaven, and cannot fairly be regarded as
using the word " repose " to represent the Nature. (Reply
to Hu Kuang Chung.) [3]

    8. This section [4] was produced at the very beginning
of the discussion, in the vain expectation that at the first

----

[1] Han Shih Lang (韓 侍 郎), Vice-President (侍 郎) of one of the
Boards of Government. Ming Tao says, in answer to the statement
quoted : " If not true, then it is false ; if not false, then it is true. How
can it be neither true nor false ? Is it not manifest, and within the comprehension of the simplest intelligence, that whatever is, is true, and what
is not, is false ? " See 粹 言, pt. i, f. 3.

[2] See 遺 書, pt. i, f. 10. See also p. 97 of this volume.

[3] See above, p. 37, n. 2.

[4] Refers to the preceding section.

glance, and in a single moment, the accumulated error of years could be rectified. Its arguments still meet with opposition on the part of some. Moreover, that I should pit my one solitary discussion against the combined wisdom of all the wise men of former generations also makes me uneasy in my mind. Hence, to-day, when I read it, I find myself, even, objecting to it on many points. For example, Kuang Chung maintains that the word "repose" is the word to express the mystery of Heaven's Law, and again that the Nature is not to be described as having both truth and error, activity and repose—which is the same doctrine as the "Chih Yen"[1] asserts when it says that the goodness predicated of the Nature is good in the sense of admirable and not good in contrast to evil. The way in which I ought to have answered him is this : Good and evil, truth and error, activity and repose, the antecedent and the sequent, the former and the latter, all receive their names from their mutual opposition. Apart from its contrast with evil, good cannot be predicated of anything. Apart from its opposition to activity, repose cannot be predicated of anything. If a thing cannot be false, then neither can it be true, and there is nothing of which these things can be predicated at all. Now, if the goodness of the Nature has no real existence for us, it follows that there is no such thing as evil. And so with truth, if it does not exist there is no such thing as error. To predicate repose implies activity. Therefore, to say that neither good and evil, nor truth and error, nor activity and repose, nor indeed any relative terms can be used to define the Nature, but that

[1] See above, p. 28 and note.

transcending the relative there is another absolute good, and absolute repose, which alone can be regarded as representing the mystery of the Nature as imparted by Heaven, is surely very strange!

Not only was the reply which I made at the time inadequate, as I have shown, but there are several other statements in which there are also omissions; as, for example, when I said that the Nature is all-inclusive, and not to be defined as repose only. This is true, but the idea should rather have been expressed thus: "Though the sphere of the Nature is repose, activity and repose are alike implied in its connotation. Therefore, the 'Yo Chi' in predicating repose of the Nature[1] is right, but when Kuang Chung uses the word repose to set forth 'the mystery of the Nature as imparted by Heaven' he is wrong." Such would be an all-round statement of the position. Again, in discussing Ch'êng Tzǔ's "true and in repose" statement, I took the word "true" as referring to the original substance, and "repose" as referring to the time before it is acted upon by the external world. This also is correct, but it would have been better to have expressed it thus: "The words 'before its manifestation' in the latter part of the sentence are the explanation of the word 'repose', and 'the five nature-principles' explain the word 'true'; but Love, Righteousness, Reverence, Wisdom, and Sincerity are to be defined as implied in the expression 'before its manifestation', and are what is meant by the 'truth' of the Nature." In this way both the idea and its expression are complete. (Reply to Hu Kuang Chung's criticism of Chu Hsi's "Essay on the Nature".)

[1] See above, p. 33, n. 1.

9.   Before the etherial element exists, the Nature is already in existence. The former is transitory, the latter is eternal. Although the Nature is implanted in the midst of the Ether, the Ether is still the Ether and the Nature is still the Nature, without confusion the one with the other. As to its immanence and omnipresence in the universe, there is nothing which is without this principle, no matter how fine or coarse the etherial element may be. It is not correct to regard the more subtile part of the Ether as the Nature and the coarser part of the Nature as the Ether. (Reply to Liu Shu Wên.)

10.   It is true that the Nature cannot be without activity, but its all-comprehensiveness is not because of its necessary possession of activity. Even if there were no activity, how could there be anything lacking in its all-comprehensiveness? The fallacy of the Buddhists lies in their falsely regarding the spirit and soul [1] as the Nature, and not in their failing to recognize that the Nature is incapable of activity. If you regard them as understanding what the Nature is, you have no right to charge them with error. Seeing that you do so charge them, you have no right to appeal to their statements that the Nature is unreal. In these passages your language is not clear, as if your own apprehension of the matter were not clear either. (Reply to P'an Kung Shu.)

---

[1] In the expression 精 神, the word 精 represents the principle of sensation, and 神 the intellectual principle ; in 魂 魄, 魂 represents the higher or intellectual soul, and 魄 the lower or sentient soul. Thus the two expressions, when analysed, seem mutually to correspond, but 精 神 again, in relation to 魂 魄, is the higher element in the psychic part of man.

11. "Our Nature is originally good. It is only after it has been acted upon by external influences that it may lose its poise and fall into evil." Such passages we may verify by reference to ourselves, and need not question them. Their proof lies in the fact that we have constantly to watch and keep guard over ourselves with reference to those things in which we are acted upon in the direction of good or evil. (Reply to Wang Ch'ing Ch'ing.)

12. Ch'êng Tzŭ said, "The Nature is Law,"[1] and Shao Tzŭ said, "The Nature is the concrete expression of Moral Order."[2] These two sayings explain one another exactly, but Shu Ch'üan in his criticism would have it that one is good and the other not. In this, not only has he failed to grasp Shao Tzŭ's meaning, but I fear that he has also failed to understand thoroughly the inwardness of Ch'êng Tzŭ's language. Further, when Mr. Fang[3] says: "Moral Law is Heaven as the self-existent," and "The Nature is Heaven as imparted to and received by the universe," he is passing on the teaching inherited from the earlier Confucianists. For, as a matter of fact, although they are not two entities, yet there is a difference in the meaning of the two terms which we must not fail to observe. Moreover, later on in the same context he says, "Although it is received from Heaven, it is neither more nor less than that which makes Heaven to be Heaven, so that it has never been regarded as two entities." But with reference to his statement : "The substance of Moral

[1] See p. 16, n. 1.
[2] See p. 6, n. 4.
[3] Probably Fang Pin Wang ; see p. 43.

Law is without activity, it is man's Mind which is the seat of activity," I say that the words " Nature " and " Mind " have each a different connotation, and this assertion cannot stand. Shao Tzŭ, too, in his statement, " The Mind is the enceinte of the Nature,"[1] is near the mark, but his language and thought are somewhat abrupt. Remember that the Mind is the ruler of the personality,[2] and that the Nature is Law inherent in the Mind, and you will not go wrong. (Reply to Chiang Shu Ch'üan.)

13. *Question.* Ming Tao says : Life is what is termed the Nature. The time preceding man's birth and the repose which then exists needs no discussion.[3] The moment you apply the term " Nature ", what you are speaking of has already ceased to be the Nature. All those who expound the Nature define it simply as what is spoken of in the dictum, " The law of their succession is goodness," the same as Mencius refers to when he says, " The Nature of man is good." [4] I Ch'uan, on the other hand, says, " What Mencius speaks of as good is the original and essential Nature." [5] How do you reconcile these two statements ?

Answer. The words, " The time preceding . . . needs no discussion," refer to the Decree of Heaven in its original substance, in contrast to it as imparted to and received by man. The words, " original and essential," refer to the perfect Law received by man, in contrast to his Physical Nature. In the phrase, " The law of their succession is

---

[1] See p. 6.
[2] Or " body ".
[3] See p. 40, n. 2.
[4] 遺 書, pt. i, f. 10.   See also p. 97 of this volume.
[5] 遺 書, pt. iii, f. 4.

goodness," [1] *the idea of the word " goodness"* is not the same as that referred to in the " T'ung Shu ",[2] but is what Mencius refers to in the passage, " If we look at the feelings which flow from the Nature, we may know that they are constituted for the practice of what is good " [3]—the reference being to the Four Terminals in their ideal perfection. (Reply to Wu Po Fêng.)

14.   "Moral Law is without form or substance ; the Nature possesses spirit and the spiritual faculty." This statement has some truth in it, but the terms " spirit " and "spiritual faculty " do not mean what we speak of as the Nature.   The error of Kao Tzŭ in saying that life is what is termed the Nature, and of the modern Buddhists in saying that functional activity is the Nature, lies just here, and is one that should be carefully studied.   Mr. Fang [4] in his statement, " It is by the Nature that the universe exists," accurately expresses the meaning of Hu Tzŭ, but to quote it as explaining the words of Shao Tzŭ is not fair, and to turn round and ridicule him as not having grasped Hu Tzŭ's idea is beside the mark.   In Mr. Fang's statement that all things in the universe exist by means of the Nature, the word " Nature " refers to the Law of the whole universe. This is what is termed "The Supreme Ultimate ".   What is there that cannot exist by it ?   Vast as the universe is, it must not be forgotten that it is corporeal ; and, although

[1] *Yi Ching*, p. 356.

[2] Mencius, p. 278.

[3] The passage referred to is in chapter vii of the *T'ung Shu*, entitled " The Teacher " (師), in which the Nature is said to consist of "Strength, Weakness, Goodness, Evil, and the Mean ".   See 大 全, bk. ii.

[4] Probably Fang Pin Wang, see below, p. 48.

as compared with men and the animal creation it has priority in time, yet from the point of view of the distinction between the corporeal and incorporeal, Mr. Fang's statement is not se very erroneous, and Chang Ju is mistaken in disputing it. (Reply to Wang Chang Ju.)

15. Such is the dignity of ancient teachings that we who come after should not of course intrude upon them with our discussions. But in relation to the question whether the Nature is good or evil, we should, apart from the ancient teachings,[1] discuss the problem from other points of view, and thus, while escaping the odium of either suppressing or avoiding difficulties, we shall still arrive at the real truth of the matter.[2] The two words good and evil are the concrete expression of Divine Law and human desire respectively. Now, to say that the Nature is not human desire is quite right, but may we go on to affirm that neither is it Divine Law ? Rather than be forced to an extreme statement of the goodness of the Nature, and the contention that it is so good that it cannot be defined, how much easier and truer would be the simple assertion that the Nature is good and can be defined ! (Reply to Hu Chi Sui.)[3]

16. "The Nature is Law."[4] Sometimes it is to be

[1] 當 舍 此 , i.e. set aside the 先 訓 mentioned at the beginning of the section.

[2] There are three courses open to the modern student ; First, to criticize our predecessors, which reverence precludes. Second, to cover their faults, avoiding the questions on which we differ from them, which would be an offence against sincerity. Third, to discuss the subject without reference to their teaching at all, which escapes both undesirables.

[3] See above, p. 24 and note.

[4] A dictum by Ch'eng I ; see p. 16, n. 1

regarded as the natural outcome of all laws, at other times
as if it were a seperate entity in itself. The Master
K'ang Chieh said, "The Nature is the concrete expression
of Moral Order,"[1] and the statement seems to be to the
point. It is also said, "When there is calm, but at the
same time ignorance of what is preserved, the Nature fails
to attain to the Mean." Now, for the Nature to attain
to the Mean is as natural as for water to be cold and fire
hot ; but the Mean is disturbed because men lose their
Nature and becloud it by habits engendered by the material
element. It is not that the Nature fails to attain to the
Mean. (Reply to Fang Pin Wang.)

17. The sentence, "The Nature is the concrete expression
of Moral Order," occurs in the Preface to the "Chi Jang
Chi".[2] Its meaning is : The Nature is what men receive
substantively ; Moral Order is the natural Law of Right
which we find in the phenomena of the universe. The Law
which we find in phenomena is really inherent in the Nature,
but when we speak of it as the Moral Order, our
idea is of something which is boundless as a vast desert [3]
and diffused in infinite variety, so that its substance is
invisible, and it is only when we seek it in our own Nature
that we see what constitutes its reality—here and nowhere
else ! The passage in "The Doctrine of the Mean"—
"Conformity to the Nature is what is termed Moral
Order"[4]—expresses the same truth. (Reply to Fang Pin
Wang.)

[1] See p. 6.
[2] See p. 6, n. 4.
[3] For this simile cf. p. 297 and note.
[4] D.M., p. 247.

18. " The Nature is the concrete expression of Moral Order." [1] When we specifically call it the Moral Order we think of it as diffused in phenomena and untraceable. When we look for it in the Mind we find that here its principles assume the concrete, fixed and unchangeable.   These principles as inherent in the Mind are what we call the Nature.   Hence, Shao Tzŭ goes on to say, " The Mind is the enceinte of the Nature." [2]   If we examine into the subject in this way we shall see where the truth and error lie. (Reply to Fang Pin Wang.)

19. Your instructive essay on the Nature and the Ether is excellent. But the word "accord" in the sentence, " 'The rule of existence [3] is that by means of which man is in accord with Heaven," is, I fear, not satisfactory, because the " rule of existence " is what is received from Heaven by Man. With reference to the sentence, " Such nourish their life and are happy thereby," [4] which you quote from the " Tso Chuan ", this is what is meant by the expression " in accord with Heaven ".   In quoting the phrase, " The Plenum of the Universe," in the " Western Inscriptions ", [5] it seems to me that your addition of the

[1] See p. 6 and note.   [2] Ibid.

[3] The allusion is to the passage in the Odes, see Legge's *Chinese Classics*, vol. iv, pt. ii, p. 541 ; cf. note on p. 54 of this volume.

[4] The passage in the " Tso Chuan " teaches that those who are able to observe Heaven's law, or " rule of existence " (則), thereby nourish their life and so obtain happiness, and this is to " accord with Heaven " Huang Tao Fu's error is in putting this " law " or " rule of existence " which is Heaven's gift, in the place of its observance, which is man's work, as the cause of this accord with Heaven.

[5] The *Hsi Ming* (西 銘), a work by Chang Tsai ; see *Introduction to Chu Hsi and the Sung School,* chap. iii.   The work is included in the 精 義, pt. ii, as well as in the 大 全.

word "expand"[1] is not happy. You should rather say,
"'The Plenum of the Universe' is none other than the
Ether, and that which we receive to constitute our corporeity
is wholly this Ether." "The Pilot of the Universe"[2]
is the Mind of the Universe, in which Law is inherent.
The Five Agents are Water, Fire, Wood, Metal, and Earth;
and their nature-principles are Love, Righteousness,
Reverence, Wisdom, and Sincerity, each of which specially
belongs to one of the Five Agents.[3] In man, these nature-
principles are all complete and invariably good ; and when
men come to be affected from without, those who preserve
a harmonious relation between their nature-principles are
good, and those who fail to preserve such harmonious
relation are not good. (Reply to Huang Tao Fu.)[4]

20. I like Han Tzŭ's[5] words, "There are five principles
which constitute the Nature." Modern teachers, however,
all mix up their teaching with Taoist and Buddhist ideas,

[1] That is, how can "fullness" be "expanded" ?

[2] Also quoted from the *Hsi Ming*, see above. The whole passage reads :
"The 'Plenum' of the Universe is the substance of my being; the Pilot of
the Universe is the law of my nature" (天 地 之 塞 吾 其 體。
天 地 之 帥 吾 其 性。). Chu Hsi's comment on this passage is :
"The 'Plenum' is the Ether, so that the substance of my being is the Ether
of the Universe ; the 'Pilot' is the Ruler, the Eternal Law of the Universe,
so that my Nature is the Law of the Universe." See 精 義, pt. ii, f. 2.

[3] Love corresponds to Wood, Righteousness to Metal, Reverence to
Fire, Wisdom to Water, and Sincerity to Earth. See *Introduction to
Chu Hsi and the Sung School*, chap. vi.

[4] Huang Ch'iao Chung (樵 仲), *style* Tao Fu, was a native of Chang
Chou (漳 州) where Chu Hsi held office. He was a very religious man
and a deep student. For days at a time, after leading his family in worship,
he would sit in silent meditation. He was the author of a commentary
on the *Book of Rites*.   [5] Han Yü.

and so divergence is inevitable. Of all the philosophers, the nearest to the truth are those of our Confucian school, who teach that the Nature in its original essence is nothing else than the substance of Love, Righteousness, Reverence, and Wisdom. According to Taoism and Buddhism, the Nature was pre-existent as an empty shell from which subsequently these four principles were evolved ; or, if not pre-existent, they still maintain that the Nature in itself is but the shell which contains within it these four principles.[1] Their modern representatives, however, do not understand their own teaching, but are content with a semblance of knowledge, and therefore cannot escape from these perplexities. Further, it having been established that the four principles constitute the substance of the Nature, the doubt is next raised as to whether they are not four separate entities heaped up within. These views of the matter are all mistaken. The essential thing to note is that that which constitutes the substance of the Nature is not something apart from the four principles, nor have the four principles form or shape so that they can be picked up and handled. It is simply that within this one all-embracing Law, while not regarding them as separated one from another as if by a wall or fence, we nevertheless recognize them as having distinctive qualities. These principles, however, are difficult to explain ; so much so that even Mencius could do no more

---

[1] The four principles, according to the " modern teachers ", do not constitute the substance of the Nature, but are contained within it as distinct from the Nature, somewhat as the contents of a vessel, though contained within it, are not part of it.

than teach men to recognize them in their manifestations[1] But Mencius did not mean that their manifestations are in the original substance of the Nature, to be called forth as they are needed ; but that, their substance being invisible and intangible, they can be recognized only in their operation, which is a simple process.[2] (Reply to Lin Tê Chiu.)

21.   Mr. Chang says : " The dictum, ' The Decree of Heaven is what is termed the Nature,'[3] is simply in praise of the exalted character of the Nature.   At this stage, man has not yet received it as his own.   It is later, at the stage represented by the sentence ' Conformity to the Nature is what is termed Moral Order ', that man embodies it as his own, and then it clothes itself[4] with the principles of Love, Righteousness, Reverence, and Wisdom."   In my judgment the dictum, " The Decree of Heaven is what is termed the Nature," means that the Nature receives its name from the fact that it is the endowment of Heaven, the original source of the moral element in his constitution, and not simply in praise of its exalted character.   What need is there for man to praise its exalted character ?   Tung Tzŭ[5] said : " The Decree is the commandment of Heaven, the Nature is the substance of life."   This may be said to approach somewhat to the meaning of Tzŭ Ssŭ, and differs from Mr. Chang's

[1] That is, in the Four Terminals, see p. 4, n. 1.

[2] Compared with the direct explanation of the four principles, which the Philosopher has just said is difficult.

[3] D.M., p. 247.

[4] 入, to enter.

[5] Tung Chung Shu (董 仲 舒), a native of Kuang Chou and scholar of the second century B.C. See 歷 代 名 臣 言 行 錄, pt. ii,下 ; the sentence here quoted occurs on f. 7.

statement. Moreover, since it is called the Nature, it is manifest that it is so called because man has received it. Here, however, it is said that at a certain stage it has not yet become man's own ! So then, Heaven in producing a man does not at once confer the Nature upon him, but deposits it in a place apart, and the man must rise and take it for himself : only then does he possess it as his own ! The exponents of this view do not realize that before man has received this Nature, according to their theory, he is already a man ! What is it that enables him to breathe and eat in the world, and so to receive this Nature ? And further, how comes this Nature as a separate entity to be placed in some particular spot, so that it may be laid hold of and deposited in the body ? Love, Righteousness, Reverence, and Wisdom, inherent in the Nature, are the substance of the Nature ; but here it is said that man embodies the Nature as his own, and afterwards it clothes itself with these principles !   This means that these four principles are placed on one side, and subsequently the Nature comes in on the other side and clothes itself with them, but where the four principles are to come from before the Nature clothes itself with them we are not informed ! (Criticism of Chang Wu Kou's exposition of " The Doctrine of the Mean ".)

22. In the " Chih Yen "[1] it is said : " The Nature consists of the faculty of liking and disliking : the noble man in his liking and disliking is actuated by Moral Law, and the ignoble man by selfishness. Study this and

[1] See p. 25, n. 2.   The passage here quoted occurs in the 學 案, pt. xlii, f. 6.

we shall understand what is meant by the expressions Divine
Law and human desire." As I read this passage, it means
that in the Nature there is no distinction between good and
evil. If it be so, then within the Nature there is simply
liking and disliking, and no standard of good and evil.
Seeing that the noble man in his liking and disliking " is
actuated by Moral Law ", Moral Law is a thing outside
the Nature. And since by studying this " we shall understand what is meant by the expressions Divine Law and
human desire ", it follows that Divine Law and human
desire synchronize with each other, and there is no
distinction between them either in respect of priority or of
authority. But what, on this assumption, are the "things"
spoken of in the passage, " Heaven in giving birth to the
multitudes of the people so ordained it that inherent in
every single thing there is its rule of existence. The people
therefore hold within themselves a normal principle of good,
and consequently approve this excellent virtue ? " [1] The
philosopher Yang Kuei Shan says, " The Decree of Heaven
is what is termed the Nature, and human desire is not the

[1] The passage is quoted from the Odes, p. 541, and occurs also in Mencius,
who quotes it to support his doctrine of the goodness of the Nature. (See
Mencius, p. 279.) Legge translates it thus :—

> Heaven, in giving birth to the multitudes of the people,
> To every faculty and relationship annexed its law.
> The people possess this normal nature,
> And they (consequently) love its normal virtue.

The second line in the original is as I have translated it, as Legge shows
in his note. " But," he adds, " the ' things ' must be understood of what
belongs to the human constitution." That, no doubt, is the case in that
particular connexion ; but the poet is stating the larger truth which
covers the special application, and it is better to translate it in the more
general sense. See next page, n. 5. Cf. Faber's *Mind of Mencius*, p. 47.

Nature."[1] This statement is correct, and Hu Tzǔ is in error in contradicting it. Nan Hsien[2] says: "Liking and disliking are the Nature." This statement in itself is harmless, it is in adding the sentences which follow that the error comes in. The writer would maintain that liking and disliking are the Nature, and that they constitute the equity of Divine Law. The noble man is the man who follows his Nature, the ignoble man brings confusion into it through human desire, and loses his standard of right and wrong. I maintain that liking and disliking are inherent in the Nature, but do not constitute the Nature ; for liking and disliking are "things",[3] and to like good and dislike evil is the "rule of existence"[4] inherent in the "things". The sentence, "Inherent in every single thing there must be its rule of existence," has the same meaning as the statement, "Form and colour are the Nature as imparted by Heaven."[5] Here it is sought to define the Nature by fastening attention upon the word "thing", while the "rule of existence" is lost sight of. Such reasoning, I fear, will inevitably prove mischievous. (From the Criticism of Hu Tzǔ's "Words of Wisdom".[6])

[1] See p. 26. I cannot find the passage here quoted in any copy of Yang Kuei Shan's writings accessible to me, but the same thought is found in the 學 案, pt. lxxv, f. 6.

[2] Chang Ch'ih (張 栻), a native of Ssǔ Ch'uan, and a great friend of Chu Hsi, though holding widely different opinions. His literary name was Nan Hsien. See *Introduction to Chu Hsi and the Sung School*, chap. iv.

[3] Cf. the passage quoted from the Odes, p. 54.

[4] Ibid.

[5] Cf. p. 54, n. 1. Here is an instance of the wider application of the "larger truth". Form and colour are the Nature of material things as ordained by Heaven.

[6] 學 案, pt. xlii, ff. 4 ff.

THE NATURE IN MAN AND OTHER CREATURES.

(SEVENTEEN SECTIONS FROM THE "CONVERSATIONS".)

1. *Question.* Do the Five Agents receive the Supreme Ultimate equally ?

Answer. Yes, equally.

Question. Does man embody all the Five Agents, while other creatures receive only one ?

Answer. Other creatures also possess all the Five Agents, but receive them partially.

2. *Question.* What is your opinion of the statement that the Nature consists of Love, Righteousness, Reverence, and Wisdom ?

Answer. It corresponds to the saying "Their realization is the Nature". But preceding this are the stages represented by the statements "The alternation of the negative and positive modes" and "The law of their succession is goodness" [1] When the Moral Law of the negative and positive

---

[1] These sentences are quoted from the *Yi Ching,* pp. 355-6. The whole passage is frequently quoted and discussed by the writers of this school and those with whom they disputed. The text reads : 一 陰 一 陽 之 謂 道。繼 之 者 善 也。成 之 者 性 也。 which I have translated : "The alternation of the negative and positive modes is what is termed Moral Law. The law of their succession is goodness ; their realization is the Nature." The first sentence is literally "One *Yin* one *Yang*", which means the *Yin* and *Yang* in alternation, not "the universal *Yin* and the universal *Yang*" as rendered by De Groot (*Religion in China,* p. 10); see *Introduction to Chu Hsi and the Sung School,* chap. vi. From this alternation of the Two Modes all things come to be. Why it is called Moral Law is seen from the sentence which follows : that which causes the one to follow the other (繼 之 者) in unfailing succession and with unfailing regularity is not a physical law merely, but ethical ; it is "goodness". And the resultant of this ethical

modes alone existed, and before ever the stage of the creation of man and other beings was reached, these four principles were already present. Even the lower orders of life, such as reptiles, all possess them, but partially and not in their perfection, on account of the limitations caused by the grossness of the Ether.

3. It is true that in the life of men and other creatures the Nature with which they are endowed differs from the very beginning in the degree of its perfection. But even within the differing degrees of perfection there is the further variation in respect of clearness and translucence.

4. *Question.* In reply to a communication from Hwang Shang Po,[1] you, sir, said, "With reference to the one source of all things, Law is uniform while the Ether is diverse ; but if we look at the variety of substance in the universe, we see that the Ether approaches more nearly to uniformity while Law everywhere varies." Would the following

alternation is the Nature—" their realization is the Nature "—which therefore is itself said to be " good ". A distinction in point of time is sometimes drawn between the two last clauses ; the clause, " Their succession is goodness," referring to the time preceding man's birth. But at whatever stage of creation—even when, as the text here states, nothing existed but the Yin and the Yang—their very alternation was Tao (Moral Law) comprising the four principles which constitute man's Nature.

[1] " Shang Po " is an official title ; the writer referred to is Huang Hao (顥). As a youth he showed considerable intelligence, and took his degree early. He held office in connexion with the Revenue, the duties of which took him frequently to Kiangsi at the time when Chu Hsi was Prefect at Nan K'ang. Huang was in the habit of visiting the Philosopher and consulting with him about his own personal difficulties. There seems to have been a strong affection between the two. At the death of Chu Hsi, Huang attended the funeral at great personal risk to himself.

be a correct interpretation of this passage? The sentence, "Law is uniform while the Ether is diverse," refers to the beginning, when the Nature was first communicated to the universe. In view of the uniformity of the all-pervading operations of the Divine Decree, Law is said to be uniform. In view of the differences in the clearness and purity [1] of the Two Ethers and of the Five, the Ether is said to be diverse. The next sentence [2] refers to the period after the Nature has been received by the universe, and means that, although there is this difference in clearness, yet in the unity of its Two Ethers and of the Five the etherial element comes nearer to uniformity, while Law, because of the varying degrees of translucence and permeability in the Ether, is very decidedly diverse. "The Doctrine of the Mean" [3] refers to the beginning, when the Nature is first communicated, while the passage in the "Collected Comments" [4] refers to the period after it has been received.

Answer. The approximation to uniformity of the etherial element is exemplified in our sense of heat and cold and of hunger and repletion, in the love of life and shrinking from death, and in the instinctive seeking for what will benefit and shunning what will be prejudicial: all this is common to

[1] 純 is "pure" in the sense of being unmixed, the opposite of 駁. It may be opaque, but it will be of one colour without admixture; it is "pure" without necessarily being "clear". 清 is the opposite of 濁 "turbid", and means pure in the sense of being "clear" or "clean"; it may be opaque, too, but without any sediment. 明, again, is "clear" as the opposite of opaque, i.e. translucent.

[2] That is, "If we look at the variety of substance, etc."

[3] The reference is to the oft-quoted dictum, "The Decree of Heaven is what is termed the Nature." D.M., p. 247.

[4] By Chu Hsi, probably containing the statement to Huang Shang Po quoted by the questioner; cf. p. 63.

man with other creatures. The diversity of Law is seen in the existence among ants and bees of the relation between sovereign and minister, in which there is manifested no more than a gleam of Righteousness; or in the existence among wolves and tigers of the relation between parent and child, in which there is manifested no more than a gleam of Love; while of the other principles you can discern nothing. It is just like a mirror, in the centre of which there are one or two spots of light and the rest is all black. Of phenomena in general, it may be said that if the endowment is great in one direction, it is at the expense of some corresponding defect in another direction, as when tender-hearted men are lacking in the judicial faculty, while men in whom the judicial faculty is prominent tend to be tyrannical; for the more Love is developed the more is Righteousness obscured, and the more Righteousness is developed the more Love is obscured.

Question. Whence comes the greater timidity of women? Is it also because of inequality in the Ether?

Answer. Love in women is confined to the feeling of affection.

5. *Question.* Men and other creatures are all endowed with the Law of the Universe as their Nature, and all receive the Ether of the Universe for their Form. Granting that the differences in men are due to differing degrees in the translucence and fulness of the Ether, I am not sure whether in the case of other creatures the differences between them are because they are imperfectly endowed with Law, or whether these also are due to the opacity and cloudiness of the Ether.

Answer. It is simply that the Ether received being limited, the immaterial principle received is also correspondingly limited. For example, the physical constitution of dogs and horses being as it is, their functions are correspondingly limited in their range.

Question. Seeing that every individual creature possesses the Supreme Ultimate in its entire substance, does it not follow that Law is universally complete ?

Answer. You may call it complete or you may call it partial. As Law it cannot be other than complete, but from the point of view of the material element it is necessarily partial. Hence Lü Yü Shu [1] says, " The Nature in other creatures approximates to that of man (as when one cat nurses another's kittens : in the writings of Wên Kung [2] there is a still more remarkable story of a cat in his home), and that of man to other creatures (as in the case of lunatics)."

6. *Question.* Seeing that the physical element differs in the degree of its opacity and grossness, does the Nature as conferred by the Decree of Heaven differ in the degree of its completeness ?

Answer. No, there is no difference in the degree of its completeness. It is like the light of the sun or moon. In

---

[1] Lü Ta Lin (大 臨), *style* Yü Shu, was one of four famous students under Ch'êng I, known as the " Four Masters ". The other three were Yang Shih (p. 26 and note), Hsieh Liang Tso (p. 322 and note), and Yu Tso (游 酢). The first two are frequently referred to in this work as Kuei Shan and Shang Ts'ai respectively. Lü Yü Shu also studied under Chang Tsai. He became a profound scholar, and received the title of Doctor of the Imperial Academy. See 宗 傅, pt. xv, ff. 42–3 ; cf. also Giles' *Biog. Dict.*, p. 561.

[2] See p. 73, n. 2. The interpolations are by the Chinese compiler of the text.

open spaces it is seen in its entirety, but under a mat-shed
it is hidden and obstructed so that some of it is visible and
some not. The opacity and grossness belong to the Ether,
and result in the Nature being hidden and obstructed as if
by a mat-shed. In man, however, this obstruction is
capable of being completely penetrated by the ethical
principle ; whereas in birds and animals, though they
still possess this nature, it is nevertheless restricted
by the corporeal element, which creates an impenetrable
barrier.[1] In the case of Love, for example, in tigers and
wolves, or Sacrifice[2] in the jackal and otter, or Righteousness in bees and ants, the penetration of this ethical
principle is, as it were, not more than a chink of light.
In the monkey, whose form is similar to man's, the
intellectual faculty is superior to that of other creatures, so
that it seems only to lack the power of speech.

7. It is not the case that man, as the being possessed
of the highest intellect, stands alone in the universe. His
mind is also the mind of birds and beasts, of grass and trees.
" Man," however, " is born endowed with the MEAN, the
attribute of Heaven and Earth." [3]

[1] Cf. Bergson's *élan vital* penetrating matter, and producing vegetism,
or instinct, or human consciousness, as the case may be. See *Introduction
to Chu Hsi and the Sung School,* chap ix.

[2] Cf. p. 21 and n. 1.

[3] Man shares the faculty of intelligence with other creatures ; what
differentiates him from them is his possession of the MEAN. There is one
Ether permeating the whole universe, but man receives it in a perfect
equilibrium, with its five qualities mutually balanced. In this respect
he ranks with the dual powers. Heaven and Earth ; cf. D.M., p. 280.
The closing sentence is quoted from the writings of Yang Kuei Shan
(龜 山 文 集); see 學 案, pt. xxv, f. 11.

8. Chi submitted to the Master the following statement
with reference to a problem which had perplexed him : The
Nature in man and other creatures, it has been pointed out,
is in some respects uniform and in other respects diverse.
It is only when we know what constitutes this uniformity
and also what constitutes this diversity, that we are in a
position to discuss the Nature itself. Now, by the activity of
the Supreme Ultimate the Two Ethers assume form ; the Two
Ethers having assumed form, the myriad transformations
are produced ; and these are the source from which men
and other creatures all proceed. Herein lies what has been
pointed out as their uniformity. But the Two Ethers and
the Five Agents, by their productive and interacting
influences, cause innumerable changes and inequalities.
Herein lies what has been pointed out as their diversity.
The source of the uniformity is in Law. The source of the
diversity is in the Ether. There must be Law, for then
only can there be that which constitutes the Nature in man
and other creatures—whence the uniformity, and the
impossibility of diversity. There must be Ether, for then
only can there be that which constitutes Form in man and
other creatures, whence the diversity and the impossibility
of uniformity. Therefore in your " Dialogues on the Great
Learning " you, sir, say : " From the point of view of
Law, all things have one source and there is no difference in
dignity between man and other creatures. From the point of
view of the Ether man receives this Law in its perfection and
unimpeded, while other creatures receive it partially and
with impediment. Herein is the cause of the necessary
inequality in respect of dignity. Nevertheless, though in

the Ether there is inequality, it is the source of that life which is common to man and other creatures ; and though in Law there is uniformity, it constitutes the Nature which makes man alone to differ from other creatures. Therefore, consciousness and activity proceed from the Ether; Love and Righteousness, Reverence and Wisdom, proceed from Law. Men are capable of consciousness and activity, as also are other creatures ; but though other creatures possess Love, Righteousness, Reverence, and Wisdom in some degree, they are incapable of them in their perfection. Kao Tzŭ took account of the Ether, but lost sight of Law.   He was trammelled by the idea of uniformity and failed to recognize diversity. This is where he laid himself open to attack by Mencius." In the "Collected Comments" you also say : " In respect of the Ether, and in the spheres of consciousness and activity, man and other creatures do not appear to differ ; while in respect of Law, the endowment of Love, Righteousness, Reverence, and Wisdom is necessarily imperfect in the inferior creatures." In this latter passage, from the statement that the Ether is uniform but that Law is diverse,[1] we see that the dignity of man is unapproachably higher than that of other creatures. In the former passage, from the statement that Law is uniform but that the Ether is diverse,[2] we see the all-sufficiency of the Supreme Ultimate, and that this dignity is not any attainment of our own. Looked at in this way all difficulty disappears. When questions are raised in regard to supposed discrepancies in the "Collected Comments" and " Dialogues ", would this be a correct answer or not ?

[1] In the passage quoted from the *Collected Comments* ; cf. p. 58.
[2] In the passage quoted from the *Dialogues on the Great Learning.*

The Master's comment on this statement was : You have discussed the subject with great clearness. It happened that yesterday evening a friend was explaining this very point to me and gave a brief statement of it, but it was not equal to yours in its consecutiveness.

9. *Question*. In the relation of parent and child in tigers and wolves, of sovereign and minister in bees and ants, in the gratitude to progenitor of jackals and otters, and the faculty of discrimination in the water-fowl and dove : [1] though the ethical principle is received in one direction only, yet if we thoroughly investigate the phenomena, we find that these creatures possess this ethical principle with unerring truth. On the other hand, all men possess the Decree of Heaven in its entirety, but it is so obscured by creaturely desire and by the etherial endowment that in some particular direction they are inferior to the brute in intelligence and power of complete development. How do you explain this ?

Answer. It is only in the one direction that the brute is intelligent, and there it is concentrated, while man's intelligence is comprehensive, embracing everything in some degree, but diffused and therefore more easily obscured.

10. *Question*. How can dried and withered things also possess the Nature ?

Answer. They all possess this Law from the first moment of their existence ; therefore it is said, " In the universe there is not a single thing without the Nature." Walking up the steps the Philosopher said : The bricks of these steps have the law of bricks. Sitting down he said : A bamboo

[1] See p. 91 n. 2.

chair has the law of the bamboo chair. You may say that dried and withered things are without the Vital Impulse, but not that they are without the law of life.[1] For example, rotten wood is useless for anything except for putting in the cooking stove. It is without the Vital Impulse. And yet each kind of wood as it burns has its own fragrance, each differing from the other. It is Law which originally constituted it so.

11. *Question.* Is there Law in dried and withered things ?

Answer. As soon as the object exists there is Law inherent in it. Even in the case of a pen—though not produced by Heaven, but by man, who takes the long soft hairs of the hare and makes them into pens—as soon as the pen exists Law is inherent in it.

It was further asked : How can a pen possess Love and Righteousness ?

Answer. In small things like this there is no need for such distinctions as that between Love and Righteousness.[2]

12. *Question.* Law is received from Heaven both by men and things. But do things without feeling also possess Law ?

Answer. Most certainly they possess Law ; for example, a ship can only go on the water, while a cart can only go on land.

13. Chi T'ung[3] said : Animals cannot live in water,

[1] That is, the same law as we see in living things.

[2] Chu Hsi's meaning is that Love and Righteousness do not belong to the functions of a pen ; none the less, the pen fulfils its own proper functions according to ethical law inherent in it.

[3] Ts'ai Yüan Ting (蔡 元 定), *style* Chi T'ung, was a pupil of Chu Hsi, to whom he was junior by five years. His home was Chien Yang in Chien

and fish cannot live on land. In animals the positive ether prevails, in fish the negative ether prevails. Those which live both on land and in the water belong to the class of the tortoise and otter.

14. Things in the vegetable kingdom receive the negative ether, while those of the animal kingdom receive the positive ether. If within these two classes we classify further : then grasses receive the negative ether and trees the positive, animals the negative and birds the positive, so that animals recline in the field, while birds nest in trees. There are animals, however, which receive the positive ether, such as the ape and monkey ; and there are birds which receive the negative ether, such as the pheasant and the falcon. In the vegetable kingdom, all receive the negative ether ; and yet here also there is the positive in the negative, and the negative in the positive.

15. In winter, flowers are slow to fall, like the Narcissus, which though brittle and weak, nevertheless retains its flower a long while ; so also with the Plum Flower and the Winter Plum. In the spring, flowers fall easily, and in summer still more easily, as in the case of the Sun-flower, the Pomegranate, and the Lotus, which hardly last beyond a single day. The fact is that in winter the Ether is correct [1] and strong, and therefore the fall of the flower is more

Chou, Fuhkien. A very able scholar, he excited the admiration of Chu Hsi, who said of him, " Chi T'ung reads difficult books with ease, while others read easy books with difficulty." When visited by Chu Hsi they would share the same bedroom and discuss philosophical questions far into the night. He died in 1198, two years before the death of his teacher. See 宗 傳, pt. xvii.

[1] The word 貞 in the text = 正.

difficult. In spring and summer, the moment the strength of the plant is put forth it is put forth to the utmost, with the result that it is not enduring.

The Philosopher also said : For the most part, large flowers fall easily. So also with fruits. For example, the pear-tree decays very easily ; when nearing its end there is a sudden outburst of fruitfulness for one year, and then it dies. This is the Ether about to disrobe.

16.   The Two Ethers and Five Agents mutually interact, and pass through a myriad transformations, so that in the production of men and things there are differences in the degree of their etherial fineness. From the point of view of the Ether as one, men and other creatures all come into being by receiving this one Ether. From the point of view of the varying degrees of fineness, the Ether as received by man is perfect[1] and free from impediment ; as received by other creatures it is imperfect and impedes. Man receiving it in its perfection, the ethical principle permeates it completely and without impediment ; while in the case of other creatures, in which it is imperfect, the ethical principle is impeded and unintelligent.   Notice, too, how in man the head is round resembling the heavens, and his feet square like the earth. He is well poised and erect. He receives the Ether of the Universe in its perfection, and therefore possesses moral and intellectual faculties.   As received by other creatures the Ether of the Universe is imperfect, and therefore birds and beasts are horizontal in form, and grasses and trees have head downwards and tail upwards. Such creatures as have

[1] See p. 115, n. 2.

intelligence have it in one direction only ; for example, birds are filial, the otter sacrifices, the dog can do no more than keep guard, and the ox no more than plough. In man, on the other hand, there is nothing he cannot know, nothing he cannot do. That which constitutes the difference between man and beast, that in which man excels, is just this.

17. *Question.* Birds and beasts, as well as men, all have consciousness, though with differing degrees of penetration. Is there consciousness also in the vegetable kingdom ?

Answer. There is. As in the case of a plant : when watered it sheds forth its glory ; when pinched, it withers and droops. Can it be said to be without consciousness ? Chou Mao Shu [1] refrained from clearing away the grass from the front of his window, " because," said he, " its impulse is just like my own." [2] In this he attributed consciousness to the plant. But the consciousness of the animal creation is not on the same plane as that of man, nor is that of the vegetable kingdom on the same plane as that of the animal kingdom. Again, there is the drug rhubarb ; when taken, it acts as a purgative, while aconite has heating properties ; [3] but their consciousness is in each case in the one direction only.

On being further asked whether decayed things also have consciousness, the Philosopher replied : Yes, they too have

[1] Chou Tzŭ, the founder of the school.

[2] That is, grass seeks to live and avoids what causes death, just as I do myself. See 遺 書, pt. iii, p. 2 ; cf. p. 338 of this volume.

[3] In Chinese medicine, drugs are classed roughly into those which are heating and those which are cooling in their properties, the latter having tonic action.

consciousness, as, when burnt to ashes by fire, and then made into broth, they will be caustic and bitter.

Following on this the Philosopher smiled[1] and said : Only just now I met the gentry of Hsin Chou, who said that vegetable things do not possess the Nature, and to-night you say that vegetable things have no Mind !

(FIVE SECTIONS FROM THE "COLLECTED WRITINGS".)

1.   The Master I Ch'uan said, " The Nature is Law." [2] From ancient times no one had ventured to give utterance to such a statement as this.[3]   The Mind is consciousness in man, and that in which Law is inherent.   The Master Hêng Ch'ü also said, " From the Great Void we have the term Heaven ; from the transformations of the Ether we have the term Moral Order ; by the union of the Void with the Ether we have the term Nature ; by the union of the Nature with Consciousness we have the term Mind."[4] The terms and their distinctive meanings are profound, but the whole statement is conclusive, and not to be gainsaid. For in the production of things by Heaven, while there is no diversity in Law, material form as received by men and things varies ; hence Mind differs in the degree of its intelligence, and the Nature differs in the degree of its completeness. As to Love, of which you speak, it is the head of the Four Virtues ; it is

[1] The smile is at the fact that, in spite of all such considerations as those to which he had just given expression. men can be found who deny that all things possess the Nature.

[2] See p. 16.

[3] It is probable that there is a mistake in the punctuation of the text here. and that the point should come after 道 , making 心 the subject of the next sentence.   The translation represents the text as thus corrected.

[4] Quoted from the Chêng Mêng.   See 精 義 , pt. iii, f. 11.

not another entity outside the Nature, and parallel to it.
In Man alone, however, is the Mind perfectly spiritual,
so that he can perfect the Four Virtues and manifest them
as the Four Terminals. In the beast, the etherial element
is deflected and impure, the mind is darkened and obscured.
Hence there are directions in which it cannot attain to
completeness. Occasionally, indeed, affection between parent
and offspring and the bond between sovereign and minister
exist in some degree, and are not eclipsed ; but in the Love
that " masters self and returns to right principle ",[1] in the
Righteousness that loves good and hates evil, there are
heights which to them are impossible of attainment ; and
yet we may not say that they are without this Nature. As
to things which have life but not consciousness: here, again,
within the restriction of the corporeal element there is still
further restriction, so that Law in this class of things,
accommodating itself to the corporeal, becomes simply
the law of one single thing. Although we cannot
predicate Love, Righteousness, Reverence, and Wisdom
of such things in the same sense as of man, yet, neither
can we say that they are wholly without these nature-
principles. The meaning of this is clear enough, and there
is no difficulty in understanding it, but Fang Shu [2] is
dull and dogged, and it is not worth while to correct him
severely. Nor is it necessary to say that Tzŭ Jung [3] does
not understand either. As to the argument from the
Buddhist doctrine of knowing the spirits : it, too, is not
relevant, because the Buddhists regard Nothingness and

[1] See Analects, XII, i, 1 (p. 114).

[2] Yü Fang Shu, see p. 72.

[3] Hsü Tzŭ Jung, in criticism of whose essay this section is wri ten.

Nirvana as paramount, and therefore look upon the knowledge of spirits as a source of life and death. According
to our Confucian cult, knowledge of spirits is the mysterious
operation of the Mind : how can we do without it ? But
to use this to define the Nature is altogether irrelevant.
Again, it is said that withered things have only the Physical
Nature, and do not possess the original Nature, which is
still more absurd, for if it were really so, other
creatures would have only one Nature while men would
have two Natures. The statement is more than ordinarily
erroneous and reprehensible, proceeding as it does from
ignorance of the fact that the Physical Nature is simply the
original Nature inherent in the physical element, becoming
one Nature in union with it, which is precisely what Chou
Tzŭ refers to when he says, " Each has its own Nature."
If there were no original Nature, whence could we get this
Physical Nature? Moreover, it is not only the philosophers
Chou, Ch'êng, and Chang, who teach this, but Confucius
also says, " Their realization is the Nature," [1] and again,
" Everything obtains its correct Nature as ordained by
Heaven." [2] Where is there any distinction here between
one thing which has the Nature and another which has
not ? Mencius also speaks of " the nature of mountains ",
and " the nature of water ". Does a mountain have
consciousness, or does water ? If we thoroughly understand
such passages as these, we shall realize that there is not a
single thing in the universe which does not possess the
Nature, and that it is only when the thing itself is non-

[1] In the *Yi Ching*, p. 356.
[2] Ibid., p. 213.

existent that the Nature is non-existent. If anything could exist without the Nature it would be, as you say in your essay, the ashes of burnt wood, or the dust which man becomes when he dies. But the ashes and the dust possess the ether of ashes and dust; and if so, they possess the nature of ashes and dust. How then can dry and withered things be said not to possess the Nature? (Reply to Hsü Tzŭ Jung.)

2. In the production of things by Heaven, some possess flesh and blood together with consciousness, such as men and beasts; some are without flesh and blood, and without consciousness, having life only, such as grass and trees; in others again life has perished, and there remain only form and solidity, odour and taste, as in withered and dead matter. Although in all these we have diversity of function, the ethical principle does not differ; and yet, following the differences of function as inherent in each individual, it cannot but differ. Hence it is that man is most spiritual, and in him the Nature of the Five Constants [1] is complete, while in birds and beasts it is obscured and incomplete. And again, in grass and trees, in withered and dead matter, it disappears together with consciousness; but Law, by which each thing is what it is, is still present. As to the statement that dead materials are without life, and thus without this Law, is it possible that there can be anything in the universe which does not possess the Nature, or that Law, immanent as it is in the universe, can leave any part of it empty and not completely filled by it? (Reply to Yü Fang Shu.)

[1] That is, the Five Cardinal Virtues.

3. With regard to Ts'ai Ch'ing's statement that minute creatures, although they possess the Nature, cannot be described as having Love, Righteousness, Reverence, and Wisdom, it is true that there is nothing in which we can discern these principles in the nature of minute creatures, yet what is there to show that they do not possess them? This species has not yet been thoroughly investigated; you need to consider the subject more carefully. Again Ts'ai Ch'ing says: In the statement, "The phrase ' Conformity to the Nature ' is used simply in reference to the fact that men and other creatures should embody the Nature in conduct," the words "The phrase . . . is used" should be omitted. This also is a mistake. The Moral Order is simply the Nature in the distinctive sense of all-pervading. It is not that Moral Order comes to be such through man's conformity to the Nature.[1] (Reply to Ch'ên Ts'ai Ch'ing.)

4. If the principle has not been received, then of course it cannot be practised. That goes without saying. But the Master Hêng Ch'ü also said, "Man's Nature approximates to that of other creatures, and the Nature of other creatures approximates to that of man." Here we have another principle introduced; for example, cats nourishing one another's kittens—in "The Writings of Wên Kung"[2] the author gives an actual instance of such a cat which was

[1] Tao, or the Mora 1Order, is not conformity to the Nature, but the Nature itself as all-pervading. Conformity to the Nature is the manifestation of Moral Order.

[2] Ssï-Ma Kuang, a statesman and historian contemporary with the philosophers Ch'êng and Chang; see *Introduction to Chu Hsi and the Sung School*, chap. ii; cf also 歷 代 名 臣 言 行 錄, pt. xv *a* ff. 10–13.

specially remarkable—is a case in which the Nature with
which they are endowed approximates to, and one might
almost say surpasses, that of man, but, and this is the pity
of it, it is cramped by its physical form. (Reply to Li
Hsiao Shu.)

5. The Nature of men and other creatures is essentially
the same ; the etherial endowment, however, necessarily
differs. When Ch'êng Tzŭ says, " The dictum, ' Conformity
to the Nature is what is termed Moral Order,' [1] is said of
both men and other creatures," and when he says, " Not men
only, but all things are so constituted," he is speaking of
the uniformity of the Nature. In the statement, " Man
receives the Ether of the Universe in its perfection, differing
therein from all else," and in the statement, " But other
creatures cannot reason, while man can," he is speaking of
the variation in the etherial endowment. Therefore, he
says again, " If you take account of the Nature
apart from the Ether, your statement will be incomplete ;
if you take account of the Ether and disregard
the Nature, it will fail in clearness. To make them two
separate entities is incorrect." [2] Ponder this statement well,
and it will be seen that the Master's meaning is far enough
removed from the teachings of Buddhism ! With reference
to what you say in the treatise you sent me, Hu Tzŭ
says exactly the same thing. (It is the chapter beginning,

[1] Quoted from the *Doctrine of the Mean*; see Legge's *Chinese Classics*,
vol. i, p. 247.

[2] See 遺 書, pt. vi, f. 2. The passage is attributed both to Ming
Tao (see p. 88) and to I Ch'uan (see p. 94). The word 二, in 二
之 便 不 是, is a verb of which 之 is the object referring to 性
and 氣.

"The philosopher Tzŭ Ssŭ said.") But the Nature is nothing else than Law, and it seems to me that it cannot be divided in this way. It is simply that, owing to the diversities in the physical endowment, Law is to some extent obscured and cannot clearly manifest itself. Law itself is one and indivisible. As to the argument quoted from Mencius: [1] Mencius is speaking of principles as applied to man only, whereas the meaning of Tzŭ Ssŭ's statement includes man and other creatures. "The Nature is uniform, it is the Ether that differs ": this sentence alone contains most profound teaching, and will well repay careful thought. If you can grasp its meaning, you will find that all your difficulties in the sayings of the saints and sages will disappear. (Reply to Hsü Yüan P'ing.)

[1] Mencius says that the Nature in men and animals differs. See Mencius, pp. 201, 273.

THE PHILOSOPHY OF HUMAN NATURE

HUMAN NATURE

BOOK II

BEING BOOK XLIII OF

THE COMPLETE WORKS OF CHU HSI

———

THE PHYSICAL NATURE

THE DECREE

CAPACITY

BOOK II

THE PHYSICAL NATURE

(Twenty-six Sections from the "Conversations".)

1. In the dictum, "The Decree of Heaven is what is termed the Nature," [1] the Decree is like a document containing instructions from a superior ; the Nature is official duty, such as the keeping of records, the settling of accounts, or the work of a district military officer or constable ; the Mind is the officer himself ; the Physical Element is the disposition shown by the officer, whether lenient or violent ; the Feelings correspond to his sitting in court and judging cases. The Feelings are thus the manifested operations ; and the Nature is Love, Righteousness, Reverence, and Wisdom. As to the statement that the Decree of Heaven and the Physical Element are bound up together : as soon as the Decree of Heaven exists, so soon does the Physical Element exist. They cannot be apart. If one is lacking, then nothing can be produced. Since the Decree of Heaven exists, Ether must also exist, for only thus can there be a receptacle for Law—if there were no Ether where could Law find its lodgment ? There is no inequality in the Nature imparted by the Decree of Heaven, but there is in the physical endowment. The Ether differs in the degree of its clearness and fulness ; but of the four principles, Love, Righteousness, Reverence, and Wisdom, not one is lacking. And yet if there be an excess of solicitude it will

[1] See D.M., p. 247.

take the form of favouritism and weak gentleness ; if there
be an excess of conscientiousness we shall be ashamed of
what we ought not to be ashamed of. Take light as an
illustration : there must be some reflecting body, whether
a mirror or a sheet of water, in order to have light. The
light is the Nature ; the mirror or water is the physical
element ; without the mirror or water the light is dispersed
and lost. Or take the five colours : if they fall where black
predominates they are all black, or if where red predominates
they are all red. In the same way everything depends on
what your etherial endowment is. Law, on the other hand,
is only good. Seeing that it is Law how could it be evil ?
What is termed evil is in the etherial element. Mencius'
doctrine asserts absolutely that the Nature is good ; and
when men are not good, it is because they allow themselves
to be " ensnared and so submerged " in evil : [1] by which he
shows that, in his view, the Nature in the beginning is
wholly good, and that afterwards evil comes into existence.
In this, apparently, he takes account of the Nature but not
of the Ether, and thus in some respects his statement is
incomplete. The Ch'êng school, however, have supplemented
this doctrine with the doctrine of the physical element, and
so we get a complete and all-round view of the problem.

The Philosopher further said : Capacity [2] belongs to the
physical element. In T'ui Chih's [3] exposition of his doctrine

[1] Mencius, p. 280.

[2] See p. 152.

[3] Han Yü, whose *style* was T'ui Chih, the great litterateur of the eighth
century. Han Yü described the nature of man as having three grades
of capacity—the Superior, the Middle, and the Inferior. " The Superior
grade is good, and good only ; the Middle grade is capable of being led,
it may rise to the Superior or sink to the Inferior ; the Inferior is evil and

of " The Three Grades " he is speaking all through of the
Physical Nature, and as such all that he says is good, except
that he ought to have made it clear that this was so.   If,
however, what he says is applied to the Essential Nature, it
is an inadequate statement ; for if it be possible thus to
divide the Nature into three grades, why stop at three ?
A hundred or a thousand would do equally well.   The
statements advanced by Hsün and Yang,[1] on the other hand,
take account only of the Ether, and not of the Nature,
with the result that they fail in clearness.   Through leaving
the Nature out of account the ethical principle is obscured.[2]

Again he said : In " The Counsels of Kao Yao " the
passage which treats of " affability combined with
meekness " and the rest of the " Nine Virtues "[3] implies
in every case the conversion of the physical element,[4] only
it does not state it in so many words.

Po Fêng[5] said: In K'ang Hêng's treatise, when he speaks
of the method by which to rule the Nature, he also refers
to the physical element.

evil only." In the Superior grade Love is supreme, and the other four
virtues are practised.   In the Middle grade Love is not wanting, but has
a tendency to its opposite and is confused with the other four.   In the
Inferior grade there is the opposite of Love, and the violation of the other
four virtues. See Legge's translation of the 原 性 (Original Nature)
in his *Chinese Classics*, vol. ii, Prolegomena, pp. 92–4.

[1] See p. 17, nn. 2 and 3.
[2] The Philosopher is here using the arguments of Ch'êng Tzŭ ; see p. 74.
[3] *Shu Ching*, p. 71.
[4] It is in correcting one virtue by its opposite, e.g. "affability" by
"dignity", that virtue in its true sense is attained to. This is to
反 氣 質, to reverse the physical element.
[5] Po Fêng was the *style* of Wu Pi Ta (吳 必 大), a student of Chu Hsi;
cf. 學 案, pt. lx·x, f. 53.

Ying[1] said : The second term in the phrase "affability combined with meekness ", and in the other similar phrases, implies effort.

To both these statements the Master assented.

Some one asked whether when the physical element is not good it can be changed or not ; to which the Master replied: It must be changed and converted, as when it is said, " If another man succeed by one effort the noble man will use a hundred efforts ; if another man succeed by ten efforts he will use a thousand. Thus, though dull he will surely become intelligent, though weak he will surely become strong."[2]

2. The Nature is Law only, but apart from the Ether of heaven and the solid matter of earth Law would have nothing in which to inhere. When this Ether is received, however, if in respect of its clearness and translucence there is neither obscurity nor obstruction, Law flows forth freely ; if there be obscurity and obstruction, but in lesser degree, then in its outflow Divine Law is victor ; if there be obscurity and obstruction in greater degree, selfish desire obtains the victory. Thus we see that the original Nature is invariably good—which is the Nature described by Mencius as " good ", by Chou Tzŭ as " perfectly pure " and "most good ", and by Ch'êng Tzŭ as the " Nature's source " and the " Original and Essential Nature "—but it is obstructed by the opacity and grossness of the physical element. Hence,

---

[1] Ying was a native of Fên Ning and a friend of Chu Hsi. His surname was Huang (黃) and his *style* Tzŭ Kêng (子 耕). Fên Ning is noted as one of the places where Chou Tzŭ held office.

[2] D.M., p. 278.

"The characteristic of the noble man is to deny the Physical Nature to be his Nature."[1] If by culture we reverse it, then the Nature of Heaven and Earth abides. In defining the Nature, therefore, we must include the physical element in order to make a complete statement.

3. When we speak of the Nature of Heaven and Earth we refer specifically to Law ; when we speak of the Physical Nature we refer to Law and Ether combined. Before the etherial element existed the Nature was already in existence. The former is transitory, the latter is eternal. Although the Nature is implanted in the midst of the Ether, the Ether is still the Ether, and the Nature is still the Nature, without confusion the one with the other. As to its immanence and omnipresence in the universe : again, no matter how fine or coarse the Ether may be, there is nothing which does not possess this Law.

4. Fei Ch'ing[2] asked for an explanation of the Physical Nature.

The Philosopher replied : The Nature of the Divine Decree, apart from the physical element, would have nothing in which to inhere. But the etherial endowment in men differs in clearness and perfection, so that the perfection of the Divine Decree also varies in the depth and fullness *of its manifestation.* The important thing is that still it cannot be styled otherwise than as the Nature. Some time ago I saw that Ping Wêng said : "I Ch'uan's theory of the Physical Nature is exactly similar to the illustrations

---

[1] Quoted from the Chêng Mêng (誠 明 篇), by Chang Tsai ; see 大 全, Bk. v ; or 學 案, pt xvii, f. 34. Cf. p. 88 of this volume.

[2] Surnamed Chu (朱).

used in Buddhist books of the salt flavour in water, and glue
in colour wash."

Question. How does Mencius' doctrine of the Nature
compare with that of I Ch'uan?

Answer. They are not the same. Mencius fastens upon
the Nature and defines it in respect of its source. I Ch'uan
defines it in combination with the physical element,
attaching importance to their not being separated. Thus
Ch'êng Tzŭ says : " If you take account of the Nature
apart from the Ether your statement will be incomplete ; if you take account of the Ether and disregard
the Nature it will fail in clearness." [1] I, also, in my
" Exposition of the Supreme Ultimate ", say :   " What
we call the Supreme Ultimate is not to be thought of
as apart from the Two Modes, nor is it to be confounded
with them." [2]

5. The Physical Nature is the Nature of Heaven and
Earth. But how does this Nature of Heaven and Earth
come to be ? The good Nature is like water. The Physical
Nature is as if you sprinkled soy and salt in it so that it all
becomes one flavour.

6. *Question.* The passages, " The unending stream of
transformations in the Universe," " Proceeding from the
one positive and one negative ether," "Endless production," [3]
" The law of their succession is goodness," all refer to
Divine Law. [4] How can it be other than good ? Mencius

[1] See p. 74, n. 2.   [2] 大 全, Bk. i, f. 2.
[3] Compare the *T'ai Chi T'u Shuo* by Chou Tzŭ, of which a translation
is given in the *Introduction to Chu Hsi and the Sung School,* chap. vi, for
the ideas, though not the exact phrasing of these sentences.
[4] *I Ching,* pp. 355–6.

refers to the same thing when he speaks of the original substance of the Nature being good. The two ethers with their reciprocal repulsion and attraction, union and contrariety, equilibrium, and deflection, naturally possess both good and evil. What is there strange then in that which is endowed with material form also possessing both good and evil? Its source, however, can only be characterized as invariably good. Is this a correct statement?

Answer. It is quite correct.

Ting Fu Chih said: You, sir, in your exposition of the passage in the *Doctrine of the Mean* which speaks of "The Great Root",[1] say that as it is called "The Great Root" it must refer to Law, and is therefore absolutely good. The moment human desire exists there is the etherial element, which also must have its source; but it was not originally in "The Great Root".

7. The Nature of all men is good, and yet there are those who are good from their birth and those who are evil from their birth. This is because of the inequality of the etherial endowment. Moreover, amid the infinite variety of phenomena in the revolutions of the Universe it may be seen that if the sun and moon are clear and bright, and the climate temperate and seasonable,[2] the man born at such a time and endowed with such an ether is possessed of a pure and bright, sincere and honest

[1] D.M., p. 248

[2] 氣 侯 is climate or "season"; 和 is neither too cold nor too hot, neither too dry nor too humid; 正 is hot when it ought to be hot, cold when it ought to be cold, etc.

disposition, and will be a good man. But if the sun and moon are darkened and the temperature unseasonable, it is due to the untoward ether of the universe, and it is not surprising if the man endowed with such an ether is a bad man. The object of self-culture is to transform this etherial endowment, but the task is exceedingly difficult to accomplish. When Mencius says : " The Nature is good," although he makes no reference to the etherial endowment and says only that " every man may become a Yao or a Shun ",[1] he means that if a man will courageously and fiercely press forward, the inequality of the etherial endowment will of itself disappear, and his task be accomplished. For this reason, Mencius does not mention the etherial endowment. If my Nature is good, what is there to prevent my being one of the holy and wise men? Nothing but the etherial endowment. For example, when a man's etherial endowment has excess of strength he is tyrannical, when it is gentle to excess he is weak. Men who excuse themselves by saying that their etherial endowment is bad, and so do not persevere, will fail ; while those who pay no regard to the injury possible from it, but go blindly on in their heedless course, will also fail. The one thing we must realize is that we must use our earnest effort and master it, cut off its excesses and restore the Mean ; then all will be well. Lien Hsi said : " The Nature consists of the five qualities, Strength, Weakness, Goodness, Evil, and the Mean." [2] Hence the object of the sages was to teach men to reverse the evil,

[1] Mencius, p. 300.

[2] T'ung Shu (通 書), chap. vii ; see 大 全 or 精 義. Note, these five are the qualities of the physical nature ; cf. p. 111.

attain to the Mean, and rest therein. Tsê Ch'ên said : " The operations of the physical element are limited, while the achievements of ethical culture are vast." [1]

8. *Question.* Mencius said, " The Nature is good," [2] which I Ch'uan says is the original and essential nature. [3] Confucius said: " Men in their Nature are nearly alike," [4] and I Ch'uan says that this refers to the physical nature. These two cases are quite clear, but in the *Doctrine of the Mean* it is said : " The Decree of Heaven is what we term the Nature." [5] I cannot tell whether this is the original and essential nature or the physical nature.

Answer. The Nature is one only. How can that which is conferred by the Divine Decree differ ? It is entirely owing to the variation in the physical element that differences develop, and these led Confucius to use the expression " nearly alike ". Mencius was fearful lest people should speak of the Nature of man as originally unlike; therefore, differentiating the Nature as decreed by Heaven from the physical element, he expounded it to his con- temporaries in this sense, and asserted that the Nature is invariably good, which is what Tzŭ Ssŭ refers to when he says : " The Decree of Heaven is what we term the Nature."

9. Ya Fu asked the question : With whom did the doctrine of the physical element originate ?

Answer. It originated with Chang and the two Ch'êngs.

---

[1] That is, ethical culture is fully adequate to overcome the demerits of the physical element.

[2] Mencius, p. 110.

[3] 遺 書, pt. iii, f. 4.

[4] Analects, xvii, ii (p. 182).

[5] D.M., p. 247.

I regard them not only as deserving much of the sages, but also as having done great service to scholars who have come after. The study of their writings makes one extremely grateful to them, for no one previously had ever given utterance to this doctrine. Han T'ui Chih,[1] for example, in his essay on " The Original Nature ", propounded his theory of " The Three Grades " ; and what he says is true, but he does not state clearly that he is speaking of the physical nature. Where can you get " three grades " in the original nature ? Mencius, in his assertion that the Nature is good, speaks of it only in respect of its origin, making no reference to the physical nature ; so that in his case, too, there must be careful discrimination ; while of the rest of the philosophers, some assert that the Nature is evil, others that it is both evil and good, whereas, if the doctrine of Chang and the two Ch'êngs had been propounded earlier there would have been no need for all this discussion and controversy. If, then, the doctrine of Chang and the two Ch'êngs stands, that of the rest is shown to be confusion.

A question was raised with reference to Hêng Ch'ü's statement : " After form is the physical nature. He who succeeds in reversing his physical nature will preserve the Nature of Heaven and Earth. Therefore the characteristic of the noble man is to deny the physical nature to be his nature." [2] Ming Tao's statement was also quoted : " If you take account of the Nature apart from the Ether, your statement will be incomplete ; if you take account of the Ether and disregard the Nature, it will fail

[1] See p. 80.
[2] " Chêng Mêng " (誠 明 篇), see p. 11 of this volume.

in clearness.   To make them two separate entities is wrong." [1]

Referring to these statements the Philosopher said : If we say that Love, Righteousness, Reverence, and Wisdom alone constitute the Nature how are we to account for the fact that in the world some are born with no such principles ? It is owing to the etherial endowment that it is so.   If you do not take the etherial element into account, your theory will not represent an all-round view of the facts, and will therefore be incomplete.   If, on the other hand, you only take into account the etherial endowment, recognizing this as good and that as evil, and disregard the unity of the source, your theory will fail in clearness.   From the time of Confucius, Tsêng Tzŭ, Tzŭ Ssŭ, and Mencius, all of whom understood the principles involved, no one had propounded this truth [until the time of Chang and the two Ch'êngs].

Ch'ien Chih asked : Is Law itself opaque and impure, according to the varying degrees of opacity and impurity in the Ether of the Universe ?

Answer.   Law in itself never varies.   It is the Ether alone that varies in this way.

Question.   If the etherial element varies in this way and Law does not, will it not follow that Law and Ether are separate ?

Answer.   Although Ether is produced by Law, nevertheless, after it has been produced, Law cannot control it. Law has its dwelling-place, as it were, in the etherial element, from which the continuous stream of daily activity

[1] See p. 74, n. 2.

proceeds ; but the Ether is strong while Law is weak. It may be illustrated thus: On the occasion of some great festival a proclamation of grace is issued remitting one season's taxes, but a local magistrate who is hard and grasping extorts the tax from the people under his jurisdiction, simply because of their proximity to him and his ability to influence the higher authority to turn a deaf ear to their petitions for relief. Here we see illustrated the coarseness of the Ether [1] and the fineness of Law. Or take as an illustration the relationship between father and son ; if the son will not follow in the footsteps of his father, the father cannot compel him. Indeed the very object of the teaching of the sages is to save such.[2]

10. The Nature is like water. If it flows in a clean channel it is clear, if it flows into a dirty channel it becomes turbid. When the physical element is clear and perfect, the Nature is received in its completeness, as in the case of man. When the physical element is turbid and defective, the Nature is obscured, as in the case of birds and beasts. The Ether is clear or turbid. As received by man it is clear, as received by birds and beasts it is turbid. In man the physical element is in the main clear, hence the difference between man and the brute, but there is also some turbidity, and, consequently, birds and beasts are not so very far removed from man.

11. Given the existence of Law, there follows the existence of the Ether. Given the Ether, there must be Law. [But in the Ether there are differences.]

[1] The 氣 is coarse like the magistrate, who is more powerful than the Emperor.

[2] Note, 這 些 子 = "these" ; 子 is an enclitic simply

Those whose etherial endowment is clear are the saints and sages in whom the Nature is like a pearl lying in clear cold water. Those whose etherial endowment is turbid are the foolish and degenerate, in whom the Nature is like a pearl lying in muddy water. " To make manifest illustrious virtue " is to cleanse the pearl from the muddy water. The brute creation also possess this Law, and in them the Nature is like the pearl dropped into the filthiest of muddy places. But their endowment is still clear [1] in some directions, so that the Nature is not wholly obscured, as may be seen in the bond between parent and offspring in tigers and wolves, in the relation between sovereign and minister among bees and ants, in the gratitude to progenitors to be seen in the jackal and otter, or in the faculty of discrimination in the water-fowl and dove. It is from such characteristics that we get the expressions " virtuous creatures " and " righteous creatures ".[2]

12. Questioned as to inequalities in the clearness and turbidity of the etherial endowment, the Philosopher said : The differences in the etherial endowment are of more than one kind and are not covered by the two words, " clear " and " turbid ". There are men whose intellect is such that there is nothing they do not understand. In such the Ether

[1] 明 is " clear " as opposed to " blurred " or " opaque " , 清 is " clear " as opposed to " muddy " or " turbid ".

[2] The first of these expressions refers to the jackal and otter. These animals are accustomed to spread out before them their prey as if offering sacrifice to the gods, and are therefore called " virtuous creatures " (仁 獸). The second expression refers to doves, in whose mating the male cleaves to one female, and because they thus observe the principles of morality as between the sexes they are called " righteous creatures " (義 獸).

is clear, but their actions possibly do not always hit the mark in respect of ethical principle, the reason being that the Ether is not rich.[1] There are others who are respectful and generous, loyal and true, in whom the Ether is rich, but whose knowledge possibly is lacking in discernment because the Ether is not clear. Follow this out and you will understand the matter.

13.   Although the Nature is the same in all men, their etherial endowment is necessarily unequal. There are those in whose endowment the Ligneous ether[2] predominates, and in them the feeling of solicitude is generally uppermost, while the manifestation of conscientiousness, the courteous spirit and moral insight is impeded ; and, similarly, there are those in whom the Metallic ether prevails, with the result that conscientiousness is prominent to the comparative exclusion of the other three terminals. So with the Aqueous and the Igneous ethers. It is only when the Two Modes unite all the virtues, and the five nature-principles are all complete, that you have the due Mean and the perfect uprightness[3] of the sage.

14.   Where the Nature is cramped by the etherial endowment, the ethical principle is able to penetrate

---

[1] 醨 here probably means " rich " or "generous " as of wine, but it may also be " pure " as the opposite of 雜 " dregs ".

[2] The Five Ethers (五 氣) are the Five Agents (五 行), see *Introd. to Chu Hsi, etc.*

[3] 中 = " mean ". Legge quotes a gloss by Chu Hsi in which he says 中 者 不 偏 不 倚。 無 過 不 及 之 名, " ' chung ' is the name for what is without deflection or inclination, which neither exceeds nor comes short " ; that is, a quality not 中 is a quality which in itself might be right, but is simply unbalanced, as an excess of generosity. The opposite of 正, on the other hand, is a quality which in itself is definitely wrong, as dishonesty.

in one direction only. Thus in a very large number of instances, there is excellence in one direction and defect in another, freedom here and obstruction there.[1] Some men have a perfect understanding of everything that is advantageous and injurious while they know nothing of moral principles, and another excels in all the arts but cannot understand books. Just as the tiger and panther know only the relationship between parent and offspring, bees and ants that of sovereign and minister, so a man may be filial to his parents and mean towards others. The Emperor Ming,[2] for example, was so affectionate to his brothers that he had a long bolster and large coverlet for them to sleep together, and continued the practice to the end of his life ; but as sovereign he killed his minister, as father he killed his son, and as husband he killed his wife. Here was a case in which there was freedom in some respects and obstruction in others, a man in whose nature there was free course for the ethical principle in one direction only, and therefore in all other directions obstruction. This was owing to the etherial endowment and also to ignorance of what is advantageous and injurious.

Question. How is it that Yao was father to Tan Chu,[3] and Kun was father to Yü ? [4]

[1] Cf. Bergson's *élan vital* ; see J. P. Bruce, *Introduction to Chu Hsi and the Sung School*, chap. ix.

[2] Ming Huang or Li Lung Chi (李 隆 基), sixth Emperor of the T'ang dynasty. See Giles' Biog. Dict., p. 450.

[3] Ibid., p. 710. The allusion here is to the passage in Mencius referring to Tan Chu ; see Mencius, p. 235.

[4] Kun was Minister of Works under Yao and Shun, and was banished by the latter Emperor for failure in the task assigned to him. He was father to Shun's successor, the Emperor Yü. See Shu Ching, pp. 23–5, 39–40.

Answer. This again is because the Two Ethers and Five Agents, at the moment of their union and revolution, differ in different cases in the degree of their clearness or turbity, and the man at his birth comes into contact with them at the very moment of this union.

15. Ya Fu said : The Nature is like the sun and moon, the turbidity of the Ether is like the clouds and mist.

The Master assented.

16. The Nature of man is like a fire buried in the ashes : when the ashes are stirred the fire brightens.[1]

17. *Question.*   People constantly speak of the nature of a man or thing being so and so ; as, for example, when it is said that the nature of one thing is hot and of another cold. Do not such statements include both the physical element and the immaterial principle with which they are endowed ?

Answer. Yes.

18. T'ui Chih's [2] theory that Capacity is of three grades and that the Nature has five grades, is superior to those of Hsün and Yang. He defines the grades of the Nature as Love, Righteousness, Reverence, and Wisdom, which is still better. But as to three grades of Capacity, we might in the same way discover hundreds and thousands of varieties, and to summarize them in this way is just the doctrine of the physical nature without the name. I Ch'uan's statement : "If you   take   account   of   the   Ether   and

[1] The allusion is to the charcoal brazier in which the live charcoal is buried in the ashes, but glows immediately the ashes are stirred.

[2] T'ui Chih is Han Yü ; see p. 80.

disregard the Nature your statement will fail in clearness ; if you take account of the Nature apart from the Ether it will be incomplete,"[1] expresses the idea exactly. For example, in teaching that in their Nature men are nearly alike but by practice grow wide apart,[2] the physical element cannot be left out of account ; and this is precisely the theory propounded by the two Ch'êngs. Lien Hsi teaches the same truth in his exposition of the Supreme Ultimate. From the time of the Han and Wei dynasties till the sudden appearance of Wên Chung Tzŭ[3] philosophers were few. In the T'ang dynasty T'ui Chih[4] appeared, whose teaching reached a higher level. Speaking generally, however, moral truth has never entirely disappeared from the world. Even though in the present generation there are none who understand these principles, there will not fail to be some in another age.

19. Questioned as to the phrase, " To make them two separate entities is wrong," the Philosopher said : You must not divide them into two separate sections, and say that the Nature is nothing but the Nature, and the Ether is nothing but the Ether. How then shall we not separate them ? By taking Ming Tao's expressions, " incomplete " and " fail in clearness," and applying them on both sides, the reason will be understood. Hence, in the statement, " To make them two separate entities is wrong," the expression, " make them two separate entities,"

[1] See p. 74, n. 2.
[2] The allusion is to the Analects, xvii, ii (p. 182).
[3] See 遺 書, pt. xix, f. 16.
[4] See p. 80.

refers to the two preceding sentences. (Ying's [1] record says: To take account of the Nature apart from the Ether, and to take account of the Ether and disregard the Nature, is to make two separate entities.) [2]

Someone asked : When Ming Tao, in his assertion that "Life is what is called the Nature", says, "The Nature is the Ether and the Ether is the Nature," [3] is this what he means by not making them two separate entities?

Answer. That, again, means that the Nature resides in the etherial endowment. When the Ether is received Law is imparted to it. This is why it is said : "The Nature is the Ether and the Ether is the Nature." But if you stop at the statement that "The Nature is the Ether, and the Ether is the Nature", then still more will you have failed to discriminate between the two.

20. It is necessary to recognize the differences in the uniformity and the uniformity in the differences. In the beginning there is no difference so far as Law is concerned, but when Law is deposited in the Ether there is likeness only in the coarser features, such as the capacity for hunger and thirst, and seeking what is advantageous and avoiding the injurious, which birds and beasts have in common with man, so that, apart from moral principles, man would not differ from them.

[1] See p. 82, n. 1.

[2] See preceding page. See also 朱 子 語 類 (*Conversations*), pt. lix, ff. 13–14, for a clear and detailed exposition of this passage.

[3] See 遺 書, pt. i, f. 10.

The Philosopher said further : The passages, "The great God has conferred on the inferior people a moral sense,"[1] and "The people hold within themselves a normal principle of good,"[2] represent the "difference". The saying, "The mass of people cast it away, while the noble man preserves it,"[3] means that we must preserve this difference. Only thus are we to be distinguished from the brute. We must not say, "The wriggling movement of the worm holds the spiritual within it; all things have the Buddha nature like ourselves."[4]

21. *Question.* The chapter commencing with the sentence, "Life is what is called the Nature,"[5] is very

[1] *Shu Ching,* p. 185.

[2] *Odes,* p. 541, *vide* p. 54 of this volume, n. 1.

[3] Mencius, p. 201.

[4] A quotation from Buddhist pantheistic statements.

[5] 遺 書, pt. i, f. 10. See also 學 案, pt. xiii, f. 29, where the text of the whole passage referred to is given. The following is a translation : Life is what is termed the Nature. The Nature is the Ether and the Ether is the Nature, and this is what is called Life. All men at their birth are endowed with the Ether, and in law there is both good and evil. But it is not that originally, when man is born, there are in the Nature these two things in opposition to each other. There are those who are good from their youth, and there are those who are evil from their youth ; but this results from the differences in the etherial endowment. Goodness is certainly the Nature, but evil cannot be said not to be the Nature. For Life is what is termed the Nature. The time preceding man's birth and the repose which then exists needs no discussion. The moment you apply the term Nature, what you are speaking of has already ceased to be the Nature. All who expound the Nature define it simply as what is spoken of in the dictum, " The law of their succession is goodness," the same as Mencius refers to when he says " The Nature of man is good ". Now that which is spoken of in the dictum, " The law of their succession is

difficult to follow. From the beginning of the passage to
the sentence, " Evil cannot be said not to be the Nature,"
makes two or three sections.

Answer. This chapter is extremely difficult, but if you
look carefully at the connexion you will understand its
meaning. The statement at the beginning : " It is not
that when man is born there are these two things in
opposition to each other," means that the Nature is good.

Question. It is true that it is stated that the Nature is
good; but following this it is said, " Goodness is certainly
the Nature, but evil cannot be said not to be the Nature."
My difficulty is that to introduce the Nature of the
etherial endowment seems inconsistent with the preceding
context.

goodness ", is like the flow of water downwards. It is all water ; some
flows to the sea itself without defilement—how can such be achieved by
human strength ? Some becomes gradually turbid before it has proceeded
far on its way ; some becomes turbid after it has proceeded some
distance in its course ; some is more turbid, some is less turbid ; but
though differing in the degree of turbidity you cannot say that the turbid
is not water. Therefore men should not fail to apply themselves to the
work of purification. By this means those who are earnest and courageous
in their efforts will be speedily cleansed ; while in those who are slow and
lazy the cleansing will be slow. When it is cleansed it is nothing else
than the original water, and you do not bring clear water to take the
place of the turbid, nor do you take the turbid water and place it in a spot
by itself. The clearness of the water represents the goodness of the Nature.
Therefore it is not that in the Nature there are the two things, good and
evil, in opposition to each other, each with a different origin. This
law is the Decree of Heaven. To follow it and accord with it is the
Moral Law. To accord with it and cultivate it so that each receives it
according to his capacity is Religion. From the Decree of Heaven to
the inculcation of it in me there is no injurious admixture in the process.
It was by this that Shun and Yü held possession of the Empire as if it were
nothing to them.

Answer. It is not the Nature of the etherial endowment which is spoken of. What is said is that the Nature was originally good and is now evil, and that it is the same Nature, but that it has been thrown into disorder by evil ; just as water is made thick by mud and sand, and yet you do not refuse to call it water.

Question. The question just asked refers to Nan Hsien's theory, does it not ?

Answer. Ching Fu's [1] treatise was issued too soon, and contained may errors and contradictions. It includes his discussion on the *Commentary on Mencius.* Many of the nobles urged him and it was difficult to withstand them.

Question. Should the words, " Man's birth and the repose which then exists," be regarded as a separate sentence ? [2]

Answer. They should be taken with the words which immediately follow, in order to complete the sense. The Nature is so-called from the time of its endowment. In " the time preceding man's birth and the repose which then exists " there was as yet no material form ; there was nothing to receive Law. How then could it be called the Nature ?

Question. How do you explain the section, " The moment you apply the term Nature, what you are speaking of has already ceased to be the Nature." (At this point the

---

[1] Ching Fu is the Nan Hsien named in the question ; see p. 102, n. 1.

[2] If taken as a separate sentence they would read : " At man's birth there is repose," and the sentence following this would be : " The time preceding needs no discussion."

writer could not recall clearly what the master's reply was, and would not venture to record it. The next evening the question was repeated, and is given below.)

Question. With reference to the statement, " All who expound the Nature define it simply as what is spoken of in the dictum ' The law of their succession is goodness '," how can the phrase " The law of their succession is goodness " refer to the Nature ?

Answer. The question raised by my friend is most germane. Here, however, it really is in reference to man that the sentence, " The law of their succession is goodness," is quoted ; for if it were quoted with a transcendental reference, it would refer to Divine Law, and Divine Law at the moment of its outflow could not be called the Nature.[1]

Question. In the passage, " Life is what is termed the Nature ; the Nature is the Ether and the Ether is the Nature "—is not the meaning that at man's birth the Nature and the Ether combine ?

Answer. When man is formed from the Ether, Law is inherent in the person so created. Then only can it be called the Nature.

Question. Some time back T'êng Tê Ts'ui questioned you with reference to the statement, " Life is what is termed the Nature." You, Sir, said : If you follow the Master Ch'êng's statement, it is all right. At that time,

---

[1] A twofold application of the dictum, " The law of their success is goodness," is possible. It may refer to Divine Law pervading the universe in the mutual succession of the two Modes, or it may refer to the same law, but as imparted to the individual. Chu Hsi says that in the passage in question it is obviously the latter. Cf. p. 56 of this volume.

although further elucidation was repeatedly sought for, you gave no answer. Afterwards, when thinking it over carefully, we recalled that this was Kao Tzŭ's statement, and if it had really accorded with that of the Master Ch'êng there would have been nothing to object to in it; but in his mind the reference was directly to the etherial element as the Nature, and thus the meaning of his statement differed from that of the Master Ch'êng.

Answer. The Master Ch'êng's words do indeed confirm the language of Kao Tzŭ as not incorrect. But if the truth really is as Kao Tzŭ contended, why should Mencius oppose him? From this we may assume that the principles enunciated by Kao Tzŭ were really wrong.[1] The Confucian school, in their discussion of the Nature, for the most part refer to the etherial element, just as the Buddhists also regard the operation of Intelligence only as the Nature.

Question. In your *Commentary on Mencius* it is said: "The teaching of the Su and Hu schools[2] in the present day is similar to this." But on examining the tenets of these two schools it looks as if they do not hold the "Ether" theory.

Answer. Their tendency is so of necessity.

Question. When the Hu School maintain that the Nature is not to be defined in terms of good and evil, does it not seem as though their desire is to represent the greatness of the Nature?

---

[1] That is, there is a verbal correspondence—the *language* was not incorrect—but the fact of Mencius' vehement opposition shows that Kao Tzŭ meant something very different from the teaching of Ch'eng Tzŭ.

[2] See J. P. Bruce, *Introduction to Chu Hsi and the Sung School*, chap. iv.

Answer. No, it is not with the idea of representing the greatness of the Nature. It is simply that they do not perceive the matter clearly. Otherwise they would not speak in this way. Ching Fu [1] also formerly held this view. But I said to him, " When everything that exists is relative, why do you want to make the Nature like a one-branched horn,[2] a thing with no correlation ? " The Master Ch'êng in his treatment of the Nature says simply : " The Nature is Law." Is this not a clear discernment of the matter ? He truly deserves well of the school of the sages.

Question. Was it the Master Ch'êng who first discerned clearly the bearing of the passage, " The law of their succession is goodness, their realization is the Nature ? " [3]

Answer. Previously no one had expressed it thus. The fact that he did is the evidence of his clear insight.

The next evening the Philosopher was again questioned with reference to the passage beginning, " Life is what is termed the Nature." We have not, it was said, wholly apprehended your meaning. We do not know whether the sentence : " The moment you apply the term Nature, what you are speaking of has already ceased to be the Nature," refers to the time preceding man's endowment with the Nature, or to the time following it.

Answer. It refers to the time following the endowment. The Nature is nothing else than the all-comprehensive

---

[1] Chang Ch'ih (張 栻), also called Chang Nan Hsien, a great friend of Chu Hsi, but holding very different views. See J. P. Bruce, *Introduction to Chu Hsi and the Sung School*, chap. iv.

[2] 尖 斜 is a perverted point leaning to one side with nothing on the other side to match it, as in the case of a cow having only one horn.

[3] *Yi Ching*, pp. 355–6.

Divine Law, but the moment you can speak of it as existing it already carries with it the etherial element. In the statement, " Apart from the Two Modes there would be no Moral Law," [1] great discrimination needs to be used.

Question. The passage following the sentence, " The flow of water downwards," [2] refers to the etherial endowment. If so, seeing that all is fixed from birth, how can we speak of the difference between " nearly alike " and " wide apart " ? [3]

Answer. It means that there is practice also.

22. *Question.* In the chapter beginning " Life is what is called the Nature ", in the passage extending from the opening sentence to the words, " But evil cannot be said not to be the Nature," [4] it appears to my poor judgment that it is the original nature combined with the physical nature that is referred to. At the very beginning of the passage the writer uses the single word " Life " which combines both natures.

Chu Hsi. But what about the word " Nature " ?

Yung said : It seems to me that the word " Nature " is also applied to both.

Yung asked further. Some time ago arising out of this very subject you used the simile of water to illustrate the Nature, and then said that the one and perfectly pure Divine Law is like water in its original clearness. The cloudiness and turbidity resulting from the complex interaction of the Two Modes and Five Agents is like water as it is defiled by

[1] Cf. 大 全, vol. i, f. 26 ; or 學 案, pt. xv, f. 22.
[2] See n. 5 on p. 97.
[3] Analects, XVI, ii, p. 182.   [4] See n. 5 on p. 97.

mud.   The possibility of restoring the cloudy and turbid
to clearness again is due to the fact that its source was
clear.   Is it not so ?

Answer.   Yes, and the lower foolish people, who are
incapable of amendment, are like water which is foul
smelling and filthy.

Question.   Can they not also be cleansed ?

Answer.   The impurity can be reduced to some extent.

From this the Philosopher went on to say : In earlier
times it was the custom for people to fill their vessels with
water at the Hui Hill Well and carry them into the city.
If after a while the water became foul, the city people had
a way of cleansing it.   They filled a bamboo pipe with sand
and stones, and, pouring the water on them, let it run
through.   By doing this several times the water would
gradually be restored to its original purity.

Some one asked : Can the lower foolish people be cleansed?

Yung said : Possibly they would not be willing to be
cleansed.

Answer.   Even foul-smelling water would scarcely be
regarded as the extreme of filth.

Question.   Would you say that when a thing has reached
the stage of being past such conversion it is more like
putrid mud ?

Answer.   Yes, that is what I mean.

Question.   The section, from " For Life is what is called
the Nature " to " like water flowing downwards ", refers
to the original nature, does it not ?

Answer.   How do you explain the phrase, " For life is
what is called the Nature " ?

Yung said : It is simply a quotation.

Yung then proceeded to ask further : In the sentence, "The time preceding man's birth and the repose which then exists needs no discussion," the writer, in the phrase, "man's birth and the repose which then exists," refers to the beginning of life ; but does he not also, in the phrase in which he speaks of "the time preceding", refer to the Divine Decree ?

Answer. Yes, and therefore the sentence in the *Yi*, "Great is the Principle of Origin, indicated by Ch'ien ; all things owe to it their beginning,"[1] refers solely to the source of Truth.[2] It is when you come to what is expressed in the sentence, "The method of Ch'ien is to change and transform so that everything obtains its correct nature as ordained by Heaven,"[3] that the Nature is in existence. The passage, "All who expound the Nature simply define it as what is spoken of in the dictum 'The law of their succession is goodness',"[4] implies the physical element.

Question. Is it not that Feeling only is included ?

Answer. Feeling includes the physical. Therefore Mencius, in his reply to Kao Tzŭ's question with respect to the Nature, said, "If we look at the Feelings which flow from the Nature we may know that they are constituted for the practice of what is good."[5] Referring to Love,

[1] *Yi Ching*, p. 213. Ch'ien is the name of the first diagram. It is also used for Heaven as one of the dual powers, Heaven and Earth. See *Introd. to Chu Hsi, etc.*, chap. vi.

[2] 誠 here is Truth in the absolute and transcendental sense, the synonym for 天命 (The Decree of Heaven).

[3] *Yi Ching*, p. 213.   [4] See p. 97.   [5] Mencius, p. 278.

Righteousness, Reverence, and Wisdom, he spoke of
solicitude, conscientiousness, respectfulness, and moral
insight ; for the Nature is invisible, but the Feelings have
their objective manifestation in deeds, and it is only by way
of the Feelings that you are able to define the Nature.

Question. To know the Nature by way of the Feelings
is just like knowing the river's source by the flowing stream.
Formerly I heard Ts'ai Chi T'ung [1] ask K'ang Shu Lin :
" Everything has two termini.   Solicitude is the terminal
of Love.   Is it the initial or the final terminal ?"   Shu Lin
regarded it as the final terminal.   Recently I heard Chou
Chuang Chung report you as saying that there ought to be
no such division at all.

Chu Hsi.   What do you say ?

Questioner.   Solicitude is the movement of the Nature.
To know the substance by means of its movements is to
know the source by means of the flowing stream.   It seems
to me, therefore, that it is the final terminal.

Answer.   That is right.

Question.   What about the section, from " It is all water "
to " but you must not regard the turbid as not water " ?

Answer.   Water here is simply the physical element.

Yung said : It seems to me that you can estimate the
degree of cloudiness in the physical element from the
strength of creaturely desire, just as you know Love and
Righteousness from the presence of solicitude and conscientiousness.

Answer.   That is true also.

Another asked : Are those in whom the Ether is clear
therefore free from creaturely desire ?

[1] See p. 65.

Answer. That cannot be asserted. The desire of taste and the desire for musical sounds are common to all. Even though the Ether with which he is endowed is clear, the man will drift into desire at the least relaxation of watchfulness and self-control.

Question. With regard to the section, from " Therefore men should not fail to apply themselves to the work of purification " to " place it in a spot by itself ", is the meaning that when men have sought the conversion of the physical element in their constitution, their success in that conversion and their return to their original nature are not imparted from without ?

Answer. It is so.

Question. Is the meaning of the section, from " The clearness of the water represents the goodness of the Nature" to " Shun and Yü held possession of the empire as if it were nothing to them ",[1] that the learner in his search for moral truth does not obtain it from without, and the sage in teaching men does not force them to act outside their natural sphere of duty ? [2]

Answer. You may gather that also from the sentence, " This Law is the Divine Decree."

23. Does not the passage, " Goodness certainly is the Nature, but evil cannot be said not to be the Nature,"[3] contradict Mencius ?

Answer. This kind of statement is difficult to explain.

---

[1] Analects, VIII, xviii, pp. 77–8.
[2] That is, the sage does not inculcate monasticism as Buddhism does.
[3] 遺 書, pt. i, f. 10 ; see p. 97, n. 5.

One cannot get the meaning all at once. I myself, as I looked at it formerly, was also perplexed. But as I read it again and again the distinction between the two passages became clear, so that now I am confident that there is no mistake and no contradiction. It is only necessary to devote time and care to the study of it, and not, with an overweening confidence in one's own ideas, declare those who preceded us to be wrong.

Question. Is the Nature in the vegetable kingdom the same as in man and the animal kingdom?

Answer. You must recognize the differences without losing sight of the uniformity, and recognize uniformity without losing sight of the differences, and then you will be right.

24. *Question.* How do you explain the section beginning: "The time preceding man's birth and the repose which then exists needs no discussion." [1]

Answer. "The time preceding man's birth and the repose which then exists" is the time before the creature, whether man or animal, is born; and before birth the term Law only can be applied, the term Nature is as yet not applicable. This is what is meant by the statement, "On its Divine side it is called 'The Decree'." The sentence, "The moment you apply the term Nature, what you are speaking of has already ceased to be the Nature," tells us that when you apply the term "Nature" man is already born, and the ethical principle has lodged in the midst of the material ether, so that what we have is

[1] See p. 97, n. 5.

not wholly the original substance of the Nature ; hence the phrase, " has already ceased to be the Nature " ; and it is this that is referred to in the words, " From the point of view of man it is called the Nature." The main idea is that it is when man possesses material form that Law becomes inherent in it, and is termed the Nature. But at the stage at which you thus apply the term Nature, it is involved in life and combined with the physical, so that it is no longer the original substance of the Nature ; and yet the original substance of the Nature has not become confused. The important thing in this matter is to recognize that the original substance is neither separate from nor confounded with the material element. In the passage, " All who expound the Nature simply define it as what is spoken of in the dictum, ' The law of their succession is goodness ' " [1] the meaning is that the Nature cannot be portrayed ; those who excel in their exposition of it simply expound it according to its manifestation in the Terminals.[2] And yet the Law of the Nature can most certainly be recognized intellectually, as when Mencius speaks of the goodness of the Nature and the Four Terminals.

25. Questioned concerning the section beginning with the words, " The time preceding man's birth and the repose which then exists," the Philosopher replied : The Master Ch'êng used the word " Nature " in the sense of the original nature, and also in the sense of the physical nature. In the case of man as dwelling in the material body it is the

[1] See p. 97, n. 5.
[2] The Four Feelings or Terminals enumerated by Mencius ; see Mencius, p. 79.

physical nature. In the phrase, "The moment you apply the term 'Nature'" the word "Nature" refers to the physical element in combination with the original nature. In the phrase, "Has already ceased to be the Nature," the word Nature refers to the original nature, meaning that the moment you predicate the physical it is no longer the original. After man's birth, the moment of repose, man has bodily form, so that he can be said to possess the Nature. Before this moment of birth and repose he has as yet no bodily form; how can the Nature, then, be predicated of him?

26. "The moment you apply the term Nature, what you are speaking of has already ceased to be the Nature"; [1] for directly you apply to it the term Nature you are speaking of it as it is in combination with the physical element. In the passage beginning with the words, "The time preceding man's birth and the repose which then exists needs no discussion," the opening phrase singles out man's birth with the repose which then exists, and, for the purposes of discussion disconnects it from the time preceding, for the term Nature cannot be applied until the appearance of the physical element, and of the time preceding the birth of man and the moment of repose we can only use the term "Heaven's Moral Law": the word "Nature" is inapplicable. This is the explanation of Tzǔ Kung's language when he said, "His discourses about the Nature and Heaven's Moral Law cannot be heard." [2] The statement that "The Decree of Heaven is what we term the Nature" points to this element in man's personality as the Nature of

---

[1] See p. 97, n. 5.   [2] Analects, V, xii (pp. 41–2).

the Divine Decree without confusion with the etherial
endowment. In the phrase, "The moment you apply the
term Nature," the Nature is referred to as in combination
with the etherial endowment. Therefore, at the very time
implied in the term used, it is already not the Nature. Lien
Hsi said, "The Nature consists of the five qualities—
Strength, Weakness, Goodness, Evil, and the Mean." [1] Lien
Hsi defined the Nature as consisting only of these five, but
there were times when he also spoke of the Nature of the
four ethical principles—Love, Righteousness, Reverence, and
Widsom. Now, the nature of the etherial endowment does
not go beyond the five qualities mentioned by Lien Hsi,
but it is still the nature of the four ethical principles ; it
is not a different nature. Indeed, the nature of the whole
universe is not outside these five—Strength, Weakness,
Goodness, Evil, and the Mean ; for if we follow up the
subject carefully we find that, vast as is the variety of
phenomena, with their thousand species and hundred
genera, beyond our powers of investigation, we still do not
get away from these five categories.

[1] See *T'ung Shu*, chap. vii (師). N.B.—These five are given as the
principles of the physical nature, not of the essential nature, of which
Chou Tzŭ himself gives the constituent principles as Love, Righteousness,
Reverence, and Wisdom. Strength is the manifestation of the positive
ether, and weakness of the negative. Each of these again is either positive,
and then it is " good ", or negative, and then it is " evil ". "Strength,"
when "good", is righteous, straightforward, resolute, majestic, and firm ;
when evil it is harsh, proud, and cruel. " Weakness," when " Good ", is
kind, yielding, meek ; when " evil " it is soft, irresolute, and false. The
Mean is the maintenance of these principles in equilibrium so that there
is no excess of the "Good" qualities, and the "Evil" are moderated so that
they come to be not Evil.

(Fourteen Sections from the Collected Writings.)

1. *Question.* Men constantly have differences in clearness and translucence, which undoubtedly are due to the etherial endowment. But the mind, necessarily following the variations in the etherial endowment, also differs to some extent. The mouth, the ear, the eye, and the mind, however, are all organs of intelligence ; how is it then that, in imparting the physical element, Heaven makes no difference in clearness and translucence in the case of the mouth, the ear, and the eye, and does so only in the case of the mind ? If we say that the ethical principle of the mind does not differ, but that it is fettered by the physical element so that it cannot maintain its translucence, we have on the other side the fact that Yi, Hui, and Yi Yin were not fettered by the physical element, and yet their righteousness in the handling of affairs was not equal to the timeliness of the Master.[1]   For we find that Mencius in discussing the three sages said that their wisdom was not equal to that of the Master. But moral insight constitutes wisdom ; can it be that these three could be filled with solicitude, conscientiousness, and courtesy, and lack only moral insight?

Answer.   The mouth, ear, and eye also differ in clearness and translucence ; for example, Yi Ya, the music-master K'uang, and Li Lou[2] possessed a very high degree

[1] See Mencius, pp. 245–8 and 69–70, where the virtues of the three sages are characterized, but declared to be still not equal to the " timeliness "—i.e. the power to meet the demands of every occasion as it arises —of Confucius, " the Master ".

[2] Yi Ya was cook to Duke Huan of Ch'i of the seventh century B.C. " A worthless man, but great in his art," his palate was said to be so delicate that he could distinguish between the waters of two rivers. See Mencius,

of clearness. It is precisely the same with Mind. Yi and
Hui were not free from the limitations of the physical
element, therefore Mencius regarded them as of a "different
way" from his own, and did not "desire to learn" of
them.[1] (Reply to Chu Fei Ch'ing.)

2. *Question.* With reference to the Nature and Decree,
those who are born sages are wholly and perfectly good,
and in them there is a clearly marked distinction between
the etherial and ethical elements, so that the two
have no entanglement with each other. In their case there
is no need to speak of the physical element. In the case
of such as are inferior to those who are born sages, although
there is no defect in Divine Law, yet, being tied to
the etherial element, the brightness of the ethical
principle is in proportion to the clearness of the
Ether, and the obscurity of the ethical principle to
the turbidity of the Ether, the two being constantly
together.[2] Hence, when referred to as the physical nature,
the idea is that the advancement and retardation of the

p. 281; cf. Giles' *Biog. Dict.*, p. 351. Li Lou, it is said, was of the time of
Huang Ti, a legendary ruler of China, *circ.* 2600 B.C. Li Lou was so "acute
of vision that at a distance of 100 paces he could discern the smallest
hair ". K'uang Tzŭ Yeh " was music-master and a wise counsellor of
Tsin, a little prior to the time of Confucius ". See Mencius, p. 164 and note.

[1] See Mencius, pp. 69–70, where Mencius says Po Yi and Yi Yin were of
different ways from his own, and gives reasons why he had no desire to
learn of them. Hui is not mentioned here, but is included in the three
mentioned on pp. 245–8, as stated above.

[2] That is, the difference between the sages and others is, that in the
one case the two elements are perfectly separate, and in the other constantly united. So says the questioner, who, however, is wrong. Chu Hsi
says the difference is not because in the one case the two elements are
separate and in the other not, but simply because of the varying degrees
in the purity, etc., of the Ether.

ethical principle depends upon the Ether, and not that the physical element in itself is the Nature and Decree.

Answer. In those who are born sages the Ether is extremely clear, and the ethical principle is unclouded. In the case of those who acquire knowledge by learning, and all below them, the clearness of the Ether varies, and the ethical principle is correspondingly affected in the degree of its completeness. (Reply to Chêng Tzŭ Shang.)[1]

3. *Question.* Hêng Ch'ü said : "From the Great Void we have the term Heaven ; from the transformations of the Ether we have the term Moral Order ; by the union of the Void with the Ether we have the term Nature ; by the union of the Nature with Consciousness we have the term Mind."[2] Does not Hêng Ch'ü in his reference to the Nature combine the Nature of Heaven and Earth[3] with the physical nature ? And in his reference to Mind does he not combine both the " natural mind " and the " spiritual mind " ?

Answer. Apart from the Ether there would be no form, and without form there would be nothing to which the goodness of the Nature could be imparted. Therefore, those who expound the Nature all start from the physical element. Inherent in it, however, is the imparted ethical

---

[1] See p. 5, n. 3.

[2] Quoted from the *Chêng Mêng*, chap. i. Chang Tsa (or Hêng Ch'ü) uses two expressions rarely used by the other philosophers, namely, " The Great Harmony " (太 和) and " The Great Void " (太 虛). The former refers to the Moral Law of the Universe, i.e. the Moral Order ; and the latter to the Nature of the Universe, the substance of being.

[3] The essential nature.

principle. The "natural mind" and the "spiritual mind" in the same way are not two separate entities. (Reply to Lin Tê Chiu.)

4. *Question.* It is stated in the *Dialogues*[1]: "But their physical element differs in clearness and perfection,[2] and creaturely desire differs in its intensity and fullness; therefore the saint and the foolish, men and animals, are at the extremes apart, and cannot be alike." The statements of this passage respecting the physical element and creaturely desire, the saint and the foolish, seem to me[3] perplexing. If we distinguish between the saint and the foolish according to the clearness and turbidity of the physical element, and between men and animals according to its perfection and imperfection; then to what can the phrase, "intensity and fullness of creaturely desire," refer? If we say it refers to the saint and the foolish, the difficulty is that the saint is free from the selfishness of creaturely desire; and if we say that it refers to men and animals, the difficulty then is that in the case of animals the differences in intensity and fullness do not apply. I fail to understand it.

[1] *Dialogues,* by Chu Hsi.

[2] The expression 偏 正, here translated "perfection and imperfection", is literally "true and deflected". It refers to the regularity and evenness or otherwise in the consistency of the ether. When the Ether is of even consistency, that is, when the proportions of the *yin* and the *yang* are correct and harmonious, the ether is said to be 正 and it is equally permeable by all the nature-principles, as in the case of man. When it is uneven, that is, when the *yin* and the *yang* are in unequal proportions, the ether is said to be 偏 and the manifestation of the nature-principles is unequal, as in the instinct of animals.

[3] 煇 (Hui) is the writer Li Hui Shu's *ming*, by which he speaks of himself. Hui Shu (晦 叔) is his *style*.

Answer. The expressions " clearness " and " perfection "
are taken from the phraseology of the *Chêng Mêng*, and
Doctor Lü [1] in his exposition of the *Doctrine of the
Mean* has further developed the subject. But he also
contrasts men with animals, and wise men and learned men
with the foolish and degenerate, and necessarily so.
Speaking in general, in man the Ether is clear and in
animals turbid, in man it is perfect and in animals
imperfect. Again, to distinguish more in detail, in the
learned we have the clear within the clear, in the
wise man we have the perfect within the perfect, in
the foolish we have the turbid within the clear, and
in the degenerate we have the imperfect within the
perfect. And in what Hêng Ch'ü refers to when he
says, " There are animals whose nature approximates to
that of man," [2] we have the clear within the turbid, and the
perfect within the imperfect. The expression, " intensity
and fullness of creaturely desire," is spoken of the human
race as a whole. If you were to classify men as possessing
or not possessing it, those who do not possess it are so few
that they could not make a class. We are therefore shut
up to this method of speech. If it presents any difficulty,
the best way is to substitute " wise men " for " saints ",

---

[1] Probably Lü Tsu Ch'ien (呂 祖 謙), *style* Po Kung (伯 恭), a
scholar of the twelfth century greatly admired by Chu Hsi, who said that
if a man would study as Po Kung he would be able to transform his physical
nature. He was a native of Kuei Lin Fu in Kuangsi, and the author
of famous works on history as well as on the " Odes " and the " Yi Ching ".
He received the title of 太 學 博 士, " Doctor of the Imperial
Academy." See *Shang Yu Lu*, pt. xv, p. 4 ; also *Giles' Biog. Dict.*, p. 561.
Cf. J. P. Bruce, *Introduction to Chu Hsi and the Sung School*, chap. iv.

[2] Cf. p. 73.

and so avoid the ambiguity.   The saints may well be
regarded as above the rest, and therefore outside the
classification.   (Reply to Li Hui Shu.)

5.   The production of a man by Heaven is like the
command of the Throne to a magistrate ; man's possession
of the Nature is like the magistrate's possession of his
office.   The duty imposed by the Throne consists of
administering the law and governing the people : how can
there be in it anything but what is good ?   Heaven in
producing a man does not fail to impart the principles of
Love, Righteousness, Reverence, and Wisdom : again, where
is there room for anything that is not good ?   But in
producing a particular being there must be the Ether, which
by subsequent consolidation furnishes the physical substance
of that being.   But the Ether in the constitution of the
creature differs in the degree of its clearness and
translucence.   When the Ether with which the individual
is endowed is clear and translucent, there is freedom from
the entanglement of creaturely desire, and we have the
saint.   When the Ether with which the individual is
endowed is clear and translucent but neither pure nor
complete, some entanglement of creaturely desire is unavoid-
able ; but it can be overcome and got rid of, and then we
have the wise man.   When the Ether with which the
individual is endowed is blurred and turbid, there is the
beclouding by creaturely desire to such an extent that it
cannot be shaken off, and we have the foolish and degenerate.
All this is the action of the etherial endowment and
creaturely desire, but the goodness of the Nature itself does

not vary. The Nature received by Yao and Shun at their
birth was the same as that of others, but because of the
clearness and translucence of their etherial endowment there
was no beclouding by creaturely desire. Therefore to be
Yao and Shun did not mean that something was added over
and above the Nature itself ; and the learner, knowing that
the Nature is good, knows that the holiness of Yao and
Shun was no forcing of the Nature. To know how Yao and
Shun became what they were is to know what is the type
and model of the goodness of the Nature ; and that the
means by which we all may day by day banish human desire
and return to Divine Law lies within what is our proper
and natural duty, a strong favouring force and free from
difficulty. (Yü Shan's Commentary.)

6. Hsiao Shu said : The expressions " Excellent " and
" Evil " probably originated in the phrase, "Strength,
Weakness, Goodness, and Evil ", in the *T'ung Shu* ; [1] and
it appears to me that the degree of clearness applies to
the Ether in its etherial form, while the terms " Strength ",
"Weakness", "Excellence", and "Evil" apply to the Ether
in the form of solid matter. " Clearness " and " turbidity "
are terms pertaining to Heaven. " Strength," " Gentleness," " Excellence," and " Evil " are terms pertaining to
earth. " Clearness " and " turbidity " are terms applicable
to knowledge ; " excellent " and " evil " are terms applicable
to capacity. " Clear " and " turbid " correspond to the
terms " wise " and " foolish ". " Excellent " and " evil "
correspond to " worthy " and " degenerate ". In those of

[1] See note on p. 111.

highest wisdom the Ether is pure as well as clear, [1] and invariably excellent. In those of greatest worth the Ether is perfect as well as excellent,[1] and invariably clear. The highest wisdom corresponds to clearness, and greatest worth to excellence. But it is not that there is any inequality; just as in the *Doctrine of the Mean*, Shun is called wise and Hui worthy.[2] Below these are those who are called wise, in whom the clear ether abounds, but possibly there is not sufficient of the excellent. In those who are called worthy there is goodness leaning to excess in the direction of either strength or weakness, but perhaps at the same time an insufficiency of clearness. This results in an incompleteness in the character of the worthy and the wise, so that their wisdom cannot be termed highest wisdom nor their worth greatest worth. Even in the case of the degenerate there are also degrees. For the difference in clearness and excellence appears to be due to differences between the positive and negative modes in the physical element. (The positive is clear and the negative turbid; the positive is good and the negative evil.) Therefore in the intricate complexity and myriad transformations of the ethers, though the main divisions are not more than these four, yet the proportions in which they interact are so unequal that the myriad varieties naturally follow. I do not know if this is correct.

[1] That is, in the genus " clear " there is the species " pure " to which highest wisdom belongs, in which case the ether is " pure as well as clear ". Similarly in the genus " excellent " there is the species " perfect ", etc.

[2] D.M., pp. 252–3. Both Shun and Hui were what they were because they chose the Mean. There is no inequality in the virtues of either the wise, as in the case of Shun, or the worthy, as in the case of Hui, because both are governed by the Mean.

Answer. Ch'ên Liao Wêng[1] speaks of "the ether of heaven and solid matter of earth". Our predecessors already had this idea. (Reply to Li Hsiao Shu.)

7. In the phrase, "Man's birth and the repose which then exists," the word "repose", it is true, refers to the Nature; but the word "birth" in itself implies the physical element. The time preceding the "birth" "needs no discussion", for the ethical principle has not as yet any means of material manifestation. Therefore at the very moment when we apply the term "Nature" the physical element is necessarily included : you cannot suspend the Nature you are describing in mid-air. The dictum, "The law of their succession is goodness," primarily describes the processes of creation and development. Ming Tao, however, is here speaking of the operation of the Nature, just as Mencius does when he says, "If we look at the feelings which flow from the Nature, we may know that they are constituted for the practice of what is good."[2]   What I Ch'uan calls "the original and essential nature"[3] is in contrast to the physical nature; although the physical element differs in respect of good and evil, yet, if you trace it to its origin and essence, the Nature is never other than good. (Reply to Wang Tzŭ Ho.)

---

[1] Ch'en Liao Wêng is Ch'ên Ch'üan (陳　瓘), who was called Liao Chai (了　齋) by his pupils.   Wêng (翁) is an honorific substitute for the second word in the sobriquet, in accordance with frequent usage.   Liao Chai was a native of Chien Chou in Fuhkien.   He was fond of books when young.   See 學案, pt. 35, fols. 1 ff.   The sentence quoted will be found on f. 3.

[2] Mencius, p. 278.

[3] 遺　書, pt. iii, f. 4.

8. P'an Kung Shu said: I should say [1] that the terms "Nature" and "Decree" apply to Law; "Virtue" and "the etherial element" apply to the person. When the Law of the Nature and Decree is embodied in the personality it is Virtue, and that which crushes [2] and submerges it is the etherial element. For Virtue cannot be other than good, it is the Ether which is unequal. Goodness is that whereby the Nature is completed and the Decree established, but the Ether by reason of its inequality constitutes an obstruction. These two elements [3] in the personality grow and diminish in relation to each other; and, following this variation in degree, the one overcomes or is overcome by the other. The phrase, "When Virtue fails to overcome the Ether," means that Virtue has no means of overcoming the inequality in the Ether. When the Ether is thus unequal it becomes relatively more powerful each day, while goodness becomes less; and so the Law of the Nature and Decree is thrown into confusion by the etherial element. Therefore it is said: "When virtue fails to overcome the Ether the Nature and the Decree follow the Ether." [4] The phrase, "If Virtue succeeds in overcoming the Ether," means that Virtue has the power to overcome the inequality in the etherial element, and goodness daily becomes more abundant, while the inequality melts away; and so the Law of the Nature and Decree lies within the sphere of Virtue. Therefore is is said,

---

[1] Lit. "Your friend Kung would submit"

[2] 牿 is used for 梏, fettered.

[3] That is, Virtue and the Ether.

[4] Quoted from Chang Tsai's *Chêng Mêng*; see p. 9 of this volume.

"When Virtue overcomes the Ether the Nature and Decree follow Virtue." I do not know if this is right.

Answer. The Ether differs also in purity ; you cannot speak of it only as crushing and submerging. But when Virtue fails to overcome the etherial element, what there is of good also proceeds from the fleshly endowment. (Reply to P'an Kung Shu.)

9.   The difference between the teaching of Confucius and that of Mencius respecting the Nature is not easy to explain in a few words.[1]   But, to express it as briefly as possible, the Master spoke of it in combination with the physical, while Mencius spoke especially of the Law of the Nature. It is because the Master spoke of it in combination with the physical that he used the term " nearly alike ", and did not say " alike " ; [2] for the reason that he realized that men cannot but differ morally, and yet have not reached the stage of being "by practice wide apart".[2]   From the point of view of Law we are told : " The great God has conferred on the inferior people a moral sense."[3]   "The people hold within themselves a normal principle of good."[4] How could there at the beginning be two Laws of our being ?   But there is that about the indwelling of this Law in man which it is not easy to find.   Mencius, therefore, in his explanation to Kung Tu Tzŭ,[5] expounded the Nature

---

[1] 質 here = 對 正, to compare.   [2] Analects, XVII, ii, p. 182.
[3] *Shu Ching*, pp. 185–6.
[4] *Odes*, p. 541 ; cf. Mencius, p. 279 ; see also p. 54 of this volume.
[5] A disciple of Mencius ; see Mencius, p. 277.

in terms of man's Capacity and Feelings.[1] For example, if you want to ascertain that water is essentially clear, and cannot get at the source, then observe its flow at a point not far from the source, and you will know that at the source itself it must be clear. (Reply to Sung Shên Chih.)

10. Questioned as to Ming Tao's words, "The time preceding man's birth and the repose which then exists needs no discussion,"[2] the Philosopher said : The repose which exists at man's birth is before there is any outgoing of the Nature. The time preceding is before the birth of the creature, when the term Nature is not applicable. The phrase, " The moment you apply the term Nature," refers to the post-natal period when Law has become inherent in the physical element, and so man's constitution is not wholly the Nature in its original substance. And yet the original substance has not come to be outside of it. It is important that we should recognize at this point that the original substance of the Nature is not confused with the physical element. In the *Great Appendix* of the *Yi* the expressions "succession" and "goodness" refer to the ante-natal period. Mencius in his dictum, " The Nature is good," refers to the post-natal period ; but even so, the original substance is still not confused with the physical element. (Reply to Yen Shih Hêng.)

[1] Mencius, p. 278.   Legge renders 才 as " natural powers "; in his note he quotes the Chinese gloss : 才＝材質。人之能也。 which he translates " man's ability, his natural powers ".   I have adopted the rendering " capacity " as best fitting the various contexts in this work.

[2] See p. 97, n. 5

11. *Question.* Ch'êng Tzŭ said: "All who expound the Nature define it simply as what is spoken of in the dictum ' The law of their succession is goodness ', the same as Mencius refers to when he says, ' The Nature of man is good.' "[1] Just now, sir, in your reply to Yen Shih Hêng you said:[2] "The dictum 'The law of their succession is goodness', in the *Great Appendix* of the *Yi*, refers to the time before birth, while Mencius in his dictum refers to the time after birth." This seems to differ from Ch'êng Tzŭ's statement.

Answer. The Master Ming Tao's language is lofty, far-seeing, comprehensive, and broad. The interpretation of it must not be restricted to its literal meaning. Such passages are many. If you hold to a rigid[3] interpretation you will find that this is not the only passage you will not be able to understand. Grasp the fact that the Nature in its origin is good, that in its issue it is still no other than good, then the meaning of the *Great Appendix* and Mencius will appear as perfectly consistent. (Reply to Ou-Yang Hsi Hsün.)

12. *Question.* The time preceding the birth of the creature is that referred to in the dictum, "The alternation of the negative and positive modes is what we term Moral Law,"[4] and in the phrase, " The permeating activity of the Divine Decree." So that the phrase, " The law of their succession is goodness," refers to the " time

---

[1] See p. 97, n. 5.   [2] See preceding section.
[3] Lit. " square ", i.e. the opposite of a round thing which will roll along the ground, while a square thing is immovable and rigid.
[4] See p. 56.

preceding ". Why, then, should it be said that " The time
preceding . . . needs no discussion " ? For to the time
before the creature is born the word " Nature " is certainly
not applicable ; it is after the creature has been born that
the term must be used. Although you say, " After man's
birth Law becomes inherent in the material form, so that
man's constitution is not wholly the Nature in its original
substance," [1] still, the inevitable presence of both good and
evil in the etherial endowment is the Nature's flow, while
the presence of good and the absence of evil in the moral
faculty is the Nature's original substance. But to both you
must apply the term Nature. The important thing for
the student is to embody in life and apply to himself what
he finds in the books he reads. Now to say, " The moment
you apply the term Nature, what you speak has
already ceased to be the Nature," I very much fear, simply
leads men to exhaust their brains upon an insoluble
problem.[2] Then again, you say [3] that the expressions
"succession" and "goodness" in the *Great Appendix*
refer to the ante-natal period, that is : it is what the
principle [4] of the Decree, which cannot as yet be called the
Nature ; while Mencius' dictum concerning the Nature
refers to the post-natal period, that is : it is what the
Great Appendix of the *Yi* refers to in the words
" Their realization is the Nature ", and not what is referred
to in the phrase " The law of their succession is goodness ".

[1] See Chu Hsi's previous answer to the same questioner, p. 123.
[2] 致 詰 = " to examine."
[3] See p. 123.
[4] 道 is used for 理, a principle or law.

On the other hand Ming Tao says, "All who expound the Nature define it simply as what is spoken of in the dictum 'The law of their succession is goodness'; the same as Mencius refers to when he says 'The Nature of man is good'." This again mystifies me.

Answer. This passage I have already explained in the section replying to Hsi Hsün.[1] There are many such passages in Ming Tao's writings. If you take them too literally you cannot understand any of them. The important thing is letting go the letter, to grasp the meaning and not allow yourself to be tied to one way of looking at a passage. (Reply to Yen Shih Hêng.)

13. The phrase, "The moment you apply the term 'Nature'" refers to what is received by man. This is Law combined with the Ether, but to be correct, since it refers directly to the Nature, you must recognize in the Ether another entity which is not to be confounded with it. As to Chiang Ch'uan's statement that the Nature of lower creatures is originally evil, how can such an idea possibly be true? Your communication is to hand. You will do well still more earnestly to ponder these truths. (Reply to Li Hui Shu.)

14. In the passage by Ch'êng Tzŭ,[2] from the sentence "Life is what is termed the Nature" to "what is called life", the meaning is : What is imparted by Heaven to the universe is called the Decree, what is received by the creature from Heaven is called the Nature. But in the permeating activity of the Divine Decree there must be

[1] See p. 124.   [2] See p. 97, n. 5.

the Two Ethers and the Five Agents interacting and consolidating; then only can there be production. The Nature and Decree are immaterial, the Ether is material. The immaterial is one all-comprehensive Law, and invariably good. The material is endless confusion and complexity, and is both good and evil. Therefore in the production of man and other creatures, this Ether, with which they are endowed in order to their production, becomes the repository of the Nature of the Divine Decree. This is how Ch'êng Tzu expounds the words used by Kao Tzŭ, "Life is what is termed the Nature," [1] and expresses the thought in the words, "The Nature is the Ether and the Ether is the Nature."

In the section, from the sentence "All men at their birth are endowed with the Ether" to the words "cannot be said not to be the nature", [2] the cause of the necessary differences of good and evil in the etherial endowment is the Law of the Nature. For in the permeating activity of the Ether it is the Nature which is the controlling factor, dividing into good and evil according to the purity or impurity of the Ether. So then it is not that within the Nature there are two mutually opposing principles; for even in the case of the evil in the Ether its Nature is no other than good, therefore evil cannot but likewise be called the Nature.[3] The Master also said, "Good and evil are both Divine Law. What is termed evil is not originally

---

[1] Mencius, p. 272.　　　　　　　　　　　[2] See p. 97, n. 5.

[3] Note the paradoxical statements, characteristic of Ming Tao, as if intended to startle the reader. The context shows clearly that they do not mean what at first sight they appear to mean. Evil is in the Nature only in the sense that it is the perversion of the good which is in the Nature.

so, but becomes so by excess or by shortcoming."[1] For
there is nothing in the universe which lies outside the
Nature. All evil is good originally, but it has lapsed

In the section, from the sentence "For life is what is
termed the Nature" to "the flow of water downwards",[2]
the Nature is simply the Nature. What words are there
to express it? Therefore even those who excel in
expounding the Nature do no more than expound it in
terms of its manifested phenomena, from which the mystery
of the Nature may be apprehended by the intellect, as when
Mencius speaks of the Four Terminals.[3] When you see
that water inevitably flows downwards, you deduce the
downward tendency of water; and similarly when you see
that the outflow of the Nature is inevitably good you deduce
its immanent goodness.

In the section, from the words "It is all water" to "each
with a different origin",[4] the subject is again illustrated
by the clearness and turbidity of water. The clearness of
the water corresponds to the goodness of the Nature. Its
flow to the sea without defilement illustrates those in whom
the etherial endowment is clear and translucent, and who
from their youth are good; such is the Nature of the Saint;
so that in him the Heavenly type is perfected. The stream
which, before it has proceeded far on its way, has already
become turbid is like one in whom the etherial endowment
is deflected and impervious to an extreme, and is evil from
his youth. The stream which becomes turbid after it has
proceeded some distance in its course, is like one who when

---

[1] See 粹 言, pt. iia, f. 2.
[2] See p. 97, n. 5.
[3] Mencius, p 79.
[4] See p. 97, n. 5

grown up follows after everything he sees, and "has lost his child-heart".[1] The varying degrees of turbidity in the stream are analogous to the varying degrees of cloudiness and impurity in the etherial element. You cannot say that the turbid is not water, and you cannot say that the evil is not the Nature. But though man is beclouded by the etherial element, and so lapses into evil, the Nature does not therefore cease to be inherent within him. Only, if you call it the Nature it is not the original nature, and if you say it is not the Nature, still it is not separate from it. Because this is so, "men should not fail to apply themselves to the work of purification." It is only when by self-culture a man overcomes the etherial element that he knows that this Nature is all-comprehensive and has not perished, that it is what in the figure is called "the original water". Although the stream is turbid the clear water is there nevertheless, so that you "do not bring clear water to take the place of the turbid "; and when it is cleansed there is no turbid water, so that you "do not take the turbid water and place it in a spot by itself". From all which the conclusion is that the Nature in its origin is good. How can there be within it two principles mutually opposed, and side by side with each other?

In the section, from the words " This Law is the Decree of Heaven" to "It was by this that Shun held possession of the Empire as if it were nothing to him ",[2] the sentence " This Law is the Decree of Heaven " includes the beginning and ending, the root and the fruit. Although the cultivation of moral principle is spoken of in relation to human affairs,

[1] Mencius, p. 198   [2] Analects, VIII, xviii, pp. 77–8.

K

still the means whereby it is cultivated are nothing else than
the essence of the Divine Decree; it is not what man by his
own wisdom can accomplish. Were it not for the saints,
man would find attainments impossible, therefore the
example of Shun [1] is used to set it forth. (A discussion
of Ming Tao's " Exposition of the Nature".)

THE DECREE.

(Nineteen Sections from the " Conversations ".)

1. The Nature is the source of all things,[2] but in the
etherial endowment there are varying degrees of clearness
and turbidity which account for the differences between
the sages and the foolish. The Decree is what all beings
alike receive; but in the rotation of the negative and
positive ethers there is irregularity in varying degrees,
which accounts for the inequalities which exist in the
happiness or misery [3] of man's lot.

[1] That is, Shun's " possession of the Empire as if it were nothing to him ".

[2] The Nature is identical with 理 (Law), the source of all things.

[3] Lit. " the five happinesses and six extremes of misery ". Of the
former : " The first is long life (壽), the second riches (富), the third
soundness of body and serenity of mind (康 寧), the fourth the love of
virtue (攸 好 德), and the fifth an end crowning the life (考 終 命)."
Of the six extremes of misery : " The first is misfortune shortening the
life (凶 短 命), the second sickness (疾), the third sorrow (憂), the
fourth poverty (貧), the fifth wickedness (惡), and the sixth weakness
(弱). See *Shu Ching*, pp. 324, 343.

2. An Ch'ing[1] asked for an explanation of the different ways in which the word "Decree" is used, sometimes referring specially to Law and sometimes to the Ether.

Answer.   They cannot be separated, for, apart from the Ether, Heaven would have no means of imparting the Decree to man, and man would have no means of receiving the Decree conferred by Heaven.

3. *Question.*   You, sir, say that the Decree is of two kinds : the one relating to wealth and honour, to life, and to longevity ; and the other relating to the difference between clearness and turbidity, perfection and imperfection, the wise and foolish, the worthy and degenerate.   The one pertains to the etherial element and the other to Law.   As I[2] look at it, the two kinds both belong to the etherial element because the differences between the wise and foolish, the worthy and degenerate, and in the degree of clearness and turbidity, perfection and imperfection, are all the result of the Ether.

Answer.   That is true.   The Nature, however, consists of the ethical principles of the Decree.[3]

4. The word "Decree" in such a sentence as "The Decree of Heaven is what we term the Nature"[4] refers to

---

[1] Ch'ên Ch'un, see p. 195, n. 2.

[2] "Hsien" (僴) refers to the speaker.

[3] The second class are all related to the ethical principles which constitute the essential nature, which is not true of the first class. Therefore, though what Hsien says is true, and the difference between the wise and foolish, etc., is due to the Ether; nevertheless, that they are what they are is also due to the ethical principles (理) in them, which constitute their essential nature.

[4] D.M., p. 247.

Law with which man is endowed ; in the passage, " These things are the Nature, but there is the Decree concerning them," [1] it refers to the measure of man's etherial endowment which varies in the degree of its fullness and depth.

5. *Question.* How does the word " Decree " in the sentences, " The Decree of Heaven is what we term the Nature," [2] and " Death and life have their Decree," differ in meaning ? [3]

Answer. " Decree " in the sentence, " Death and life have their Decree," includes the etherial element, which varies in fullness and depth. " Decree " in the sentence, " The Decree of Heaven is what we term the Nature," refers only to Law. It should be remembered, however, that that which is decreed by Heaven is never really separated from the etherial element ; none the less, the statement in the *Doctrine of the Mean* refers to Law. Mencius in the sentence " These things are the Nature, but there is the Decree concerning them ", [1] includes the etherial endowment and the sensations of taste and colour in the term " Nature " ; and the word " Decree " in the sentence, " These things are the Decree but there is also the Nature," [4] includes the etherial element. The statement, " The Nature is good," [5] again, refers to what transcends the etherial.

6. *Question.* With regard to the statement that " the Master seldom spoke of the Decree " [6], the cardinal virtues, Love, Righteousness, Reverence, and Wisdom, are all alike decreed by Heaven, but in the Decree relating to honour,

---

[1] Mencius, p. 365.   [2] D.M., p. 247.   [3] Analects, XII, v, 3, p. 117.
[4] Mencius, p. 366.   [5] Mencius, p. 110   [6] Analects, IX, i, p. 80.

life, and longevity there are different degrees. How do you explain this ?

Answer. All are decreed by Heaven.   Those whose etherial endowment is pure and bright are saints and sages, and they receive the ethical principle in its completeness and perfection. Those in whom the endowment is clear and translucent are eminent and refined ; those in whom it is simple and generous are gentle and genial ; those in whom it is clear and elevated are honourable ; those in whom it is abundant and generous are rich ; those in whom it is enduring and extended are long-lived ; those in whom it is feeble and deteriorating, attenuated and turbid (one copy reads : Those in whom the endowment is decaying and solitary are the poor, the mean, and the short-lived), are the foolish and degenerate, the poor, the mean, and the short-lived. Whenever Heaven by means of the etherial element produces a man, a large number of other creatures are produced at the same time.

The Philosopher said further: That which Heaven decrees, it is true, is one and homogeneous, but in the etherial endowment we find inequalities, and all depends on what that endowment is like; if it is generous, the ethical principle is perfect. I have said before that the Decree is like letters patent conferred by the Throne. The Mind is like the officer sent to his office. The Nature is like the duty of that office : the prefect has the duties belonging to the office of prefect, and a magistrate those of magistrate. But duty is one, and only one. Heaven in producing a man instructs him in numerous ethical principles, and thereby entrusts to him numerous duties (another copy reads : The ethical principle is one only).   The etherial endowment is like the emolument ; honourable status is like high office, lower status is like a small post ; wealth is like high pay, and poverty like small pay ; longevity is like filling the office for two or three years and then having a second term ; shortness of life is like one who does not even complete his term ; and when the Throne sends a man to his office there follows in his wake a numerous retinue.

7. *Question.*   For Yen Yüan " the time decreed unfortunately was short ".[1]   When Po Niu died Confucius said, " It is decreed, alas ! "[2]   In regard to his obtaining office or not, Confucius said, " That is as decreed."[3]   Is there no distinction between " decree " in these cases and in the dictum, " The Decree of Heaven is what we term the Nature " ?[4]

Answer.   The Decree in its true meaning proceeds from Law, its variations proceed from the physical element.   The important thing is that in both cases it is imparted by Heaven.   Mencius said, " That which happens without man's causing it to happen is the Decree " ; but man ought himself to fulfil his part, then whatever he meets with is the Decree in its true sense.

Out of this arose the question : At the present time the school which expounds the mystical meaning of numbers according to K'ang Chieh's theory[5] teaches that all is fixed and unchangeable.   What do you say ?

[1] Analects, VI, ii, p. 49.

[2] Ibid., VI, viii, p. 52.

[3] Mencius, p. 241.

[4] D.M., p. 247.

[5] See J. P. Bruce, *Introduction to Chu Hsi and the Sung School*, chap. ii.

Answer. All you can do is to gather the main trend of growth and decay, diminution and increase, in the negative and positive ethers. The saints and sages, however, did not emphasize this teaching. Those who in the present day expound K'ang Chieh's theory of numbers as teaching that every single event, and every single thing has its moment of success or failure—all such are superficial in their exposition.

8. Wên Yi asked: In the plaint of Confucius, "It is killing him. It is decreed, alas!"[1] does the word "decreed" refer to the etherial endowment?

The Philosopher replied: Life, death, longevity, and brevity of life, it is true, are the endowment of the Ether. You have only to look at Mencius' words, "These things are the Nature, but there is the Decree concerning them."[2]

Tsê Chih[3] asked: What about the word "Decree" in the phrases, "Without recognizing the Decree,"[4] and "To know the Decree of Heaven"?[5]

Answer. It has not the same meaning. In the sentence, "To know the Decree of Heaven," the meaning is to know whence this Law is derived. Take water as an illustration. All know it to be water, but the sage knows its source. In the sentence "Without recognizing the Decree", however, the reference is to the Decree of death, life, longevity, wealth, and honour. But Mencius said again, "A man

---

[1] Analects, VI, viii, p. 52.   [2] Mencius, p. 365.

[3] Possibly Liu Tsê Chih, cf. 朱 子 年 譜, pt. iv, p. 54; but more likely Lin Tsê Chih; see p. 300.

[4] Analects, XX, iii, 1 (p. 218).   [5] Ibid., II, iv, 4 (p. 11).

should receive submissively the Decree in its true meaning."[1]
If, in defiance of natural laws, he "stands beneath
a precipitous wall",[1] then he has not received it in its true
meaning.

9. Li Chih quoted the saying, "The Master was mild
and yet dignified, majestic and yet not fierce, respectful and
yet easy"; [2] and with reference to it asked : Those who
receive the clear and translucent ether are saints and sages ;
those who receive the clouded and turbid ether are foolish
and degenerate ; those in whom the ether is generous are
wealthy and honourable ; those in whom it is attenuated
are poor and lowly.   All this is true, but when the sage
receives the clear, translucent, equable, and harmonious Ether
of the Universe he ought to be without any defect, and yet
the Master was poor and lowly.   How was that ?   Can it
be that his horoscope was unpropitious ; Or is it that his
endowment was inadequate ?

Answer. It is because there was a deficiency in the
endowment.   His clear and translucent ether could only
secure his being a saint and sage ; it could not guarantee
his being wealthy and honourable.   Those in whom the
endowment is elevated are honourable ; those in whom it is
generous are rich ; those in whom it is extended are long-
lived.   In the poor, lowly, and short-lived the reverse is the
case.   Although the Master was endowed with the clear
and translucent ether and was therefore a sage, while on
the other hand his endowment was low and attenuated, and
therefore his lot was one of poverty and lowliness.   Yen Tzŭ

[1] Mencius, p. 326.   [2] Analects, VII, xxxvii, p. 71.

was not even equal to Confucius, being endowed with the contracted ether, and so was short-lived as well as poor.

Question. The negative and positive ethers should be equal and homogeneous, and therefore the worthy and degenerate ought to be in equal proportions. How is it that the noble-minded are always few and the ignoble always many?

Answer. It is because the phenomena of the two ethers are so complex and intricate as to make equality impossible. Take coins thrown in gambling as an illustration : [1] it is very rarely that they turn up all alike, more often they are mixed. It is simply that the Ether, either at an earlier or at a later stage is alloyed and complex ; the Ether received, therefore, cannot be perfectly fitting, and so cannot be evenly proportioned. For example, in any one day, it may be cloudy or bright, windy or rainy, cold or hot, clear and sparkling, or keen and biting ; so that you may see many changes in the course of one day.

Question. Although the Ether is alloyed and complex, yet after all there are but two ethers, the one negative and the one positive ; how can there be all this inequality?

Answer. It is not as you put it. If there were but a single negative and a single positive ether, then there would be equality. But it is because of the infinite variety and complexity of their phenomena that we cannot meet with that which would be exactly suitable.

---

[1] The allusion is to the process of gambling by which several coins are thrown by the gambler on to a stone slab ; if all are obverse or all reverse the gambler wins, if they are mixed he loses. Obviously it is a rare and lucky chance that gives them to the gambler.

Question. In that case Heaven and Earth[1] produce the saints and sages by accident and not intentionally.

Answer. Whenever it is the intention of Heaven and Earth to produce a saint or sage the Ether is there in due proportion, and thus the saint or sage is produced. The very fact that he is produced seems to show that it is by the will of Heaven.

10. Ching Tzŭ[2] asked a question about natural proportions in the etherial endowment.

Answer. There are those in whom the etherial endowment is generous and their happiness is full, or the Ether is attenuated and the happiness is meagre. Those in whom the etherial endowment is bright and glittering have abundance of riches; those in whom it is weak and feeble are in humble station. When the Ether is extended there is long life; when it is contracted there is premature death. This is a necessary law.

Question. Is there any foundation for the doctrine of spirits and fairies?

Answer. Who says not? They certainly exist. But their work is generally speaking difficult. It is only when they lay aside everything else, and concentrate on the task in hand, that they can accomplish it.

---

[1] Note: the expression " Heaven and Earth " is here used interchangeably with the term " Heaven " alone; cf. the last sentence in the answer to this question. See J. P. Bruce, *Introduction to Chu Hsi and the Sung School*, chap. xii.

[2] Li Fan (李 燔), *style* Ching Tzŭ, a native of Nan K'ang, where Chu Hsi held office, and a disciple of the Philosopher. After Chu Hsi's death he was invited by the Governor of Nan K'ang to the post of President of the " White Deer College ", associated with Chu Hsi's name.

He said further: I saw in a famous temple pictures of the patron saints representing them [1] as majestic and heroic. It must be that they stood out thus as heroes among men. Thus Miao Hsi, in praise of a Buddhist priest, says, "Originally if it had not been for this religion he would certainly have been a great chief." And the sight was enough to convince one that the remark was true. How could riches, honour, gain, advancement, music, women, or avarice hold ensnared a man with such a countenance? He regarded them all as powerless to move him.

Some one asked: If the Buddhists had not picked him up, would he have followed our Confucian cult?

Answer. He was still not of the sort who "without a King Wên rouse themselves ",[2] but simply a man of independence and individuality, a man who in all that he did must be conspicuous. If a sage had taken him up, probably he would have been all right. But at that time our teaching was obscure and eclipsed. Scholarship consisted of stilted phrasing. Such a man as this could no more be controlled by such pedantic teaching than a dragon or tiger. He was bound to break loose very soon. There can be no doubt of that. The serious thing is that it went so far that good men were led away by these Buddhist saints.

11. *Question.* With reference to the statement, "Riches and honour are decreed,"[3] how did the low and mean, such

---

[1] 人 物 here means a man's appearance. It is frequently so used in modern speech.
[2] Mencius, p. 330.　　　　　　[3] Analects, XII, v, 3, p. 117.

as appeared in after ages, obtain riches and honour in the time of the three dynasties of Yao and Shun ? [1]

Answer. In the period of the three dynasties of Yao and Shun they did not attain to riches and honour. That they did so in later generations was because it was so decreed.

Question. In that case the etherial endowment is uncertain, is it not ?

Answer. For those endowed with this kind of ether to be born in a favourable time [2] is because the Decree is favourable. For the same phenomenon to appear in another than this particular age is because there is what is spoken of as " the natural endowment just fitting the age ". For example, that 400,000 men died at Ch'ang P'ing was because they fell into the hands of Po Ch'i. [3] That he should be the one they should come into collision with, was owing to the Decree.

12.   When the saints and sages are in high position it is because their Ether is equable and harmonious.   When otherwise it is because their Ether is unequal in its flow. Therefore in some the Ether is clear, and these are intelligent but without wealth.   In others the Ether is turbid, and they are wealthy but without knowledge.   In both cases the

---

[1] That is, of Yao, Shun *and* Yü.

[2] The first " 此 " (this ether) refers to the ether of the " low and mean " ; the second (this time) to the " later generations " in which they obtain " riches and honour ".

[3] The allusion is to the incident which took place in a war between the feudal states of Ch'in and Chao in the third century B.C. Four hundred thousand men of Chao were treacherously put to death at a place called Ch'ang P'ing, after surrendering to the enemy under Po Ch'i, the commander-in-chief of the Ch'in forces. See Giles' *Biog. Dict.*, p. 629.

determining factor is in the proportions of the Ether. Yao, Shun, Yü, Kao, Wên, Wu, Chou, and Shao[1] all received the Ether in its perfection, whereas the Ether as received by Confucius, Mencius, Yi, and Ch'i[2] was imperfect. In the period of the Five Dynasties, after exceedingly turbulent times, there again appeared numerous saints and sages as though in the revolving cycle the statesmen of the patriarchal times came round once more. (The Yang record says: It is the same principle as is expressed in the saying, "A great fruit which has not been eaten.")[3] It is like a man's renewal of energy when he awakes from a deep sleep. (The Yang record adds: Now, however, is a time of deceit and folly from which we have not yet awakened. When the extreme of disorder fails to reach its limit in the

[1] All these are celebrities mentioned in the Shu Ching. The first three are the three famous emperors, Yao, Shun, and Yü. The third was Shun's minister Kao Yao. Then follow the two kings Wên and Wu, and lastly the two dukes, Chou and Shao, mentioned in the *Books of Chow*. See *Shu Ching*, p. 420.

[2] For Yi and Ch'i, see Analects, V, xxii. They were Po Yi and Shu Ch'i, sons of King Ku Chu. "Their father left his kingdom to Shu Ch'i, who refused to take the place of his elder brother Po Yi. Po Yi in turn declined the throne, so they both abandoned it and retired into obscurity. When King Wu was taking his measures against the tyrant Chou, they made their appearance, and remonstrated against this course. Finally, they died of hunger, rather than live under the new dynasty." See Analects, p. 45 and note. They were thus a noble instance of the ether being favourable to virtue, but not to material wealth or power.

[3] The quotation is from the Yi Ching (p. 106). The picture is of one large specimen of fruit which remains on the tree, the one survivor of the autumn gathering. The passage occurs in a chapter which treats of the decay of the power of the good, but with hope of its return. "Small men have gradually displaced good men and great, till but one remains; and the lesson for him is to wait. . . . A change for the better will shortly appear" (See Legge's note, pp. 106–7.)

course of fifty or sixty years, the Ether becomes fixed in its
dormant condition and does not revive.   Alas, the pity
of it !)

13.   The Philosopher was questioned about I Ch'uan and
Hêng Ch'ü's theory of the Decree and Chance.[1]

Answer.   What is termed the Decree is like the command
of the Emperor to occupy some official post.   The degree
of simplicity and ease, of complexity and difficulty, and the
question where one can succeed and where not, belong to the
Decree of the particular period.   All one has to do is to go
and occupy the post.   Therefore Mencius says simply:
" Everything is decreed."[2]   But there is what is truly called
the Decree and what is only indirectly so.[3]   What I mean by
the true Decree is what Heaven appoints for me at the
beginning, such as loyalty in serving my prince and filial
piety in serving my father, in which many principles are
included.   The differing degrees of fullness and depth, on the
other hand, pertain to the etherial endowment, which though
it would not be right not to call it the Decree, is still not the
true Decree.   " Death under handcuffs and fetters "[4] cannot be described as not the Decree, for the simple reason
that it results from a perverse ether with which the subject

---

[1] I Ch'uan was asked the difference between the decree and chance
(遇 " to meet with ") ; and replied that "to meet with " calamity or not
is decreed—thus denying the existence of chance.   Hêng Ch'ü is not so
clear ; he said that to explain the difference in recompense for the same
deeds was as difficult as to explain the difference between decree and
chance.   See 遺 書, pt. xviii, f. 23.

[2] See Mencius, p. 325.

[3] For the force of the word 正 see Mencius, p. 325.

[4] See Mencius, p. 326.

was originally endowed, but to call it the true Decree would be wrong. Therefore the noble man " trembles as if on the brink of a deep gulf, or treading on thin ice ",[1] because his desire is to receive submissively the Decree in its true meaning, and not that which is only indirectly termed such. Again, if a man says he is destined to die in water or fire, he does not, on that account, himself leap into the water, or fire, and die. But what is needed to-day is to regard it simply as the Decree, and not concoct a number of fine distinctions, saying, this is the Decree and that is Chance, these are uniform and those are diverse.[2]

14. *Question.* Does the exclamation of Confucius, " It is decreed, alas ! "[3] mean that [in the case of Po Niu] the proportion of the Ether determining his life was exhausted at this point ?

Answer. It was that he received his endowment in just this way. The Decree is like what we have said before concerning man's mind. There are two kinds of Decree, not two Decrees. There is the Decree which includes the physical, and there is the Decree which is wholly Law.

15. *Question.* In that part of the " Literary Remains "[4] in which the Decree is discussed, what is the meaning of the passage in the commentary, " The sages were not ignorant of the Decree, but in human affairs they did not fail to use their utmost endeavour " ?

---

[1] See Analects, VIII, ii (pp. 72–3).

[2] Probably referring to Hêng Ch'ü's remark about the difference in recompense for the same deeds (行 同 報 異); see J. P. Bruce, *Introduction to Chu Hsi and the Sung School*, chap. vi.

[3] See Analects, VI, viii (p. 52).

[4] The 二 程 遺 書.

Answer. For man there is certainly the Decree, but he must not fail to " receive it submissively in its true meaning",[1] as taught in the words, " He who understands what the Decree is will not stand beneath a precipitous wall."[1] If a man, saying "It is decreed", goes and stands beneath a precipitous wall and the wall falls and crushes him, it cannot be attributed solely to the Decree. In human affairs when a man has done his utmost you may talk of the Decree.

16.   Hêng Ch'ü said, " The unchangeable thing is the length of a man's life." It is important to bear in mind that this too is changeable, but the statement is true in the main.

17.   *Question*. With reference to the statement, " That which happens without man's causing it to happen is the Decree " : [2] in the case of Pi Kan's death,[3] from the point of view of Law it may be called the Decree in its true sense, but not surely from the point of view of the etherial element.

Answer. How can you say so ? " Death sustained in the discharge of duty is the Decree in its true sense." [4] When one who ought to die does not die, that is to lose the Decree in its true sense. This kind of passage must be looked at broadly, as when Mencius said, " Death under handcuffs

---

[1] See Mencius, pp. 325–6.   [2] Mencius, p. 235.

[3] Pi Kan was uncle to the tyrant Chou, the last Emperor of the Yin dynasty, 1153–1122 B.C. Owing to his remonstrances against his nephew's tyranny he was thrown into prison, where to escape death he feigned madness. " Pi Kan, persisting in his remonstrances, was barbarously put to death, the tyrant having his heart torn out that he might see, he said, a sage's heart." See Analects, XVIII, i, i (p. 195).

[4] Mencius, p. 326.

and fetters is not the Decree in its true sense,"¹ you must
have regard to what Mencius himself meant. And again, in
the case of Kung Yeh Ch'ang, who, "although he was put
in bonds, had not been guilty of any crime,"² if he had died
in bonds you could not have said his was not the true Decree.
He could say with truth, " My innocence or guilt rests with
myself." How the ancients by their death could establish
virtue,³ and what they could accomplish after their death
may be seen in this. It is what Mencius refers to when
he says, " I will let life go and choose righteousness,"⁴ and
again, " The determined officer never forgets that his end
may be in a ditch or a stream ; the brave officer never forgets
that he may lose his head." ⁵ Let the student get a clear
grasp of this principle, and when face to face with the choice
between gain and loss, he will willingly give himself up to be
cut in pieces. He must be set, too, like a wall 10,000 rods
high.⁶ But now-a-days, if there be a question of choice
between even small gain or injury, there is calculating
comparison. How can it be correct to speak of death in the
case you mention as not the Decree in its true sense ?

18. " Heaven and Earth have a mindless Mind " ; " The
Fu diagram represents one positive mode as produced under

¹ Mencius, p. 136.
² Kung Yeh Ch'ang was the son of Confucius. Nothing is known as
to the cause of his " bonds ". See Analects, V, i, p. 36.
³ Analects, xv, viii, p. 161. ⁴ Mencius, p. 287. ⁵ Ibid., p. 265.
⁶ That is, so that no temptation can get over his resolute will. The
word rod (𠀋) is a measure equal to 7 or 8 feet.

the negative : this is the Mind which delights in creating " ; [1]
" The great God has conferred on the inferior people a moral
sense " ; [2] " The way of Heaven is to bless the good and
punish the evil " [3]—these passages indicate that there is
a Person, as it were,[4] ruling in it all. The Mind is His
agent, and the Feelings are His purpose.

The further question was asked : [5] How may we know
what are the Feelings of Heaven and Earth ?

Answer. Man is true and great, whence we may know
that the Feelings of Heaven and Earth are true and great.
But the truth and greatness of Heaven and Earth are
absolute ; there is never anything false, there is never anything small in them.

19. *Question.* When we consider the inequalities of the
Decree, does it not seem as if there is not really One who
imparts it to man, but rather that the two ethers in their
intricate complexity and inequality follow wherever they
happen to strike, and, knowing that these inequalities do

[1] This passage is quoted from Chu Hsi's commentary on the *Yi Ching*.
It must be taken in conjunction with the passage in the *First Appendix*
which says : "Do we not see in Fu the mind of Heaven and Earth ?" See
Yi Ching, p. 233. Legge in his note on the same page says : " ' The Mind
of Heaven and Earth ' is the love of life and of all goodness that rules
in the course of nature and providence."

[2] *Shu Ching*, p. 185.

[3] Ibid., p. 186.

[4] The translation here given is literal, as also on p. 147. The discussion
of its import goes to the heart of Chu Hsi's teaching, see *Introd. to Chu
Hsi, etc.*, chap. xii. Here it is sufficient to say that the Translator regards
the phrase as meaning a Person, i.e. the Supreme Personality ruling in the
universe.

[5] The 又 suggests that there was a previous question not recorded,
to which the preceding paragraph is the answer.

not proceed from man's own powers, people speak of them as decreed by Heaven ?

Answer. They simply flow from the Great Source. The phenomena may be such as would lead one to think that there is not really One imparting the Decree ; but that there is a personal Being above us by whose command these things come to pass, seems to be taught by the "Odes" and "Records"—in such passages, for example, as speak of the wrath of the Supreme Ruler. But still, this Ruler is none other than Law. In the whole universe there is nothing higher than Law and hence the term Ruler. In the passage which says, "The great God has conferred on the inferior people a moral sense," [1] the very word "confer" conveys the idea of One who exercises authority.

Question. "Great is Yüan, the principle of Origin, indicated by Ch'ien ! From it all things derive their beginning" ; [2] "The method of Ch'ien is to change and transform so that everything obtains its correct Nature as ordained by Heaven" ; [2] "All things fill the universe in an endless succession of production and reproduction" ; "The sun goes and the moon comes " ; " The cold goes and the heat comes " [3]—in the phenomena referred to in these passages, and in the causes at work in the rushing wind, the torrent of rain, the rivers' flow, and the mountain peaks, is it that the Empyrean truly possesses the power which controls the creative and transforming processes ; or is it simply that the Supreme Ultimate is the PIVOT on which all transformations turn, and therefore that the universe is what it is by a process of self-evolution ?

[1] *Shu Ching*, p. 185.   [2] *Yi Ching*, p. 213.   [3] Ibid., p. 389.

Answer. This is the same question as the one already answered.

(THREE SECTIONS FROM THE "COLLECTED WRITINGS".)

1. People reckon the happiness, longevity, and prosperity of men by the time of their birth in its conjunction with the Celestial Stems and Terrestrial Branches,[1] together with the quality of the Ether indicated by them.[2] Although the art is apparently simple, it nevertheless frequently happens that the calculations of its disciples are not very successful in detail.   For the means whereby Heaven and Earth produce all things are no other than the

---

[1] The Celestial Stems (天 杆) and Terrestrial Branches (地 支) are the ideographs used to denote the days of the month and the sixty years of the Chinese cycle.   There are ten of the former and twelve of the latter, of which two numbers sixty is the least common multiple ; so that the two series, combined together in fixed order, give sixty different combinations, one for each year of the cycle.   The Celestial Stems represent the Five Agents, two stems for each Agent, corresponding to which are the five planets, Jupiter, Mars, Saturn, Venus, and Mercury.   Each planet bears the name of its corresponding Agent, and is represented by the same combination of Stems.   Thus Jupiter is the Wood Planet, Mars the Fire Planet, Saturn the Earth Planet, Venus the Metal Planet, and Mercury the Water Planet.   The Terrestrial Branches represent the twelve signs of the Zodiac, and the twelve periods into which the day is divided.   Each of these signs, in both series, represents either the Yin or the Yang according to the order of their notation, the odd numbers referring to the latter and the even numbers to the former ; and in combination they represent different proportions of these two modes of the Ether. From this it will readily be seen how men's horoscopes may be made to indicate the proportions of the Two Modes in their etherial endowment, with variations *ad infinitum*.

[2] 納 音 is the kind of ether, whether Ligneous or Caloric, etc., indicated by the horoscope.

Two Modes and Five Agents. Their contraction and
expansion, their diminution and increase, their intricacy and
transformations, are truly beyond the power of human
investigation ; while the difference between the wise and
foolish, between the highly placed and the lowly, does not
represent more than a hair's breadth of difference in the
degree of translucence and fulness in the Ether imparted
to the creature. Is it to be supposed that such a science
can be easily understood ? Mr. Hsü is a Confucian scholar
and understands this science. He thinks deeply, and most
of his pronouncements are accurate, and confirmed as correct.
If those who are high-minded come into contact with him
and seek to know their horoscope, not only will his art
be adequate to win their faith in the art itself and increase
its fame, but it will also enable them to realize that the
proportion in which the etherial endowment was received by
them at birth is even as thus reckoned, and so learn that
wealth, honour, and fame are not to be obtained by coveting
them, nor poverty, lowliness, and calamity to be avoided by
man's skill. They will therefore take the straight path and
follow Destiny and their own virtuous resolves. Thus, at
one go, evil habits will be changed, and there will be a return
to those customs of honesty, incorruptibility, and modesty,
which have been handed down to us from our ancestors—
all this may be achieved by the help of Mr. Hsü. But none
the less will he teach those who are sons to rely on filial
piety, and those who are statesmen to rely on loyalty, for
their true destiny. " When neither premature death nor
long life causes a man to hesitate, but, cultivating his
personal character, he awaits them, whatever the issue may

be—this is the way in which he establishes his destiny." [1]
(A Preface on the subject of Destiny written for Hsü
Tuan Shu.)

2. *Question*. My strong desire [2] is exhaustively to
investigate the laws of the universe, but the phenomena
are so multifarious that I cannot find any point at which
to begin. At present all, I can see is that riches and
honour are not to be obtained by coveting them, and poverty
and lowliness are not to be avoided by our own efforts.

Answer. What you say is from the point of view of
Destiny ; you must further consider, from the point
of view of Righteousness, whether you ought to seek them
and whether you ought to avoid them ; and still further,
from the point of view of duty, you must examine your
own desires as to why you seek or avoid them. Moreover,
you must know whether it is gain or loss, glory or shame,
which will have the greatest effect upon your own moral gain
and loss, advantage and injury, and so have that whereby
you will be able to take a stand. (Reply to Chu Fei
Ch'ing.)

3. *Question*. The fact that some men are long-lived
and others suffer premature death is due to the Ether ; the
fact that some are wise and some are foolish is also because
of the Ether. Longevity and premature death proceed from

---

[1] Mencius, p. 325.   [2] 比 = 必.

the Ether, and therefore, while all alike receive life, there is a difference between Yen Tzŭ and the Robber Chih. The wisdom of the wise and the foolishness of the foolish both proceed from the Ether, and therefore, while both alike are in their essential Nature good, there are different types of men such as Yao and Chieh.[1]   Now I thought that the Ether of the Universe was one, that the cause of long life and premature death was this Ether, and that the source of the difference between the wise and the foolish was this same Ether. But when we think of the Robber Chih, an extreme instance of folly and yet long-lived, and Yen Tzŭ, the acme of wisdom and yet subject to premature death, it looks as if the Ether of longevity and the Ether of wisdom were not the same. Ming Tao in his epitaph on Ch'êng Shao Kung says : " Having regard to the trouble he met with in his time, that his days could not be many was well. My son ! So pure and yet so contracted was the Ether he received ! " Considering this carefully, it would seem that the Ether differs in clearness and in extension. Because it is clear, we have the wise man ; but though clear it is contracted, and therefore the measure of his life is contracted. Because it is turbid, we have the foolish man ; but though turbid it is extended, and therefore the measure of his life is extended. I am not sure whether I am correct or not.

[1] Yen Tzŭ was the favourite disciple of Confucius, and the Robber Chih was a famous robber of the same period ; see Mencius, p. 161 and note. Yao was the famous sage emperor. Chieh was the notorious tyrant emperor, the last of the line of Hsia, and overthrown by T'ang, the founder of the Shang dynasty. See *Shu Ching*, p. 170.

Answer. Your explanation is correct. It is the same
with honour and wealth. But before the Three Dynasties [1]
the proportion of the Ether was generous and abundant,
and therefore the clear Ether was unfailingly full and
extended, so that the saints and sages were at the same time
honourable, long-lived, and wealthy. Afterwards it came to
be the opposite. (Reply to Chêng Tzŭ Shang.) [2]

CAPACITY. [3]

(THREE SECTIONS FROM THE " CONVERSATIONS ".)

Question. What is the difference between the Feelings
and Capacity ?

Answer. The Feelings are the roads and paths issuing
from the Mind. Capacity is the power of the Feelings to
emanate from the Mind in a particular way. For example,
solicitude may be earnest or otherwise : the difference is due
to a difference in Capacity.

Question. In that case the operations of the Mind and
Capacity are of the same class.

Answer. Capacity is the power of the Mind, it is made
up of etherial force. The Mind is the controller and ruler ;
it is in this that its greatness consists. The Mind may be
likened to water. The Nature is the law of water—the
principle, as it were, which resides in water as still; Feeling is
the principle which works in water as moving; Desire is the

---

[1] That is, the three Emperors, Yao, Shun, and Yü.
[2] See p. 5, n. 3.   [3] See p. 123, n. 1

flow of water extending to an overflow ; Capacity is the physical force by reason of which it is possible for water to flow, the difference in the rapidity of its flow corresponding to the difference in Capacity.   This is what I Ch'uan means when he says, " The Nature is the endowment of Heaven, and Capacity is the endowment of the etherial element." [1]

2.   The Nature is the law of the Mind.   The Feelings are the activities of the Mind, Capacity is the power of the Feelings to act in a certain way.   Feeling and Capacity are in fact nearly alike.   But the Feelings are called forth by contact with object, their roads and paths are crooked and curved ; Capacity is their power to be so.   Bear in mind that the web of consciousness with its innumerable threads proceeds wholly from the Mind.

3.   Some one asked : In the " Collected Comments " it is said, " Capacity is akin to ability."   What is the difference between these two ?

Answer.   The word " Capacity " refers to the principles. The word "Ability" refers to their operation.   In the passage, " When people see the bare and stripped appearance of the mountain they think it was never finely wooded,"[2] Mencius uses the word *ts'ai* with the " wood " radical [3] with the meaning of " suitable in operation ".   In the sentence, " It is not owing to their natural capacity conferred by

---

[1] 遺 書, pt. 18, f. 19.   [2] Mencius, p. 283.
[3] 材, " finely wooded ", is the same word as that rendered " ability " above.

Heaven that they are thus different," [1] the reference is to moral principles.

Question. The word "Capacity" is used with reference to its explaining mental operations. The word "ability" includes the corporeal, does it not?

Answer. Yes, it includes the corporeal, hence you speak of useful abilities.

Question. Is it not similar to the word materials?
Answer. Yes.

(ONE SECTION FROM THE "COLLECTED WRITINGS".)

1. The use of the word "Capacity" by Mencius and Ch'êng Tzǔ is different. As the teachings of saints and sages, we learners of a later generation would not venture to criticize. But on such a subject as this we need only to realize the truth and recognize it in our own persons in order to understand it; nor shall we fail to apprehend the reasons for the correctness and accuracy or otherwise of our predecessors. Thus in the "Collected Comments" [2] it is pointed out that Ch'êng Tzǔ is very detailed, while in what Mencius says lacunæ have not been altogether avoided. To-day we are guided solely by Ch'êng Tzǔ and gather from his teachings what we need to make up what is lacking in Mencius. Thus nothing is lost to truth, and, at the same time, the writings of both are found to be not seriously conflicting. (Reply to Lin Shu Ho.)

[1] Mencius, p. 280.　　　　[2] The Collected Comments of Chu Hsi.

THE PHILOSOPHY OF
HUMAN NATURE

BOOK III

BEING BOOK XLIV OF

THE COMPLETE WORKS OF CHU HSI

———

MIND

BOOK III

MIND

1.   Chih Tao [1] said :   Mind is the Supreme Ultimate.
Lin Chêng Ch'ing said : Mind is indwelt by the Supreme
Ultimate.   Chih Tao raised the question with the Master.

The Master replied :   Such points are very minute and
difficult to explain.   It would seem that Mind is both active
and passive.   " Its substance is termed Flux,[2] its law is
termed Moral Law, and its operation is termed Spirit." [3]

Chih Ch'ing [4] in expanding and explaining this statement
said : The Master's teaching is very ripe, he expresses himself easily, and always explains a subject thoroughly.

---

[1] Surnamed Chao (趙) ; cf. p. 337.

[2] The word is Yi (易), the same as that which occurs in the title of
the *Yi Ching* (The Canon of Changes), the book on which the philosophy
of our school is professedly based ; cf. J. P. Bruce, *Introduction to Chu Hsi
and the Sung School*, chap. x.   " Yi," here translated " Flux ", is
used to represent the substance of Mind, the material of which it is composed.   The word itself in such a connexion inevitably reminds us of the
doctrine of all things as a perpetual flux and reflux, enunciated by
Heraclitus.   But in the Sung School there was a further development
of its meaning, as indicated here in the text.   Cf. *T'ung Shu*, f. 19 1352 義,
pt. i, f. 19) ; also Complete Works, book xlix, f. 16.

[3] Cf. note 1 on p. 159.   The whole sentence is by I Ch'uan ; see
遺 書, pt. i, f. 4.

[4] Chih Ch'ing was the *style* of Huang Kan (黃 幹), a native of Foochow,
who held office in Hupeh and Anhui.   He was a disciple and son-in-law
of Chu Hsi, and assisted his teacher and relative in the commentary on
the *Li Chi* (Book of Rites) ; see Giles' *Biog. Dict.*, p. 335.

Huo Sun asked : In the statement, "Its substance is termed Flux," what is meant by the word "substance"?

Answer. Substance is not substance as used in contrast to operation, but rather in the sense of material,[1] as if we said, the material of which Mind is composed is to be defined as Flux, and Law is the Nature. Passages of this kind need to be taken not too literally. The word "mind", for example, has its different connexions ; as in the statement by Mencius, "Love is man's mind,"[2] in which Love is said to be man's Mind and Mind is regarded as in combination with Law ; while in the passage, "There was Yen Tzŭ, for three months his Mind did not offend Love,"[3] Mind is the ruler and is said to do nothing contrary to Love.[4] We must look at the connexion and then we shall be right.

2. The law of the Mind is the Supreme Ultimate, its activity and repose are the Two Modes.

3. Mind alone is absolute.

4. *Question.* Is the spiritual faculty in man the Mind or the Nature ?

Answer. The spiritual faculty is Mind and not the Nature. The Nature is Law.

---

[1] Cf. the same double meaning of the English word.

[2] Mencius, p. 290.

[3] Analects, VI, v (p. 50). N.B.—Yen Tzû in the original passage is referred to by his name Hui (回).

[4] That is, instead of Love being identical with Mind it is spoken of as if it were a principle distinct from Mind.

5.   *Question.*   With regard to consciousness : is it the spiritual faculty [1] of the Mind that is thus conscious, or is it the action of the Ether ?

Answer.   It is not wholly etherial.   There is first the law of consciousness.   But Law in itself cannot be conscious : there must be union with the etherial element before there can be consciousness.   Take for example the flame of this candle, it is because it receives this rich fat that we have so much light.

Question.   Is the efflux from the Mind Ether ?

Answer.   No, it is simply consciousness.

6.   *Question.*   Mind is consciousness and the Nature is Law.   How do the Mind and Law come to be united as one ?

Answer.   You must not think of their being made to unite.   They start united.

Question.   How do they start united ?

Answer.   Law apart from Mind would have nothing in which to inhere.

7.   Mind is the pure and refined portion of the Ether.[2]

8.   Expounding the word " mind " the Philosopher said : One word will cover it, namely, Life.   "The highest attribute of Heaven and Earth is the production of life."[3]

---

[1] *Ling* (靈) and *Shên* (神) both mean " spirit ", with this difference, that *shên* is substance and *ling* operation, a favourite distinction with the Chinese philosopher.   Because of this meaning of *ling*, it has often the meaning of intellect, or intellectual ; and may be good or evil, whereas *shên* is only good, like the Nature in its source as distinguished from its flow.

[2] The Ether is regarded as of two kinds, the grosser and denser portion becoming physical, and the finer or purer portion becoming mind or spirit.

[3] *Yî Ching*, p. 381.

It is by receiving the Ether of Heaven and Earth that man lives ; therefore the Mind must love, for Love is life.

9.   In your consideration of the Mind you must combine the ideas of immensity [1] and permeating activity, and then add that of the Vital Impulse.[2] Ch'êng Tzŭ, too, defined Love as the life-producing Mind of Heaven and Earth ; which means that immensity is an attribute of Heaven and Earth, and that in the production of things their activity permeates the universe in endless production and reproduction.

10.   Mind and Law are one.   Law is not a separate entity side by side with Mind, but inherent in Mind.   Mind cannot be confined : it issues forth as phenomena present themselves.

At this the Philosopher smiled and said : Saying this makes one smile.   It is just like a library with all the books removed and a lamp lighted : on all sides and in every corner it will be flooded with brilliant light just as it is here at this spot.[3]   To-day, however, few people are able to look at the matter in this way.

11.   *Question.*   Mind as a distinct entity possesses all laws in their completeness, so that the good manifested

[1] The expression " immensity " refers to the power of the Mind to penetrate in thought to an infinity of distance, whether in space or time ; cf. pp. 170-1.

[2] See J. P. Bruce, *Introduction to Chu Hsi and the Sung School*, chap. xiii.

[3] That is, instead of the shadows created by the books obscuring the light.   It must be confessed that the application of the simile is difficult to follow.   It suggests the Philosopher's favourite doctrine of the Ether and Law.   Cf. p. 164.

undoubtedly proceeds from the Mind. But what about the evil manifested, which consists entirely of the selfishness of the material endowment and creaturely desire ? Does this also proceed from the Mind ?

Answer. It is not indeed the original substance of the Mind, but it also proceeds from the Mind.

Question. Is this what is called the " natural mind " [1] ?
Answer. Yes.

Tzŭ Shêng, following on the above, asked : Does the " natural mind " include both good and evil ?

Answer. Yes, both are included.

12. *Question.* Is there any connexion between bodily movements and the Mind ?

Answer. How can it be otherwise ? It is the Mind which causes bodily movements.

Question. Before there are any stirrings of pleasure, anger, sorrow, or joy, the body exercises its functions ; for example, the eye sees and the ear hears. Is this before or after the activity of the Mind ?

Answer. That, as yet, there are no stirrings of pleasure, anger, sorrow, or joy, is one thing ; but sight, hearing, and locomotion also imply the presence of Mind. If the Mind is ignorant of the bodily movements, then it is not present and has not noticed them, in which case to say " before activity " is not applicable. " Before activity " does not mean that the Mind is steeped in unconsciousness. It is

[1] The " natural mind " (人 心) is contrasted with the " spiritual mind " (道 心) in the *Shu Ching*, p. 61.   See also p. 19 of this volume, n. 1.

spoken of the Mind as continually awake, and not as though
it were asleep, as your way of expressing it would suggest.

13.   *Question*.   Solicitude and conscientiousness,
pleasure, anger, sorrow, and joy, are, it is true, the outcome
of the Mind, as may be clearly and easily seen from the
fact that before their issue is the time of perfect stillness
and repose.   But it cannot be like a log of wood.   The eye
and ear have their automatic sight and hearing, and the
hand and foot their automatic movements.   What I do not
understand is what this period is called.

Answer.   When there are no stirrings of pleasure, anger,
sorrow, and joy, it is the Mind which has not as yet put
forth its activity.   The movements of the hand and foot
are purely bodily movements.

14.   *Question*.   The Five Agents become in man the
Five Organs,[1] but the Mind possesses the principles of the
Five Agents.   Is this because the Mind is formless spirit ?

Answer.   Mind as a bright and active thing belongs to
the Igneous class,[2] and therefore it can have numerous
principles inherent in it.

15.   *Question*.   How do you explain the statement that
man's heart is both corporeal and incorporeal ?

Answer.   The heart [3] as one of the internal physical
organs is certainly a concrete thing.   What modern scholars

[1] See p. 20, n. 1.   [2] Fire is one of the Five Agents.
[3] The word " heart " is the same word (心) as is elsewhere rendered
" mind ".   Like the word " heart " in English it has the meaning of the
physical " heart " as well as of " mind ", and both are discussed and
compared in this and the following section.   It has not been possible to
retain the same rendering throughout.   The reader, however, will bear in
mind that in Chinese only one word is used.

speak of as the Mind to be " held fast " or " let go ",
" preserved " or " lost "[1] is unfathomable in its spiritual
intelligence. Thus the physical heart if diseased can be
cured by medicines, but this Heart is not to be healed by
Calamus and China Root.

Question. In that case is Law which is inherent in the
Mind incorporeal ?

Answer. The Mind as compared with the Nature has
something more of visible traces, and as compared with the
Ether it is in the nature of the case more spiritual.

16. *Question by I Kang.* You, Sir, once said : " The
Heart is not this particular piece of flesh." I venture to
suggest that the whole person is the Heart, and that this
particular organ is no more than the pivot.

Answer. Not so. This is not the Heart but the home
whence the spiritual intelligence of the Mind goes forth and
to which it returns. When people's hearts are diseased it
is the home of their Mind which is suffering ; so it is
with the rest of the organs. The Mind cannot be without
activity ; it must always be within the confines of the
body, just as the magistrate of this county, Chien Yang,
must always be in his Magisterial Office : only thus can
he administer the affairs of his district.

I Kang said : But Ch'êng Tzŭ said : "Let your mind
be in your breast,"[2] by which he meant, did he not, that
the Mind should be in its home and not outside ?

Answer. Not necessarily so. It is as if he said the

[1] Mencius, p. 285.
[2] 遺 書, pt. vii, f. i ; cf. ibid., pt. iii, f. 3.

Mind must not be in the foot, or in the hand, but in the body as a whole.[1]

17.   Han Ch'ing[2] asked: Is not the passage, "The Mind is like a library ; on all sides and in every corner it is flooded with brilliant light just as it is here at this spot,"[3] like the Buddhist illustration of a monkey in a room with six windows ? Whichever way he calls there is an echo?

Answer.   The Buddhist teaching on Mind has a great deal in it that is good.   Former philosophers declared that it was better than that of Yang and Mo.[4]

18.   The word "Mind" is itself a *radical*.[5]   Hence the words "Nature" and "Feeling" are both derived from the word "Mind".

19.   Chang Tzŭ combined the Nature and Consciousness as the explanation of the term Mind. This, I think, cannot be quite correct because it assumes another consciousness outside the Nature.

---

[1] Lit. "in these", i.e. in the body and its members.   The "Mind" is not in the physical "breast" any more than in any other part of the body.   "Breast" is merely a form of expression for the person.   It is a popular way of saying "preserve your mind" (存 心).

[2] Fu Kuang (輔 廣) *style* Han Ch'ing, a native of Ch'ing Yüan (慶 源) and disciple of Chu Hsi, a man of singularly pure spirit and keen intellect ; he was specially gifted as a poet.   See 宗 傳, pt. xvii, f. 20.

[3] See p. 160 and n. 3.

[4] Yang Chu and Mo Ti ; see Mencius, p. 158.

[5] One of the 214 root ideographs of which all the ideographs in the Chinese language are compounded.   The word 性 (nature) is composed of 忄 (mind) and 生 (birth), and in the word 情 (feeling) the 忄 (mind) also occurs as its *radical*.

20. The daughter of Fan Ch'un Fu[1] said, "How can the Mind have outgoing and incoming?" I Ch'uan said, "This woman did not understand Mencius, but she understood the Mind."[2] This remark should be noted. It refers to the quotation from Confucius by Mencius, "Its outgoing and incoming cannot be defined as to time or place."[3] Elsewhere this saying of I Ch'uan's is given as: "This woman Ch'un understood the Mind, but the Mind is easy to understand; she did not, however, understand what Mencius meant."

21. The Mind that is perfected is like a clear mirror which is free from blemishes. If you look into a mirror with patches which do not reflect, the effect will be that your own person appears blotchy. In the present day the conduct of many is marred by a number of follies and blemishes because their vision of themselves is imperfect. The Mind is essentially formless spirit;[4] all laws are complete within it, and all phenomena come within the sphere of its knowledge. In these days people are for the most part perverted by their physical nature, and beclouded by creaturely desire. Thus their minds are darkened and

---

[1] Fan Tsu Yü, *style* Ch'un Fu (涫 夫), was a scholar of the eleventh century. He assisted Ssü-Ma Kuang in the compilation of his history. See 尚 友 錄, pt. xvii, f. 5.

[2] 外 書, pt. xi, f. 5.

[3] Mencius, p. 285. Legge in his note quotes a comment by Chu Hsi, thus: "Mencius quoted these words of Confucius to illustrate the unfathomableness of the spiritual and intelligent mind, how easy it is to have it or to lose it, and how difficult to preserve and keep it, and how it may not be left unnourished for an instant."

[4] 大 全, book xxxii, f. 6.

they are unable to perfect knowledge. This is why the saints and sages placed such emphasis on the exhaustive investigation of principles.

22. Again, take as an example a graduate in his studies. First he would study this, and then he would study that; again, he must learn penmanship, and then he must learn the poetic art; and so the whole mind is scattered. For this reason I Ch'uan taught that the mind should not be used in any but the one direction. He would have the student exclude penmanship and essay-writing from his studies. This was not prejudice, but in accord with right principles. Men have only one mind; it is not reasonable to divide it in so many directions. If you give only spare scraps of time to the proper use of the mind, to what good will it lead? It does not help the original object of study in any sense. Further, consider those scholars of ancient times who were experts in essay-writing. They have, it is true, an undying fame, but who of them to-day can be regarded as men of knowledge? At the beginning, it is true, they had bent their minds in the one direction only [but in the opposite sense] and so in their case also the mind was scattered. But to attain to "making the desires few" and to "preserve this mind" is extremely difficult. Even of the saints, T'ang and Wu, Mencius says that they were what they were "by conversion".[1] Conversion means to return; that is, to return and receive again the original mind. For example, the passage which says T'ang "did not come within the sound of lewd music, nor approach

[1] Mencius, p. 371.

dissolute women, nor seek to accumulate property or money ",[1] means simply that his desire was to preserve this mind. Look at the book *The Hound of Lü*.[2] To receive one hound was so grave a thing that repeatedly and earnestly the Grand Guardian warned King Wu against accepting it. From this we may see how desires should be feared : whether great or small there must be no carelessness with regard to any of them.

23. *Question.* Lü Yü Shu [3] said : " Before activity is put forth the substance of the Mind is present in its entirety, brightly luminous. After activity is put forth you have the operation of the Mind." Nan Hsien criticizes the statement, contending that it is " brightly luminous " after activity is put forth. Is this not somewhat beyond the mark ?

Answer. The criticism has no meaning in it. Ching Fu [4] was exceedingly clever, but not sufficiently exact in his

[1] *Shu Ching*, p. 180.

[2] Ibid., p. 345. Legge renders the word 獒 in the plural, " Hounds ", and says in his note : " The critics generally understand the term in the text in the singular—I know not why. There is nothing in the Book, and no ancient references to it, which should make us do so. We more naturally take it in the plural, and it seems to me more likely that several hounds, and not one only, would be sent to King Woo." It is generally understood, however, by Chinese scholars that the hound was of a very rare species, large in size, and regarded as exceedingly valuable. In any case, here the context shows conclusively that Chu Hsi understood it as a single hound, and therefore the word must be translated in the singular.

[3] See p. 60, n. 1.

[4] Chang Ch'ih (張 栻), Ching Fu, and Nan Hsien were his *tzŭ* and *hao* respectively. He was Chu Hsi's great friend, but holding very different views. See J. P. Bruce, *Introduction to Chu Hsi and the Sung School*, chap. iv.

study of philosophy. Mr. Lü[1] is simply criticizing I Ch'uan's statement that "all who discourse on the Mind refer to it as having already put forth activity."[2] But later, I Ch'uan corrected his former statement thus : "This statement, I admit, is not accurate. The Mind is one. Some refer to its substance—that which is 'still and without movement'; others refer to its operation—that which, 'when acted upon penetrates forthwith all phenomena.'[3] We must have regard to the nature of its manifestation." This is an all-round statement and faultless. Generally speaking the sayings of the saints and sages are terse, presenting only the germs of truth; these are developed by later teachers, and then expanded and added to. We must see to it, however, that we get at the original meaning of the saints and sages; otherwise at what point shall we begin in our development of their teachings ?

24. *Question.* The Mind is essentially an active thing. I do not understand whether before activity is put forth it is absolutely still and in repose, or whether the repose condition holds within it the principle of activity.

Answer. It is not that the principle of activity is contained in the repose. Chou Tzŭ said, "Repose is the *non-ens*" and "activity is the *ens*".[4] But repose is not non-existence. It is called the *non-ens* as being without form. The meaning is not that it is existent because of its activity, but that it is so named because of its manifestation. Hêng Ch'ü's way of combining the Nature and the Feelings is

[1] Lü Yü Shu, quoted above. [2] 學 案, pt. xxxi, f. 18.
[3] *Yi Ching*, p. 370.
[4] *T'ung Shu*, chap. i; see 大 全, book ii, f. 9; or 精 義, pt. i.

excellent.[1] The Nature is passive, the Feelings are active, and the Mind combines both the active and passive. We refer to its substance or to its manifestation according to the point of view. The moment the passive state is past, the principle of movement is present. I Ch'uan said, "At the moment between the active and passive states [2] the ear cannot hear and the eye cannot see, but the principle of both hearing and sight is there." And when movement takes place it is still that same thing which was passive.

Ch'un [3] raised the question of I Ch'uan's theory that "The principle of activity is the Mind of Heaven and Earth".[4]

Answer. Activity is not the Mind of Heaven and Earth; it simply reveals the Mind of Heaven and Earth. For instance, in the tenth month,[5] do we not have the Mind of the Universe? It is permeating all things just as before. Of the Four Ultimata: [6] Yüan, the Principle of Origin, is the season when the young sprouts begin to shoot up; Hêng, the Principle of Beauty, is the season of growing foliage; Li, the Principle of Utility, is the fruit-bearing season; and Chêng, the Principle of Potentiality, is the season when the fruit returns to the place of its rest. If in the end there were no such return to rest there would be no Yüan. But because there is the return to rest Yüan springs forth from it. When Yüan has completed its course

---

[1] 學 案, pt. xviii, f. 14. [2] 當 中 時 ＝ 動 靜 之 中.

[3] Probably Ch'ên Ch'un; see p. 195, n. 2.

[4] 大 全, pt. xxvi, f. 16.

[5] That is, in the winter when all is still and apparently lifeless.

[6] *Yüan, Hêng, Li, Chêng,* the principles of Origin, Beauty, Utility, and Potentiality.

Chêng returns, and when Chêng has completed its course Yüan returns, and so on for ten thousand ages in endless revolution. It is completely expressed in the words, " The Decree of Heaven ! How profound it is and undying ! "[1] In the tenth month all things are stored up, and leave no traces, until the positive ether is again active, when the Mind that produces all things becomes once more manifest.

Question. Is not the return of the positive ether[2] in the case of men the first sprouting of goodness ?

Answer. As goodness, it is the first sprouting of goodness. As virtue, it is that first thought of repentance and turning towards goodness which arises in the midst of the darkness—this is a " return ". The sudden awaking from sleep is a picture of the " return ". Or when, the repression of moral principle in man having reached its climax, there is a sudden clearing of the channel, which, although slight, is still the earnest of the full flowing stream—this again is a " return ". The principle has countless transformations and, whenever you find it, it is always profound and mysterious.

25.   The Mind is most spiritual. So fine is it that it penetrates the very point of a hair, or the smallest blade of grass, and I become conscious of them. So great is it that there is not a single place from nadir to zenith, or within the four points of the compass, where it is not present. Back through the countless ages of the past, or forward through the unknown periods of future time, my

---

[1] *Odes*, p. 570.

[2] Compare the Fu Diagram in the *Yi Ching*, p. 107, and Legge's note on pp. 108–9.

thought reaches to the end of them the very moment it proceeds from my Mind. It is unfathomable in its spiritual intelligence, most intangible, most spiritual and marvellous in its orderliness ! And yet, though there is no one who does not possess this Mind, most men know only the desire for gain, till the Mind becomes completely submerged in it. At home or abroad, all that they seek is pleasure and self-indulgence ; their every thought, the moment it is born, is of these things.

26. *Question.* The word " Mind " never occurs in the " Analects ", while Mencius constantly speaks of man's Mind, and discusses it again and again ; as in the expressions, " Extend this heart," [1] " Seek the lost mind," [2] " Perfect the mind," [3] " The child heart," [4] " Preserving the mind." [5] Was this not because the disciples of Confucius themselves knew and understood all about the Mind, and did not trouble the sage to discourse upon it, whereas by the time Mencius appeared the world had very much changed, men had become inferior in ability to the ancients, and therefore Mencius did his utmost to teach them what the Mind is in its origin ?

Answer. Although Confucius did not discourse on the Mind, yet he could not have replied to the questions of his disciples on Love if he had not understood Mind, for Love is Mind. Only at that time they did not use the word " Mind ". Study this passage carefully, and you will find that there is no great difficulty in it.

[1] Mencius, p. 15.   [2] Ibid., p. 290.   [3] Ibid., p. 324.
[4] Ibid., p. 198.   [5] Ibid., p. 285.

27. Question by Li Tê Chih. Ming Tao when repairing a bridge had to choose some long beams. Afterwards, every time he saw a specially fine forest he immediately began mentally to measure the trees. From this he began to discourse to his students on the desirability of not having anything on the mind. It seems to me obvious that you must think about everything in order to understand them. How could he say : you must not have anything on your mind ?

Answer. How can you not think about things ? But the right course is, when the matter is ended, not to keep it on the mind any longer. Ming Tao had one beam in his mind. He still fell short of the people of to-day who have several beams in their minds. The Buddhists have the idea of consciousness being like a stream of flowing water. Water naturally flows on, but if there be several leaks in the channel the flow will be checked.[1]

28. Question. It is said : " Let your mind be in your breast." [2] What should be the mind's attitude to thought about phenomena, and the response to external influences ?

Answer. Thought and responsiveness are indispensable, but the mind should be concentrated on the thing in hand.

Question. In that case, then, when the external impression is received the mind must be fastened on the matter before us, but when the matter has been dealt with the mind must not continue to busy itself with it.

[1] That is, the mind should set aside all thought about things which have been dealt with and pass on to other duties, just as water flows on—unless, indeed, the channel is leaky.

[2] 遺 書, pt. vii, f. 1 ; cf. ibid., pt. iii, f. 3.

Answer.   Certainly, that is how it should be.

29.   *Question*.   In the passage, "Man's mind should be living, permeating in all directions without limit, and not confined to one spot,"[1] what is the meaning of " living ? "

Answer.   If the mind is without selfishness, it can expand and enlarge.   Living is the opposite of dead.

30.   The mind into which " anxiety arising from external things can find no entrance " is the mind in which " there is a controlling principle and is therefore filled ". The mind into which " evil arising from external things can find no entrance " is the mind in which " there is a controlling principle and is therefore empty ".[2]   When this is made the controlling principle in one's mind and nothing else has any existence in it, where is it possible for evil to enter ?   How otherwise can it be described than as empty ?   But in the writer's statement, " The mind in which there is a controlling principle is empty," the words, " there is a controlling principle," in themselves imply being filled.

The Philosopher said further :   The sentence, " The mind in which there is a controlling principle is filled," means that when one's mind has within it a controlling principle, anxiety arising from external things can find no entrance : what is this but to be filled ?   The sentence, " The mind in which there is no controlling principle is filled," means that when one's mind has no controlling principle, evil arising from external things comes in and fills it. How can this be described otherwise than as filled ?

[1] 粹 言, pt. ii, f. 40.   [2] 學 案, pt. xv, ff. 7–8.

31.   *Question*.   What is meant by concentration ?

Answer.   Concentration means not to lose the mind in this or that direction.   Concentration is the opposite of mind-wandering.

Question.   What about thought upon things that need to be thought about ?

Answer.   There is no objection to that ; but there should be no incoherent thinking, and the thought should be on one thing only.   To be thinking about a certain thing and then to let your thoughts go off to something else will not do.

32.   " When the mind is fixed, importance is attached to calmness of speech." [1]   The meaning of this statement is :   Speech is the outcome of the mind.   If the mind be fixed there will be careful discrimination in the use of language, with the result that it will carry the accent of assurance, and will be calm and deliberate.   When the mind is not fixed, confusion prevails within, while language flows forth without previous thought, and is shallow and hasty in consequence.   This,[2] too, is the fruit of the action of the will upon the physical element.[3]

33.   *Question*.   Does the statement, " The Mind is the enceinte of the Nature," mean that the Nature is enclosed in the Mind ?

The Master nodded assent, and said :   Yes, but Hêng Ch'ü's statement, " The Mind unites the Nature and the

[1] 遺 書, pt. xi, f. 4.

[2] The 此 (this) refers to the passage quoted at the beginning of the paragraph.

[3] An allusion to the teaching of Mencius on the will moving the physical element (志 動 氣) and vice versa ; see Mencius, p. 65.

Feelings," [1] is not to be improved upon. Mencius often
spoke of the Mind, but said nothing so exact as this. If
you consider it carefully you will see that in the books
of the other philosophers there is nothing even approaching
this.

34. Fang Pin Wang in a letter asked the following
question: The statement, "The Mind is the enceinte of
the Nature," should be explained as meaning that the Mind
is the seat of that ruling principle which controls
the personality. K'o Hsüeh [2] says that the expression
'enceinte' means to enclose. The Mind contains these
principles [3] as a city wall [4] does its inhabitants.

Chu Hsi replied: Fang's statement is too vague. [5]

Question. Who is it that explains the external operation
of the Mind as the exhaustive investigation of principles?

Answer. It is a statement of the Kiangsi School.

Questioner. The manifestation of the Mind in speech
cannot be regarded as the external operation of the Mind, [6]
because in that case the external operation of the Mind
would be wholly dependent on the brief moment of time
occupied in speech, and what dependence could be placed
upon it?

Answer. The Hunan School [7] all take this view.

[1] 學 案, pt. xviii, f. 14.　　[2] Surnamed Chêng, see p. 3.
[3] That is, the principles of Nature.
[4] 郭 郭 "The outermost walls enclosing the city and suburbs."
[5] Lit. "slow", i.e. not crisp and clear.
[6] 是 refers to 用 心 於 外, immediately above.
[7] The Hu (胡) School, founded by Hu An Kuo (see p. 24), also called
the Hu Hsiang School, see p. 28, n. 4. Nan Hsien (see p. 102) was a
prominent representative of this School; see 學 案, pt. l, f. 3.

Question.   When Mencius spoke to the King of Ch'i [1] his
desire was by means of speech to help him, but if he had
depended only on speech he would have failed, would
he not ?

Answer.   Yes.

Question.   " The necessary existence of life in the seed
corresponds to the necessary existence of Love in man."
Thus life is taken to illustrate Love.   The life of the seed
is the principle of life, so that the principle of life is
regarded as Love.   Is it not so ?

Answer.   It certainly should be so.

The Philosopher further explained Nan Hsien's [2] state-
ment`that the active manifestation of the Mind's substance
is incessant.   When it is manifested it should be preserved
and be master of whatever phenomenon it is dealing with.

K'o Hsüeh said : How can the Mind wait till after its
manifestation before it controls the phenomenon ?

Answer.   If you force the meaning of a passage in this
way you will find many seeming mistakes in Nan Hsien's
statements.

35.   In the statement, " The Mind moulds [3] the virtues

---

[1] Mencius, p. 194.   [2] Chang Ch'ih (張 栻).

[3] The word 妙 generally means " wonderful " or " mysterious " ;
I cannot find that there is any other instance of its use as a verb meaning
" to fashion " or " mould ", except as this sentence is referred to in other
parts of this work.   The sentence is from the writings of Hu Wu Fèng
(see 學 案, pt. xlii, f. 12), and means that the province of the mind is
to mould the powers or virtues of the Nature and Feelings, and so unite
them in harmonious operation.   It is similar to Hèng Ch'ü's saying, " The
Mind unites the Nature and Feelings " (心 統 性 情), see p. 174.
運 用 is the object of the verb 主 宰 ; and the statement means that
the Mind is like a pivot, controlling the operations of the Nature and Feelings.

of the Nature and Feelings," the word "moulds" means to direct their activities.

36. I Ch'uan said at first that all who discoursed on the Mind referred to Mind as manifested. Subsequently he acknowledged that this statement was not correct.[1] Wu Fêng,[2] however, adhered to the earlier statement; and, regarding Mind as already manifested and the Nature as not yet manifested, he contrasted the one with the other in this sense. The *Chih Yen* is full of such statements.

37. The expression, "the natural mind,"[3] refers solely to that which is affected by the material body. The possessor of bodily form we call man; add the ethical element and you have what is termed Moral Law; and that which has consciousness is termed the Mind.

38. "The positive ether is clear; when it prevails the virtuous nature operates: the negative ether is turbid; when it prevails creaturely desire becomes active."[4] You need only to examine and test your own thoughts and you will find it so. When man's mind is empty and still, it will follow naturally that it is pure and clear. When it is clouded by creaturely desire, it is sunk in the densest darkness. This is how the turbid negative ether comes to be predominant.

[1] See p. 168 and n. 2.
[2] The son of Hu An Kuo and author of the *Chih Yen* (Words of Wisdom); see p. 23, n. 2.
[3] Contrasted with the "spiritual mind" (道 心); see p. 19, n. 1.
[4] Quoted from the *Chêng Mêng* (誠 明 篇), by Chang Tsai; see 大 全, pt. v, or 宗 傳, pt. iv, f. 13.

N

39. " When the mind is enlarged it can enter into every-thing [1] throughout the universe. . . . The mind of the man of the world rests within the narrow limits of the senses," and therefore cannot enter into everything [1] throughout the universe. It is the sage alone—he " who develops his Nature to its utmost, and so does not allow his mind to be fettered by what he sees and hears "—whose mind is large enough to embrace all things, so that " under the whole heaven there is not a single thing which he does not look upon as he looks upon himself." [2] All other distinctions are lost in this distinction between greatness and littleness.[3] " Mencius means the same thing when he says, ' By developing the mind to the utmost we understand our Nature and know Heaven.' " [4] For to develop the mind to the utmost is to enlarge it to its utmost. When it is enlarged to its utmost we understand our Nature, we know Heaven, and there is no trace of egoism.[5]

Tao Fu [6] asked : To-day, we who have not, like the

[1] Cf. D. M., p. 261.

[2] Quoted from the *Chêng Mêng* (大 心 篇), see above.

[3] " Littleness " refers to the sentence above, in which Chang Tsai speaks of the heart of the worldly man as so small that it confines itself to what it sees and hears.

[4] See *Chêng Mêng*. For the quotation from Mencius, see Mencius, p. 324, and Legge's note.

[5] When the mind embraces all things there is nothing outside it. The opposite of this is egoism, or 有 外 之 心.

[6] Tao Fu may have been either one of three of Chu Hsi's disciples whose surnames were respectively Huang (黃), Chao (趙), and Yang (楊), but whose *style* in all three cases was Tao Fu. For Huang Tao Fu, see p. 50. Yang Tao Fu was a disciple of Chu Hsi in the latter's declining years, and a faithful companion at the time of his disgrace ; see *Chu Tzŭ Nien P'u* (朱 子 年 譜), pt. iv, f. 44. Chao Tao Fu (*ming* 必 愿),

sages, attained to such development of the mind, must we
not also extend it so as to influence others ? [1]

Answer. Although we have not attained to that standard
we must still learn to say that beyond the senses there is
a realm of principles which cannot be seen or heard. If
we have not learned so much, how can the mind be extended?
The important thing is that this is what Hêng Ch'ü meant; [2]
it does not follow, however, that it is what Mencius meant. [3]

Tao Fu. For Mencius' real meaning we must rely upon
the passages quoted in the *Dialogues on the Great
Learning* ? [4]

Answer. Yes, Mencius' meaning is simply that when
your investigation of principles is perfect the mind naturally
attains to the fullness of its utmost capacity, and not that
you must enlarge it in order to understand your Nature
and know Heaven.

Tao Fu. But simply as Hêng Ch'ü expresses it, it is
very difficult to carry out.

Answer. That is just Hêng Ch'ü's way of talking at
times, as though he were carried away by his imagination.
The mind is large by nature [why talk of enlarging it] ?

was the grandson of Chao Ju Yü, Chu Hsi's friend and the Emperor Ning
Tsung's Prime Minister; see J. P. Bruce, *Introduction to Chu Hsi and the Sung
School*, chap. iv. He held office in various provincial posts, in all of which
he followed the principles of government adopted by his grandfather.
The education he received from the same source also bore fruit in ripe
scholarship and a well-balanced mind.

[1] The meaning of 推 is the same as in Mencius, p. 20, q.v.

[2] That is, in the statement quoted on the previous page.

[3] That is, in the passage (p. 324) referred to by Chang Tsai.

[4] A work by Chu Hsi ; see J. P. Bruce, *Introduction to Chu Hsi and the
Sung School*, chap. iv.

Passages like this really mean that from an exhaustive
investigation of phenomena there follows naturally and
freely communion with all things. This is " from the study
of the lowly to understand high things " ; [1] and the meaning
of Mencius is precisely the same.

40.   In the passage, " When the mind is enlarged, it can
enter into everything throughout the universe," [2] the
expression " enter into " [3] is like what is spoken of as " the
universal embodiment of Love in actions ", and means that
the principle of the mind permeates everywhere like the blood
circulates in the body. If there is a single thing into which
it does not enter, its permeation is incomplete, and it fails
perfectly to embrace all things, which is egoism.   For
selfishness produces separation between the ego and the non-
ego, so that they stand opposed the one to the other. The
result is that even towards those dearest to us there is no
assurance of a perfect altruism. " The egoistic mind,"
therefore, " cannot be one with the Mind of Heaven." [2]

41.   *Question.*   In the statement, " When there is anything which the mind does not enter into, it is egoistic," [3]
which is the meaning of the expression " enter into " (*t'i*) ?

Answer.   It means to import the mind into the
phenomenon, and so to investigate it as to grasp its
principle.[4]   It is the same meaning as that of the

[1] Analects, xiv, xxxvii, 2, p. 153.
[2] *Chêng Mêng,* 大 心 篇.   [3] Cf. p. 350.
[4] Cf. Bergson's doctrine of intuitive sympathy as the means whereby
" we get into the heart of things in the making " ; see *Eucken and Bergson,*
by E. Hermann, pp. 149–152.

expressions "investigation of things" and "perfection of knowledge"; [1] and differs from that of *t'i* [2] meaning substance as contrasted with its manifestation.

42. Hêng Ch'ü said: "When there is anything which the mind does not enter into, it is egoistic"; [3] and again, "The egoistic mind cannot be one with the Mind of Heaven." [3] For Heaven is great and altruistic, embracing all things; when in my investigation of things there is one principle in them which eludes my search, my mind is egoistic and unlike the Mind of Heaven.

43. Someone asked: What is meant by egoism?

Answer. It means: When there is selfish thought, obstruction arises between the subject and object. We see only ourselves, and everything external is regarded as having no relation to the self. Such is egoism.

44. *Question.* How can the mind by means of moral principle be in communion with external things to an unlimited extent?

Answer. The mind is not like a horizontal door which has to be made larger by force. [4] You must clear away the obstructions arising from creaturely desire, and then it will be pure and clear with no limit to its knowledge; in investigating the principles of phenomena there will be free communion. Hêng Ch'ü said, "Do not allow the mind to be fettered by the senses"; "When the Mind is enlarged

---

[1] G. L., p. 222.   [2] The same word as *t'i*, to enter into.

[3] *Chêng Mêng,* 大 心 篇.

[4] It is upright and of adequate size; all that is needed is to clear away the obstructions, and then there will be no difficulty of access.

it can enter into everything throughout the universe." [1] The expression, " To be in communion with external things by means of moral principle," means this unobstructed communion. Merely to guard the senses of hearing and sight naturally has a narrowing effect.

45. " The Mind is the principle of life." [2] This sentence was recorded by Chang Ssŭ Shu.[3] I question whether there is not some statement omitted. It must be that when the text was corrected it was accidentally lost.

Po Fêng [4] said : Why was it included in your work, *Modern Thought* ?

Answer. How dare I do other than record it.? But I fear there is some defect. These four words are not adequate to express the idea.

46. The Mind is the principle of life ; man possesses Mind, and the Mind dwells in a material form and thereby man lives. The solicitous mind is the principle of life." [5] How do you explain this ?

Answer. The Mind of Heaven and Earth [6] which gives birth to all things is Love. Man by his endowment receives

---

[1] *Chêng Mêng,* 大 心 篇.

[2] A statement by I Ch'uan ; see 學 案, pt. xv, f. 28. The word translated " principle " is *tao* (道). Its meaning is somewhat obscure, as the text indicates. It is probably equivalent to *tao li* (道 理) = " principle ", a frequent use of the word.

[3] A pupil of I Ch'uan ; see 遺 書, pt. xii, f. 22.

[4] Wu Pi Ta (吳 必 大), *style* Po Fêng ; see p. 17.

[5] See 學 案, pt. xv, f. 28.

[6] The use of this expression here is in the same sense as that of " The Mind of Heaven " in the next section ; cf. J. P. Bruce, *Introduction to Chu Hsi and the Sung School,* chap. xiii.

this Mind of Heaven and Earth and thereby his life. Hence the "solicitous mind" in man is also the principle of life.

47. The statement, "The Mind is the principle of life,"[1] means that the Mind is the principle which produces life. The statement, "The solicitous mind is the principle of life in man," means that we receive the Mind of Heaven and thereby live. To give birth to things is the Mind of Heaven.

48. *Question.* In the section on the Mind as the principle of life, does not the first part, "The Mind is the principle of life,"[1] refer to the Mind of Heaven and Earth as giving birth to all things; and the latter part, "The solicitous mind is the principle of life in man,"[1] to the Mind of Heaven and Earth as received by man to be his Mind? For in Heaven there is nothing but this Law, and apart from material form Law would have nothing in which to inhere. Hence the statement, "Man possesses Mind, and Mind dwells in a material form, and thereby lives."[1] The first part corresponds to the statement, "The law of their succession is goodness"; [2] the latter part to the statement, "Their realization is the Nature."[3]

Answer. To make the first part, "The Mind is the principle of life,"[1] refer solely to Heaven is not correct either; for Law is one all-comprehensive Law, and man is inseparably united to Heaven and Earth.

49. Let the mind go, so that it may be broad and tranquil; and it will be enlarged. Do not let it be prepossessed by the divisive influence of selfish thought, and it

[1] See p. 182.   [2] *Yi Ching*, p. 355.   [3] Ibid., p. 356.

will be enlarged. With the mind enlarged it naturally follows that there will be no hastiness; if we meet with calamity there will be no fear; if we meet with prosperity there will be no exultation; for in a very little while calamity may give place to prosperity, and prosperity to calamity. Hsün Tzŭ said, "The noble man with a mind enlarged will be one with the Divine, and in accord with Moral Law. If his mind be small he will be inspired by awe and righteousness and be self-controlled."[1] For with the noble man, when his mind is enlarged it is the Mind of Heaven, when it is small it is the watchful and reverent mind of King Wên,[2] and both are good. With the ignoble man, if his mind is enlarged it will be reckless, if it be small it will be petty and narrow, selfish and miserly, and both are bad.

(THIRTY SECTIONS FROM THE COLLECTED WRITINGS.)

1. Man lives by the union of the Nature with the Ether. But given this union we find, when we analyse it, that the Nature pertains to Law and is formless, while the Ether pertains to form and is material. The former as pertaining to Law and formless is altruistic and invariably good; the latter as pertaining to form and material is selfish and potentially evil. The manifestations of the former, since it is altruistic and good, are all the workings of Divine Law; the manifestations of the latter, since it is selfish

---

[1] See 子 書 二 十 三 種, 元 七, pt. ii, chap. iii. A note on this phrase in the work referred to says: 天 而 道 = 合 於 天 而 順 道.

[2] See *Odes*, p. 433.

and potentially evil, are all the actions of human desire. Hence the distinction between the " natural mind " and the " spiritual mind " in Shun's admonition to Yü.[1] For this distinction is a root distinction, and not to be explained as excess or shortcoming in the action of the Ether, with subsequent lapse into human desire. But the statement does not go beyond the term " natural mind ", and implies, surely, that it is not necessarily wholly evil. It does not go beyond the term " unstable ", and equally implies that it is not necessarily foredoomed to become criminal. But seeing that it pertains not to Law but to form, its lapse into evil and even crime is not difficult. This is the reason for its "instability ", and herein it differs from the " spiritual mind ", which is infallibly good and never evil, is stable and never falls to one side or the other, has its standard, and can be relied upon. In regard to these two, therefore, we must use the utmost discrimination and singleness, and so make the altruistic and invariably good the perpetual master of our entire personality and of all our conduct, while the selfish and potentially evil must be allowed no place in our lives. Then, in everything we do and say, there will be no need to choose between excess and shortcoming: it will spontaneously and unfailingly accord with the Mean. (Whenever you begin your examination of anything you should first consider and decide upon its goodness or otherwise, and then proceed to consider whether it accords with the Mean or not. By "discrimination and singleness "[1] you examine

---

[1] See *Shu Ching*, p. 61 ; also J. P. Bruce, *Introduction to Chu Hsi and the Sung School*, chap. x.

its goodness or otherwise ; then by " sincerely holding fast the Mean " [1] there is neither excess nor shortcoming, and the Mean is attained to naturally. You do not seek the Mean by means of discrimination and singleness.) This was the real meaning of Shun's admonition to Yü recorded in the " Preface ".[2] The manifestations of the Ether are not directly regarded as wholly evil, with no allowance for times when it is clear and translucent, pure and unadulterated, as suggested in your treatise. But such clearness and translucence, purity and unadulteratedness, seeing that they belong to the accidental condition of the material Ether, can do no more than retain connexion with Law and assist its animating influence. They cannot be regarded as the spiritual mind, or as a substitute for discrimination and concentration. In Mencius, for example, although he speaks of the Ether as the " restorative influences of the night ",[3] nevertheless that which it is desired to retain by them resides in the moral mind, and he does not directly regard such influences as paramount. Again, although he speaks of " nourishing the ether ", yet the power it employs for this resides in " the accumulation of righteous deeds " ; [4] he does not directly select the non-excesses and shortcomings of the Ether with a view to nourishing them. In your treatise you place too much emphasis on the word " Ether ". I will not, therefore, examine your other statements. For

[1] See *Shu Ching*, p. 61.

[2] The Chinese Preface to the *Shu Ching* reputed to be written by Confucius; see *Shu Ching*, p. 1. This admonition of Shun to Yü, however, is not specifically mentioned in the Preface, but in the body of the work, p. 61, as above.

[3] Lit. " night-ether ", Mencius, p. 284.   [4] Ibid., p. 66.

example, the distinctions you make between the "medium ether", the "excess ether", and the "inadequate ether", seem to me to be at fault, but as they do not affect the subject of the "minuteness of the spiritual mind" it is hardly worth while to discuss them. (Reply to Ts'ai Chi T'ung.)[1]

2. I have received your letter and two essays replying to Hu Piao. Your criticism of Mr. Lü's treatise[2] on the *Doctrine of the Mean* is most trenchant, and very striking. But there are some points not clear. Permit me to set out in order my reasons for saying so, and I beg you will submit them to your friends for their criticism. Your reply to Kuang Chung[3] on the faults peculiar to the scholar[4] hits the mark exactly, but in my opinion the chief fault lies in the fact that in ordinary times the illumination of principles is imperfect and the nurture of the mind immature, so that when affairs present themselves there is no preparation for dealing with them. To say that at the very time when affairs crowd in upon us we should make a careful investigation of the Mind's origin, means that in addition

[1] See p. 65, n. 3.

[2] Probably Lü Tsu Ch'ien (呂 祖 謙); see p. 116, n. 1. Or possibly the reference is to Lü Yü Shu, whose writings were, in fact, criticized by Nan Hsien; see p. 458. I have not been able to find the treatise referred to.

[3] Hu Kuang Chung, see p. 37, n. 2.

[4] The idea combated in the following argument is that we can attain to perfection by understanding the mind (識 心) as a pre-requisite, and that this should be done in the time of the mind's activity and when its workings and springs of action can be investigated.

to the task of dealing with these affairs we have at the
same time the further thought of investigating the Mind
itself. Thus with the Mind we examine the Mind, and the
difficulty and complexity of our task are intensified. Moreover, the importance of using such effort before we meet
with affairs is lost sight of. This makes me question your
line of reasoning. The essence of Confucian teaching is to
put the investigation of principles first, because each
individual thing [1] has its own law. This must be first understood, and then the phenomena of the Mind will be seen
to have in each case a standard by which their character [2]
may be estimated. The *Shu Ching*—in such expressions
as "Divine social arrangements", "Divine social
distinctions", "Divine appointments", and "Divine
retributions"[3]—and Mencius—in the words, "The relations
of all things may be thus determined, and it is of the
greatest importance to estimate the actions of the mind"[4]
—both express this same idea.[5] If we fail first to "extend
our knowledge to the utmost" in respect to this fact, and

[1] "Thing" here refers to the mental faculties ; see p. 54.
[2] For the force of 輕 重 長 短, see Mencius, p. 20, verse 13, in
reference to which Legge says in his note : "心 爲 甚 means that the
mind, as affected from without, and going forth to affect, may be light
or heavy, long or short, i.e. may be right or wrong, and that in different
degrees, etc."
[3] *Shu Ching*, pp. 73-4.
[4] Mencius, p. 20 ; see note 2 above.
[5] That is, that each individual thing has its own law as stated above ;
the 此 in 皆 謂 此 也, and in 若 不 於 此, refers to the same
as that referred to in the sentence 須 先 明 此 above, viz. the statement immediately preceding 凡 一 物。有 一 理 (each individual
thing has its own law).

are content with knowing and understanding how the Mind comes to be what it is—and that vaguely, with no standard to guide us—then how is it possible for either the content, or the manifestations, of the Mind to accord with eternal principles ? Consider, moreover, the teachings of the Buddhists on rigid posture and hard discipline.[1] They indeed observe and contemplate the Mind, and yet with it all we cannot in their company attain to the moral ideal of Yao and Shun, simply because, not recognizing the Divine Law, they regard Mind alone as ruler ; and thus there is no security against falling into selfishness. This accords with a saying of our predecessors that the sages regard Heaven, and the Buddhists regard Mind, as the foundation of things. In your treatise you speak of the mind being continuously emptied of *anxiety and evil*. I grant this so far as the original substance of the mind is concerned, but when you have regard to human desire and selfishness in which the mind has so long been submerged, how is it possible in one day suddenly to attain to this standard ? The sages therefore insisted that the mind must be rectified, that " to rectify the mind there must first be sincerity of thought, and that to be sincere in thought, knowledge must first be extended to the utmost ".[2] When efforts are made in this order, then the true mind is attainable, and with it a return to its original state of emptiness ; but this is not to be achieved in a single day. You, however, speak baldly of the mind being continuously so empty. Again you say :

[1] Lit. " Holding a dusting-brush with the hands erect (i.e. in a forced rigid position), carrying water and fuel ", all as acts of self-discipline.

[2] G. L., p. 222.

" If the Mind be understood, it will be successful in whatever direction it may be employed." Here again you are mistaken in representing the process as too rapid, and so fall into error. According to the teaching of the Confucianists, there must be perfect righteousness and spirituality in order to succeed in whatever direction the mind may be employed. Then indeed you may say that the mind is continuously emptied of *anxiety and evil*.[1] When Mencius speaks of " preserving " and " losing ", "outgoing " and " incoming ",[2] his meaning surely is that the mind should be held fast and preserved ; for one must suppose that he did not use such expressions with the idea merely that the mind should be understood. If we can constantly hold fast and preserve it, then the reverent care of which you speak will be perfect. If this be perfect it will be the same whether in activity or inactivity, and the mind will be continually preserved. You insist, too, that we should seek it in activity, with the idea of avoiding the onesidedness of inactivity, overlooking the fact that the result must be a leaning to the onesidedness of activity. The man, however, who can claim to hold fast and preserve his mind is one who surpasses even Yen Tzŭ. Again, you say that it is by understanding the mind that we can guard it. As to which my[3] fear is that the method is all too easy. The Master Ming Tao said, " If we can enter into things with joy, we need not fear inability to guard the mind."[4]   We

---

[1] 可 得 而 語 矣, i.e. your statement that the mind is continuously emptied would then stand; see above.

[2] Mencius, p. 285 ; cf. Legge's note *in loco*.

[3] 僕 refers to the speaker.   [4] 學 案, pt. xiii, p. 5.

must adopt this attitude; only thus will our position be unassailable, without flaw, and free from vitiating errors. According to your esteemed opinion this preservation of the mind is to be sought for in its manifested operations, which is exactly the idea of the Buddhists when they speak of sparks from the flint and lightning,[1] while you appear to pay little attention to the work of prolonged leisurely nurture. Hence the search for it is too hasty, its attainment is with apprehension, the reliance upon it is weak, and its manifestation too evanescent. What the *Yi Ching* expresses as "with broadness of mind continuing in what has been attained to",[2] means the unwillingness to fall into this error. (Reply to Chang Ch'in Fu.)[3]

3.   The position of the Buddhists is that we need only to understand the one Mind, but, as a matter of fact, they themselves do not know what the mind-substance really is. Although they assert that all laws have their origin in the Mind, they really hold that there is a law external to it.[4] Hence there is no room in their philosophy for the First Cause of the Universe, and their doctrine of subject and object is incomplete. But those who teach this doctrine know enough to make them mask their position on both sides,

---

[1] Possibly refers to their quality of instantaneousness.

[2] *Yi Ching*, p. 416.

[3] Chang Ch'ih (張 栻); see J. P. Bruce, *Introduction to Chu Hsi and the Sung School*, chap. iv.   Ch'in Fu was probably his *style* in early life and was subsequently changed to Ching Fu, the *style* by which he is referred to in his biographies.   That Ch'in Fu is identical with Nan Hsien (Chang Ch'ih's literary name) is clear from a passage in the 近 思 錄, pt. i, f. 5.

[4] That is, that outside the Mind there is another Law.   To this doctrine Chu Hsi replies: "No, how can there be two 'Laws' in the ultimate sense?"   See below.

and, skilfully veiling their ideas, persistently decline to say in so many words that outside the one Mind there is another First Cause. According to the account of Mind given by our sacred Confucian cult the " Divine social arrangements", " Divine social distinctions ", " Divine appointments ", and " Divine retributions ",[1] " solicitude ", " conscientiousness", " moral insight ", and " courtesy ",[2] are all included in it, and there is no law external to it. Mencius said therefore, " He who develops his Mind to the utmost understands his Nature. Understanding his Nature he knows Heaven. By preserving his Mind and nourishing his Nature he serves Heaven."[3] Here, then, we have Heaven and Man, the Nature and the Decree, *united in one :* how can there be two " Laws " in the ultimate sense ? But those who to-day propound this theory maintain on the contrary that external to the Mind there is another First Cause ; that apart from Love there is another method by which the Nature may be developed, and the Decree perfectly embodied. I fear that this only means an ungrateful disregard of the teachings which the saints and sages have bequeathed to us, and of their lifelong devotion to learning and inquiry into truth. I fear also lest this theory should spread and, exposing itself to attack by heretics, seriously involve our doctrine. (Reply to Chang Ch'in Fu.)

4. In seeking to regain the lost mind [4] it is not necessary to explain what it is, but through the hours of the day, in its various activities, continuously and carefully to watch it, not allowing it to get beyond control ; and in course of

[1] *Shu Ching*, p. 73.
[3] Ibid., p. 325.
[2] Mencius, p. 79.
[4] See Mencius, p. 290.

time the result will appear naturally, the moral nature will be illuminated, and steadfastness attained, without any abnormal expenditure of effort. (Reply to Li Shu Wên.)

5. The sentence in the *Commentary on the Yi*,[1] " Although free from heart depravity it is still not in accord with right principle," really includes both activity and inactivity. If in a time of solitary leisure I am affected by the external world and ought to respond in some particular way, but my mind remains rigidly and obstinately unresponsive, then, although there is the absence of heart depravity, the inaction is in itself out of accord with right principle. Or if I ought to respond to a certain phenomenon in a certain way, but I actually respond to it in a different way, then, although not necessarily proceeding from intentional selfishness, this alone is out of accord with right principle. Seeing that it is out of accord with right principle, what is it if it is not depravity ? We must not depend solely on rectitude and carefulness for this preservation and nurture, thinking that if I preserve the Mind in this way, there will be no heart depravity. On the contrary, we must bear in mind that it is possible for carefulness to fail through anxieties and distractions, and pave the way for falseness and heart depravity. In what you say about the modern heresy with respect to understanding the Mind you strike at the very root of the error. What the learning of the ancients emphasized in the preservation of the Mind was to extend it so as exhaustively to investigate the laws of the universe. What the moderns

[1] A commentary by Ch'êng I. It is included in the 二 程 全 書, and entitled 伊 川 易 傳.

mean by understanding the Mind is by reliance upon it to stand outside the laws of the universe. With the ancients, therefore, the more exalted their knowledge was, the deeper was the humility which characterized their Reverence ; while with modern scholars, the loftier their discussions are, the greater is their arrogance and licence—from which you may judge of the correctness or otherwise of their teachings. (Reply to Fang Pin Wang.)

6.   It is not necessary to go out of one's way to get rid of the natural mind ; it needs only that the spiritual mind shall rule. That is, if the natural mind is to be rendered powerless to play the robber, it must be by the spiritual mind. But this is exceedingly difficult to secure, so sudden and rapid are the movements of human desire. (Reply to Chêng Tzŭ Shang.)[1]

7.   The intellectual powers of the Mind, when they manifest themselves on the plane of ethical principle, constitute the "spiritual mind" ; [1] when they manifest themselves in the region of desire, they constitute the "natural mind".[2] (Reply to Chêng Tzŭ Shang.)

8.   *Question.* The Mind of man is a spiritual [3] thing. It is true that by day, before there has been any response to external phenomena, it is still and without activity ; [4] it is also true that, in this state of inactivity, the Mind is

[1] See p. 5, n. 3.   [2] See *Shu Ching*, p. 61.

[3] "Spiritual" (靈) here is a different word with a different meaning from that in the expression "spiritual mind" (道 心). In the former case it is spiritual in the sense of pertaining to spirit, or the intellectual part of man's being in contrast to the physical. In the latter case it is spiritual in the sense of morally pure and good.

[4] *Yi Ching*, p. 370.

continuously awake and not blindly unconscious; while in dreams of the night again the Mind is active as in thought by day. When dreams cease, however, and there is no return to consciousness, we have deep sleep, and at such times to speak of the Mind as still and without activity is a mistake; for when the mind thus sinks into unconsciousness, and that unconsciousness is so deep that there is as total an absence of knowledge or perception of things as in rocks and trees, hardly differing indeed from the unconsciousness of death itself, the expressions "still" and "without activity" are not applicable. But what mystifies me is this: Where is the mind-substance at such times, and where is what we call the spiritual faculty? What is the difference at such times between the sage and the common man? And what ought the inquirer to make the object of his search in such phenomena?

Answer. Waking and sleeping are the active and inactive states of the Mind. Thought and absence of thought are the active and inactive phases of its active state. Dreams and dreamlessness are the active and inactive phases of its inactive state. But the waking state belongs to the positive mode, and sleep to the negative mode, waking to the clear, and sleeping to the turbid ether. Waking is under control, and sleeping not. Therefore the mystery of that stillness, and, when acted upon, that penetration to all phenomena,[1] *referred to in the "Yi"*, can only be predicated of the waking state. (Reply to Ch'ên An Ch'ing.)[2]

[1] See *Yi Ching*, p. 370.

[2] Ch'ên Ch'un (陳 淳), *style* An Ch'ing, also called Ch'ên Pei Hai (北 溪), was a native of Fukien. He was first interested in ethical

9. *Question.* On thinking over your statement, "Waking and sleeping are the active and inactive states of the Mind, etc.," the subject presents itself to my [1] mind in this way : All men possess the two ethers. The spirit has its origin in the positive and the body in the negative ether. Mind enters into these two ethers and resides in both alike, whether active or passive. It is the home of the spirit and the ruler of the body. By day the negative ether subsides and the positive is in operation. Since the positive is active, the spirit is in motion, and, the body responding to the movement of the spirit, the waking condition results. At night the positive ether subsides and the negative is in operation. The negative is passive ; the body, therefore, is rigid, the spirit is inert, and the result is sleep. When the spirit is active the substance of the invisible psychic powers and of consciousness is clearly manifested ; its budding life can be seen, as when, with the return of the positive mode, the whole world puts on the garment of spring. This is how it is that the Mind, whether still or affected by the external world, is under control   When the spirit is inert the substance of the invisible psychic powers and of consciousness sinks into hidden depths : it is silent and leaves no traces of its existence ; just as, in the winter months,[2] every sign of life

study by reading Chu Hsi's *Modern Thought* (近 思 錄), and became his pupil at Chang Chou.   Chu Hsi spoke of him as "eager and indomitable".   He was the author of a glossary of philosophical terms (性 理 字 義), and the first to use the term Hsing Li (性 理), which formed part of the title of his book.

[1] 湻, used for 淳, refers to the writer Ch'ên Ch'un ; see note above.

[2] 坤 = 陰, the negative mode, 純 = wholly ; thus 純 坤 之 月 are the months wholly under the influence of the negative mode, i.e. winter months.

throughout the universe is hidden beyond our power to
search it out. This is why the Mind, whether still or affected
by the external world, differs in sleep from the wondrous
mystery of waking hours, and there is the absence of control.
Nevertheless, there is that within which does not perish ;
there still remains the unfathomable mystery. You call
it and it answers ; you startle it and it responds ; so that
it is still not without some control, nor is it without a wonder
of its own. Therefore, speaking broadly, the waking state
is positive and the sleeping state negative, in which the Mind
is respectively active and passive. More particularly, the
thought of the waking hours is the activity of the active
state, the positive within the positive mode. The absence
of thought in waking hours is the inertness of the active
state, the negative phase of the positive mode. The dreams
of sleep are the activity of the passive state, the positive
phase of the negative mode ; while dreamless sleep is the
inertness of the passive state, the negative phase of the
negative mode. Again, to show their complex interaction
still further, thought divides itself into good and evil
thoughts, in which the clearness of the positive ether and
the turbidity of the negative ether affect the activity of the
active state. The absence of thought is divisible into the
right and wrong kinds of responsiveness to phenomena,
in which the clearness of the positive ether and turbidity
of the negative ether affect the inertness of the active state.
Dreams are good and bad according as the activity of the
passive state is affected by the clearness and turbidity of
the two ethers respectively. And in dreamless sleep there
is a difference in the degree of responsiveness to external

impressions corresponding to the difference between the clearness and turbidity of the two ethers by which the inertness of the passive state is affected. Thus we have the active and the passive in continuous alternation and complex interaction. The sage and the ordinary man are one, and yet differ in the translucence and turbidity of their positive and negative ethers respectively. The sages, whether active or inactive, are actuated by singleness and in them purity and perfection are paramount, while the masses are mixed in their motives and uncertain. But from this may be seen how great are the consequences attaching to earnest study.

Answer. Correct. (Reply to Ch'ên An Ch'ing.)[1]

10. *Question*. In Ch'êng Tzŭ's doctrine of the mind controlling the mind,[2] it appears to me that the double use of the word "mind" is best explained as referring to the distinction between the natural mind and the spiritual mind. That is: In the one case the "mind" is the spiritual mind and refers specially to right principle and right conduct;[3] in the other case, the "mind" is the natural mind and refers

---

[1] See p. 195, n. 2.

[2] The allusion is to one of I Ch'uan's sayings; see 學 案, pt. xv, f. 10. The whole sentence which is here referred to reads: 以 心 使 心 則 可。人 心 自 由 便 放 去 也。(You must use the mind to control the mind; if a man's mind is allowed to go free it will be lost.)

[3] See Mencius, p. 283, where these expressions occur, and to which the phrase as here used probably alludes. Legge, in his note *in loco*, explains it thus: 理 = 心 之 體, the mental constitution, the moral nature; and 義 = 心 之 用, that constitution, or nature, acting outwardly."

to the physical element. To say that the mind should control
the mind means that the spiritual mind should rule the
entire personality, and the natural mind obey its behests.

Answer. It is so too. But if you look at the Master
Ch'êng's meaning, you will see that it is no more than that
you should be master of yourself. (Reply to Ch'ên An
Ch'ing.)

11. *Question.* Recently, I understood you to say that
some years ago, when you were at T'ung An, from hearing
the sound of a bell you learned the method of conserving
the mind. At first I [1] did not understand how this could
be, but on further examination I saw that it would be so.

Answer. That was not the real meaning of what I said
at the time about hearing the sound of a bell. All I said
was that the time of the outgoing and incoming of man's
mind is indeterminate, for before the sound of one stroke
of the bell had ceased my mind had already changed many
times. (Reply to Chang Ching Chih.)

12. Hu Wên Ting [2] said, "That which neither rises
into consciousness nor subsides is the substance of the Mind.
That which rises and subsides is the Mind's operation. If
we can hold fast and preserve the Mind, though in one
day there may be a hundred risings and subsidings, the
Mind will maintain its character." This is well said, but
the reader must remember that what is referred to as not
rising or subsiding is not a solid immovable thing without

---

[1] 顯 父 refers to the writer, Chang Ching Chih.
[2] Hu An Kuo, the founder of the Hu School; see p. 24.

consciousness ; nor is there, amid the hundred risings and
subsidings, a separate thing which does not rise or subside.
But when the Mind is luminous and wholly without selfishness, then you have the original substance of the Mind,
" still and without movement " ; [1] and when its risings and
subsidings are alike according to right principle, then you
have what is described as " acted upon and forthwith penetrating all the phenomena of the universe".[1]
(Reply to Shih Tzŭ Chung.)

13.   Your treatise on Mind is excellent, except that it
would be better if it were more concise and restrained. Your
questions on the mind controlling the mind are good too,
for Ch'êng Tzŭ's meaning also is that you should be master
of yourself, and not allow the mind to become scattered
or wandering. It is the same idea as that of Mencius when
he speaks of " holding fast and preserving the mind " or
of " seeking the lost mind ".[2] How can it mean to use
one mind to control another ?   But in the present day the
words " examine " and " understand" are brought into the
discussion, and so we get the ideas of " seeking "
and " seizing ", which are altogether different from the
spirit of the expressions " hold fast", " preserve ",
and " rule", as used by the saints and sages. Though the
point is a fine one, it is essential that we should clearly
understand it ; otherwise we shall slip into the heresy of
the Buddhists. (Reply to Shih Tzŭ Chung.)

14.   In the essay you sent me you say : " The Master in
discussing Love regarded 'the mastery of self' as the

[1] See *Yi Ching*, p. 370.   [2] Mencius, pp. 285, 290.

important thing ; [1] the Buddhists in discussing the Nature
regard the negation of Mind as supreme, denying Kuei
Shan's doctrine that the Mind cannot be non-existent."
According to my view, what is termed self—so termed in
opposition to external things—is a selfish recognition of
self, which gives rise to a calculating comparison and produces liking and desire.   This, therefore, ought to be
mastered.   If it is mastered, there naturally follows the
" return to right principle ",[2] which is Love.   The Mind
has a real existence.   It is pure, undivided, penetrating,
and all-pervading in its influence.   The perfect development of the Nature and the practice of the Moral Law
both proceed from this.   You, however, regard it as vain
and would get rid of it, and yet you yourself recognize that
this would not do, and therefore say "there is the true
Mind which must be preserved" (this is the language of
your essay) ; and so after all there is a Mind !   In this
case how can the theory of the negation of Mind be wholly
right ?   And how can those who do not assert this doctrine
be wholly wrong ?   Suppose you take the negation of Mind
to be correct, then, I contend, the mastery of self presupposes
Mind, for how otherwise could one master himself ?   Or
if you take self-mastery to be a reality, then make it your

[1] Analects, XII, i, 1 (p. 114).
[2] Ibid. 禮 here is almost equivalent to 理 ; cf. Legge's note in loco.
Soothill renders the word as " what is right and proper ", and, like Legge,
quotes Chu Hsi's gloss, 禮 者 天 理 之 節 文 也, " Li
is the restraints and graces of Divine Law", see Soothill's Analects of
Confucius, pp. 557-8.   It is probable that the sage in his use of the
word in this passage had the Divine Law in mind more than its
" restraints and graces ".

business to practise it, and that is all that is required.
Again, why speak of self-mastery in one connexion and of
the negation of Mind in the other, as if they had their
origin in two different sources, and so cause inconsistency
in your statements ?   (Reply to Li Po Chien.)

15. The Mind is a unity. What is called
" Intelligence " is also the Mind. Your idea of seeking the
Mind and using the Mind by means of " Intelligence ",
feverishly trying to get hold of it in various ways, I fear
is a mistake. Not only is it exactly like pulling up the
young corn,[1] but, in itself, it is not so good as in daily life
to be guided by reverent care and never to lose sight of it.
Then naturally the real Mind will be unclouded ; when acted
upon by external things it will penetrate them ; and be
" intelligent " with respect to everything without waiting
to be made so. Therefore Confucius spoke of self-mastery
and return to right principle,[2] and not of making oneself
intelligent or exercising reverent care. Mencius speaks only
of holding fast and preserving the mind, or of letting go
and losing it, and does not say that it is by intelligence
it is preserved and by unintelligence it is lost. The Master
Hsieh,[3] although he liked to define Love in terms
of Consciousness, nevertheless did not speak of being

[1] An allusion to one of the illustrations used by Mencius, in which he
tells of the " man of Sung ", who, grieved that his growing corn was not
longer, pulled it up, and said to his family : " I am tired to-day, I have
been helping the corn to grow long," upon which his son went and found
it withered. See Mencius, pp. 66–7.

[2] Analects, XII, i, 1 (p. 114).

[3] Hsieh Shang Ts'ai, see p. 322, n. 3.

conscious of the Mind, but said, "The Mind must have consciousness." (Reply to Yu Ch'êng Chih.)

16. The mind-substance is originally in repose, and yet it cannot but have movement. Its operation is originally good, and yet it is possible for it to lapse into the not-good. Now its movement and lapse into evil cannot be called the original character of the mind-substance, and yet it cannot be termed otherwise than Mind. It is only because it has been beguiled by external things that it becomes evil. The former sages therefore said only, "Hold it fast and you will preserve it. (If it is preserved and thus is in repose, then its movement will not be otherwise than good) ; let it go and you will lose it (It is thus that movement results in the lapse into evil) ; its outgoing and incoming cannot be defined as to time or place (Its outgoing and loss, its incoming and preservation, are without any set time or place. They depend wholly on the way in which men hold the mind fast or let it go)." [1] In this sentence the Mind's substance and operation, its source and issue, truth and falsity, depravity and rectitude, are all included ; and from it we see that not to hold fast to it is to let it go, that its non-outgoing is its incoming : there is no middle position for it to rest in. According to your argument the rectitude of the Mind consists in the outgoing and incoming having their set time ; in which case the indeterminateness of the outgoing and incoming of which Confucius speaks is a disease of the Mind, and he ought not to have categorically concluded his statement with the words "It is

[1] Mencius, p. 285.

the Mind of which this is said ! " [1]   (Reply to Yu Ch'êng
Chih.)

17.   The instructive communication and treatise on Mind
which I have received from you are excellent, though, as
it appears to me, somewhat incomplete. For the incoming
and preserved mind is the true mind, and the outgoing
and lost mind is also the true mind, but has become lost
through the seductions of its environment.[2] You say that
the preserved mind and the lost mind, the outgoing and the
incoming mind, are alike produced by the seductions of the
environment. Thus in addition to the preserved mind there
is still another true mind.[3] But, in that case, why did
Confucius not speak of it? Tzŭ's Chung's [4] contention
contains the same error. Tzŭ Yo [5] too would combine the
outgoing and lost mind with the incoming and preserved
mind, and not distinguish between the true and false,
but regard both as an unfathomable mystery. Both
these ideas are wrong. My recent reply to these
two correspondents [6] was not altogether complete. The
reply [7] which I made later to Yu Ch'êng Chih was somewhat
more satisfactory. I now send you a copy of it, in the
hope that you will let me have your instructive opinion
upon it. As to the Mind's substance and manifestation,
however, with its origin and issue, although it is to

[1] This sentence immediately follows on the others quoted above.

[2] Cf. Legge's note on the passage referred to ; see Mencius, p. 285.

[3] If the preserved mind, as well as the lost mind, is the result of the
seductions (!) of its environment, then there must be still another " true "
mind which seeks to bring it back from its seductions.

[4] See pp. 199–200.   [5] See pp. 206–8.

[6] See p. 208 for reply to Tzŭ Yo.   [7] See pp. 202–3.

be distinguished as to its truth and falsity, depravity and
rectitude, it is none the less unfathomable in its mystery ;
and, although it is unfathomable in its mystery, it is none
the less to be distinguished as to its truth and falsity,
depravity and rectitude.   I do not know what your exalted
opinion may be.   (Reply to Ho Shu Ching.)

18.   I have studied your treatise on Mind.   You say,
" The mind of the sages is like a mirror or a sheet of still
water : the Divine Law in them is pure and perfect."   In
this sentence you are speaking of the preservation of the
mind.   But although it is true that the sages, without the
special effort of holding fast the mind, continually preserved
it, while ordinary men preserve it by holding it fast ;
nevertheless, when ordinary men do thus preserve it, it does
not differ from the mind as preserved by the sage ; it is
simply that if they do not hold it fast they fail to preserve
it.   The mind preserved is the spiritual mind, the mind
lost is the natural mind.   But the Mind is one : it is not
that really there are these two minds, each a separate entity
without any connexion the one with the other, but only that
different terms are used to distinguish between preserving
and losing.   It is true that when it is lost it is not the
original state of the mind ; but neither must you say that
there is another mind which is both preserved and lost, outgoing and incoming, waiting to return to its source, and
that we are to seek to exchange it for still a different mind
which has no distinction between preserved and lost, outgoing and incoming.   There is only this one Mind.   The
failure to preserve it is in itself to lose it, not to lose it is to

preserve it.   There is not the smallest conceivable middle ground.   The student, therefore, must be earnest in holding fast and preserving the mind.   For even between Shun and Yü there was the warning to cultivate discrimination and singleness.[1]   And as in the case of peace and danger, good government and disorder in the world, although in the time of the sages Yao and Shun there was peace and good government and no danger and disorder, still you would not say that the expressions " peace " and " danger ", " good government " and " disorder ", cannot be applied as a whole to the time of Yao and Shun.   If you were to do so you would be falling into the same heresy as the Hu School, who maintain that there is no distinction between good and evil in the Nature.[2]   I beg you to consider the subject once more, and give me your views.   (Reply to Ho Shu Ching.)

19.   Mind as referred to in the sentence, " Hold fast to it and you will preserve it," is itself the original substance, and there is no need to seek for another.   But when the holding fast is long continued and mature, there naturally ensues resting in righteousness and moral principle, and

[1] See *Shu Ching*, p. 61.

[2] Ho Shu Ching's position is, that the preserved mind and the lost mind are two different entities ; or, if they are one, there is another, the true mind, which has no such distinction as that between preserved and lost, which means that it has no distinction between good and evil — the Hu heresy.   With this Hu heresy in his mind, Chu Hsi combats their favourite argument that the Nature cannot be said to be good because that would imply that it was evil, and uses the illustration of the times of Yao and Shun, to which, though there was no confusion whatever, the opposite term " peace " is applied.   Similarly, the term " preserved " may be applied to the mind which has not gone, and yet may go, astray.

the absence of evil activity; in which case what is called "stillness" will manifest itself without any so-called "examination" and "understanding". You, however, would make out that in this momentary holding fast and by the application of "examination" and "understanding" you may arrive at "stillness". I fear that the substance of the Mind as still cannot be understood in this way and that what you call "examination" and "understanding" is but to accelerate movement and activity, and lapse into care and vexation. The same idea is expressed in the Master Ch'êng's statement, "The moment thought comes into existence the Mind is already manifested; therefore, while nurture is possible before its manifestation, to bring it into accord with the Mean before its manifestation is not possible." But the Mind is one, and the expressions "hold fast" and "preserve" cannot mean that there are two minds, each holding fast to the other in the same way as two wrestlers grasp each other and will not let go. The Master said further,[1] "Let there be concentration and no absent-mindedness; let there be no activity unless in accord with right principle;[2] then there will be self-control and the preservation of the mind." The countless utterances of the saints and sages, if you trace them to their beginning and follow them to their conclusion, you will find have no other meaning. (Reply to Lü Tzŭ Yo.)[3]

---

[1] 亦 曰 refers to Ch'êng Tzŭ.

[2] 禮 here is equivalent to 理; see p. 201.

[3] Lü Tsu Chien (呂 祖 儉), *style* Tzŭ Yo (子 約), pupil of Chu Hsi, and brother of the more famous Lü Tsu Ch'ien (呂 祖 謙).

20. The expressions "holding fast" and "letting go", "preserving" and "losing", represent the instability of the natural mind, but the spiritual mind which is "but a spark" is no other than this same mind. You are mistaken when you interpret these four sentences[1] as referring, not to man's Mind,[2] but to the mystery of its activity and inactivity, without beginning or ending, without location, without corporeity. You are wrong, too, when you say : "Even in the wild restless turning to and fro which does not know where to rest, although not the original Mind, you may see the impossibility of restraint of the Mind's essence" ; for if the mind-essence is really as you say, why should you disapprove of its not knowing where to rest and say "It must find its rest in reverent care?" (Reply to Lü Tzŭ Yo.)

21. Everyone regards the passage on preserving and losing the mind as teaching that the selfish actions of the natural mind are due to relaxing hold of it and losing it, but forgets that preservation is simply by holding fast this very same mind. Tzŭ Yo says the terms "preservation" and "loss", "outgoing" and "incoming", alike express the excellence of the Mind's unfathomable spirituality and intelligence ; hence he makes no distinction between true and false. In both these respects he is wrong. The truth is : the preservation and loss, the outgoing and incoming,

---

[1] That is, sentences in Mencius in which the expressions quoted occur ; see Mencius, p. 285.

[2] 人 心 here probably means not the "natural mind" specifically, but man's mind in a general sense.

of the Mind are indeed the operation of its unfathomable spirituality and intelligence ; [1] but its truth and falsity, its error and rectitude, the beginning and ending of its activity and inactivity, must be distinguished. (Reply to Lü Tzŭ Yo.)

22.   Your account of the natural mind and spiritual mind is very good, for if the spiritual mind is allowed to rule, then the natural mind is transformed into the spiritual mind. For example, food and dress are originally the outcome of the natural mind, but, as is shown in the *Hsiang Tang*,[2] in the case of the sage they proceed wholly from the spiritual mind. (Reply to Huang Tzŭ Ching.)

23   It is asked whether the doctrine of the contemplation of the Mind as taught by the Buddhists is true.

My reply is : The Mind is the agent by which man rules his body. It is one and not divided. It is subject and not object. It controls the external world and is not its slave. Therefore, with the Mind we contemplate external objects, and so discover the principles of the universe. According to this theory, however, and contrariwise, we examine the Mind by means of an external object ; that is, in addition to this my Mind, I have another Mind external to it, by which it is controlled. But is this thing that we call Mind

[1] Chu Hsi himself says that the terms " preservation " and " loss ", etc., express the operation of the unfathomable spirituality, etc., but not the *excellence* of them as Tzŭ Yo says they do.   By saying they express the *excellence* of the unfathomable spirituality Tzŭ Yo excludes everything not excellent, such as falsity.

[2] The title of book x in the Analects.   The passages referred to are in chaps. vi to viii (pp. 94–7).

P

one entity or two ? Is it subject or is it object ? Is it
free or is it the slave of the external ? We do not need
to be told in order to see the fallacy of it all.

Someone may say : If this argument is correct, how are
we to explain such expressions in the writings of the saints
and sages as " Discrimination and singleness ",[1] " Hold fast
and preserve it ",[2] " Perfect the Mind and understand the
Nature ",[3] " Preserve the Mind and nourish the Nature ",[4]
and " See them in front of you and resting on the yoke ".[5]

I reply : [6] The apparent similarity but essential difference between this theory and such sayings in the classics
is just like the difference between wheat and tares [7] or
vermilion and purple, and the student must discriminate
between them. When we read of the instability of the
natural mind [8] and the budding of human desire, or of the
smallness of the spiritual mind [8] and the mystery of Divine
Law, we must remember that the Mind is one, and that
different terms are used simply to express its accord or
otherwise with what is right.

The meaning of the phrase " discrimination and singleness " [9] is to fasten upon what is right and discern all that

---

[1] *Shu Ching*, p. 61. [2] Mencius, p. 285. [3] Ibid., p. 324.

[4] Ibid., pp. 324-5. [5] Analects, XV, v, 3 (p. 160).

[6] The answer is first given in general terms, and then in detailed sections
corresponding to the sayings quoted by the questioner, and in the same
order.

[7] Yu, 莠, is a weed, very similar in appearance to the young sprouts
of corn.

[8] *Shu Ching*, p. 61.

[9] The first of the sayings quoted in the question, " To fasten upon what
is right and discern all that diverges from it," explains "discrimination"
(精) ; " to discard everything that is opposed to it and restore all that is
in accord with it," explains " singleness " (一).

diverges from it, to discard everything that is opposed to it and restore all that is in accord with it. If we can do this we shall indeed " hold fast the Mean ",[1] and be free from either excess or shortcoming. The phrase does not mean that the spiritual is one mind and the natural one mind, and that there is another mind by which we make the mind discriminating and single.

The meaning of the phrase, "hold it fast and preserve it," is not that one mind is used to hold fast and preserve the other; nor is the meaning of "letting go and losing it"[2] that one mind is let go and lost by another. When the Mind is held fast by the Mind itself, then the lost is saved ; when it is let go and not held fast, then the preserved is lost. But "holding it fast" is also to be explained as not allowing the doings of the day to fetter and destroy the natural goodness of the virtuous nature,[3] and not that we are to sit in rigid posture and preserve a manifestly useless " intelligence " ! [4]

" To perfect the Mind " [5] means "to investigate things ",[6] "to study exhaustively the laws of the universe ",[7] and " to be possessed of a wide and far-reaching penetration ",

[1] *Shu Ching*, p. 61.

[2] Occurs in the same connexion as " hold fast and preserve it ". See Mencius, p. 285.

[3] Alluding to the context of the saying, " hold it fast," in Mencius ; cf. the whole of chap. viii, Mencius, pp. 283–5.

[4] As the Buddhists do.

[5] This paragraph explains the third of the sayings quoted in the question, but not wholly ; part of it, viz. " understanding the Nature", is explained in the next paragraph in connexion with the phrase "nourishing the Nature ".

[6] G.L., p. 222.

[7] Ibid., p. 229.

and so to have that by means of which we may develop to their utmost extent the principles inherent in the Mind.

"To preserve the Mind" means "to maintain inward correctness by seriousness, and to regulate outward conduct by righteousness",[1] as in what has already been said in explanation of the expressions, "discrimination and single-ness," and "holding fast and preserving the Mind". There-fore by perfecting the Mind we can understand our Nature and know Heaven, because, the substance of the Mind being unclouded, we are able to search into this Law as the Self-Existent. By preserving the Mind we can "nourish our Nature and serve Heaven",[2] because, the substance of the Mind being not lost, we can obey this Law as the Self-Existent. How can this be regarded as one mind perfecting another mind, or one mind preserving another mind, like two things holding each other and not letting go?

The passage, "See them in front of you and resting on the yoke," is in reference to the preceding expressions, "sincere and truthful," "earnest and serious."[3] For what it means is: If sincerity and truthfulness, earnestness and seriousness, do not perish from the Mind, then we cannot go anywhere but we shall see them facing us; and not that we see our Mind in front of us. Moreover, what rhyme or reason would there be in saying that the body is here and the Mind in front of us, or the body in the carriage and the Mind resting on the yoke?

To sum up: The teaching of the sages is, that with the Mind we exhaustively investigate principles, and by

[1] *Yi Ching*, p. 420. [2] Mencius, p. 325.
[3] Analects, XV, v, 2 (p. 159).

following these principles we determine our attitude to external things, just as the body uses the arm, and the arm the hand. Their doctrine is even and clear, their attitude broad and calm, their principles real, and the practice of them spontaneous. The teaching of the Buddhists, on the other hand, is with the Mind to seek the Mind, with the Mind to use the Mind, like the mouth gnawing the mouth, or the eye gazing at itself. Its methods are uncertain and feverish, its course is dangerous and clogged, its principles are hollow, and its tendency antagonistic to what is right. These, then, are the reasons why I maintain that, though in phraseology there are some points of similarity to that of the sages, their teaching is essentially different. And yet who but the high-minded with careful reflection and clear discrimination can avoid error on such a subject ? (Treatise on the Contemplation of the Mind.)

24. *Question.* Hêng Ch'ü said, "Let the mind be expanded widely"; and again, "If we are large-minded we shall possess penetration in all things, if we are small-minded everything will be wrong." [1] Sun Ssŭ Miao [2] said, " Be great in courage but small in mind." My own explanation of these two statements is that Hêng Ch'ü was speaking of the mind-substance, while Ssŭ Miao was speaking of its manifestation. I do not know if I am correct or not.

Answer. The mind, of course, ought [3] to be large in some directions and small in others. If you insist upon forcing

[1] 宗 傳, pt. iv, f. 19.
[2] A scholar of the seventh century ; see 尙 友 錄, pt. iv, f.17 ; also Giles' *Biog. Dict.*, p. 695.
[3] 合 = 合 當.

the letter of the text, then all thinking becomes impossible. (Reply to P'an Tzŭ Shan)

25.   We must turn inwards and examine our own mind. We must examine it in its outgoing and incoming. We shall preserve it just in so far as we hold it fast. Our labour must be continuous and unbroken. (Reply to Li Hui Shu.)

26.   *Question.*   I [1] once said that the student should constantly preserve his mind in rectitude and singleness, and not allow the smallest shadow of selfish thought to intrude itself.   Then it will follow naturally that there will be an inward controlling principle, and the mind will not be scattered and wandering, and we shall come very near to the comprehension of the original substance of spirituality and intelligence.   But if we would really and truly understand the original substance of this spirituality and intelligence, we must also cultivate daily intimacy with moral principle, and eradicate selfishness : only thus shall we attain to an understanding of the original mind-substance.

Answer.   You need to get rid of a lot of superfluous methods and useless verbiage ; to look only at what is meant by the saying, "Hold it fast and you will preserve it" ; [2] and not add redundant comments.   (Reply to Li Hui Shu.)

27.   Scholars of the present day for the most part busy themselves for the most part with irrelevant matters, and do

----

[1] 煇 refers to the questioner Li Hui Shu (李 晦 叔) ; 煇 was his *ming.*

[2] Mencius, p. 285.

not realize that the mystery of the Mind is the source of all phenomena.[1] Those who do know can do no more than, with beetling brows and glaring eyes, shout and swear away the views they are opposing, asserting that this alone is the virtuous mind and original nature, and that it is invariably good. They do not realize that if there is no holding fast and preserving it, no practical conduct, no explanation, and no thorough examination, then all this beetling of the brows and glaring of the eyes resolves itself into selfish thought and human passion, and the more earnestly sincere it is the more wild will it be. You must not fail carefully to examine and studiously avoid this error. (Reply to an anonymous questioner.)

28. I regard the theory that the Mind has neither birth nor death[2] as very nearly akin to the Buddhist doctrine of transmigration. In the production of things by Heaven and Earth "it is man who receives the ethers in their highest excellence, and is therefore the most spiritual of all beings".[3] What we call Mind is the psychical faculty and consciousness, as seen in the hearing and sight of the ear and eye. In the case of Heaven and Earth, there never has been and never can be either creation or dissolution; but in the case of man and all other creatures, on account of their material form, there is both beginning and ending. If we understand that Law is one but its functions are diverse, then

[1] See p. 217 ff.

[2] A tenet of the Hu School; see 學 案, pt. xlii, f. 8.

[3] Cited from the *T'ai Chi T'u Shuo*; see J. P. Bruce, *Introduction to Chu Hsi and the Sung School*, chap. vi.

why need we devise this theory of the Mind being without
birth or death, and startle the ear of the student. (Extract
from Chu Hsi's "Criticism of Hu Tzŭ's *Words
of Wisdom*".)[1]

29. Now between "holding fast and preserving" the
Mind on the one hand, and "letting go and losing"
it[2] on the other, there can be no gap. Seeing that we
recognize it as lost and seek it,[3] it follows that the Mind
exists. It is said that the Mind which is lost cannot be
held fast and again preserved; we can only lay aside our
quest, wait for some other time when we see the Mind's
manifestation in some other direction, and then follow it
up and hold it fast.[4] But in this interval, while you are
waiting to see its manifestation, there is a break in the
Mind's continuity, and no means of renewed activity. Even
if you could see its manifestation again and hold it fast,
what you thus hold fast would not be the whole Mind but
only a part.[5] When, so far as its original and entire
substance is concerned, not a single day's labour has been
used in nourishing the Mind, to expect to be able "to
expand and fill it so that it may be great as Heaven itself",
seems to me contrary to all reason! (Extract from Chu
Hsi's "Criticism of Hu Tzŭ's *Words of Wisdom*".)[1]

[1] The treatise *Words of Wisdom* (知 言), by Hu Wu Fèng, is to be
found with Chu Hsi's criticisms in the 學 案, pt. xlii, ff. 2-12.

[2] Mencius, p. 285.

[3] Ibid., p. 290.

[4] Cf. the *Chih Yen* (see note 1), from Chu Hsi's criticisms, of which
the whole paragraph is taken.

[5] 一 端, i.e. one only of the 四 端.

30 *Question by Ch'en An Ch'ing*. Some time back I[1]
wrote a treatise on Mind in which I said : " The Decree
of Heaven, how profound it is and undying ! "[2]   That
by means of which it rules over the production of things
is the Mind of Heaven. Man receives the Decree of
Heaven and so is born ; and because this by which Heaven
gives me birth is received by me in its entirety to be lord
of my complete personality, and in its entirety to reside in
me, spiritual and intelligent, continuously illuminating and
unclouded, living and imperishable—this we call the Mind
of Man. Its substance, answering to what are termed the
principles[3] of Origin, Beauty, Utility, and Potentiality,
is inherent in me as the nature-principles—Love, Righteousness, Reverence, and Wisdom.[4]   Its operation, answering
to what are termed the ethers of spring, summer, autumn,
and winter,[5] is manifested in me as the Four Feelings—
solicitude, conscientiousness, courtesy, and moral insight.[6]
Therefore, though the substance resides in a very minute
spot,[7] that which constitutes it the substance is really as
great as Heaven and Earth ; the countless laws of the
universe are present in their completeness, and there is not
a single thing outside their scope. Although its operation

---

[1] 淵 refers to the questioner Ch'en Ch'un (*style* An Ch'ing) ; see p. 195, n.

[2] *Odes*, p. 570.

[3] 道 = 道 理, principles.

[4] See J. P. Bruce, *Introduction to Chu Hsi and the Sung School*, chap. vii.

[5] Ibid., chaps. vii and xi.

[6] Ibid., chap. xi.

[7] 方 寸 is a term for the " mind " or " heart ", and, of course, has
that meaning here, but the force of the expression in this connexion is
in its literal meaning.

proceeds from a very minute spot, yet that which constitutes its operation is really in union with the pervading activity of Heaven and Earth; the countless phenomena of the universe are united by it, and there is not a single law which does not operate in them. Herein lies the mystery of the Mind; it unifies activity and repose, the manifest and the hidden, the external and the internal, the source and the issue, to the exclusion of all barriers. But man is fettered by the impurity of the Two Ethers and Five Agents which fall to his lot, to which is added the entanglement of the desires of the senses; and thus the Mind is cramped by material form, it cannot be enlarged in a lofty sympathy and unselfishness, nor has the spiritual faculty any means of ruling in the Mind. Those who would give full substantiality to this Mind so that it may continually be the ruler of their entire personality, must see to it that their energy in perfecting knowledge is adequate, their cultivation of seriousness whole-hearted, and their inward light brilliant and pure, and thus rise above the material endowment and human desire. My original mind-substance, in so far as it is equal in greatness to Heaven and Earth, is brightly illuminating in every direction, so that there is not one principle which is not luminous. In the original operation of my Mind, in so far as it is in union with the all-pervading activity of Heaven and Earth, there is nothing to divide or separate, and there is not even a momentary cessation of life. Thus, before being affected by the external world, the Mind is pure and brilliant, clear as a mirror and poised evenly as a balance, truly able to stand before God, with all laws established within. After being

affected by the external world, the favourableness or un-
favourableness, as well as the degree, of the response depends
upon this particular phenomenon.[1] For this Law is all comprehensive, and resides in every single thing *as the law of
its individual existence* ; as is said in the *Yi Ch'ing* : "The
method of Ch'ien is to change and transform so that everything obtains its correct nature as ordained by Heaven,"[2]
and without the smallest error. The Mind, therefore, does
not linger with a matter that has once been dealt with. In
repose the substance of Heaven and Earth remains—one
source with an infinite plurality of phenomena. In activity
the operations of Heaven and Earth go forth—an infinite
plurality of phenomena but united in one unity.
The substance constantly enfolds its operation within itself,
and its operation is never separated from the substance.
The substance and its operation are united in one revolving
unity, and this is wholly that Divine Law which daily and
continuously manifests itself in motion and rest. Now,
following this, what I have received in its entirety from
Heaven becomes in me the assurance of a return to the
source, and I too, like that Decree of Heaven so profound,
may be "undying".[3] This, I apprehend, is in brief, the
way in which man may preserve his mind.

---

[1] 應 = "response to", or "reception of". The response to or
treatment of a particular phenomenon by a mind such as is here described
depends entirely on the nature of that phenomenon, just as the treatment of a man by a perfectly good man will depend entirely on what kind
of man the former is. The treatment will be perfectly appropriate to
the subject treated.

[2] *Yi Ching*, p. 213.

[3] See p. 217.

Wang Ch'êng—style Tzǔ Chêng—said:[1] Your way of treating the subject is most excellent, but what you say about the mind-substance being as great as Heaven and Earth, and its operation as in union with the all-pervading operations of Heaven and Earth, needs substantiating, and I would be glad to receive your further instruction.

I therefore prepared another supplementary treatise as follows : The statement, that the mind-substance is as great as Heaven and Earth, is made from the point of view of Law ; for permeating the whole universe there is but one Law as the ultimate reality, the pivot of creation and transformation, received alike in all ages by men and all other creatures. Yet among all creatures it is man who is Spirit. So true is this that I embody and receive congregated in my Mind all those principles which are comprehended in that one Law, and which constitute what is termed the Nature. But although these principles are thus congregated in my Mind and become my Nature they are never severed from the Divine. What in my Mind is called Love, is the Divine principle of Origin ; what in my Mind is called Reverence, is the Divine principle of Beauty ; what in my Mind is called Righteousness, is the Divine principle of Utility ; what in my Mind is called Wisdom, is the Divine principle of Potentiality.[2] They are really identical and not simply used as illustrations. The Moral Law of Heaven is all-comprehensive and the Law of my Mind is all-comprehensive ; the Moral Law of Heaven is limitless and the

[1] Ch'ên An Ch'ing tells Chu Hsi what Wang Ch'êng had said in criticism of his essay.

[2] See J. P. Bruce, *Introduction to Chu Hsi and the Sung School*, chap. vii.

Law of my Mind is limitless; the Moral Law of Heaven enters into every single thing without exception, and there is not one thing in the universe which is not Divine, and the Law of my Mind also enters into everything without exception, and there is not one thing in the universe which is not my Mind. (What is there that is not done by the Mind? What principle is there not inherent in the Mind?) In all the world how can there be anything outside the bounds of my Nature, or not included within the Law of my Mind. From the point of view of Law only it is the all-comprehensive universe, and we do not think of it as in its close relation to myself. But when I call it the substance of my Mind, then, from the point of view of Law as it is inherent in me, there is an arch-controller and its operations are traceable. This is why the Mind is most spiritual and most wonderful. To whatever point Law reaches, the thought of my Mind follows it. If in its greatness it reaches to infinitude, or if it be so fine as to pierce things indescribably minute, the Mind penetrates and permeates all. If it reaches back to the most ancient time, or forward ten thousand generations, the Mind comprehends all. Whether it be near or distant, a foot or ten thousand miles, it is all alike. Even though it extend to "establishing order in heaven and earth, and nourishing all things",[1] it still does not go beyond the fullness of the original mind-substance: it is not something accomplished outside its sphere. This is what Chang Tzŭ means when he says: "The egoistic mind cannot be in union with the Mind of

[1] D. M., p. 249.

Heaven." [1] The statement, that the operation of the Mind is in union with the all-pervading operations of Heaven and Earth,[2] is made from the point of view of the pervasiveness of Law. For Law pervades and revolves throughout the universe without a moment's cessation. Of all things and all phenomena, large and small, coarse and fine, there is not one which is not pervaded by Divine Law. This Law I receive into my Mind in its entirety, and being in my Mind there is not a moment when it is not productive and in union with the all-pervading activity of Heaven and Earth. Let men's desires be pure, and their feelings far-reaching, with no barrier in their all-pervading operations, then they will be continually in union with the all-pervading operations of Heaven and Earth. Take, for example, the feeling of solicitude. In the case of those who are near, it is manifested in family affection. When we are affectionate towards those to whom we ought to be affectionate it is the pervading activity of the Decree of Heaven. I simply unite with it in its pervading activity, and then I do not defraud the objects of my affection. If there is the slightest lack, it is because Divine Law is impeded in the sphere of family affection, and its pervading activity ceases. Or in a wider circle, in the sphere of love to men, such as the obligation to comfort the aged, to treat the young tenderly,[3] and to be apprehensive for one falling into a well,[4] this, too, is the pervading activity of the Decree

---

[1] Chêng Mêng, 大 心 篇.

[2] See p. 220, and Wang Ch'êng's criticism, to which this passage is an answer.

[3] Analects, V, xxv, 4 (p. 46).

[4] Mencius, p. 78.

of Heaven. I simply unite with it in its pervading activity, and so do not fail in cherishing, in comforting, and in being apprehensive. If there be failure in the slightest degree, it is because Divine Law is impeded in the sphere of love to men, and its pervading activity ceases. Or, in a still wider circle, in the sphere of kindness to inferior creatures, such as sparing the young sapling, saving the life of pregnant animals, and avoiding the destruction of young creatures,[1] this, too, is the all-pervading activity of the Decree of Heaven. I simply unite with it in its pervading activity and so do not injure the growing, the pregnant, and the young. If there be the slightest injury, it is because Divine Law is impeded in the sphere of kindness to inferior creatures, and its pervading activity ceases. And the same is true of the response of all the Four Feelings in all the affairs of everyday life. If in only one thing there is not the appropriate response, it is because in that one thing Divine Law is impeded. If in a single moment of time there is lack of union, it is because in that moment of time Divine Law is impeded. But if in all the innumerable threads of life we follow the simplicity of the laws of Heaven, and there is on the part of the Mind an all-round carrying of them into effect, then in its operation it will be one with the principles of Origin, Beauty, Order, and Potentiality, in their all-pervading activity throughout the universe. This is why Ch'êng Tzǔ refers to the saying in the *Yi Ching*. "Through the changes and transformations produced by Heaven and Earth, plants and trees

---

[1] See Li Chi, *Sacred Books of the East*, vol. xxvii, p. 221.

grow luxuriantly," [1] to represent the picture of the fullness
and growth of a mind ruled by sympathy. But we must
have the substance great as Heaven and Earth, then only
can we have the pervading operation of Heaven and Earth.
And we must have the pervading operation of Heaven and
Earth, then only can we have the substance great as Heaven
and Earth. We must remember, however, that they are
really two separate entities.

Wang Ch'êng criticized this supplementary treatise [2]
somewhat more closely, saying further : The Decree of
Heaven, the Nature, and the Mind, although not separate
entities, yet have each their own sphere which must not
be mistaken. In your discussion of the mind-substance
you ought to be content to show the Mind's connexion with
the Nature and with Heaven, for then what is there to
which such a statement would not apply? Once we understand this clearly, half a sentence, or a word even, will be
enough to make your meaning plain. You need to give the
matter further consideration and investigation.

On thinking over the matter further it seems to me [3] that
speaking in the ontological sense it is still correct to say,
" The mind-substance is as great as Heaven and Earth,
and its operation is in union with the all-pervading activity
of Heaven and Earth," but to express it only in this way
would be to fall into the opposite error of speaking on too
lofty a plane, and of not bringing the subject into touch

[1] *Yi Ching*, p. 420.

[2] That is, Ch'ên An Ch'ing's treatise ; cf. p. 220.

[3] Ch'ên An Ch'ing again states his own opinion in reference to Wang
Ch'êng's further criticism.

with our own faults. It seems best simply to speak from our own point of view in our daily experiences, and say, " That which is all-comprehensively within is the substance ; that which is affected by the external world and responds thereto is its operation," as the most pertinent statement of the matter. I recall that the saints and sages spoke in simple common speech. I fear that my ideas must all go beyond the truth, and trust that you will correct them.

Answer.[1] This treatise is indeed excellent. If you take a still broader view in your consideration of the subject, your understanding of it will be all the more exact. Moreover, do not be content to confine your study to the direct investigation of the metaphysical aspect of the subject. Devote some labour also to the study of daily practical affairs, of the teaching of the classics, of the lessons of history ; then the subtle and the coarse, the external and the internal, will be united together in perfect union, and there will not be a single principle lost sight of. (Reply to Ch'ên An Ch'ing.)

[1] That is, by Chu Hsi.

THE PHILOSOPHY OF
HUMAN NATURE

BOOK IV

BEING BOOK XLV OF
THE COMPLETE WORKS OF CHU HSI

———

THE MIND, THE NATURE, AND THE FEELINGS

THE STEADFAST NATURE

FEELING AND MOTIVE

THE WILL AND THE ETHER. THE WILL AND MOTIVE THOUGHT

BOOK IV.

THE MIND, THE NATURE, AND THE FEELINGS.

(TWENTY-ONE SECTIONS FROM "THE CONVERSATIONS".)

1.   The Nature corresponds to the Supreme Ultimate. The Mind corresponds to the Two Modes. The Supreme Ultimate is inherent in the Two Modes and is inseparable from them, but the Supreme Ultimate is the Supreme Ultimate, and the Two Modes are the Two Modes. So it is with the Nature and Mind. As is expressed in the saying: "One and yet two, two and yet one." The philosopher Han[1] defined the Nature as Love, Righteousness, Reverence, Wisdom, and Sincerity, and the Feelings as Pleasure, Anger, Grief, and Joy. This was an advance upon the teaching of the rest of the philosophers with respect to the Nature. But in his doctrine of the Three Grades he dealt with the material element only, and did not take the Nature into account.

2.   *Question.* That which is imparted by Heaven to men and other creatures is the Decree, that which is received by them from Heaven is the Nature. The ruler of the personality is the Mind. Is it the case that some obtain from Heaven that which is bright and clear, true and great, and that this is "Illustrious Virtue"?[2]

---

[1] See p. 77, n. 3.
[2] G. L., p. 220.

Chu Hsi. How do you distinguish between Mind and the Nature ? How do you place the word " Illustrious "? What is the difference between " receive " and " obtain " ? What are the distinguishing features of " men ", " other creatures ", and the " person " ? Does " Illustrious Virtue " pertain to Mind or to the Nature ?

Questioner. The Nature is concrete, but if you take into account affection by the external world and the response thereto, emptiness of self and the resulting clearness, then the meanings attached to the word " Mind " are many.

Answer. Of these two, to speak of one is to imply the other. They cannot be separated, and are perforce difficult to distinguish. To be without the Mind would be to be without the Nature and vice versa. Hence Mencius in his account of the Mind and the Nature always associates the two. He speaks of Love, Righteousness, Reverence, and Wisdom as the Nature ; and then of the solicitous mind, the conscientious mind, the courteous mind', and the discriminating mind.[1] You need to study the subject still more thoroughly.

3.   Although the Nature is formless it consists of concrete principles. Although the Mind is a distinct entity, it is formless and therefore can contain innumerable principles It is desirable that people should examine this for themselves, and so arrive at the truth.

4.   The Nature is essentially without form, but consists of concrete principles. The Mind is as though it had form, but its substance is really formless.

[1] Mencius, p. 79.

5. The Nature consists of the concrete principles contained in the Mind. The Mind is the seat of the assemblage of those principles.

6. The Nature is Law. The Mind is the receptacle which holds and stores the principles of the Nature, the agent which distributes and sets them in operation.

7. To the Mind the Nature stands in the relation of substance. The Mind holds the Nature within it like the stuffing of cakes, for the simple reason that it is in virtue of its possession of the Nature that it possesses these principles.

8. When you have succeeded in describing a thing, and when you have succeeded in naming it, you may claim clearly to understand it. The Mind and the Nature are also very difficult to define.

Answer. A definition which I have already given is: The Nature is the law of the Mind; the Feelings are the Nature in action; and the Mind is the ruler of the Nature and Feelings.

9. The Nature is undefinable. We are able to assert that the Nature is good because we observe the goodness of the Four Terminals. From these we infer the goodness of the Nature, just as we know the purity of the stream from the purity of its source. The Four Terminals are feelings, while the Nature consists of principles. The issues are Feelings, the source is the Nature. It is the same principle as when you infer the presence of an object from the shadow it casts.

10.   Po Fêng[1] raised the question of the Nature as having both a pre-active and a post-active state.

Answer.   The moment the Nature has put forth activity you have Feeling.   The Feelings are divisible into good and evil, while the Nature is wholly good ; and the Mind includes both the Nature and the Feelings.   Generally speaking, in defining the Nature you must remember that in its origin it is the Decree received from Heaven.   Its endowment thus has its source *outside itself*, and it cannot, as in the case of the Mind, be defined by a single word. The Confucian scholars of the Han dynasty, however, in their explanation of the dictum, " The Decree of Heaven is what we term the Nature "[2] made use of such expressions as, " The Ligneous disposition is Love ; the Metallic disposition is Righteousness " ; and did so advisedly : they did not adopt them heedlessly.   The student should examine these expressions closely.

At this point the Philosopher sighed and said : Granted that if you do not clearly open up the matter and are content with simple nurture, you will attain your object and even save some strength ; nevertheless, if you would expound and teach, you must combine investigation with carefulness in teaching, and thus, it may be, avoid disrespect to the ancients.

11   A long time ago I saw a statement by Wu Fêng[3] in which he spoke only of the Mind in contrast to the Nature, leaving no place for the Feelings.   Subsequently

---

[1] Wu Pi Ta, style Po Fêng, a pupil of Chu Hsi; cf. 學 案, pt. xlix, f. 53.
[2] D.M., p. 246.   [3] Hu Wu Fêng, see p. 25, n. 2.

I saw the statement by Hêng Ch'ü that the Mind unites the Nature and the Feelings,[1] and recognized it as exceedingly valuable, because it gives us the true application of the term "Feeling", and accords with Mencius' treatment of the subject. Mencius says, "A solicitous mind is the terminal of Love."[2] Now Love is the Nature, and Solicitude is Feeling. Here then, we have the Mind recognized in Feeling. Again he says, "Love, Righteousness, Reverence, and Wisdom have their root in the Mind."[3] Here we have the Mind recognized in the Nature. For the Mind includes within it both the Nature and the Feelings. The Nature is the substance and the Feelings are its operation.

12. Most people define the Nature first and the Mind afterwards, whereas it would seem as if the Mind should come first. The ancients also in their construction of the ideographs made the "Mind" ideograph first: the words "Nature" and "Feeling" being both derived from the word "Mind". It is true that it is at man's birth that he first receives these principles, but at the very moment of birth they are inherent in the Mind. Then again Love and Righteousness are the Nature, but Mencius speaks of the "Heart of Love and Righteousness".[4] Solicitude and conscientiousness are Feelings, but Mencius calls them the "solicitous mind" and the "conscientious mind".[5] It is because the Nature is the Law of the Mind, and the Feelings are the operation of the Nature. Now by defining the Mind first, men are taught to recognize a head to the Nature

[1] See 學 案, pt. xviii, f. 14.   [2] Mencius, p. 78.   [3] Ibid., p. 336.
[4] Mencius, p. 283.   [5] Ibid., p. 79.

and the Feelings, and a receptacle for the principles of the
Nature. If we put the Nature first, it gives the impression
of an additional mind present in the Nature. Hêng Ch'ü's
statement, "The Mind unites the Nature and the
Feelings," is excellent.

13. The Nature is that which precedes activity, the
Feelings follow activity; and the Mind includes both the
pre-active and the post-active states. For the Mind's pre-
active state is the Nature, and its post-active state is
Feeling, as is expressed in the saying: "The Mind unites
the Nature and the Feelings." Desire is Feeling in its
manifestation. The Mind is like water, the Nature is the
stillness of water at rest, Feeling is the flow of water, and
Desires are the waves. But waves are good and bad. So
with desires: there are good desires, as when "I desire
virtue"; [1] and there are evil desires which rush out pre-
cipitately like wild and boisterous waves. For the most
part, evil desires destroy the Divine Law, as when a dam
bursts and carries with it universal destruction. When
Mencius speaks of the Feelings as constituted for the practice
of what is good,[2] he refers to the Feelings as they ought to
be. As they flow from the Nature they are infallibly good.

14. The Mind must be thought of as ruler. In activity
and repose alike it is ruler. It is not that in repose the
Mind is unemployed, and only rules when there is activity.
When I say "ruler" I mean that an all-comprehensive
supreme ruler dwells within. The Mind unites and controls

---

[1] Analects, VII, xxix, p. 68.   [2] Mencius, p. 278.

the Nature and Feelings ; but it is not united with the Nature and Feelings in such a way as to form one entity, without any distinction.

15. *Question.* When a man is unoccupied and his mind empty, clear, and unclouded : is not this the Ether, and his spontaneous activity the Nature ?

Answer. The empty, clear, and unclouded is the Mind. Law, which dwells within in its entirety and without the slightest defect, is the Nature. Activity in response to affection by the external world is Feeling. Hêng Ch'ü puts it well when he says, " From the Great Void we have the term Heaven ; from the transformations of the Ether we have the term Moral Law."[1] This is said of the universal. " By the union of the Void with the Ether we have the term Nature ; by the union of the Nature with Consciousness we have the term Mind." This is said of men and other creatures.

16. *Question.* What is the difference between the Mind, the Nature, and Feeling ?

Answer. Ch'êng Tzǔ said : " The Mind is like the seed corn : the principle of life contained in it is the Nature ; the putting forth of life on the part of the positive ether is Feeling."[1] Extend this principle and you will find that it is so with everything that exists.

17. Mencius, in his account of the Nature, did not speak directly of the Nature. What he said was, " If we look at

[1] *Chêng Mêng*, 太 和 篇 ; see 大 全 or 精 義 also 學 案, pt. xvii, f. 11.

[2] 宗 傳, pt. iii, f. 7. The statement is by I Ch'uan, see p. 333.

the Feelings which flow from the Nature we may know that they are constituted for the practice of what is good."[1] From the goodness of the Feelings you can infer the goodness of the Nature.

The Philosopher said further : In the case of solicitude and conscientiousness, for the most part we infer the Nature from things contrary to its principles. It is when we see something calculated to wound that the feeling of solicitude is stirred ; it is when we do something hateful that the feeling of conscientiousness is stirred. In the case of "serving one's parents" and "obeying one's elder brother",[2] the Nature is manifested in spontaneous accord with these principles.

18. *Question.* In your comment on "perfecting the Mind" and "understanding the Nature",[3] you, sir, say : "The Mind is without substance: the Nature is its substance." How is it so ?

Answer. The Mind is a hollow receptacle : the Nature constitutes its inward content. The principles of the Nature are contained in the Mind, and when activity is put forth that which is put forth pertains to the Nature. It is not that there is a perceptible object inside called the Nature ; it is simply the inherent rightness of Law which constitutes the Nature. A man ought to act in a certain way : this is what constitutes his Nature. As to the passage in Mencius beginning with the words : "The feeling of solicitude is the terminal of Love " ;[4] these four sentences refer to the

[1] Mencius, p. 278.   [2] Ibid., p. 189.   [3] Ibid., p. 324.
[4] Ibid., p. 79.

Nature, to the Feelings, and to Mind, which it would be well to consider in conjunction with Hêng Ch'ü's dictum: "The Mind unites the Nature and the Feelings."

19.   The meaning of the statement that the Mind unites the Nature and the Feelings is this: When the Mind is still and as yet without movement,[1] the principles of Love, Righteousness, Reverence, and Wisdom are present; when it is active we have Feeling. Some assert that the state of repose is the Nature, the activity the Mind, but this is dividing the Mind into two separate compartments, the Mind and the Nature. It is not to be accounted for in terms of activity and repose. Everything has Mind, and within, it is hollow like the heart of a chicken or pig which you have in your food, and which when you carve it you see to be hollow. Man's Mind is like that: it consists of such hollow places in which numerous principles are stored. If we take into consideration the whole universe with eternal time, and apply this reasoning, we shall recognize that in the whole heaven and in the whole earth there is nothing which does not have its origin here; and that this is what constitutes the mystery of Man's Mind. Law inherent in man's Mind is what we call the Nature. The Nature is like the soil of the Mind: that which fills the Mind is simply Law. The Mind is the seat of the spiritual intelligence, the ruler of the entire personality. The Nature consists of numerous principles received from Heaven and contained in the Mind, the manifestations of which in knowledge and thought are all Feelings. Hence the statement: "The Mind unites the Nature and Feelings."[2]

[1] *Yi Ching*, p. 370.

[2] See above.

20. *Question.* You have discussed the Mind from the point of view of man's personality. Can you take what we learn from man's personality and apply it to the universe ?

Answer. The Decree of Heaven pervades all things ; the agent by which these principles are controlled is the Mind of Heaven ;[2] that which possesses these principles is the Nature of Heaven, as, for example, the law which produces the four seasons ; and those influences which are put forth and nourish all things are the Feelings of Heaven.

21. If we illustrate the relation between the Mind and the Nature by a grain of corn,[3] the envelope represents the Mind, from which in some cases there develops millet and in other cases rice ; the cause of the difference in the development from the different seed represents the Nature. The agent of the development is the Mind ; its province is simply to produce. Or we may illustrate by the taking of medicine. The healing which follows is its medicinal property; whether it is warm or cold in its property is its Nature ; and the warm or cold effect as actually experienced after it has been taken is its Feeling.

(TEN SECTIONS FROM "THE COLLECTED WRITINGS".)

1. Tso Hsü[4] said : "Feelings proceed from the Nature and therefore stand in contrast to the Nature. The Mind has consciousness of both, and can unite and control both.

---

[1] As in the preceding section.

[2] 其 心 is the Mind of Heaven. 是 理 are the principles of the Nature which, in the universe at large, as in man, are controlled by Mind.

[3] See 235, n. 2.   [4] Fêng Tso Hsü ; see p. 35, n. 5.

In a pre-active state, apart from a uniting factor, there would be inertness and nothing more ; in the post-active state apart from a uniting factor there would simply be confusion." This passage is good, but to regard inactivity as the Mind is wrong. If the Mind is originally inactive why should Mencius "at forty attain to an unperturbed mind"?[1] If we recognize that the pre-active state is the Nature, that the post-active state is Feeling, while the Mind connects the activity and repose and is present in both, then we shall have the true account of all three. In the "Words of Wisdom" it is said, "The Nature exists in all things throughout the universe, the Feelings follow the activities of the universe, and the Mind moulds the virtues of the Nature and the Feelings."[2] This statement is very exact. (Reply to Fêng Tso Hsü.)

2. "The Mind rules the Nature and the Feelings."[3] This principle is well understood, and time will not permit any further argument in its support. But, as I view it, the fact that in the pre-active state consciousness is unclouded shows unmistakably that the Mind is ruler of the Nature ; and the fact that in the post-active state there is perfect order shows unmistakably that the Mind rules over the Feelings. The "Mind" connects the hidden and the manifest, it unites the higher and lower, it is everywhere present, and cannot be described in terms of extension or form. (Reply to Hu Kuang Chung.)[4]

---

[1] Mencius, p. 61. The words "unperturbed" and "inactive" are the same in the original.

[2] 學 案, pt. xlii, p. 12 ; see p. 32 of this volume and note.

[3] Ibid., pt. xviii, f. 14.

[4] See p. 37, n. 2.

3.   It is granted that you cannot say that before activity is put forth the Nature and the Feelings are non-existent, but neither can you say that they are one and without any distinction ; nor can you say that there is no time when the Mind is empty and still.   For before activity is put forth, countless principles are contained within it ; but the concrete in the midst of the formless, and the activity in the stillness, are as yet wholly without manifestation or location,[1] and therefore this state is described as equilibrium.   After activity is put forth, the concrete principles contained within operate in the midst of the activity.   (Reply to Hsü Yen Chang.)

4.   I do not know what your later opinion may be on your teaching as to the distinction between the Mind and the Nature.   The Nature consists of principles, the Feelings are their outflow and operation.   The Mind's consciousness is the agent by which these principles are possessed and the Feelings put into practice.   Take Wisdom for example : the principle by which we know the difference between right and wrong is Wisdom—a principle of the Nature ; that by which we actually regard a particular act as right or wrong is Feeling ; and the agent which possesses the principle and is conscious of the distinction made is the Mind.   These distinctions are subtle, but if they are examined with discrimination they will be understood.   Affection, respect, the sense of obligation, and discrimination,[2] pleasure, anger,

---

[1] 奠 = " to settle ", as also does 著.

[2] Note :   These correspond respectively to Love, Righteousness, Reverence, and Wisdom, and stand for the Four Feelings more usually given as Solicitude, Conscientiousness, Courtesy, and Moral Insight.

grief, and joy are all Feelings. From what has been said the rest may be easily inferred. (Reply to P'an Ch'ien Chih.)

5. The principles of Origin, Beauty, Order, and Potentiality,[1] are the Nature; production, growth, maturity, and storage are the Feelings; the agent which causes production by the principle of Origin, growth by the principle of Beauty, maturity by the principle of Order, and storage by the principle of Potentiality, is Mind. Love, Righteousness, Reverence, and Wisdom are the Nature; solicitude, conscientiousness, courtesy, and moral insight are the Feelings; and the agent by which Love is affectionate, by which Righteousness hates evil, by which Reverence is courteous, and by which Wisdom knows, is the Mind. The Nature is the law of the Mind, the Feelings are the operation of the Mind, and the Mind is the ruler of the Nature and Feelings. Ch'êng Tzŭ's statement, " Its substance is termed Flux, its law is termed Moral Law, and its operation is termed Spirit,"[2] is just this idea.

The Philosopher went on to say : When we speak of the Divine self-existence we refer to what is termed the Moral Law of Heaven ; when we speak of the Divine immanence we refer to the Decree of Heaven. He said further : the statement, " To give birth to things is the Mind of Heaven and Earth," expresses the same thought.[3] (Treatise on the Four Ultimata.)

---

[1] See J. P. Bruce, *Introduction to Chu Hsi and the Sung School,* chap. vii.

[2] See p. 157, notes 2 and 3.

[3] The phrase " The creative Mind of Heaven and Earth " expresses the same idea as the immanence of the Divine Decree referred to in the preceding sentence.

6. The possession of form implies the possession of Mind ; the principles received by the Mind from Heaven are termed the Nature, and the movements of the Nature when affected by the external world are termed the Feelings. These three all men have. The distinction between the sage and the rest of men is not that the sage has them and that others have not.[1] But in the case of the sage the Ether is clear and the Mind true, therefore the Nature is complete and the Feelings are without confusion. The student should preserve his Mind so as to nourish the Nature and control the Feelings. You say that in the sage the Mind is non-existent, and go on to maintain that we ought not to keep anything in our Mind for a single moment.[2] But among all those benefits which Heaven has given to us [3] how comes it that there is just this one thing that is a useless drag upon us ? (Reply to Hsü Ching Kuang.)

7. *Question.* The Nature in its beginning is only good ; there is no evil originally which can be attributed to it. It is the Principle of Origin, the first of the Four Attributes, Love the parent of the Five Cardinal Virtues. This is what is implied in Mencius' dictum, "The Nature of man is good," [4] what Ming Tao means when, quoting the statement "The law of their succession is goodness ",[5] he says it refers to the manifested operations of the Nature, the Mind of the Four Terminals.[6] How then can you describe it as one with Feeling ?

[1] Cf. Mencius, p. 288.
[2] The Buddhist idea.
[3] Ibid., p. 294.
[4] Mencius, p. 110.
[5] *Yi Ching*, p. 356.
[6] Mencius, p. 79.

Answer. The Nature from beginning to end is wholly good: you must not say that it is at the beginning that the Nature is wholly good. Could you, in line with what your statement suggests, say that the Nature in the end is evil ? If the manifested operations of the Nature are not Feelings, what are they ? What you may say is that the Feelings in their beginning are wholly good and without any evil. In the phrase, " If we look at the feelings which flow from the Nature," I do not think that the word *jo* (if we look at) means " to accord with ". [1] (Reply to Wang Tzŭ Ho.)

8. *Question.* Mencius said, " If we look at the Feelings which flow from the Nature we may know that they are constituted for the practice of what is good " ; and Chou Tzŭ said, " When the five nature-principles act in response to affection by the external world there comes the distinction between good and evil." [2] This again connects both good and evil with activity. Can it be that Mencius is speaking from the standpoint of the condition prior to the activity of the Feelings, and Chou Tzŭ from the standpoint of their post-active condition ?

Answer. The Feelings are not necessarily wholly good, but in their origin they are constituted for doing good, and not for doing evil ; it is when they are perverted, that they issue in the practice of evil. [3] Mencius spoke of them in

---

[1] Ibid., p. 278 ; cf. Legge's note on the word 若 (*jo*), in which he quotes the view of its interpretation referred to here.

[2] See the " T'ai Chi T'u Shuo " ; cf. J. P. Bruce, *Introduction to Chu Hsi and the Sung School*, chap. vi.¶

[3] See Legge's note on the original passage ; Mencius, p. 278.

their original perfection ; Chou Tzŭ spoke of them both in
their original perfection and as they are when perverted.
Chuang Tzŭ has the same idea when he speaks of forsaking
Heaven and violating the Feelings. (Reply to Chang Ching
Chih.)

9. Ch'êng Tzŭ in his later writings clearly states that his
statement that the Mind refers to the post-active period
was inaccurate.[1] It is not easy to avoid slight error at some
time or other. If we follow his later statement there will be
no mistake ; for the Nature is the substance, the Feelings
are its operation, and the Mind connects the two. We must
keep to the Master Hêng Ch'ü's statement : "The Mind
unites the Nature and Feelings" ; his way of expressing it
is very exact. (Reply to Fang Pin Wang.)

10. "Before there are any stirrings of pleasure, anger,
sorrow, or joy, the Mind may be said to be in a state of
equilibrium."[2] This is the Nature. "After they have
been stirred, and they act in their due degree, there ensues
what may be called a state of harmony."[3] This is Feeling.
Tzŭ Ssŭ in writing this desired the student to recognize
what he said as referring to Mind. The Mind ! How
wonderfully it "moulds the virtues of the Nature and
Feelings" ![4] (Reply to Chang Ching Fu.)[5]

---

[1] 學 案, pt. xxxi, ff. 13–14. The Philosopher referred to is I Ch'uan.
See p. 168 of this volume.

[2] D.M., p. 248.

[3] Ibid.

[4] 學 案, pt. xlii, f. 12 ; see p. 32 and note.

[5] Chang Chi'h (張 栻) ; see J. P. Bruce, *Introduction to Chu Hsi and the
Sung School*, chap. iv.

THE STEADFAST NATURE

(Fourteen Sections from the "Conversations".)

1. *Question.* How do you explain Ming Tao's statement : "The highest attainment is with broadness of mind to be actuated by a high altruism, and to respond naturally and fittingly to each phenomenon as it presents itself"?[1]

Answer. If with broadness of mind we are actuated by a high altruism we shall not be "full of anxious thoughts";[2] if we respond naturally and fittingly to each phenomenon as it presents itself we shall not be in the position of having "only our friends follow us and think with us".[3] It is just the same idea as in the passage which speaks of a man being partisan and not catholic, or catholic and not partisan.[4] I used to regard this section as calculated to confuse one, but

[1] Quoted from the *Essay on the Steadfast Nature* (定 性 書), by Ch'êng Ming Tao ; see 明 道 文 集, pt. iii, ff. 1–3. The essay, which covers little more than two pages, was written as an answer to the question : "How is it that, even with a steadfast nature, we cannot but be active, as though we were one with the external world ?" (定 性 未 能 不 動。猶 累 于 外 物 何 如。). See 學 案, pt. xiii, f. 11. The question was propounded by Chang Tsai, and therefore the essay is often referred to as "The Essay on the Steadfast Nature in reply to Hêng Ch'ü". The word 順, in the passage quoted, includes the ideas of appropriateness and a spontaneous ease in the response to the external things. 廓 然, which I have translated by the phrase "with broadness of mind", indicates the sphere in which the "high altruism" operates, corresponding to the 物 來, the sphere in which a natural and fitting response is called for.

[2] That is, irresolute and unsettled. The allusion is to a passage in the *Yi Ching*, p. 389 ; the complete sentence is : "Full of anxious thoughts you go and come."

[3] Ibid. This is a continuation of the sentence quoted above.

[4] Analects, ii, xiv (p. 14).

now I have come to see that its arguments are particularly clear.

2. Shun Pi asked : Is not the essay on "The Steadfast Nature" very difficult to grasp?

Answer. No, it is not very difficult. The title, "Steadfast Nature," sounds somewhat strange. The word "Nature" means Mind. Ming Tao's style is very comprehensive. At the first reading one fails to understand or grasp his full meaning, but with more careful study the divisions of the subject and their mutual relation become clear. This treatise was written when he was at Hu and was still very young.[1]

3. Ming Tao's treatise, "The settled Nature," gushed out from his mind, as if there was some power behind pushing the ideas out so rapidly that he could not get them all into writing.

Chih Ch'ing [2] said : This is exactly what is described as the language of a creator of truth.

Chu Hsi. Yes, but throughout the whole treatise one fails to find any indication of how to make a beginning.

Fei Ch'ing.[3] Does not the sentence, "With broadness of mind to be actuated by a high altruism and to respond naturally and fittingly to each phenomenon as it presents itself," [4] furnish the point of departure?

[1] See J. P. Bruce, *Introduction to Chu Hsi and the Sung School*, chap. iii.

[2] Huang Kan (黃 幹), *style* Chih Ch'ing, one of Chu Hsi's most honoured disciples. After some years of official life, he himself became a teacher of philosophy and had many followers, who gave him the name Mien Chai (勉 齋).

[3] Surnamed Chu (朱).

[4] See p. 245.

Chu Hsi. This represents the goal. Moreover, in the present age men's selfish desires in innumerable forms distract and distress them with no means of escape: how can they be "actuated by a high altruism"? Their conduct is all contrary to principle, how can there be the natural and fitting response to their environment?

Tao Fu.[1] It is as you said the other day, sir, "We must preserve our mind."[2]

Chu Hsi. It does not lie with you to preserve it. Whatever remedy you find for the distraction and distress of the Mind you cannot regain its lordship. You must perceive and understand the principles of the universe without the slightest admixture of selfish motives, then you will succeed ; as is expressed in the saying : "The point where to rest being known the mind is settled."[3] Otherwise, you will find that selfish desire becomes like a live dragon or tiger, impossible to master.

4. *Question*. It is said in the treatise on the "Settled Nature,"[4] "The things to be feared are for the most part self-concentration and the calculating mind.[5] With self-concentration there cannot be the action appropriate to the circumstances in which response to a phenomenon is called for.[6] With the calculating mind there cannot be the spontaneity of clear insight." What is your opinion ?

[1] See p. 178, n. 6.

[2] 這 箇 refers to the mind.

[3] G.L., p. 220 ; see Legge's quotation from Ying Ta in his note on p. 221.

[4] See p. 245, and note.

[5] 智 (wisdom) is good ; but to 用 智 (lit. "to use wisdom ") is bad, i.e. to rely on calculating cleverness.

[6] 應 迹 = 應 事 物 之 迹 , see p. 253.

Answer. This treatise from beginning to end has only these two thoughts. I Ch'uan's style is to divide clearly into sections. Ming Tao generally favours continuous discourse. At first it seems to lack a governing unity, but when carefully grasped you perceive the unity and connexion running through the entire work. " In the study of the noble-minded the highest attainment is with broadness of mind to be actuated by a high altruism, and to respond naturally and fittingly to each phenomenon as it presents itself." [1] There is a great deal that follows after, but it says no more than is expressed in these two sentences. *The passage in the Yi Ching :* " When one's resting is like that of the back, and he loses all consciousness of self ; when he walks in his courtyard and does not see any of the persons in it," [2] expresses the same idea as the phrase, " With broadness of mind to be actuated by a high altruism." The passage in Mencius, " What I dislike in your wise men is their boring out their conclusions," [3] expresses the idea of the phrase, " Respond naturally and fittingly to each phenomenon as it presents itself." In the passage, " Only

[1] See p. 245, n. 1.

[2] *Yi Ching*, pp. 175–6. Legge explains the hexagram referred to as denoting " the mental characteristic of resting in what is right ", of which the symbolism is taken from different parts of the human body. One of these parts is the back, of which Legge says in explanation of this passage : " The back alone has nothing to do with anything beyond itself—hardly with itself even. So should it be with us, resting in principle, free from the intrusion of selfish thoughts and external objects. Amidst society, he who realizes the idea of the hexagram is still alone, and does not allow himself to be distracted from the contemplation and following of principle." See ibid., p. 177. It is this attitude of mind which Chu Hsi says corresponds to Ming Tao's " high altruism ".

[3] Mencius, p. 207.

let one in the midst of one's anger straightway forget the
anger and consider the right and wrong of the principle
involved," [1] the phrase "straightway forget the anger"
answers to the phrase, "With broadness of mind to be
actuated by a high altruism," and the phrase, "consider the
right and wrong of the principle involved," answers to the
phrase, "respond naturally and fittingly to each phenomenon
as it presents itself." If you thus study the passage carefully you will get at its meaning.

5. In Ming Tao's essay in reply to Hêng Ch'ü's question
on our experience that "even with a Steadfast Nature we
cannot but be active," [2] his idea is that we should neither
despise external things nor banish them from us. People
of the present day in their disapproval of some external
things reject all, and in banishing things are nevertheless
led away by them ; whereas true goodness is neither to reject
them nor drift with them, but in all cases to respond to them
in exactly the right way. [3] For Hêng Ch'ü's idea is that we
should cut ourselves off from the outward, and make steadfast the inward ; while Ming Tao's idea is that we should
harmonize the outward and inward in one unity. Alike in
activity and repose the Mind should be steadfast, then in the
response to external things we shall naturally avoid being
in bondage to them. If the Mind is steadfast only in the
time of repose, then it is to be feared that in the time of
activity we shall be ensnared by external things.

<hr>

[1] Quoted from the *Essay on the Steadfast Nature*, see p. 245.
[2] Ibid.
[3] 曲 當 = 恰 當.

6. *Question.* In the case of the sages, the Mind is steadfast alike in activity and in repose. Is what is described as "steadfast" the substance?

Answer. Yes.

Question. Does it mean that the Mind remains steadfast when evil things approach and affect us, or when both good and evil things approach and affect us?

Answer. When evil things approach us they do not affect us, and of course there is no response from myself.

Question. What about good things?

Answer. There is response in every case where there should be response, and just in proportion to the degree of the approach. But through all I myself remain steadfast.

Question. When "the Master bewailed *Yen Yüan* exceedingly",[1] wherein did the steadfastness appear?

Answer. There was response which was in accord with right. We must also with broadness of mind be actuated by a high altruism, and respond naturally and fittingly to each phenomenon as it presents itself: I have thought this over often, and regard it as an all-round statement of the truth.

7. *Question.* I do not clearly understand the nature of the steadfastness in the case of the sages.

Answer. "The point where to rest being known there is steadfastness."[2] Look only at this one sentence and you will get at the meaning. In everything in the universe there is the right point in which to rest. Know this, and naturally the Mind will not be moved by external things.

[1] Analects, xi, ix, 1, p. 104.
[2] G.L., p. 220.

Question. Shun "cried out and wept toward the pitying heavens".[1] "When Hsiang was sorrowful he was also sorrowful ; when Hsiang was joyful he was also joyful."[2] When Shun acted in this way in what respect could he be said to be steadfast ?

Answer. This is a case of response where there should be response ; when that is the case there is steadfastness. To respond where there should be no response is confusion ; not to respond when there should be response is to be dead.

8.   *Question.* "It is the constant rule of Heaven and Earth by means of the Mind to fill all things, and yet to do so spontaneously and without effort of the Mind. It is the constant rule of the sages by means of the Feelings to be in harmony with all things, and yet to be so spontaneously and without effort of the Feelings. Therefore in the study of the noble-minded the highest attainment is with broadness of mind to be actuated by a high altruism, and to respond naturally and fittingly to each phenomenon as it presents itself."[3] What about the learner who has not yet attained to this ?

Answer. Although we may not have attained to this, yet such is the ideal. "With broadness of mind to be actuated by a high altruism" is to expel selfish motives, to act in given circumstances in harmony with the principle indicated by those circumstances. Suppose a case in which you yourself recognize that you should act on certain principles towards a certain man, but from motives of

[1] See Mencius, p. 218.
[2] Ibid., p. 223.
[3] The whole passage is quoted from Ming Tao's *Essay* ; see p. 245.

partiality you accord this treatment to some other man. This is the opposite of just, and does violence to those principles, so that there cannot be the fitting response. The saint has the saint's measure of altruism, the sage has the sage's, the learner the learner's.

Question. I certainly dare not ask what is the measure of altruism attainable by saints and sages as though I could attain to it ; but what should be the attitude of the learner ?

Answer. Simply let him preserve his mind and overcome selfish desire. These two sentences are complete ; " high altruism " expresses the matter comprehensively ; " natural and fitting response " expresses in detail what is comprised within it. Altruism is ingenuousness ; it corresponds to the passage—" The Decree of Heaven, how profound it is and undying ! " [1] " Fitting response " corresponds to the passage—" The method of Ch'ien is to create and transform so that everything obtains its correct nature as ordained by Heaven." [2]

9.   The phrase, " With broadness of mind to be actuated by a high altruism," corresponds to the expression, " Still and without movement." [3] " To respond naturally and fittingly to each phenomenon as it presents itself " corresponds to " When acted upon it penetrates forthwith to all phenomena ". [3]

10.   " It is the constant rule of Heaven and Earth by means of the Mind to fill all things, and yet to do so

---

[1] *Odes,* p. 570.
[2] *Yi Ching*, p. 213.
[3] Ibid., p. 370.

spontaneously and without effort of the Mind. It is the constant rule of the sage by means of the Feelings to be in harmony with all things and yet to be so spontaneously and without effort of the Feelings." [1] In this passage the phrases, "fill all things" and "be in harmony with all things", correspond to "With broadness of mind to be actuated by a high altruism"; while the phrases, "without effort of the Mind" and "without effort of the Feelings", correspond to "respond naturally and fittingly to each phenomenon as it presents itself". Self-concentration makes high altruism with broadness of mind impossible, and then there cannot be the action appropriate to the circumstances in which response to a phenomenon is called for; a calculating use of wisdom makes a natural and fitting response to each phenomenon as it presents itself impossible, and then there cannot be the spontaneity of clear insight.

11.   In Ming Tao's statement: "There cannot be the action appropriate to the circumstances in which response to a phenomenon is called for," the expression *ying chi* means the circumstances in which response to a phenomenon is called for. As to the Mind, it is not yet active.

12.   *Question.* Yesterday, arising out of the statement that Ch'êng Tzǔ attributed self-concentration to the Buddhists, Wei Tao [2] quoted from Ming Tao's essay in reply to Hêng Ch'ü. You, sir, replied: But this refers to the selfishness of people generally. It was objected

---

[1] Quoted from Ming Tao's *Essay on the Steadfast Nature.*

[2] Wei Tao was a disciple of Chu Hsi. His surname was Yeh, and his *ming* Chih Tao (葉 知 道).

that if we take the expressions, " self-concentration,"
" calculating use of wisdom," with the expression "checking
anger" which follows, then the statement seems limited
in its application; but if we have in mind the complete
sentences, " If there be self-concentration there cannot be
the action appropriate to the circumstances in which response
to a phenomenon is called for," and, " If there be calculating
wisdom there cannot be the spontaneity of clear insight,"
we shall realize that what is referred to is very wide. You,
sir, said : That is true ; but Ming Tao was speaking of men's
selfishness in a general sense. Wei Tao then referred to the
theory of looking at one's reflection in a mirror, and the
theory that advocates aversion from external things. You
said: These also are selfishness. The selfishness of ordinary
men and the self-concentration of the Buddhist are one
and the same selfishness. But Ch'êng Tzŭ was not specially
referring to the self-concentration of the Buddhist. You
then said : This was said by way of admonition because
of Hêng Ch'ü's error.[1] But there are some whose minds[2]
are naturally empty and therefore are not able to respond
to their environment ; and there are those who are immersed
in a self-induced emptiness and will not respond to their
environment ; and both are self-concentration. If we can
with openness of mind be actuated by a high altruism,
then the exalted will not fall into a vacant solitariness,[3]
and the lowly will not be entangled by creaturely desire ;

[1] That is, in the question which was the occasion of Ming Tao writing
his " Essay " ; see p. 249, and p. 245, n. 1.

[2] 中 = 心.

[3] As do the Buddhists.

as a matter of course we shall be able "to respond naturally and fittingly to each phenomenon as it presents itself".[1]

13. The Master referred to the fact that men's feelings are easily stirred and difficult to control; that anger is the most difficult to control, but that in the midst of the anger we can rapidly check it and consider the right and the wrong of the matter involved. Formerly he said that when we thus consider the right and wrong of the matter we shall see ourselves to be right and the other to be wrong, and thus the contention is intensified. Afterwards he came to see that this was a mistake and that Mencius is right when he says : "The noble man will say 'I must be lacking in love' and will examine himself and be loving . . . The perversity and unreasonableness of the other, however, are still the same . . . Then he will say 'This is simply a lost man ! ' "[2]

14. *Question.* The sages, one would think, never wore an angry countenance.

Answer. Why should they never wear an angry countenance ? When one ought to be angry the anger ought also to be manifested in the countenance. For example, it would not be right to go and reprove a man when he is wrong with a smile on your face.

---

[1] The whole of this section appears to form one question to which no answer is recorded, unless one or all of the instances in which 先 生 曰 occurs are taken as the Philosopher's answers. But in that case the dialogue could not be consecutive, and the 先 生 曰 is not generally used in this manner. It seems most probable that this is given as the only record of the conversation received by the questioner.

[2] Mencius, pp. 209–10.

Question. In that case the quality of the anger would be affected, would it not ?

Answer. When Heaven is angry there are the reverberations of thunder. When Shun cut off the four criminals it was right for him also to be angry. But in the midst of the anger there should be moderation, and when the matter is past the anger should subside and not revive.

(ONE SECTION FROM THE " COLLECTED WRITINGS ".)

The expression "Steadfast Nature" means the attainment of the original quality of the Nature by the completion of the work of preservation and nurture. When the Nature has become steadfast it remains the same whether in activity or repose, and there is no difference between the internal and external. Is it not because of their steadfastness that Heaven and Earth are Heaven and Earth, and that the sages are sages ? The study of the noble man, too, aims solely at steadfastness. Therefore " with broadness of mind to be actuated by a high altruism " is what makes Love to be the substance ; and what makes Righteousness its operation is the "natural and fitting response to each phenomenon as it presents itself". When Love is established and Righteousness practised, then the Nature is made steadfast and activity is everywhere unified, as expressed in the term "Chêng".[1] Why, then, should he be in haste and in a fever of anxiety about putting away external temptations ? The reason why ordinary men fail

---

[1] Chêng (貞) means " correct and therefore true ", i.e. it is 定, fixed or steadfast.

in steadfastness, however, is not because the Nature was originally defective, but because its Love has been violated by self-concentration, its Righteousness has been injured by calculating cleverness, and so the Feelings are beclouded and feverish anxiety prevails. They do not think of turning upon themselves and eliminating the evil, but fix their attention upon hatred of external things as their object, and seek illumination in solitude. The result is that the more they toil and expend their energy, the more beclouded is the illuminating principle within them, and they are all the more feverishly anxious and self-ignorant. When " the resting is like that of the back " [1] we shall be free from self-concentration. When we can " accomplish things by natural processes " we shall be free from a calculating cleverness. To be oblivious of both subject and object is not oblivion. If we act in accordance with right principle we shall not assert the subjective at the expense of the objective ; and if we do not assert the subjective at the expense of the objective, we shall attain a high altruism and be in harmony with our environment, in which case what is there of all things external that can entangle us ? The pleasure and anger of the sages, because they were actuated by a high altruism and were in harmony with their environment, were the perfection of the Divine Law. The pleasure and anger of the mass of men, because they are actuated by self-concentration and calculating cleverness, are the ebullitions of human passion. Discard anger and cherish altruism, observe principles and act in harmony with them : these are the prescriptions for examining oneself and eliminating

[1] *Yi Ching*, p. 175 ; cf. n. 2 on p. 248 of this volume.

the evil. Now it is not for us who come after to criticize Chang Tzŭ's philosophy, but, in view of his way of forcing arguments and his lack of wide penetration and mature consideration, there could not but be doubts on this subject. It was for this reason that Ch'êng Tzŭ issued his treatise ; his aim was profound. (Discussion of the " Steadfast Nature".)

FEELING AND MOTIVE

(FOUR SECTIONS FROM THE "CONVERSATIONS".)

1. *Question.* Are Motives the operation of the Mind, or the emanation from the Mind ?

Answer. The operation of the Mind is emanation from the Mind.

Question. Feelings are also emanations ; what, then, is the difference ?

Answer. Feelings emanate from the Nature. Feeling refers to the character of the emanation ; Motive is what determines its character. For example, when I like a certain thing, that is Feeling ; the wherefore of my liking it is the Motive. Feeling is like a boat or a cart, Motive is like the man's use of them.

2. *Question.* Motives issue from the Mind ; it is also said that Motives come after Mind, so that their emanation is still controlled by the Mind. But when selfish motives abound the Mind also follows them. Is it not so ?

Answer. Certainly.

3. Li Mêng Hsien asked : What is the difference between Feeling and Motive ?

Answer. Feeling is the ability to act; Motive is the consideration in various ways of how to act. Motives come into operation after, and because of, the existence of the Feelings.

4. *Question.* "The Decree of Heaven is what we term the Nature";[1] the plenum of the body is the Ether; affection and stimulus by the external world are Feeling; the ruling faculty is the Mind; that which determines the direction is the Will; that on which thought is fastened as its objective is the Motive; and the driving force is Desire.

Answer. The correctness or otherwise of these statements is a matter of speculation. The important thing is in discussing the subject not to be hurried, but to exercise a wide penetration with mature consideration; thus in course of time it will become clear. I have heard the Master[2] say that the definition of terms is exceedingly difficult to determine. For example, in defining the Nature there is the Nature of Heaven and Earth and there is the physical nature; in defining Love, I Ch'uan sometimes speaks of Love in the universal sense and sometimes in the particular sense. Such distinctions must be thought about quietly and thoroughly understood.

THE WILL AND THE ETHER. THE WILL AND MOTIVES

(SIX SECTIONS FROM THE "CONVERSATIONS".)

1. The Nature is Divine Law, with which all things are endowed so completely that there is not a single principle

[1] D.M., p. 247.
[2] Probably Li Yen P'ing; see J. P. Bruce, *Introduction to Chu Hsi and the Sung School*, chap. iv.

lacking. The Mind is the ruler of the entire person. The Motives are the emanation of the Mind. Feelings are the movements of the Mind. The Will is the direction of the Mind, and is stronger than Feeling or Motive. The Ether is what constitutes the fleshly element and the plenum of the body ; it is more corporeal and coarser than the rest.

2. The direction [1] of the Mind is termed the Will ; the direction of the sun is termed time. The ideograph "will" is derived from the ideographs "towards" [2] and "mind". The ideograph "time" is derived from "towards" [3] and "sun". The idea in the formation of the ideograph for "time" was taken from the sun's forward movement as seen, for example, at noon or daybreak. The Will is the direction in which the Mind moves, going straight forward. [4] Motives are the working processes, backwards and forwards, of the Will ; they are the feet of the Will. All the doing of business and calculating and going to and fro of the Mind are the Motives. Therefore Hêng Ch'ü said : "The Will is altruistic and the Motives are egoistic."

3. *Question.* What is the difference between Motive and Will ?

[1] 之 = 至.

[2] The old form of 志 was composed of 之 and 心. Dr. Chalfant gives its probable original as 㞢, of which 㞢 is the original of 之 ; see *Early Chinese Writing*, pl. xxii.

[3] The 土 in 時 was originally 之 ; cf. the old form 㞢 given above.

[4] Chu Hsi thus explains these ideographs as expressing the idea of motion, but the old form of 志, as given by Dr. Chalfant (see n. 2), suggests rather the idea of will as "that which issues from the heart". See *Early Chinese Writing*, pls. xxii and viii.

Answer. Hêng Ch'ü said: "The difference between the two terms 'Motive' and 'Will' is that Will is altruistic and the Motives are egoistic, Will is strong and Motive is weak, Will is positive and Motive is negative."

4. *Question.* Motives are the outcome of the Mind; how do they compare with the Feelings and the Nature?

Answer. Motives are closely allied to Feelings.

Question. What about the Will?

Answer. The Will is also closely allied to the Feelings. But the Mind is originally "still and without movement";[1] its first activities are called the Motives. Hêng Ch'ü said: "The Will is altruistic, and the Motives are egoistic." This appears to be well said. The Will is clear, Motives are turbid; the Will is strong, the Motives are weak; the Will is assertive, Motives are in the background. You need only to consider this carefully and you will see that it is so. The Motives we speak of are for the most part selfish. Of the Will it is said: "The Will of even a common man cannot be taken from him."[2]

5. The Will pertains to the positive element in the universe, and the Ether is the negative.[3]

6. When the Ether is concentrated it naturally energizes the Will, as the ancients were nourished in their activity and rest.

---

[1] *Yi Ching*, p. 370.   [2] Analects, X, xxv (p. 88).

[3] The fact that 氣 is here contrasted with 志 and said to be 坤, the negative mode, shows that it is used in a limited and narrow sense. It is not the primordial ether, which is both positive and negative, but the negative ether which becomes solid matter and the physical element in man's being, in contrast to the positive, " the pure and bright portion of the ether," which becomes spirit. It is to the latter that the will pertains.

(One Section from the "Collected Writings".)

1. The Ether is one. When it is controlled by the Mind, it becomes resoluteness; when under the control of the body it is passion. (Reply to Li Hui Shu.)

THOUGHT
(Six Sections from the "Conversations".)

1. Tê Fu said: Thought is perspicacity. Learning without thought is labour lost,[1] simply because there is no thought. How then can it be maintained that we must not think?

Answer. Yes indeed, if we must not think, of what value would the books left us by the sages be?

2. A question was asked about thought and distraction.

Answer. Without thought you cannot know what the Mind is; it is when you apply thought that you know that the Mind is thus subject to distraction. You know it gradually, but also by mental application.

3. Learning originates in thought; it is by thought that intelligence is evoked.

4. Ts'ai asked a question about Ch'êng Tzŭ's words: "When you seek to cease from thought, you find that thought does not cease."

Answer. You must not try to cease from thought. Simply exercise care and all anxious thought will die away.

5. *Question.* Hêng Ch'ü said: "When undisciplined thoughts[2] abound the constant mind becomes less; when

[1] Analects, II, xv (p. 14).
[2] Lit. "guest thoughts", i.e. thoughts that come in from outside, not under the mind's control, and hankering after the impossible.

the mind practised in error prevails the true mind is not perfected." Is there any difference between the expressions "undisciplined thoughts" and "the mind practised in error"?

Answer. Yes, there is a difference. "Undisciplined thoughts" are thoughts that overflow like a flood. "The mind practised in error" is the mind which in the past has by practice become contaminated and obtained the mastery on the wrong side. The "true mind" is the moral mind.

6. *Question.* The manifestations of the mind in thought are both good and evil. It seems to me that evil thoughts are of two kinds: there are those which appear in the thoughts and proceed from within unconsciously. There are others which arise from external temptations and so stir the thoughts. The way to exclude depravity is to be unremittent in effort, to examine the mind's outgoings in thought, and not allow them when wrong to be actualized in deed. In temptations arising from external things there must be watchful care over sights and sounds, speech and actions. But the most important thing is to maintain seriousness: if there be seriousness, then there will be a dignified interaction of the bodily and mental functions, the inward and the outward, and no injurious divorce between the two.

Answer. To say that there are two kinds of evil thoughts is undoubtedly correct. But after all, those which appear unconsciously in thought are also from outside. The Divine Law is one, and if there be anything evil it does not proceed from the Divine Law; if it does not proceed from the Divine Law it must come from outside. Sights and sounds, speech and actions, include both the outward and the inward, and must not be referred to as if they were purely external functions. If in your thought you make one set of functions to be internal and another set of functions to be external, then the internal and external are separated the one from the other, which is an impossible idea. There must be sincerity in thought and watchfulness in action, then there can be the proper interaction of the internal and external functions.

(SEVEN SECTIONS FROM THE "COLLECTED WRITINGS".)

1. Man's mind is never without the principle of thought. When thought is called for we ought to think, and not make painful efforts to banish and crush thought, and so fall into the evil of unrest. (Reply to Wu Po Fêng.) [1]

2. *Question.* How may we "repress desire"? [2]

Answer. Simply by thought. In learning there is nothing more important than thought. It is thought that can repress desire.

Some one said : If thought be not correct it is inadequate to repress desire; this is how it happens that the business of life is injured. How about thoughts which are not depraved?

Answer. Thoughts which are not correct are simply desires. To think on the right and wrong, the ought and ought not, of the thing desired, can never be other than correct. (Reply to the students at the Tu Ch'ang District School.)

[1] A pupil of Chu Hsi ; his *ming* was Pi Ta. See 學 案, lxix, f. 53.
[2] *Yi Ching*, p. 317.

3. The expressions "guard your mind" and "make the mind true" do not mean that we are to be immersed in a condition of no-thought; but that we should be constantly on the watch, think upon what we ought to think upon, and not violate moral principle. (Reply to Kuo Hsi Lü.)

4. In the "investigation of things" and "perfecting of knowledge",[1] even though the response to environment be natural and easy, how can there be neglect of thought when approaching any matter? And still more, when we have not attained to that condition, how can we fail to exercise repeated thought? (Reply to Ch'ên An Ch'ing.)[2]

5. To consider the principle involved in an affair after the time has come for dealing with it, or to consider the principle of anything when the time for taking it in hand is past, is to fail of attainment from lack of forethought. On the other hand, to discuss it beforehand is to fall into the error spoken of as thinking about what is not my business[3] and so creating confusion of thought. But with prolonged effort there will appear a way of settling this difficulty. (Reply to Ch'êng Tzŭ Ch'ing.)

6. What you say as to thoughts being so multifarious that the breast becomes solidified and clogged, is what all learners deplore, but it is very difficult to rid ourselves of them all at once. It is better to use the mental energy devoted to such thought and devote it to the investigation

[1] G.L., p. 222.
[2] See p. 195, n. 2.
[3] See Analects, XIV, xxviii, p. 150.

of principles ; let us be earnest and whole-hearted in the latter direction, and the things that trouble us in the former direction will unravel themselves without any effort of ours to solve them. (Reply to Wang Tzŭ Ho.)

7. In answer to a question on the subject of thought and distraction, someone has said the Mind is really without thought ; for the most part its consideration is of things past or of things still to come. I say that the relation between Mind and thought is that of the substance and its operation, and it is for this reason that the knowledge of the future and the memory of the past are united together so that there is not a single thing outside its scope.[1] If only we can be careful and so hold it fast, then we may have it in its perfection and be free from anxiety as to distraction. Your anxiety as to distraction, and your statement as to the Mind being originally without thought, show that you have not grasped the distinction between substance and operation. And further let me ask how can your theory of the Mind being originally without thought cure the evil of distraction which already exists ? (Record of Doubts.)

---

[1] That is, of the Mind.

THE PHILOSOPHY OF
HUMAN NATURE

BOOK V

BEING BOOK XLVI OF
THE COMPLETE WORKS OF CHU HSI

MORAL LAW

LAW

VIRTUE

BOOK V

MORAL LAW

(FOURTEEN SECTIONS FROM THE "CONVERSATIONS".)

1. The term Moral Law[1] includes both substance and operation, both its hidden essence and its wide manifestation.

2. The word Tao means a road. Generally speaking it is the road which all men follow; while Li[2] refers to each principle as distinct and marked off from the rest.

Arising from this the Philosopher quoted K'ang Chieh's statement, "Tao is a road. But Tao itself is invisible; it is in men's actions as they walk along this road that it is made manifest. It is like the road itself—so level that it can be travelled upon for countless myriads of years, and all men find their way to it."[3]

3. *Question*. How do you distinguish between Tao and Li?

Answer. Tao is a road, Li is like the veins of bamboo.

Question. Is it like the grain in wood?

Answer. Yes.

Question. In that case the two terms would seem to be alike.

---

[1] The word for Moral Law is *Tao* (道). In many contexts it is impossible to translate, particularly in this book (Book V), largely taken up as it is with controversies with Taoists, whose use of the word is different from that of Chu Hsi.

[2] Li (理) is the word for Law, the immaterial element in the Universe.

[3] This statement is by the philosopher Shao Yung, canonized as K'ang Chieh. It will be found in the 學 案, pt. ix, f. 8.

Answer. The content of the word Tao is wide; Li consists of numerous vein-like principles included in the term Tao.

The Philosopher further said : The term Tao calls attention to the vast and comprehensive ; the term Li calls attention to the minute and infinitesimal.

4. *Question.* Viewing the universe comprehensively, " The sun sets and the moon rises, the cold passes and the heat returns," [1] " the four seasons pursue their course, and all things are continually being produced." [2] This is the pervading and manifested operation of Tao. Speaking in a collective sense, does the continuity of this going and returning, creating and transforming, without a single moment's cessation, constitute the substance of Tao ?

Answer. Your explanation of substance and operation is right, but you ought not to use the word "collective," because then you are including the operation. Take only the immovable and abiding element, and you have what is the substance. For instance, the flow of water, the cessation of its flow, or the lashing into billows—these are its operation ; the unchanging power to flow, to cease from flow, or to be lashed into billows—this is the substance. Or take the human frame : the body is the substance, the sight of the eye, the hearing of the ear, and the movements of hand and foot, are its operation. The hand is the substance, the movements of the fingers in picking up things are its operation.

[1] *Yi Ching*, p. 389.
Analects, XVII, xix, 3 (p. 190).

Ch'un[1] quoted the *Commentary on the Analects*[2] as saying, "The past is past, but the future joins on without the break of a single moment." This is essentially what the substance of Tao is.

Answer. That is the idea.

5. *Question.* The other evening it was said that there is no fixity in the relation between substance and operation, but that it varies according to circumstances. What if we take all phenomena together and regard them as one vast substance and operation?

Answer. The relation between substance and operation is nevertheless fixed. The present is the substance, the emerging future is its operation. The body is the substance, its movements and activities are its operation. Heaven is the substance; that " all things owe to it their beginning"[3] is its operation. Earth is the substance, that "all things owe to it their birth "[4] is its operation. From the point of view of the positive mode, the positive is the substance and the negative its operation; from the point of view of the negative mode, the negative is the substance, and the positive its operation.

6. *Question.* You, sir, said sometime ago, "Reverence is the substance"; now you say, "Reverence is the graceful expression of Divine Law, the pageantry of human affairs," which is more like operation than substance.

Answer. Your people in Kiangsi have a particular way

[1] Probably Ch'ên Ch'un ; see p. 196 and note.
[2] Chu Hsi's own " Commentary ".
[3] *Yi Ching*, p. 213.
[4] Ibid., p. 214.

of talking about substance and operation. When you have divided a thing into sections you say it is the operation and not the substance. For example, a foot rule without the divisions into inches is the substance ; with the division into inches, it is the operation. A scale without the dots marking the different weights is the substance ; with these dots, it is the operation.[1]   Or again, a fan has the handle, the bones, and the paper pasted on : this is the substance ; when one waves it you have its operation.

Yang Chih Chih asked about the term substance.

Answer. The inherent fitness of a thing is the substance.

7. What we call Moral Law is not something out of the ordinary which has to be sought. It is what we commonly speak of as moral principle, and not some other Tao which needs suddenly to be discovered and seized by me, and so recognized as Moral Law. It is no more than the ordinary principles of everyday life, by which we know that this is right and that is wrong. The recognition of right in everything is Moral Law. In the present day the Buddhists talk of a Tao which is to be apprehended suddenly. But Tao is not a thing which can be felt and handled.

8. The Moral Law is the Law followed by all in the past and in the present. The kindness of the father, the filial obedience of the son, the benevolence of the sovereign, and the loyalty of the minister, are one principle common to all people. Virtue is the reception of this Law in one's

---

[1] A Chinese scale is a steelyard with the different weights indicated by brass brads.

own person ; just as, when the sovereign cannot but be benevolent and the minister loyal, it is because they have received this Moral Law within themselves, and therefore manifest this disposition. Yao cultivated it and attained to the virtue of Yao. Shun cultivated it and attained to the virtue of Shun. From before heaven and earth, from the incarnation of the Imperial Hsi,[1] in all there has been but this one Moral Law ; from the ages of the past right up till now there has been no other. Only in each generation there appears one who stands out as leader; but he is leader because he has received this truth into his own personality.[2] It is not that Yao had one Moral Law, and Shun another, while King Wên and the Duke Chow, with Confucius, each had theirs. Lao Tzŭ said, "When Tao is lost people follow after Virtue,"[3] which shows that he did not understand either of these terms. To distinguish them as two separate entities is to make Tao an empty abstraction. Our Confucian school teaches that they are simply one entity ; it is as common to all the ages, and not from the point of view of the individual man, that it is termed Tao. Virtue is this Tao received in its entirety by the individual personality. Lao Tzŭ says, "When Tao is lost, people follow after Virtue, when Virtue is lost people follow after Love, when Love is lost people follow after Righteousness."[3] But if we separate

[1] Fu Hsi, the first of the Five Emperors of the legendary period, supposed to have been miraculously conceived by his mother ; see Giles' *Biog. Dict.*, p. 233.

[2] Showing that the apparent exception is no exception.

[3] See the *Tao Tê Ching*, chap. xxxviii ; cf. *The Sayings of Lao-Tzŭ*, by Lionel Giles, p. 25.

T

Tao from Love and Righteousness we have no ethical principal at all. In that case how can it be Tao ?

9. The Master in consequence of some remark said : Modern scholars exhaust their efforts in the search for the transcendental instead of beginning with what is near.

Someone replied to this : It is indeed the case that the fault of modern scholars is too great a love for the transcendental. I Ch'uan, however, was asked, " What is Tao ? " and he replied, " It is seen in conduct." Ming Tao, too, was asked, " What is Tao ? " and he taught the student to seek the answer in the relation between father and son, sovereign and minister, older and younger brother. All the Masters spoke in the same sense. In these there was no talk of the lofty and distant.

Answer. That was certainly Ming Tao's teaching, and yet in the relationship between father and son, elder and younger brother, sovereign and minister, there is, in each case, the principle of inherent right, which is Tao.

10. It is just this principle which is universally indispensable. For instance, the Buddhists and Taoists discard human relationships, and yet they pay reverence to their teacher as to a father, they regard their younger brethren as sons, their seniors as elder brother teachers, and their juniors as younger brother teachers. The only thing is that they are all imitations.

11. " The incorporeal is termed Tao, the corporeal is termed the vehicle of manifestation." [1] The Tao is the

---

[1] *Yi Ching*, p. 377.   But cf. Chinese text, Imp. Edition, pt. xiv, f. 21.

ethical principle which every phenomenon has ;   the vehicle
is the corporeal vestigia which every phenomenon has.   Tao
must have its vehicle of manifestation, and the vehicle of
manifestation must have its inherent Tao.   That is,
" Inherent in every single thing there must be its rule of
existence." [1]

12.   *Question.*   Is it correct to say that the substance
is termed the Nature and its operation Moral Law ?

Answer.   Moral Law is simply the comprehensive term
for these cardinal principles and must not be regarded as
their operation.   Love, Righteousness, Reverence, Wisdom,
and Sincerity are principles, and Moral Law unites them
in one comprehensive term.

Chih Ch'ing [2] said : The term Moral Law appears to
combine both substance and operation.   For example, when
we say that these principles are termed Moral Law we are
referring to it as substance ;   and when we say, " Conformity to the Nature is what we term Moral Law," [3] we
are referring to its operation.

Answer.   This saying in its higher application refers
to Heaven, and in its lower application refers to man.

13.   Chêng Ch'ing asked : How do you regard Shao
Tzŭ's statement, " The concrete expression of Moral
Law " ? [4]

Answer.   This is what is taught by all the Masters, but
by none is it expressed so exactly as by Shao Tzŭ.   When
the doctrine is first stated there does not seem to be even

[1] See p. 54, n. 1.   [2] See p. 246, n. 3.
[3] D.M., p. 247.   [4] See p. 6, n. 4.

the semblance of a meaning in it. But the truth of the statement, "The Nature is the concrete expression of Moral Law," may be apprehended with certainty. We need not talk about empty and far away things : only let us turn inwards and study our own personality, and we shall know whether this principle really exists or not. For this reason I said once before, " If we would know the reality of Moral Law, we must seek it in our own Nature." Shao Tzŭ abruptly said not more than a few sentences in his " Preface to the Chi Yang Chi," but what he said was most excellently said.

14. When Kuei Shan [1] regarded the satisfying of hunger with food and the quenching of thirst with drink as Tao, he lost the " Tao " in the " manifesting vehicle ", and lost the " rule of existence " in the " thing ".

The Philosopher said further : In the passage, " The Moral Law may not be left for an instant : if it could be left it would not be Moral Law," [2] it is what cannot be left that is called Moral Law. If we regard the common actions of everyday life as Moral Law, then in all that we do there is nothing that is not Moral Law. But in that case, why should the noble man be " cautious and apprehensive " ; [3] why should he still study the action of Moral Law ? It is because "it must not be left" that he must walk in conformity with Moral Law. Take speech for example : You would hardly say that the act

---

[1] Yang Kuei Shan ; see p. 26, n. 1.

[2] D.M., p. 248.

[3] As the author of the saying quoted above admonishes us ; see ibid.

of speaking is Moral Law; there must be Love, Righteousness, Reverence, and Wisdom in the speech before you can say that there is Moral Law. If you take ordinary bodily movements to be Moral Law, why should you say further that " it must not be left ".[1]

(NINE SECTIONS FROM THE " COLLECTED WRITINGS ".)

1. The infinite greatness of the substance of Moral Law, and at the same time the necessity that the student in his study of it should be "accomplished, distinctive, contemplative, and all searching ",[2] and not allow error even to the extent of a hair's breadth : this is what the saints and sages exhibited in discoursing upon Moral Law. Therefore, having said, " It sends forth and nourishes all things, rising up to the height of Heaven," [3] and so pictured its vastness, they of necessity go on to say, " It embraces the three hundred rules of ceremony and the three thousand rules of demeanour," [3] in order fully to recover its extreme minuteness. And in their instruction to the scholar in the task of "actualizing Moral Law by the cultivation of virtue", having spoken of "perfecting its breadth and greatness ", they of necessity go on to show that " none of its exquisite and minute points may be omitted ".[4] Modern teachers in expounding the meaning of Moral Law are very different. In discussing its vastness, they rejoice in its comprehensive completeness, but dislike research into its

---

[1] There must, or ought to be, "tao " in what we do, but you cannot say therefore, that what we do is " tao " *per se* ; otherwise, why should the *Doctrine of the Mean* say " it must not be left ".

[2] D.M., p. 292.   [3] Ibid., p. 286.   [4] D.M., pp. 286–7.

ramifications ; they delight in its transcendent mystery, but gloss over its infinitesimal minuteness. So far as its "broadness and greatness" are concerned, they do not differ materially from the sages, but they do not examine into its "exquisite minuteness" ; so that even in respect of what they call its "broadness and greatness" they are not in a position to discuss the true account of its entire substance. (Reply to Chao T'i Chü.)

2. Is it maintained that Tao is lofty and distant, inscrutable [1] and mysterious, and beyond the possibility of human study ? Then I answer that Tao derives its very name from the fact that it is the principle of right conduct in everyday life for all men, that it is like a road which should be travelled upon by the countless myriads of people within the four seas and nine continents. It is not what the Taoist and Buddhist describe as Tao, empty, formless, still, nonexistent, and having no connexion with men. Is it maintained that Tao is far removed from us, so vast as to be out of touch with our needs, and that we are not called upon to study it ? Then I say that Tao, present as it is in all the world in the relation between sovereign and minister and between father and son, in down-sitting and uprising and in activity and rest, has everywhere its unchangeable clear law, which cannot fail for a single instant. For this reason the saints and sages exerted themselves and gave us their instruction so as clearly and perfectly to manifest its meaning, both in its vastness and minuteness, in its fineness of detail and broad outlines ;

[1] 元 is for 玄.

and the student of their books must not be satisfied with examining the letter only, for the mere pleasure of analysis and synthesis, he must discuss their teachings intelligently, and examine them exhaustively, in order to remember them, practise them, and manifest them in the business of life ; only thus can he fulfil his mission and take his place in the universe. He must not examine the letter only for the mere pleasure of tracing out and compiling. When, therefore, Tzŭ Yu quoted the Master as saying : "When the man of high station is a disciple of Moral Law he loves men ; when the man of low station is a disciple of Moral Law he is easily ruled," the Master endorsed his words.[1] How different is "the study of Moral Law", as presented to us here, from the teaching of the scholars of this age ! (Reply to Chou I Kung.)

3. You regard the heretical doctrine of Tao as useless, and therefore go on to make the Tao itself a useless thing. Can that be right ? On the contrary, while the word "Love" refers directly to the mystery pertaining to man's Mind, the word "Tao" is the comprehensive term for the moral nature common to all. Therefore, although the description of it combines both the individual and the transcendental, there are not really two entities, the *Doctrine of the Mean* says, "Moral Law is cultivated by Love." [2] Hu Tzŭ also says, "If a man has not Love, the essence of Moral Law is gone," which conveys the same idea. (Reply to Lien Sung Ch'ing.)

[1] Analects, XVII, iv, 3 (p. 183).
[2] D.M., p. 269.

4. *Question*. There is only one Law of Heaven and Man. The root and fruit are identical. When the Moral Law of man's Nature is perfected, the Moral Law of Heaven is also perfected. The realization of the fruit does not mean separation from the root. Even those whom we regard as saints spoke only of perfecting the relationships of human life. The Buddhists discard man and discourse on Heaven, and thus separate the fruit from the root, as if they were two horns of a dilemma [1] of which you must choose one and reject the other. The presence of the Four Terminals and the Five Cardinal Virtues in man's nature they regard as masking the Nature. [2] The indispensable relationships between father and son, sovereign and minister, husband and wife, senior and junior, they regard as accidental. They even go so far as to regard Heaven and Earth, the Two Modes of Matter, men and other creatures, as phantasmal transformations. They have never so much as inquired into their reality, but simply assert the Nature of the Great Void. Now there are no two laws in the universe ; how then can they take Heaven and Man, the root and fruit, summarily asserting the one and denying the other, and yet call this Tao ? When their perceptions are so partial, so small and incomplete, what possibility is there of the familiar doctrine of a perfect union between the transcendental and the lowly ? Those who follow the sacred Confucian school, on the other hand, "from the

---

[1] Note : the 歧 and the 有 所 擇 = " separate . . . and present them as a case for choice ".

[2] 理 障 is a Buddhist expression, meaning that these principles hide the true nature from us ; cf. 遺 書, pt. xviii, f. 15 ; 學 案, pt. xvii, f. 44.

study of the lowly understand high things " ; [1] they advance
from the humble accomplishments of " sprinkling and
sweeping, answering and replying, advancing and
receding ". [2] Whether in food and drink or in the relation
between the sexes, they were never lacking in seriousness.
For " the Moral Law which the noble man follows after
is far-reaching and yet mystical ". Far-reaching, it
embraces the whole of his daily life ; mystical, it is Divine
Law. With this Divine Law, then, in daily life—in the
relation between sovereign and minister, father and son,
husband and wife, senior and junior, or when engaged in
the toasting and pledging of social intercourse, or when
eating, resting, seeing, and hearing—there is not one sphere
of activity which is not under the guidance of Law, and
not one that can be confused ; for wherever there is confusion Divine Law has perished.[3] " Therefore the noble
man is never lacking in seriousness." [4] By this means the
Mind is held fast with firmness, the practice of good is
mature, and so the hidden and manifest are blended, the
outward and inward are united ; and Moral Law dwells
within me ! What is there in Buddhism adequate
to express this ! What Buddhists call " Intelligence " is
no more than a glance at the connecting thread. The
reality and unchangeableness of Divine Law and man's
Mind they have not apprehended. What they call
" culture ", also, is nothing more than control of the Mind

[1] Analects, XIV, xxxvii, 2 (p. 153).

[2] Ibid., XIX, xii, 1 (p. 207).

[3] The charge against Buddhism is the " confusion " of the social
relationships.

[4] Cf. Analects, XII, v, 4 (p. 117).

and sitting in silence. Discarding human relationships, destroying the Divine Law, they reap no good that can be perceived. As you, sir, said : after all, they fail even to get near a solution of the problem. " Before the stirrings of pleasure, anger, grief, and joy," is the condition when " the Nature is still and without movement".[1] Here we have the Mind of Heaven and Earth, the Source of the universe. There are not two sources in the universe ; therefore the transformations of Ch'ien and K'un, and the classification of species, all proceed from this one source. Every form, produced and reproduced, has each the Nature of Heaven. This is the reason for the inseparableness of the creature from its source.[2] Receiving its spiritual essence we become man, and within the confines of the four cardinal principles it resides, inscrutable, formless, still, and, it would seem, unnameable. Tzŭ Ssŭ, having regard to the absence in it of any leaning to one side or the other, called it The Mean. Mencius, having regard to its perfect purity called it Good. The Master [3] having regard to its life-producing substance called it Love. The terms differ but the thing named is the same, and is not separable from everyday life. This is why you said that its meaning is manifest without our seeking it. Formerly I read many books from different points of view, but failed to grasp their main drift ; I studied vaguely such subjects as Heaven and Earth, the Two Modes, man and other creatures, good and evil spirits, but did not find any principle of unity. With the truth near me, I was seeking it afar off, suffering probably from the mistake of over-eagerness in my search. I

[1] See *Yi Ching*, p. 370.   [2] Lit. " fruit from the root ".   [3] Confucius.

also heard that in the discourses of the Master Kuei Shan [1]
it is said : " Before we speak of perfecting the Mind, we
must understand what the Mind is ; after we have realized
this clearly and distinctly, we may proceed to discuss the
idea of perfecting it " ; and my former explanation accorded
with this exactly.   But " Moral Law cannot be left for
a single instant ".[2]   In everyday life it is brightly shining ;
why should there be any waiting to search for it ?   This
is what you, sir, have enjoined and taught, and I could
not venture to do other than respectfully receive your
teaching.   As to the misleading character of the mirror
and image illustration, were it not for your teaching my
understanding of the truth would have been in considerable
peril.   Formerly, in a time of leisure and meditation, as
I perceived its all-comprehensive, omnipresent, and all-
pervading attribute,[3] and realized that every single thing
in the universe is manifested in it, it seemed to me that the
figure of the mirror and image was approximately suitable ; I therefore expanded it and elaborated the statement
of the hawk and fish, regarding this as an apt simile.   You
showed the error of this by reference to the Great Void and
the myriad phenomena.   After considerable study I fully
realized that my statement was not correct.   If it were,
then the hawk and fish, on the one hand, and my Nature, on
the other, would become two separate entities.   Examining
carefully your meaning, it is that there must be some reason
why, when the hawk and fish come into existence, they are

[1] Yang Shih ; see p. 26, n. 1.   [2] D.M., p. 248.

[3] 充 周 ＝ 充 滿 周 遍, i.o. 無 所 不 到 ; 洞 達 ＝ 無
所 不 通.

hawk and fish, and that the cause is in the presence of the
substance of Moral Law.   The hawk flies and the fish leaps
not by the individual choice of the hawk and fish, but
because of the Divine Law imparted to them in unceasing
flow.[1]   Between " not forgetting " and " not assisting the
growth "[2] *of the physical nature* Divine Law flows in its
operation with not a hair's breadth of selfishness ; which
is exactly the same idea.   This is what Ming Tao calls
" uniformity ".[3]   Such is my unworthy opinion.   I should
like to know, sir, whether or not it accords with yours.
For the rest, such as the doctrine of life and death, good
and evil spirits, I must wait till I have opportunity of
receiving your instruction in person.

Answer. Your communication accords with my own mind
in all respects.   It shows your fine ability.   I now know
surely that my former expectations were not mistaken.
There are one or two points not quite accurate, but they
are not of very great moment.   I am now travelling and
unsettled, and therefore unable to reply point to point.   I
would advise you still to apply yourself to discriminating

---

[1] The illustration of the hawk and fish is taken from a stanza in one of
the Odes (pt. iii, bk. i, ode v), which reads :—

> The hawk flies up to heaven ;
> The fishes leap in the deep.
> Easy and self-possessed was our prince ;—
> Did he not exert an influence upon men ?

Upon which Legge's note says : " The hawk rises in the sky, and the fishes
leap about in the deep,—without an effort ; it is their nature so to do.   So
there went out an influence from King Wên, unconsciously to himself. "
This spontaneous flying and leaping is here attributed to Tao, the Divine
Moral Law.   See Odes, p. 445 and note.

[2] See Mencius, p. 66.

[3] That is, the uniformity of nature in man and other creatures.

study, and your ideas will gradually become true
and correct. (Reply to Liao Tzŭ Hui.)

5. Chang Yüan Tê's [1] explanation of Tao as the walk
of life is certainly too wide, and you, Tzŭ Yo,[2] are right
in contradicting it; but his use of the word "walk" is
nevertheless not without reason. When, therefore, you
neglect to follow this up and analyse his argument for him,
but, taking a different line, answer him by quoting Ch'êng
Tzŭ's simile of the boundless desert,[3] it is not surprising
that you yourself are conscious of having fallen into the
error of being neither clear nor relevant. (Ch'êng Tzŭ in
his statement is comparing Moral Law with Righteousness
so that his simile has a natural appropriateness and is
without fault.) The effect of your method of answering
his argument is that you and he are talking about two
different things [4] which have no connexion with each other.
This is because your [5] own perceptions are not perfectly
clear, and so you cannot avoid resorting to guesswork,
generalizing,[6] and forced statement, with the result that
you branch off into superficial and vague arguments, and
are unable to make your meaning clear. According to my

---

[1] Chang Hsia (張 洽), *style* Yüan Tê, was one of Chu Hsi's most
prominent disciples. He was a native of Ch'ing Chiang (清 江).

[2] Tzŭ Yo was another disciple, surnamed Lü, to whose communication
this section was a reply. See p. 207, n. 3.

[3] See 遺 書, pt. xv, f. 11 ; cf. also p. 291 of this volume and n. 1.

[4] 彼 東 我 西 = "He is on the east side and I am on the west side."

[5] Lit. "my," but = "one's own," and refers to Tzŭ Yo, to whom
this section is addressed.

[6] 籠 罩 = to cover, or include, in a basket, hence to generalize.

idea, Tao obtains its name simply from the principle of inherent right present in all phenomena. Yüan Tê says baldly that it is the walk of life, in which he is certainly wrong. If at the time, however, you had contented yourself with answering him by saying that Tao is the road along which we ought to walk, you would have succeeded in making your own [1] idea clear in his language, and the phrase "boundless desert" would also have its place in your argument. Further, with regard to your reference to the expressions "negative and positive modes", "the relation between sovereign and minister and between father and son," "the corporeal and incorporeal," and the simile of "the boundless desert": if we first combine and then analyse them, the negative and positive modes, the relation between sovereign and minister and between father and son, are all phenomena, the actions of man ; while the corporeal consists of the varied species of the myriad phenomena—each one of which has within it the principle of right, what we call Moral Law, the road along which we ought to walk—and the incorporeal is the void of the boundless desert. If we speak of it from the point of view of the incorporeal, its "boundless desert" character is certainly the substance, and its manifestation in phenomena its operation. If we speak of it from the point of view of the corporeal, then phenomena constitute the substance and the manifestation of the principle its operation. You must not combine them and say that the incorporeal is the substance of Moral Law, and "the five duties of universal obligation" its operation. What Yüan

[1] See p. 285, n. 5.

Tê says, from the sentence "Tao cannot act of itself" onwards, is without error, and yet you argue against it. (The answer says what is so far true, but as a reply is irrelevant.) Referring again to a later statement, you say, "The incorporeal is termed Tao, and constitutes the principles of things, the corporeal is the manifesting vehicle and constitutes the things themselves."[1] You would do well to cast everything else aside and confine your argument to these two sentences ; for if you get these clear, the rest will of its own accord become perfectly clear and complete. (Reply to Lü Tzŭ Yo.)[2]

6. *Question.* The reason why I cannot agree with Yüan Tê's explanation of Tao as the walk of life is that the word "walk" is not adequate to express the meaning of the word Tao; you must also include the reason for the walk.[3] But still, in order to find the one, was it necessary to look for two ? I therefore used Ch'êng Tzŭ's simile of the "boundless desert", anxious that Yüan Tê should search deeply into this great substance, and by meditation perceive the mystery which lies beyond the perception of the senses ; then, as a natural consequence, he would realize that the word "walk" was altogether inadequate. If I had said "the road along which we ought to walk ", then I fear he would not have been able to grasp the idea of "universal obligation",[4] nor would the origin of Tao have

[1] *Yi Ching*, p. 377, where, however, the passage is translated differently ; cf. the Chinese text, Imp. Edition, pt. xiv, f. 21.

[2] See above.

[3] See p. 285 for the argument to which this whole question refers.

[4] See D.M., p. 270.

been easy to explain by such language. The corporeal
is the incorporeal. When the *Commentary on the Yi*[1]
says, "The most subtle is law," it is the incorporeal
which is referred to, and when it says "the most manifest
is phenomena", it is the corporeal which is referred to.
The substance and operation have one source, the manifestation and the subtle principle are inseparable. Therefore, though there is the distinction between the corporeal
and incorporeal, they are still but this one ethical
principle.

Answer. The fault in Yüan Tê's statement I have fully
explained already.[2] But your way of stating the case will
not meet his point. I fear you can only see yourself
right and have not carefully examined what I said. You
say that the law according to which we ought to walk constitutes the universal obligation, and that the phrase,
"void like the boundless desert," represents the origin of
Tao. This really does not amount to a serious statement,
and is not what I would have expected of Tzŭ Yo. That
you can write this is in itself sufficient to account for your
other statements not being correct. You must lay hold
of the truth that there is only this one natural principle
of right. When we use the phrase, "void like the boundless desert," it is not that there is any such entity in
addition to this principle. As to the corporeal and incorporeal there certainly is a difference. You have to
divide them and say that this is substance and that is
operation, before you can say that they have one source.

[1] That is, the Commentary by Ch'êng I.
[2] See pp. 285–7.

You have to say that this is phenomenon and that is its principle, before you can say that they are inseparable. If they were merely one entity there would be no need to speak of one source, and of their being inseparable. (Reply to Lü Tzŭ Yo.)[1]

7.   The Su school[2] say : " Lao Tzŭ taught us about Tao, but said little of the manifesting vehicle, because, if the student confines himself to the knowledge of the vehicle, then Tao will be obscured ; he therefore excluded Love and Righteousness and rejected Ceremony and Music, in order to make clear the Tao."[3]   I explain the word " Tao " as the general term for Love, Righteousness, Ceremony, and Music, and these four are the substance and operation of the Tao.   The cultivation of Love and Righteousness, and the development of Ceremony and Music by the sages, were in order to manifest the Tao. For the Su school to say that Love and Righteousness were excluded, and Ceremony and Music rejected, in order to manifest the Tao, is to discard the multiples two and five in order to find ten.   This surely is wrong !   (Criticism of the Su Huang School's *Exposition of Lao Tzŭ*.")[4]

8.   The Su school say : " Heaven's Moral Law cannot be expressed in words ; what can be so expressed is its similitude.   The understanding know the true by means of the similitude, and the ignorant by fastening upon the

[1] See above.

[2] See J. P. Bruce, *Introduction to Chu Hsi and the Sung School*, chap. iv.

[3] 學 案, pt. xcix, f. 25.   See also *Tao Tê Ching*, chap. xix ; cf. W. Gorn Old's *The Book of the Simple Way*, p. 54.

[4] 學 案, pt. xcix, f. 24.

U

similitude fall into error." [1] My position is this : The
sages explained Moral Law as the relation between
sovereign and minister, father and son, husband and wife,
elder and younger brother, and between friend and friend ;
what I ask is, do these express Moral Law or only its
similitude ?   Does fastening upon these and acting
accordingly mean that we shall fall into error ?   But why
really should Tao be inexpressible in words ?   It is only
because men do not realize that Tao and the manifesting
vehicle are never separate, and seek it in the inscrutable
and formless, that they use such language.   (Criticism of
the Su Huang School's *Exposition of Lao Tzǔ*.)

9.   A principle is invisible ; it is only in actions and
speech that right and wrong are perceived.   The more
minutely we investigate and understand it, the more
exquisitely fine the principle appears.   When the ancients
spoke of " investigating things " and " perfecting knowledge ",[2] they meant no more than that we should make
a beginning at this point.   (Reply to Hu Chi Sui.) [3]

LAW.

(Sixteen Sections from the " Conversations".)

1.   Law is like a piece of thread with its strands,
or like this bamboo basket.   Pointing to its rows of
bamboo splints, the Philosopher said, One strip goes this
way ; and, pointing to another strip, Another strip goes

---

[1] Ibid., f. 25 ; cf. *Tao Tê Ching*, chap. i ; see *The Book of the Simple Way*
by W. Gorn Old, p. 25.

[2] G.L., p. 222.

[3] See p. 24, n. 1.

that way. It is also like the grain of the bamboo : on the straight it is of one kind, on the transverse it is of another kind. So the mind possesses numerous principles.

2. Whether great, as in heaven, earth, and all things, or small, as in the activities and rest of ordinary life— in all alike is the Law of the Supreme Ultimate and of the Two Modes.

3. In all things throughout the universe there is nothing that is not relative. Given the negative mode, there is the positive ; given Love, there is Righteousness ; given good, there is evil ; given speech there is silence ; given movement, there is repose.[1] And yet there is but one principle, as when a man walks out, or when he returns, it is with the same pair of foot. It is like the breath of one's mouth : in expiration it is warm and in inspiration it is cold.

4. Whether high or low, fine or coarse, root or fruit, there is but one Law.

5. Whenever you consider principles you must apprehend clearly the fountain-head ; in all subsequent stages it is still this Law which is diffused in the infinite variety of phenomena. Confucius in his teaching enunciated principles on any and every subject as they were presented to him, but did not point out one supreme general principle. But if you take things which are all about us, and generalize concerning them, you will perceive a general law. Mencius drew attention to this

---

[1] See 遺 書, pt. xv, f. 20.

in his teachings ; while Chou Tzŭ made it specially clear
in his doctrine of the Supreme Ultimate. Take, for
instance, the feeling of solicitude : if from this you trace
backwards you will arrive at Love, which is inherent in
the Mind ; but Love is the Principle of Origin, one of
the Divine Attributes, and the Principle of Origin is the
positive and active mode of the Supreme Ultimate. Thus
by tracing backwards stage by stage we arrive at the
fountain-head. If now, we apprehend the Supreme
Ultimate clearly, we shall certainly be able to recognize
the numerous laws and principles of the universe as all
proceeding from it. In every single phenomenon there
is a principle, and nothing is without its principle.

6. Some truths are obvious, and it is best to give
expression to them in free and easy terms. To clothe
them in tortuous language is mischievous.

7. Throughout the universe this principle is present
in everything, even in insignificant things ; for " the
Decree of Heaven is what we term the Nature ".[1] But the
principle is formless, with nothing in which to inhere,
except in the affairs of everyday life. These two are
never separate ; in every single thing there is its law,
therefore "the noble man makes an extensive study of all
learning ".[2] It might seem as if extensive study were an
unimportant matter, but those many principles are all
to be found here, and all proceed from the one source.
Therefore, whether fine or coarse, great or small, all alike
are made use of and mentally grasped, for the simple

[1] D.M., p. 247.   [2] Analects, VI, xxv (p. 57).

reason that there is nothing extraneous to me. When all are thus understood, knowledge is perfectly developed, and becomes full-orbed and complete.

8. The "Great Learning" speaks of "investigating things",[1] but not of an "exhaustive investigation of principles",[2] because to investigate principles is like clutching at vacancy with nothing to lay hold of. When it simply says "investigate things", it means, through the corporeal vehicle to seek the incorporeal Moral Law ;[3] and when we do that we find that the two are inseparable, so that there is no need to say more than "investigate things". "Heaven in giving birth to the multitudes of the people so ordained it that inherent in every single thing there is its rule of existence."[4] This is what is meant by Tao. Where do you find it said that every thing is itself a rule of existence ?

9. This principle is infinite. It is present all around us ; it runs through all the myriad threads of the web of life. Drawing circles with his finger, the Philosopher said : See, there is circle within circle. Horizontally it is so, perpendicularly it is so, backwards and forwards it is all so. If we express it from the point of view of

[1] G.L., p. 222.

[2] Ibid., p. 229. In the original text of the G.L. the word translated by Legge as " investigation " in the phrase " investigation of principles " is a different word from that used in the phrase " investigating things '. It means " exhaustively to search for ". Chu Hsi's point is : You " investigate " or " examine " a phenomenon or thing ; you " search for " its principle.

[3] Alluding to the passage in the *Yi Ching* ; cf. p. 288 of this volume.

[4] *Odes*, p. 541.

the Two Modes, the Supreme Ultimate is the Supreme
Ultimate, and the Two Modes are its operation. From
the point of view of the Four Symbols, the Two Modes
are the Supreme Ultimate and the Four Symbols are its
operation. And again, from the point of view of the
Eight Trigrams, the Four Symbols are the Supreme
Ultimate and the Eight Trigrams its operation.

10. This principle is so great as to include Ch'ien and
K'un,[1] and sustain the processes of creation and transformation ; it is so minute as to penetrate the finest
hair.[2] All-comprehensive and all-pervading, we must
nevertheless ascertain what it is that it comprehends.

11. *Question.* When Ch'êng Tzŭ said, "It is the law
of the universe that everything has its correlative and
nothing stands alone" ; why did he go on to quote the
passage, "unconsciously the feet begin to dance and the
hands to clap" ? [3]

Answer. If it be true that there is nothing which
does not have its correlative, and we realize what it means,
it is indeed a matter for astonishment and laughter. As
to the Two Modes, now, they have a correlative, but what
is the correlative of the Supreme Ultimate ?

Questioner. The correlative of the Supreme Ultimate
is the Infinite.

---

[1] The dual creative Powers ; see J. P. Bruce, *Introduction to Chu Hsi
and the Sung School,* chap. vi.

[2] 豪, 釐, 絲, and 忽 are four measures of which the largest is so small
that the word itself means infinitesimally minute ; and of this the smallest
of these measures is equal to one thousandth part.

[3] 遺 書, pt. xi, f. 4 ; cf. Mencius, p. 190.

Answer. This is only referred to in one sentence. Of the Five Agents, Earth appears to be without any correlative, and yet each one has its correlative. The Supreme Ultimate is the correlative of the Two Modes as shown in the statement: "The incorporeal is what we call Tao, the corporeal is what we call the manifesting vehicle."[1] But the correlation is a cross-relation. Earth is the correlative of the other Four Agents, Metal, Wood, Water, and Fire, because the four have their location, while Earth has not; so that these also are correlated. (Pi Ta records:[2] The reason is that the Four Agents are all pervaded by Earth.) The Hu School[3] say that good is not to be contrasted with evil. But evil is the negative of good, just as you have Love and not-Love; why should they not be contrasted? If not, then everything in the universe will appear to be one-sided like a single-branched horn,[4] and nothing can be predicated of anything.

12. *Question*. It is said, "It is the law of the universe that everything has its correlative and nothing stands alone. Given movement there must be repose, given the negative there must be the positive, and so on to bending and straightening, diminishing and growing,

---

[1] See p. 287.

[2] Wu Pi Ta, *style* Po Feng; see 學 案, pt. lxix, f. 53.

[3] See J. P. Bruce, *Introduction to Chu Hsi and the Sung School*, chap. iv.

[4] 尖 斜 is a point leaning on one side, with nothing on the other side to match it.

flourishing and decaying ; nothing is excepted."[1] Is this naturally so ?

Answer.   It is all naturally so. " One " is the correlative of " two ", and the corporeal of the incorporeal.   But in the case of " one " there is a correlation within it, as, for example, in the case of an object in front of me, there are its back and front, its higher and lower parts, its inside and outside. " Two," also, has its own correlatives. Although it is said that everything has its correlative and nothing stands alone, yet there is an aloneness which nevertheless also has its opposite ; for example, on the chessboard, in each pair of squares the two are mutually correlative, but there is one in the centre which is simply an empty track, and apparently without any correlative ; but this track stands in contrast to the whole three hundred and sixty squares.[2]   It is what we speak of

---

[1] Cf. 遺 書, pt. xv, f. 20, where a similar statement is made. See p. 39, n. 2.

[2] There are two Chinese games played with a board divided into squares. The one is named *Hsiang C'hi* (象 棋), and is said to have been invented about 1120 B.C.   It is doubtless connected in origin with the western game of chess. The game is played with thirty-two men on a board of sixty-four squares ; the board, however, differs from that used in the western game in that there is a gap between the fields of the two opponents popularly called the Yellow River. The other game is called *Wei Ch'i* (圍 棋). Its origin is ascribed to the Sage-Emperor Yao.   The game is played with 360 black and white pieces on a board with eighteen rows of eighteen squares each. The pieces are placed not in the squares, but on the points of intersection of the dividing lines and of the union of the latter with the boundary lines. Of the places thus formed there are 361. It is the board used in the second of these two games that is referred to in the text.

as the One in contrast to the All, Tao in contrast to the vehicle of manifestation.

13. *Question.* With regard to the passage, "Void like the boundless desert . . . lead men to enter the beaten path,"[1] when Ch'êng Tzŭ uses the expression "beaten path", does he not mean the way in which men ought to act, and that of everything we ought to do, the principle exists beforehand, so that when we are about to do a thing we do not need to search for its principle.

Answer. What it says is that before the case exists there is its law ; for example, the law of the relationship between sovereign and minister exists before there is sovereign or minister ; the law of the relationship between father and son exists before there is father and son. It cannot be that before the relationships of sovereign and minister, father and son exist, the law of those relationships is non-existent, and that it is when they come into existence that the principle is implanted in them.

---

[1] 遺 書, pt. xv, f. 11. The whole passage reads : 沖 漠 無 朕。
萬 象 森 然 已 具。未 應 不 是 先。已 應 不 是 後。
如 百 尺 之 木。自 根 本 至 枝 葉。皆 是 一 貫。不 可
道 上 面 一 段 事。無 形 無 兆。却 待 人 旋 揉 排 引
入 來。敘 入 塗 轍。既 是 塗 轍。却 只 是 一 箇 塗 轍。
"Void like the boundless desert, but filled with innumerable Forms like a dense forest ! Before the response [i.e. to a particular phenomenon] is not before, and after the response is not after. Just as a tree a hundred feet high is one unity from the root to the topmost branch and outermost leaf, so you must not say that the transcendental is a thing by itself, formless and trackless, waiting for man specially to prepare and bring into his personality, and so lead him into the beaten path. Seeing that it is a beaten path there is only one beaten path."

Question. What does the sentence, "Seeing it is a beaten path, then there is only one beaten path," mean?

Answer. In any one phenomenon there is but one principle: whether subtle or coarse there is one law running through it and no other. The moderns can see only the first part, its formlessness and tracklessness; and speak of it as a vast emptiness. They have not realized that though it is "Void like the boundless desert", it "is filled with innumerable Forms like a dense forest". For example, the Buddhists speak only of Vacuum and the Taoists speak only of the Non-ens, but do not realize that it is filled with innumerable principles.

Question. In the sentence "'Before the response' is not before, and 'after the response' is not after", does the word "response" mean response to phenomena?

Answer. "Before the response" means before the response to a particular phenomenon, and, similarly, "after the response" means after the response to a particular phenomenon. Before the response of course is "before" in time, but the event responded to is subsequent, and after the response is made, is, it is true, "after" in time, but the principle of the response is antecedent.

14. *Question.* It is said: "The good and evil in the universe are both Divine Law."[1] Of the schools of Yang

---

[1] Quoted from Ch'êng Ming Tao's writings; see 遺 書, pt. ii, A, f. 2. The whole passage is: "The good and evil in the universe are both Divine Law. What is called evil is not evil originally, but it comes to be such by excess or shortcoming, as is exemplified in the schools of Yang and Mo."

and Mo[1] the one went too far and the other not far
enough,[2] but they both started from Love and Righteousness. To call these Divine Law is right, but can the great
wickedness of the world be called Divine Law?

Answer. Originally it was Divine Law, but it has
been perverted and so come to what it is.   For example,
cruelty is the reverse of solicitude. Arson and murder, too,
are the extreme of wickedness, but the use of fire for the
cooking of food, and the killing of a man that ought to be
killed : are not these Divine Law?   It is simply from
the perversion of it that wickedness springs.   Ethical
principle has both its obverse and reverse.   Obedience
to it is right, disobedience to it is wrong.   It is because
Law exists that evil exists.   Like the muddy stream of
a sewer : if in the beginning there had been no clean
water there could not have been this muddy stream.

15. Some one asked with reference to the statement,
"Good and evil are both Divine Law"[3] : In the case of
excess or defect, or in the case of many small wickednesses,
it is granted that you may still call them Divine Law.
But how can the great sin and wickedness of the world
also be Divine Law?

Answer. The original mind which man has at the

---

[1] Yang Chu and Mo Ti were philosophers of the fourth and fifth centuries
B.C., whose views were combated by Mencius. Yang was the apostle of
egoism and Mo of altruism. See Legge's Prolegomena to Mencius, chap. iii.

[2] Mo Tzŭ in his doctrine of universal love went too far, i.e. he went
beyond the Mean, while Yang Tzŭ in his egoism did not come up to
the Mean.

[3] See above.

beginning is wholly good, but very early it becomes clouded by the desire for pleasure and shrinking from pain. For instance, violence and robbery are the reversal of the solicitous mind : this is a case of man himself reversing the Divine Law.

Huo Sun asked : If it is a reversal of Divine Law, how can it be said that good and evil are both Divine Law ? Is it not that the wickedness of violence and robbery originally issued from the feeling of shame and hatred ; that lust and covetousness originally issued from the feeling of solicitude ; and that both became wrong by excess, but that in their issue at the beginning they were both Divine Law ?

Answer. This statement of the problem is also good. But with reference to what is called reversal, in the Four Terminals themselves there are mutual contrasts ; for example, the feeling of shame and hatred is the opposite of solicitude, the sense of right and wrong is the opposite of the feeling of modesty and humility. What you say is also a good interpretation, and from it I now see the meaning of a former statement of yours which I could not understand. You said, "In the exercise of human wisdom reject the disingenuous, in the exercise of human courage reject the tyrannical." In these two sentences I could follow your meaning. But when you said, "In the exercise of human love reject covetousness," I could not understand you. Now, however, when you say that covetousness originally issues from the feeling of love, what you said then becomes clear and is also right. When one's thought dwells upon it, how easy it seems for the perfectly good man to contract the faults of carelessness and indulgence, leniency and covetousness.

16. Chi Jung Fu asked : What is the meaning of the statement, " To accord with Law pertains to the thing done ; Righteousness is in the heart " ?

Answer. The phrase, " To accord with Law," applies to the thing as done in accordance with Law, " Righteousness " is that by which we are able to do it in accordance with Law. Righteousness implies choice and rejection. The *Commentary on the Yi*[1] says : " In the thing itself it is Law, in the management of the thing it is Righteousness."

(FIVE SECTIONS FROM THE "COLLECTED WRITINGS".)

1. All in me that is not the body is Law. What I have to do is not to allow the body and its passions to rule, and see to it that they wholly follow this Law. It is not that outside my person there is another entity which we call Law. To drift into some side course is not what can be called attaining. (Reply to Lü Tzŭ Yo.)[2]

2. The saying, " By the art of Meditation to enter Tao,"[3] means that when thought reaches the point that its stream is cut off, Divine Law is perfectly manifested. This again is incorrect. True thought IS Divine Law ; its continuous flow and operation are nothing else than the manifestation of Divine Law. How can it be that we are to wait till the stream of thought is cut off before

[1] By Ch'êng I.   [2] See p. 207, n. 3.
[3] Referring to the Buddhist Meditation Trance.

Divine Law is manifested ?   Moreover, what is this that
we call Divine Law ?   Are not Love, Righteousness,
Reverence, and Wisdom, Divine Law ?   Are not the
relationships of sovereign and minister, father and son,
elder and younger brother, husband and wife, friend and
friend, Divine Law ?   If the Buddhist really apprehends
Divine Law, why must he act contrary to and confuse,
cut off, and destroy all these, beclouding his own mind,
and losing his true knowledge of himself ?   (Reply to
Wu Tou Nan.)

3.   You say : "For the Buddhist, apart from the one
Intelligence, there are no distinctions ; for him phenomena
have no existence. For us Confucianists, of all phenomena
there are none which are not Divine Law."   This statement is correct, but for us Confucianists also, these
distinctions are not apart from Intelligence.   But within
this Intelligence there are the differences of height and
depth as of heaven and earth, and the infinite variety of
things, of all which, not even the smallest hair can be
changed.   This is exactly expressed in the expressions,
"Divine social arrangements," "Divine social distinctions," "Divine Appointments," and "Divine re-
tribution." [1]   (Reply to Chan Chien Shan.)

4.   The most subtle is Law, the most manifest is
phenomenon ; the substance and operation have one
source ; the manifestation and the subtle principle are
inseparable.   For from the point of view of Law the
operation is latent in the substance, which is what is meant

[1] *Shu Ching*, p. 73.

by "one source". From the point of view of the phenomenon, the subtle principle cannot be outside the manifestation, which is what is meant by "inseparable". (Reply to Wang Shang Shu.)

5. Divine Law is all-comprehensive; but the very fact that it is called Law implies the existence of ramifications. Therefore the four virtues of which it consists, Love, Righteousness, Reverence, and Wisdom, have in the nature of the case each its own principle, and there is no confusion between them. Before their manifestation we do not see any clue to their character and are not able to describe them as any one particular law; therefore we use the term all-comprehensive. It is not that within the comprehensive there are no distinctions, and that subsequently Love, Righteousness, Reverence, and Wisdom come into existence one after the other, as four visible things. You must bear in mind that Divine Law is simply the general term for Love, Righteousness, Reverence, and Wisdom, and that these four are the several component principles of Divine Law. (Reply to Ho Shu Ching.)

VIRTUE.

(FIVE SECTIONS FROM THE "CONVERSATIONS".)

1. The *Doctrine of the Mean* distinguishes between Moral Law and Virtue when it speaks of the five relationships as "the universal Moral Law",[1] and of Wisdom, Love, and Courage as "the universal Virtues".[2]

[1] D.M., p. 270.   [2] Ibid., p. 271.

The sovereign has the Moral Law of the sovereign, the minister that of the minister, and Virtue is the practice of Moral Law. Therefore the sovereign is ruled by love, the minister by seriousness, and love and seriousness should be termed Virtue and not Moral Law.

2. In the expressions " perfect Virtue " and " perfect Moral Law ",[1] Moral Law is that which is followed by all men in common. Virtue is that which the individual receives for himself alone. Of the expressions " complete virtue" and "supreme goodness",[2] complete virtue is what the person receives,[3] supreme goodness is what the person attains to. Of the terms sincerity, ingenuousness, honesty,[4] and truth, singleness of mind is what we call sincerity, complete self-expression is what we call ingenuousness ; as it is in the heart it is honesty, as manifested in objective fact it is truth.

3. Virtue is what we obtain from Heaven ; when by study we obtain it, we obtain the very thing that pertains to our own duty.

4. To serve one's parents is the virtue of filial piety, to serve one's elders is the virtue of fraternal respect.

[1] Ibid., p. 286.   [2] G.L., p. 227.
[3] There is a play on the word " virtue " here. In Chinese it is " tê ", and the word " to receive " is also " tê ", different ideographs but the same sound. The allusion is to a sentence in the *Li Chi* 德 者 得 也, " Virtue means realization *in oneself* " ; see *Li Ki*, vol. ii, p. 95, and Legge's note.
[4] Fu (孚) is hardly distinguishable from Ch'êng (誠), sincerity ; see *Yi Ching*, p. 199 and note on p. 200. The word " honesty " is here adopted to distinguish from " sincerity " occurring just before, but of course in its older sense of " true-heartedness ". Cf. p. 431.

Virtue is what is received into the heart. Before serving one's parents and following one's elder brother, to already possess a perfectly filial and fraternal mind : this is what we term Virtue.

5. The Master asked : How do you regard the section in the *Literary Remains*[1] which says, " If we wish to hold the Divine Law firmly, the secret lies in Virtue " ?

Pi Ta[2] replied : The *Doctrine of the Mean* says, " Only by perfect virtue can the perfect Moral, Law be realized." [3]

The Master remained silent for some time, until Pi Ta asked him what he thought, when he replied : This also is correct, but you are only quoting. What really is Virtue ?

Pi Ta. It is simply this ethical principle. When by study and practice we translate it into conduct, and show that it is our own certain possession, then we are able to preserve and not to lose it.

Chu Hsi. How do you explain the sentence : " Ordinarily you may see the evidence of it in Virtue " ?

Pi Ta replied by quoting Hêng Ch'ü's explanation of Virtue as " guarding whatever moral principle we receive in the proportion in which we receive it ".

Chu Hsi. You must receive it before you can guard it. According to this explanation you still have not acquired a thorough understanding of the word "Virtue". Moreover you say : " It is simply this ethical principle "; but you must be continually watchful, and make the principle

---

[1] *The Literary Remains of the Brothers Ch'êng*, by Chu Hsi.
[2] See p. 295.
[3] D.M., p. 286.

which is in you such that action is certain to be in accordance with it. For example, when sitting in meditation alone before serving my parents and my sovereign, and before holding intercourse with my friends, there must already be in me the perfectly filial and fraternal, loyal and faithful disposition, which so inspires my conduct that in serving my parents I cannot be other than filial, in serving my sovereign I cannot be other than loyal, in intercourse with friends I cannot be other than faithful, and this spontaneously "without waiting for special preparation".[1] For as cherished in the heart it is called Virtue,[2] as seen in action it is called conduct. The *Yi* says : "In the noble man his conduct is the fruit of his completed virtue,"[3] which expresses exactly the idea that Virtue is seen in all kinds of action. When Virtue is perfected in me, it is as though there were a man in me, who of necessity is filial and fraternal, loyal and faithful, and would not in any wise do anything that is not filial and fraternal, loyal and faithful. It is something like the Taoist's idea of nurturing a child into existence within one. Everything pertaining to human desire, this man will in no wise consent to let me do. Therefore it is said : "The completion of the study of them by silent meditation, and the securing of the faith of others without the use of words, depended on their virtuous conduct."[4] What this means is : Although as yet it is not expressed

[1] See p. 297 and n. 1.
[2] Though not yet put into practice, if it is received into the heart, it is Virtue.
[3] *Yi Ching*, p. 416.
[4] Ibid., p. 378.

in words, yet being cherished in the heart, this kind of conduct is already determined upon, after which there must be watchfulness, concern, and nurture. The reason why there must be such nurture is to guard against any break. Ch'êng Tzǔ's statement that we must secure that faith of others in us which will be independent of words means that before speech or action there is already this perfectly virtuous "man," in me,[1] but without as yet any visible manifestation. Therefore it is said, "It is hard to picture it in words."

[1] See above.

THE PHILOSOPHY OF
HUMAN NATURE

BOOK VI

BEING BOOK XLVII OF
THE COMPLETE WORKS OF CHU HSI

———

LOVE

BOOK VI

LOVE

(FORTY-NINE SECTIONS FROM THE "CONVERSATIONS".)

1. Some one asked : Is Truth the all-comprehensive and inactive, and Love the flowing forth of Law ?

Answer. From the point of view of the Nature Love does not flow forth either,[1] but its energy-producing principle includes the four cardinal virtues.

2. It is after we have received this Vital Impulse,[2] and are thereby in possession of life, that we have Reverence, Wisdom, Righteousness, and Sincerity. From the point of view of priority Love is first, from the point of view of greatness Love is greatest.

3. To-day we shall endeavour to understand what is the meaning of the word "Love". The saints and sages expounded it frequently, one in one way and another in another. Their use of words and the meanings attached to them differ, but when we have definitely ascertained what the meaning is in each case, and when we have collected together and carefully examined their statements

---

[1] That is, Love does not differ from Truth, so far as flowing forth is concerned.

[2] The Vital Impulse is Love (仁), the parent of all the virtues, as is repeatedly taught throughout Book VI ; cf. especially pp. 314, 315, 316. See also J. P. Bruce, *Introduction to Chu Hsi and the Sung School*, chap. xiii.

—scattered as they are like the stars—we shall find that this is the invariable interpretation, and that it is everywhere consistent. In the definition of Love as " The principle of affection and the virtue of the mind ", which is given in the *Collected Comments*,[1] affection is solicitude, and solicitude is Feeling ; its principle is Love. In the phrase, " The virtue of the mind," virtue, again, is simply affection, because the reason why Love is called the virtue of the mind is that it is the source of affection. The two elements which make man to be man are Law, which is the Law of Heaven and Earth, and Ether, which is the Ether of Heaven and Earth. Law is without traces and invisible, so that it is only in the Ether that we can see it, and if we would understand the meaning of Love, we must think of it as manifested in an all-comprehensive, mild, and gentle Ether.[2] This Ether is the positive springtime Ether of Heaven and Earth, its Law is the life-producing Mind of Heaven and Earth. If now we turn to man's own personality and suppose him to possess this Law, what do we find ? The moment he possesses it he is good in precisely the same way,[3] and free from drought in the same way, as Heaven and Earth.[4] If we examine the

---

[1] A work compiled by Chu Hsi ; 愛 (*ai*) = the emotion love ; 仁 (*jên*) = the disposition love.

[2] *Jên* (Love) is a principal or law and purely immaterial, but Law can only be discerned in the Ether as its medium of manifestation ; hence the meaning of each of the four nature-principles is seen in the Ether, which in the case of *Jên* is all-comprehensive, mild, and gentle.

[3] 恁 地 = thus, i.e. man exhibits the same characteristics as Heaven and Earth.

[4] " Drought," i.e. the opposite of " life-producing ".

many passages in which the saints and sages discuss Love
we find that they all have the same meaning.   Confucius
described it to Yen Tzŭ as " The mastery of self and the
return to right principle ".[1]   To master, and so get rid
of self, is obviously this very idea.   It is not something
that must be arranged for the occasion ; in every one it
is from birth a perfect, all-pervading thing.   This
principle has no separate selfish element ; the man who
is ruled by it looks upon other men as one with himself,
he looks upon lower creatures as one with himself.   When
the altruistic principle has free course, there cannot but
be this kind of outlook. The disciples of Confucius
inquired only as to what we should do to practise Love ;
as to what Love is in itself they all knew already.   Modern
scholars on the other hand are ignorant of what it is ; how
then can they speak of practising it ?   Consider further
the Master Ch'êng's statement, " In the narrow sense it
is but one, in the comprehensive sense it includes the
four."   The statement above this : " The Principle of
Origin, of the Four Attributes, corresponds to Love in
the Five Cardinal Virtues," seems to imply that there
is a great Love and a small Love.   What Ch'êng Tzŭ
speaks of as love " in the narrow sense " is the small
Love, which is simply the one thing, Love.   What he
speaks of as love " in the comprehensive sense " is the
great Love, and includes Reverence, Righteousness, and
Wisdom, in addition to Love.   When described in this
way we are apt to think there are two kinds of Love, forgetting that Love is only one.   Although we speak of

[1] Analects, XII, i, 1 (p. 114).

it in the narrow sense, all these many principles are included in it; and when we speak of it in the comprehensive sense it is still these principles which are included in it.

Chih Tao said: Is it not like the spring, the season when things are born, which already enfolds within it the growth of summer, the fruitage of autumn, and the storage of winter?

Answer. The spring is the season when things are born. In summer, autumn, and winter there is still the same ether flowing onward; but in spring we have the idea of the new-born burst of glory. In the summer, after the fruit becomes fixed, this Vital Impulse gradually becomes old.

Huo Sun said: We can certainly recognize the mild and gentle ether as Love, and if we consider it as including the four virtues, then naturally there is refinement, the sense of obligation, and clear discrimination.

Answer. Yes.

4. Whenever and wherever Love penetrates, whatever should be Righteous will be Righteous, and whatever should be Reverence or Wisdom will be Reverence or Wisdom. Consider, also, the storing operations throughout the universe: how can there be any cessation of them? All have the Vital Impulse latent in them. Just as seeds or peach and apricot kernels, if sown, will spring into life, and are not dead things—which accounts for the use of the word *jên* as the name for a kernel[1]—so we see all

---

[1] A play on the word *jên* (仁), " Love," of which a secondary meaning is " kernel ".

things possessed of this Vital Impulse. Thus spring is the Vital Impulse itself; summer is the production of things in their profusion; in the autumn we see this Vital Impulse gradually gathering itself in ; and in the winter we see it stored in the storehouse.

The Philosopher further said : Spring and summer are the progression, autumn and winter are the retrocession ; just as in breathing, when exhaled the breath is warm, when inhaled it is cold.

5. It is manifest that we should [1] use our efforts in all kinds of virtuous conduct, but how are we to ascertain what they are ? All kinds of virtuous conduct are summed up in the Five Cardinal Virtues, and the Five Cardinal Virtues are summed up in Love. Therefore Confucius and Mencius simply taught men to seek Love. To seek Love is to make seriousness the ruling principle, and thus to seek the lost mind. If we can do this we shall have found the truth.

6. Some one asked an explanation of the statement : " To preserve the mind—this is Love."

Answer. To preserve the mind we must not be overcome by selfish desire, we must apply ourselves with energy to everything we meet with requiring our attention. We must not allow ourselves to be led away by external things, but keep an extremely watchful guard. If we continually preserve our minds, then, in dealing with all affairs, " although we may not hit the centre of the target, we shall not be far from it." [2] Anxious thought

[1] 合 = 合 當, " ought."   [2] D.M., p. 234.

and inward distraction are because we are unable to preserve the mind. When we fail to preserve the mind, we are unable to see what we ought to see, or hear what we ought to hear.

Question. Does not the secret of it all lie in seriousness ?

Answer. Seriousness is not a separate thing, it is constantly to stir up the mind. People fly [1] through the days and never stop to collect their minds.

The Philosopher said further : Although Love appears to have the quality of strength and directness, it really is a mild and gentle thing. But in its operation it manifests several phases ; there must be moral insight, courtesy, and judgment, these three, before the deed of Love is complete. But when the deed is done, these three retire and Love remains mild and gentle, because its original nature is such. Men only see the moral insight, refinement, and judgment ; but to say that these are the fundamental qualities of man is wrong. Spring is essentially mild and gentle, and therefore gives birth to things : this is why we say that Love is the spring.

7. Some one asked about the statement : " To preserve the mind—this is Love."

Answer. This sentence is very good, but in the sentence following, " If a thing is in harmony with the mind do it, if not, then do not do it," the writer has digressed, and is treating of what pertains to Righteousness and not Love. Moreover, we need only to take

---

[1] 鶻突. Giles gives the meaning as " to swoop down like a hawk ".

Mencius' statement, " Love is man's mind and Righteousness is man's path," [1] in order to see the difference
between Love and Righteousness.   For " Love is the
virtue of the mind " ; when we preserve the mind there
can be nothing but Love.   For example, when the sage
speaks of " The mastery of self and the return to right
principle ",[2] he simply means that when we have put
away selfish desires the mind will be continually preserved, and is not at this point speaking of conduct.   When
you say, " If a thing is in harmony with the mind, do it,"
you have stepped over the boundary and trenched upon the
ground covered by the phrase, " Righteousness is man's
path."   But the ability to practise Righteousness is by
the operation of Love.   The student must constantly preserve his mind, then he will be able to estimate both the
phenomenon that presents itself and the law it embodies,
and so do what he ought to do.   This is the teaching of
Confucius and Mencius.   Therefore we must put the
pursuit of Love first ; for Love is the source of all laws,
the foundation of all phenomena, and we must first know
it, we must first preserve and nourish it : then we shall
have the *point d'appui*.

8.   The virtue of the ear is alertness, the virtue of the
eye is clearness, the virtue of the mind is Love.   Think
over the meaning of these statements and study them.

Take the expression, " The principle of affection," and
study and consider it with respect to your own mind, and
you will see what Love is.

[1] Mencius, p. 290.   [2] Analects, XII, i, 1 (p. 114).

Love is mild and gentle, soft and yielding. Lao Tzŭ said, "The soft and yielding belong to the class of living things, the strong and hard belong to the inanimate." This represents the idea of Love. How could you sow seed upon stone ? Gentle like the mildness of spring ! Buoyant like the richness of new wine ! These are the true similitudes of Love.

What is received from Heaven at the beginning is simply Love, and is therefore the complete substance of the Mind. But Love branches out into four divisions : the first division is the Love of LOVE, the second is the Righteousness of LOVE, the third is the Reverence of LOVE, and the fourth is the Wisdom of LOVE—one substance with four members united under the headship of LOVE. The Mind contains only these four, and all things and all events proceed from them.

The different characteristics of heaven's four seasons are very manifest. The spring gives birth to things ; in summer they grow, in autumn they are reaped, and in winter they are stored. But, although divided into four seasons the Vital Impulse runs through them all; even in the severity of frost and snow there is still the Vital Impulse.

When we define Love in terms of life we are going back a stage ; but we need to recognize the purpose of Heaven and Earth in giving me birth.

Note anything which is hard, such as a block of stone: whatever it comes to be it will be lacking in Love.

Note what takes place when there is a mild and gentle, soft and yielding spirit : by this come " filial piety and fraternal submission, the foundation of Love".[1]   In the case of the block of stone you can neither sow seed in it nor reap fruit from it.   You can see the idea in the proverbial expression: "A hard heart"; when a man is hard hearted, how can you talk with him ?

In each of the expressions, solicitude, conscientiousness, courtesy, and moral insight, there is a combination of the meanings of two words. " Solicitude " combines the word " grief ", which is the initial word, with "distress ", which means pain ; " conscientiousness " combines the word "shame ", meaning shame at my own wickedness,[2] with " hatred", meaning hatred of wickedness in others ; " courtesy " combines the word " humility ", having reference to myself, with "complaisance ", having reference to others ; the expression "moral insight," explains itself.[3]

As soon as Love exists it produces Reverence ; therefore Love answers to the spring, and Reverence to the summer. Righteousness represents decision and restraint, and when you obtain Wisdom you reach the end ; therefore Righteousness and Wisdom answer to autumn and winter.

When, having thus clearly understood Love, we come to practise it, we must "master self and return to right principle ".[4]   "When we go abroad we must behave to

<hr>

[1] Analects, I, ii, 2 (p. 3).

[2] " The sense of the shame which we usually call conscience " ; see Faber's *Mind of Mencius*, p. 114.

[3] 是 非, lit. : " right and wrong," or " true and false ", with the idea of discrimination between them, which is " moral insight ". Faber calls 智 (here translated " wisdom ") "Moral Knowledge " (see *Mind of Mencius*, p. 98).   Legge also says, " It will be seen how to 智, ' knowledge,' ' wisdom,' he (Mencius) gives a moral sense."   See Mencius, p. 79, note.

[4] Analects, XII, i, 1 (p. 114).

everyone as if we were receiving an honoured guest, we must employ people as if assisting at a great sacrifice, and we must not do to others what we would not wish done to ourselves." [1] This is to practise Love.

9.   Chou Ming Tso asked about Love.

Answer.   The saints and sages in their discourse sometimes referred to the essential principle, as in the sentence, "Love is man's Mind" ; [2] and at other times referred to the practice of Love as in the sentence, "To master self and return to right principle."

10. Love is spontaneous, reciprocity is produced voluntarily ; Love is natural, reciprocity is by effort ; Love is uncalculating, and has nothing in view, [3] reciprocity is calculating and has an object before it.

11.   The earlier philosophers, in teaching men to seek Love, spoke only of its profound depth, its mildness and purity, including all ethical principles.

12.   Love is the principle of affection, and altruism is the principle of Love ; therefore, if there is altruism there is Love, and if there is Love there is affection.

13.   Chou Ming Tso : To be cleansed from selfish desire is Love.

Answer.   To say that when we are cleansed from selfish desire Love in its substance is manifested, is allowable ; but you must not say that to be freed from selfish desire is Love.   For example, the light of the sun and moon

---

[1] Ibid., XII, ii (p. 115).   [2] Mencius, p. 290.

[3] 覷 當 底 = a visible object facing one.

when covered by clouds and mist is invisible, but you could not point to the disappearance of the clouds and mist and say that that is the sun or moon. And so water, when mixed with sand and stone, is certainly not in its original condition, but when you have removed the sand and stone and have nothing but water left, you do not say that the absence of the sand and stone is the water.

14. Yü Chêng Shu said : The absence of selfish desire is Love.

Answer. To say that when selfish desire is absent we have Love is allowable, but to say that the absence of selfish desire is Love is incorrect. For it is simply that when selfish desire is absent Love is made manifest, just as when there is nothing to choke the channel water can flow freely.

Fang Shu [1] said : To be one with all things in the universe is Love.

Answer. The absence of selfishness is antecedent to Love ; to be one with all things in the universe comes after Love. Let there be no selfishness and Love will follow ; let there be Love and there will follow the oneness with all things in the universe. (It is important to distinguish between the two.) What after all is Love like ? If we wish to understand the meaning of the term, we must consider the three words, Righteousness, Reverence, and Wisdom together. If we really wish to see the typical expression of Love, we must practise "the mastery of self and the return to right principle ".[2] (Love as

[1] Li Fang Shu, a friend and pupil of Su Tung P'o, the poet.
[2] Analects, XII, i, 1 (p. 114).

explained by the modern schools is like sauce which all say is sweet, and yet they have never tasted it, and do not even know what sort of flavour sweetness is.) The sages never explained it; it simply rested with the learner to embody it in his own person.

15. The word Love is expressive of breadth, and represents the entire substance. The words solicitude and tender affection express its essential similitude.

16. Love is the root, solicitude is the young sapling, while "attachment to parents, love of the people, and kindness to other creatures",[1] are its expansion in branches and leaves.

17. *Question.* In your written reply to the Hu Hsiang school,[2] you, sir, used the word "affection" to explain Love; what was your meaning?

Answer. It was because Shang Ts'ai[3] laid too much stress on the word "Consciousness", and so he bordered on the "Meditation" doctrine.

Question. Kuei Shan,[4] however, analysed the term "solicitude", did he not?

---

[1] Mencius, p. 352.

[2] See p. 28, n. 4.

[3] Hsieh Liang Tso (謝 良 佐), *style* Hsien Tao (顯 道), a native of Shang Ts'ai (上 蔡), in Honan. His literary name was Shang Ts'ai from the name of his birthplace. He studied under both the brothers Ch'êng, and himself established a school called the "Shang Ts'ai School". (Cf. p. 324.) He seems to have been of a restless, impulsive disposition, but an earnest student with phenomenal memory. See 學 案, pt. xxiv; 宗 傳, pt. xv, f. 21ff. Cf. pp. 348–9 of this volume.

[4] See p. 26, n. 1.

Answer. Kuei Shan's statement : "The universe is one with myself, etc.," is also too wide.

Question. Does this refer to the substance of Love ?

Answer. It is not the substance but the capacity of Love. Love, it is true, has consciousness, but to say that consciousness is Love is not correct. It is also true that Love can be one with the universe, but to call oneness with the universe Love is not correct. For example, in speaking of a room, without discussing whether its pillars are made of wood or its partitions of bamboo, we say it is so large, it contains many things. So with the phrase, "oneness with the universe," it simply expresses the capacity of Love. (From the mention of the word "Meditation" arose the subject of "Capacity".)

18. *Question.* Scholars of the Ch'êng school explained Love as "Consciousness".[1] The K'ê Chai Chi[2] does not agree with it. What is your opinion ?

---

[1] In the *Literary Remains* Ch'êng Ming Tao is recorded as saying, "In medical books a hand or foot which is numb is said to be 不 仁 (lit. : 'without love')"; and from this he draws an illustration of Love. For Love is the recognition of all things as one with myself, while the lack of love means that I am unconscious of any connexion of other things with myself, as in the case of the hand or foot when it is paralysed or numb ; see 遺 書, pt. ii, A, f. 2. This is what is meant by the "Consciousness" theory. The absence of "consciousness" in this sense, is the "non-recognition of ethical principle"; see pp. 332-3. The analogy is elsewhere still further applied to the term "solicitude" (惻 隱), one of the Four Terminals or Feelings, corresponding to Love (仁) as one of the Four Principles. The two characters *ts'ê* (惻) and *yin* (隱) mean "pain" or "pity" and "distress". When a limb is numb it is insensible to "pain" and there is no feeling of "distress", and is therefore said to be 不 仁 (without Love), just as in the ethical sphere to lack "solicitude"

Answer. Love cannot be separated from affection. The Shang Ts'ai school all reject affection as the explanation of Love. They had regard to I Ch'uan's statement "Universal affection is not Love.[1] Love is a principle of the Nature,[2] affection is Feeling". But I Ch'uan did not say that affection is not Love. If anyone had asked him the question, he would certainly have said: "Affection is the feeling of Love, and Love is the principle[3] of affection." In this way we can understand the matter. The pity is that those of this school have taken hold of that one idea, and so explain Love wholly by "Consciousness", to the detriment, it would seem, of its true explanation in terms of the emotion love. As a consequence of this, having passed over the true

is to be lacking in the manifestation of Love (仁). A section of Ch'êng Tzŭ's disciples, led by Hsieh Shang Ts'ai (cf. p. 322), gave an excessive emphasis to this explanation, excluding the idea of "affection" (愛) from the term "Love" (仁), and so restricting the latter to the idea of "consciousness". See p. 368. They became a separate school, distinguished by the "Consciousness Theory".

[2] The writings of Shih Tzŭ Chung (石 子 重), a disciple of Chu Hsi, a native of Tai Chou, and at one time in office at T'ung An, where Chu Hsi first held office. His literary name was K'ê Chai (克 齋), the name of his home.

[1] A direct contradiction of Han Yü's statement in the *Yüan Tao* (原 道) that "universal affection is Love" (博 愛 之 謂 仁). Han Yü interpreted *jên* (仁) in terms of *ai* (愛) like other scholars who preceded the two Ch'êngs; but the latter philosophers maintained that the word could not be explained simply in terms of *ai* (愛), although this is its basal idea. See p. 362.

[2] Love, Righteousness, etc., are called the 五 性, the five nature-principles.

[3] Lit. nature or nature-principle.

application of the word "Love" they have no proper definition of it to give. The passage, "When people see a child about to fall into a well, they will all without exception experience a feeling of alarm and distress," [1] bears on this closely. The saints and sages in expounding Love all start from this passage.

Question. Does not consciousness also have the Vital Impulse ?

Answer. Certainly, but to explain Love in terms of consciousness is too cold. Consciousness pertains more to intellect, and only in a small degree to Love. Love is the idea of harmony. But to add another sentence would be repetition. You must study it for yourself and you will get the meaning.

19. The Hunan school [2] in their exposition of Love have all of them, for many years, been in the habit of propounding a speculative theory without any foundation for it. I saw recently that Wang Jih Hsiu, in explaining Mencius, said, "The Ch'i Lin is a lion." [3] Love is essentially solicitous, mild, and generous, but, as described by them fictitious notions are imported into it, and the idea of fierceness is added, as if it actually had beetling brows and glaring eyes. It is just like Wang Jih Hsiu's saying that the Ch'i Lin is a lion, attributing to this harmless creature the appearance of one devouring all kinds of beasts. All this proceeds from the use of the word "consciousness". (The Ch'i Lin did not eat raw flesh or

[1] Mencius, p. 78.

[2] See p. 175, n. 7.

[3] The " Ch'i Lin " is a fabulous animal said to be a species of giraffe, and which it would be utterly incongruous to speak of as a " lion ".

raw vegetable, while the lion, as soon as it hears the sound of any beast, seizes it and tears it to pieces.)

20. As the "principle of affection" Love is referred to in the narrow sense of one of the four nature-principles ; as the "virtue of the mind" it is referred to in the comprehensive sense as including all the four.[1]   Therefore, speaking collectively the four virtues are all virtues of the mind, but Love is the ruling virtue; speaking severally, Love is the principle of affection, Righteousness is the principle of obligation, Reverence is the principle of respectfulness and courtesy, and Wisdom is the principle of moral discrimination.

21. The statement, "Love is the principle of affection," regards Love as divided into four. Love is the principle of affection ; affection for men or for other creatures is the manifestation of this principle. Righteousness is the principle of obligation, Reverence is the principle of respectfulness, Wisdom is the principle of moral discrimination. Principles are invisible : it is from affection, the sense of obligation, respectfulness, and moral insight, that we know that there are the principles Love, Righteousness, Reverence, and Wisdom in the mind —what are termed the virtues of the mind.   But this ability of Love thus to include the four virtues is in its pervading operation, what is called, "preserving in union the conditions of great harmony."[2]   Love is a principle of life.   To be without Love is to be dead.   Man is never without Love, it is simply clouded by selfish desire ; when

---

[1] See p. 312.   [2] *Yi Ching*, p. 213.

he "masters self and returns to right principle",[1] Love is found to be still present.

Chih Ch'ing[2] said : Selfish desire is not an additional thing, it is simply the mind's perverted condition.

Wang Chêng Fu asked : The minister Tzŭ Wên three times took office and three times retired from office, and the sage could not say that he was actuated by Love ; [3] but Kuan Chung was pronounced as having Love.[4] Why was this ?

Answer. The thrice taking office and thrice retiring was a private matter. When Kuan Chung came out, it was really to accomplish a work of Love. For example, one man perishes suddenly where he sits or stands,[5] another relying on his integrity suffers a violent death for righteousness' sake. Really it is the man who relying on his moderation, dies for righteousness' sake who is counted good, while the man who dies where he sits or stands reaps no benefit.

Hwan Ya Fu asked a question about the passage which speaks of sacrificing one's life in order to preserve in its completeness, and seeking life at the cost of injuring Love.[6]

Answer. The desire for life inevitably means the heart's unrest. If when principle demands death, the

---

[1] Analects, XII, i, 1 (p. 114).

[2] Huang Kan (黃 幹), *style* Chih Ch'ing, a disciple of Chu Hsi ; see p. 246, n. 2.

[3] See Analects, V, xviii, 1 (p. 43).

[4] Ibid., XIV, xvii (p. 145–6).

[5] Referring to the fixed posture of the Buddhist ascetic who remains in that posture until he dies. The point of the argument is in the difference between the selfish motives, on the one hand, and the altruistic motives, on the other, in the cases cited.

[6] Analects, XV, viii (p. 161).

sacrifice of life is made, then, though the body dies, the principle abides.

Ya Fu said : It is important to collect all the passages which refer to Love and study them together.

Answer. This is indeed a quick method, but it is not a good method. It is best to study the passages in order. Although, sometimes, after you have understood the meaning of a particular section, it may seem to you as if you have forgotten it, nevertheless, suddenly, as you grasp the meaning of another section, you will find that the idea comes back to you with perfect clearness.

22. Someone asked for an explanation of the sentence. " Love is the virtue of the mind." [1]

Answer. Righteousness, Reverence, and Wisdom are all contained in the Mind, while Love is all-comprehensive. Speaking of these separately, Love's special province is affection. Speaking of them collectively, Love includes the other three.

Some one asked : What is meant by saying that Love has the Vital Impulse ?

Answer. It is because of the Vital Impulse that mind is a living thing. There must be this mind [2] before we can know humility, before we can know conscientiousness, and before we can know right and wrong. If the mind is not living how can we know humility, conscientiousness, and the difference between right and wrong ? Further, it is like the birth of things in spring : when the growing season of summer comes it is the life that grows, when

---

[1] See p. 312.

[2] " This mind " refers to " Love " (仁).

the fruiting season of autumn comes it is the life that yields fruit, and in the consummating season of winter it is the life that is consummated. In the ripening of all kinds of grain, when the process has reached to seven- or eight-tenths of the fruitage, if the root is cut off the life perishes, and not more than the seven- or eight-tenths of the grain are obtained. If the life does not perish the ten tenths may be reached. This is reaped and stored, and apparently the life ceases ; but in the following year, if it be sown, there will be the return of life. The various philosophers of the past have differed in their study of Love. But the modern definition of it as the principle of affection means that in "the mastery of self, and the return to right principle"[1] we require nothing else than that we should preserve this affection, and that "the mastery of self and return to right principle" is not in itself Love. "To make friends of the most virtuous scholars, and take service with the most worthy of the great officers,"[2] also means nothing else than that there should be a manifestation of this affection. It is so with all the rest.[3]

23. *Question.* How do you explain the definition, "The principle of affection and the virtue of the mind"?[4]

Answer. A principle is in the Nature. Because in the Nature there is this principle of affection, therefore when it is manifested there is unfailing affection. Ch'êng Tzŭ

[1] Analects, XII, i, 1 (p. 114).
[2] Ibid., XV, ix (p. 161).
[3] All the rest of the passages in the Classics on Love (仁).
[4] See above.

said : " The mind is like the seed, the nature-principle of its life is Love."[1]   The expression " The nature-principle of its life " corresponds to the expression " The principle of affection ".

24.   In saying that altruism is Love, altruism must not be regarded as parallel to Love.   Altruism is simply the absence of selfishness ;   when there is no selfishness Love has free course.   When the Master Ch'êng said " Altruism is near to it " he did not mean near in the sense of being like it, but when there is altruism Love is present, therefore he used the word " near ".   For example, the passage " To know what is first and what is last is to be near the truth "[2] does not mean that the truth consists in what is first and what is last, but that when we know these we are near the truth.   Just as when you remove the dam the water flows freely, but the flow of water is not made by the removal of the dam.   The water is there originally, but dammed up ;   as soon as the dam is removed it flows.   Love is there originally, but is cut off by selfishness ;   when one's selfishness is conquered and removed that which then acts is Love.

Huo Sun said :   Altruism is the substance of Love, and Love is Law.

Answer.   You need not explain it in this way : to do so is a futile lack of discrimination.   What is needed is simply the absence of selfishness.   When there is the absence of selfishness there is the absence of anything which beclouds Law.   With people of the present day joy

[1] 遺 書, pt. xviii, f. 3.
[2] G.L., p. 221.

is selfish joy, anger is selfish anger, grief is selfish grief, fear is selfish fear, affection is selfish affection, hatred is selfish hatred, desire is selfish desire. If we can master our selfishness and "with broadness of mind be actuated by a high altruism",[1] then joy will be altruistic joy, anger will be altruistic anger ; grief, fear, affection, hate, desire will all be altruistic. This matter is very important in its consequences.   What Yen Tzŭ learned from the Master was simply that "the mastery of self and the return to right principle is Love".[2] In the study of a book one should shun most of all the vice of expounding it according to one's preconceived ideas, and trying to make the book accord with them, not realizing that they do not represent the real meaning of what we are reading. We ought to make our explanation accord with the author's meaning, and if in our endeavour to make that meaning clear we find that there are obscure passages, then compare them with our own ideas.

Hu Wu Fêng[3] said : "Man may be lacking in Love, but the mind never." This is most excellently said. Love may be hidden by man's selfish desires and so rendered invisible, but it is still present in the mind. It is like the sun and moon, which are originally bright and clear, and though hidden by the clouds, are still bright and clear ; or like water which, though dammed up by mud and therefore not flowing, still possesses the flowing nature. Therefore

---

[1] See p. 245.
[2] Analects, XII, i, 1 (p. 114).
[3] See p. 25, n. 2.

"the mastery of self, and the return to right principle",[1] is Love only in the sense that when we have conquered selfish desire we find Love still present. Or it is like a mirror which originally was bright and clear, but because of the dust has become blurred; if you wipe away the dust you will find the brightness and clearness still there.

26. *Question*. In the "Remains" the use of the expression "pu jên" by the medical profession is borrowed to explain Love.[2] In another paragraph it is stated that the medical school call insensibility to pain "pu jên".[3] Again, unconsciousness, the non-recognition of ethical principle, is regarded as being without Love. And yet again, the subject is explained in terms of consciousness.

Answer. Yes, but the "Consciousness" is consciousness with respect to principle.

Question. Is this in accord with the teaching of Shang Ts ai[4] or not?

Answer. No, it is different; Shang Ts'ai explained "Consciousness" as the first stage in recognizing this mind.[5]

Question. What do you think of Nan Hsien's[6] statement

---

[1] Analects, XII, i, 1 (p. 114).

[2] 遺 書, pt. ii, f. 2.

[3] Lit. "without love".

[4] Hsieh Liang Tso, whose literary name was Shang Ts'ai; see 學 案, pt. xxiv, f. 1. Cf. p. 323 of this volume.

[5] That is, the ethical mind; 此, "this," refers back to 理, "principle," in Chu Hsi's preceding answer.

[6] The literary name of Chang Ch'ih (張 栻), Chu Hsi's friend and opponent; see J. P. Bruce, *Introduction to Chu Hsi and the Sung School*, chap. iv.

that Shang Ts'ai's account of "consciousness" is different from the "Intelligence"[1] of Buddhism?

Answer. When Shang Ts'ai says : "It flows forth from the mind," he does not differ a great deal from Buddhism. Your statement that consciousness of pain represents the faculty of consciousness with respect to principle is good, but it is the second stage. For a satisfactory explanation you must ask : How do we know pain ? Where does the pulse come from?[2] Whence does this consciousness proceed?

Some one said : If we do not discover the source we have not reached the immaterial principle, but are speaking only of what is material.

Answer. True. The passage in which I Ch'uan speaks of the nature of the seed-corn is very good.[3]

27. *Question.* What is meant by the whole breast being filled with solicitous mind ?[4]

Answer. The word "breast" refers simply to the hollow parts of the body.

Question. Does it mean that at birth man possesses the solicitous mind in its fullness ?

[1] The same word as that which is translated "consciousness" above. The expressions 覺 and 知 覺 cannot be consistently rendered by one word in English. Sometimes the idea is mere sensation, sometimes fully developed intelligence. Most often it is expressed by the more general term "consciousness". As used by Ming Tao to illustrate Love it is "Consciousness". As representing the teaching of the Buddhists "Intelligence" is the best rendering. Its use by Shang Ts'ai hovers between the two.

[2] See p. 342.

[3] 宗 傳, pt. iii, f. 7 ; see p. 235 of this volume for translation.

[4] 遺 書, pt. iii, f. 3 ; cf. ibid., pt. vii, f. 1.

Answer. It is so regarded in the present day. When what I do is not satisfactory and I feel dissatisfied, this is the solicitous mind. Lin Tsê Chih [1] once said, " A man as high as seven feet, if he receives a pin prick in his body will feel the pain."

Question. Such being the case with my body, will it be the same in my conduct of affairs ? [2]

Answer. The response to environment by the Mind is infinite in its multifariousness. If in every single instance there is this solicitous mind, then it is Love ; if in one instance it is absent, then it is to that extent not Love.

Question. Is the original mind in such a case still present ? [3]

Answer. Up till now I have not thought out whether it is present or not ; according to the principle of the thing it is present, but not in the particular spot in which this feeling of solicitude is lacking. For example : " Within the sea-boundaries all are the king's servants ", [4] but there is one district where the people do not submit to the king's sway, and rebels set themselves up as princes and rulers. In such a district there is no king ; and yet the king is there, but he cannot be relied upon. You must not say, however : " The Divine Law is in some other place and not here, [5] I can let my selfish desire have full play and it will not matter ". Wang Hsin Po was in a room with

---

[1] See p. 12, n. 2.

[2] That is, will one minute fault cause " pain and distress " ?

[3] That is, in the case where " in one instance the feeling of solicitude is absent ".

[4] Allusion to *Odes*, p. 360.

[5] Lit. " only there."

Fan Po Ta, who asked him : " Ought not a man to regard everything in the universe as falling within the sphere of his Love ? " Wang pointed to the window sill and asked Fan : " Should the window fall within the sphere of one's Love ? " Fan was silent. To my thinking he ought to have replied : " If this window does not come within the sphere of my Love why do I not smash it ? " If in a man's conduct of affairs, every case is dealt with rightly, then every case has come within the sphere of his Love. Take the window for instance : to be treated properly, it should be papered [1] in some part or other, and not be smashed without reason.

Question. " Love regards all things as one." [2] When matters have actually come before us for action, then we have the means of dealing with them ; but before they are actually present we are not in a position to enter into them. What is your opinion ?

Answer. Even when they are not actually present the principle is, and when they are present we deal with them in accordance with it.

28. *Question.* How does the solicitous mind include the four Terminals ?

Answer. Solicitude is manifested at the time of the first movement of the mind. Conscientiousness, moral insight, and respectfulness are possible only when solicitude has become active ; they are seen only in its movement. Take for example the four seasons ; apart from the vital ether

---

[1] The window supposed would be one of lattice-work covered with thin paper which has to be renewed from time to time.

[2] 學 案 , pt. xiii, f. 18.

of things in spring, what growth could there be in summer? What would be reaped in autumn? Or what would be stored in winter?

29. The Principle of Origin is the beginning of the production of things by Heaven and Earth. The *Yi* says: "Great is Yüan, the Principle of Origin, indicated by Ch'ien! All things owe to it their beginning".[1] "Perfect is Yüan, the Principle of Origin, indicated by K'un! All things owe to it their birth".[2] From this we learn that the Principle of Origin is the thread running through all stages in the production of things by Heaven and Earth. Yüan is the Vital Impulse, in Hêng it becomes the development of the Vital Impulse, in Li it is its fruitage, and in Chêng its completion. It is the same with Love. Love is essentially the Vital Impulse, the feeling of solicitude; if this Vital Impulse is wounded, the feeling of solicitude is called forth. Conscientiousness also is Love manifesting itself in Righteousness; courtesy is Love manifesting itself in Reverence; and moral insight is Love manifesting itself in Wisdom. If a man have not Love how can he have Righteousness, Reverence, and Wisdom?

30. *Question.* Ch'êng Tzŭ said: "Love is 'To maintain inward correctness by seriousness, and to regulate outward conduct by righteousness'".[3] How can these be regarded as Love?

Answer. These too are Love. If we can attain to the perfect cleansing from selfish desire, and Divine Law have

[1] *Yi Ching*, p. 213.
[2] Ibid., p. 214.
[3] Ibid., p. 420.

free course, all these may be termed Love. For example :
" Wide learning and earnest purpose, eager inquiry and
thought with self-application—Love is in these " ;[1] or " To
master self and return to right principle "[2] is also Love ;
" When you go abroad, to behave to everyone as if you were
receiving an honoured guest, to employ the people as if
assisting at a great sacrifice,"[3] are also Love ; " In private
life to be sedate, in handling public business to be
serious, in intercourse with all to be ingenuous,"[4] are
also Love. Whatever path you follow, once entered upon,
only let it be followed till the goal of perfection is reached ;
then all are equally the paths of Love.

31. " Probably in every case when ' the mind cannot be
held firmly '[5] it is lacking in love.'" In view of this statement[6] the question was asked : The original substance
of the mind is calm, empty and clear, free from the entanglement of even a hair's breadth of selfish desire, in
which case the virtue of the mind does not fail to be preserved. The inability to hold the mind firmly is the result of
the confusion caused by selfish desire, which means the
wandering of the mind, and the perishing of its virtue.

Answer. According to your statement, it is because
of the inability to hold the mind firmly that Love is said
to be lacking. But in this instance, the phrase " lacking
in Love " means that it is because of the lack of Love that
there is the inability to hold the mind firmly.

---

[1] Analects, XIX, vi (p. 205).
[2] Ibid., XII, i, 1 (p. 114).
[3] Ibid., XII, ii (p. 115).
[4] Ibid., XIII, xix (p. 135).
[5] 學 案, pt. xiii, f. 17.
[6] By Chu Hsi.

32. *Question*. How do you explain Chou Tzŭ's not removing the grass from the front of his window, and the remark that its Vital Impulse was the same as in himself? [1]

Answer. It was just that accidentally he saw what accorded with his own impulse.

Question. Was Hêng Ch'ü's reference to the braying of the ass [2] intended to illustrate the spontaneous activity of a man's original instinct?

Answer. Certainly it was so, but he also heard it accidentally. In the case quoted of the grass according with Chou Tzŭ's own impulse, would not the leaves of a tree also have a likeness to himself? And in the case of the braying of the ass being akin to one's own calling out, would not the neighing of the horse be equally akin?

Question. Was Ch'êng Tzŭ's use of the phenomenon of the production of things by Heaven and Earth the same? [3]

Answer. He also observed this by accident simply, and then gave utterance to it in order to teach others. But you must not suppose that all you need is to observe the phenomenon of the production of things.

Question. "In observing young chickens we can observe Love." This illustration surely is to the point, expressing as it does the first manifestation of the Vital Impulse. [4]

[1] Refers to an incident in Chou Tzŭ's life, and his answer to a request for an explanation; see 遺 書, pt. iii, f. 2.

[2] 遺 書, pt. iii, f. 2.   [3] 遺 書, pt. xiii, f. 29.

[4] The "vital impulse" is regarded as a manifestation of *jen* (仁 = Love). It represents the instinctive love of life which characterizes all living things, corresponding to the Divine love of life manifested in the love of creating things, as shown in the preceding examples. Here there is a further extension of the idea.

Answer. It is simply because of the transparency of their skin that observation is possible. In the full-grown bird it is not that Love could not be observed, except for the fact that the skin is thick.

33. Pi Ta[1] said: When Tzǔ Hou[2] heard of the birth of a prince he rejoiced greatly, but was sad at the sight of starving people eating a meal.[3] Chêng Ch'un remarked on this as rejoicing with those that rejoice and grieving with those that grieve. Lu Tzǔ Shou[4] said: "He simply made the incident a text." You, sir, asked him: "Have you thought about it thoroughly?" He answered: "All things are one in matter and one in substance; it is when that which resides in me is perfectly altruistic and without egoism that there can be the absence of all separating barriers, and I can rejoice with those that rejoice, and grieve with those that grieve."

Answer. That is so far true, but it only represents a part of the matter. When Chêng Ch'un said this, he was indeed using the incident merely as a text, without really understanding the matter. What sort of egoism is there in earth and wood for instance? And yet they have no union with other things. Man, however, possesses this mind originally, and therefore, if he be perfectly altruistic

---

[1] Wu Pi Ta, *style* Po Fêng: see 學 案, pt. lxix, f. 53.

[2] Chang Tsai (張 載), whose style was Tzǔ Hou.

[3] 遺 書, pl. iii, f. 2.

[4] The second of the three brothers—Lu Tzǔ Mei, Lu Tzǔ Shou, and Lu Tzǔ Ching. Lu Tzǔ Shou's *ming* was Chiu Ling (九 齡). The family home was Chin Ch'i (金 谿) in Fuhkien. He was associated with his younger brother, Tzǔ Ching (子 靜), as a teacher of philosophy. Both were contemporaries and opponents of Chu Hsi.

and without egoism, all things will be under his control,
and there will be nothing to come between them and him.

34.   Love is latent in the feeling of solicitude : this is
Love as substance.[1]   When several things are accomplished
each action contains its own bit of Love and this is its
operation.[2]

35.   The inclusion of the four virtues in Love is like
the union of the six ministers under the headship of the
Prime Minister.

36.   If thought as soon as it springs up is firmly held,
that is Love ; but if the thought as soon as it springs up
goes astray, then it is robbed of its Love ; if when it ought
to dispense deeds it errs, it is robbed of its Reverence ;
if when it ought to be gathering in it errs, it is robbed of
its Righteousness ; if when it ought to be still and at rest
it errs, it is robbed of its Wisdom. This principle is present
in everything.

37.   Spring is the beginning of the year.   From it
proceed summer, autumn, and winter—all born of
the spring.   Therefore Love is said to include the four
virtues for the simple reason that the four are one.   But
as to three Yüan—in Yüan, the principle of Origin, there
are included the principles of Origin, Beauty, Utility, and
Potentiality ; and conversely the principles of Origin,
Beauty, Utility, and Potentiality have each its Yüan, or

[1] 骨, lit. " bones ", as the framework of a thing, or the ribs of a fan.

[2] 業 is equivalent to 事, which is an " event " in contrast to 物,
a " thing ", or " operation " in contrast to " substance ".

principle of Origin. If we grasp this idea, the statement that Love includes the four virtues will be clearer.

38. *Question.* I Ch'uan said: The Vital Impulse in all things is fully capable of observation. What is your opinion?

Answer. At the beginning of life, when things are not far removed from their source, it is certainly easy to observe; but when branches are formed and leaves are put forth in their luxuriance, it is not easy. As in the case of the child falling into the well, the feeling of solicitude and alarm is Love in its elementary stage, and when we meet with it we can easily perceive it. But in the case of "instituting a government dispensing Love"[1] it is so far-reaching[2] that we cannot see where the Love is.

39. *Question.* In the "Literary Remains" it is said: "In feeling the pulse we may see what Love really is."[3] Does not this mean a sincere seeking after it?[4]

Chu Hsi. Is it the one who feels the pulse that represents Love, or the pulse itself?

---

[1] See Mencius, p. 78. In the case of solicitude concerning a child who has fallen into a well, it is easy to watch and analyse the springs of Love, but in the case of government with its complicated and far-reaching organization, often masking its "love" in law and severe punishment, it is not by any means so easy.

[2] Mencius, p. 22.

[3] The origin of the saying was in an interview between Ming Tao and Hsieh Liang Tso. While sitting together one was feeling the other's pulse and Ming Tao remarked, "In feeling the pulse we may see what love really is." See 遺 書, pt. iii, f. 1.

[4] Just as the physician in feeling the pulse is intent and sensitive to its slightest beat.

Questioner. The act of feeling the pulse represents Love.

Chu Hsi. If that be the case, then, when feeling the pulse, we ought also to cherish the resolve to embody Love in practice.[1]

Chu Hsi further asked Fei Ch'ing:[2] What is your opinion of Chung Ssŭ's[3] statement?

Fei Ch'ing: According to my[4] view it is the same as in the case of the young chicken.

Chu Hsi. How?

Fei Ch'ing. The young chicken represents Love.

Chu Hsi. What about feeling the pulse and embodying Love in practice?

Fei Ch'ing. The pulse is the permeating flow of the blood. By feeling the pulse we can perceive Love.

Chu Hsi. Yes, it is probably so. The blood pervades the whole body; it is so also with the principle of Love.

The Philosopher further asked: How do young chickens represent Love?

Tao Fu[5] said: You, sir, once said it was because of the tenderness which characterizes the beginning of their life.

Chu Hsi. Looked at in this way the meaning is somewhat clearer, for at this time they drink, they peck their food with perfect self-possession, and as yet have no

[1] That is, Chu Hsi does not agree with the questioner that "*feeling* the pulse" represents Love; see below.

[2] Surnamed Chu (朱).

[3] The original questioner.

[4] 伯 羽 is Chu Fei Ch'ing.

[5] See p. 178, n. 6.

experience of the alarms of fighting and raiding. This it is that represents Love.

40. *Question.* With reference to altruism, is it correct to say that it is the principle of Love, that Love is a principle of flowing movement and the putting forth of life, and that it is for this reason that altruism as embodied in man is termed Love? [1]

Answer. This is not easy to answer. The statement, " Altruism as embodied in man is Love," is somewhat faulty ; but if we really understand what is meant by it, we shall recognize that it is well said. 'It was on this account that Ch'êng Tzŭ also said : " Altruism comes near to Love." For Love belongs to the connotation of the word " man ". You possessed it originally, you brought it with you at your birth,[2] but because of the lack of altruism it has been covered up and choked so that it cannot flow forth ; if you can attain to altruism, Love will have free course. It is like the water in a dyke, which, obstructed[3] and clogged by sand and earth, ceases to flow ; if you can remove the obstructions the water will flow freely. It is not that you go outside and bring in fresh water to throw into the dyke ; the water was in the dyke originally but was impeded by foreign substances. Remove the obstruction and the water has free course. In the saying, " To master self and return to right

---

[1] Chu Hsi's answer seems to imply that this passage is from Ch'êng Tzŭ's sayings. I have not succeeded in finding either this or the one immediately following.

[2] 合下 = 生下來.

[3] 窊 靫 to obstruct ; 窊 = 閼 a failure of water ; 靫 = 鞹 to oppose.

principle is Love,"[1] to master self and return to right principle is nothing more than removing the egoism. If we can remove the egoism Divine Law will naturally have free course. It is not that having mastered self we seek another Divine Law and implant it within. Therefore it is said : " Altruism comes near to Love."

Questioner. Altruism is the quality by which we can exercise sympathy and affection. Sympathy is the bestowal of Love, affection is the operation of Love. Affection is the outflow of Love, sympathy extends this feeling of affection for the object loved, so that it actually reaches that object. Is it not so ?

Answer. What you say is not incorrect, but your definitions are not related to each other, and so there is nothing in them to excite interest. If philosophy were only studied in this way what would it accomplish ? The reason why no progress is made is just because in the study of phenomena no interest is excited.

Question. Ought we not in our explanation to retain the word " altruism " as it occurs in the first part of the sentence ?[2]

Answer. Yes, sympathy and affection both originate in the Love principle. But apart from altruism how can there be either the one or the other ?

Question. Is not affection the initial outflow, but not as yet applied to the object, and sympathy the quality by which we can import ourselves into the object ?

Answer. The outflow of Love is simply affection.

[1] Analects XII, i, 1 (p. 114).
[2] Refers to the opening sentence of this section on p. 343.

Sympathy is that which applies the affection, and affection is that which is applied by sympathy ; but for the sympathy applying the affection, the affection could not reach to the object loved—there could be no " attachment to parents, love of the people, or kindness to other creatures ",[1] but simply a feeling of affection. If there were no affection there originally, what would there be to extend ? It is like the clearing of a dyke : the water is there originally, and therefore when the dyke is cleared the water flows. If there were no water in the dyke originally, how could there be a flow of water when the dyke is cleared ? On the other hand, although there is water there, how can it flow out if the dyke is not cleared ? The water is the feeling of affection, that which clears the dyke is sympathy.

41. *Questioner.* It is said : The doctrine of Love is exhaustively expressed in the one word " Altruism ". Altruism is the principle of Love. It is because altruism is embodied in man that it is called Love. What I say is that Love is a principle in itself, and that altruism is the work of self-mastery arrived at its goal. Therefore altruism leads to Love. The sentence, " Altruism as embodied in man is Love," may be expressed thus : When one's egoism has been wholly eliminated, if we look solely at man's personality, it is seen to be Love. The word " embody " suggests " bony framework ".[2] Its meaning

[1] Mencius, p. 352.

[2] As the " bones " are in the body, forming its framework, so is altruism embodied in man's personality. Note, the word *t'i*, " to embody," is the same word as that translated " enter into ", and " sympathy " in the sentences following.

is the same as in the sentence, "They enter into all things and there is nothing without them,"[1] and the construction is the same as in the sentence, "The Principle of Potentiality is the faculty of action."[2] It is not the word meaning sympathy.[3]

Answer. Altruism is the method of Love ; man is the material of Love. Where man is there is Love ; for, having physical form, he possesses the principle of life. If there is no selfishness with its separative barriers, the entire substance of man's personality is Love. If there were no physical form, the Vital Impulse would have no seat of unity. The statement that the word "embody" means sympathy is also allowable. Sympathy is to import one's self into the object and so study it, as in the sentence, "Kind and considerate treatment of the whole body of officers," in the *Doctrine of the Mean.*[4]

42.   The term "Love" is not derived from altruism, but from man ;[5] hence the statement, "It is when altruism as embodied in man is Love."

43.   "Altruism as embodied in man is Love." Love is a permanent principle of man's mind. If altruism, then

[1] D.M., p. 261.

[2] See *Yi Ching,* p. 403 (Ch. Ed., pt. i, f. 5). This sentence is quoted simply to assist in the interpretation of the word *t'i* (體). *Kan* (幹) = "a framework ". When any "action" is performed, it must "embody" wisdom, i.e. it must contain wisdom within it as the "framework" on which it is built ; then only will it be satisfactorily performed. Similarly "altruism" (公) must be "embodied" in man.

[3] Chu Hsi shows that there is no practical difference between these two uses of the word *t'i*; see the end of this section.

[4] D.M., p. 272.

[5] That is, from the ideograph 人 .

there is Love ;   if egoism, then there is not Love. But you must not therefore regard altruism as Love. It must be embodied in man before it can be Love. Altruism, sympathy, and affection, all may be employed to explain Love.   Altruism is antecedent to Love, sympathy and affection are subsequent ; because where there is altruism there can be Love, and where there is Love there can be affection and sympathy.

44.   Someone asked :   In the statement, " Sympathy is Love's bestowal, affection is Love's operation," what is the difference between " bestowal " and " operation ? "

Answer.   That which is bestowed by sympathy is the affection ; if there is not sympathy, then, although there is affection, the affection cannot reach its object.

45.   *Question*.   In the statement, " Sympathy is Love's bestowal, affection is Love's operation," what is the difference between " bestowal " and " operation ? "

Answer.   Bestowal is the flowing forth from one's own person, operation refers to the thing done. The extension of the self is sympathy, it is the outflow from self reaching its object ; affection is the first beginning of it. Affection is like water, and sympathy is like the flow of water.

The Questioner again asked : You, sir, said that affection is like water, and that sympathy is like the flow of water. After I [1] went away, and thought it over, it seemed to me that this was not quite accurate. I would prefer

---

[1] 淯 is for 淳 (Ch'un) and is the questioner's way of referring to himself, Ch'ên Ch'un ; see p. 195, n. 2.

to say that Love is like water, that the affection is like the quality of humidity in water, and that sympathy is like the flow of water. I do not know what you think of it.

Answer. You are right, what I said yesterday was incorrect.[1]

46. "Sympathy is Love's bestowal, affection is Love's operation." The two expressions "bestowal" and "operation" must on no account be transposed.[2] Such virtues were only possible to Confucius and Mencius. The rest from Hsün and Yang downwards were unable to attain to them, and therefore their statements could be altered. Formerly it was said: "Completeness of self-expression is what we call ingenuousness, and completeness in the representation of an object sympathy." I Ch uan said, "Completeness in the representation of an object can express no more than the idea of truth, the extension of one's self to the object is termed sympathy."[2] For the sentence, "Sympathy is the extension of the self," is the only true explanation of "bestowal". Such passages as this need to be studied very minutely.

47. *Question.* Hsieh Hsien Tao,[3] the first time he met Ming Tao, was full of self-confidence because of his wide learning; he knew every word in the books of History. Ming Tao said, "Honoured sir, you have a prodigious memory, but is it not what might be character-

[1] See p. 345.
[2] 遺 書, pt. xxiii, f. 1.
[3] Hsieh Liang Tso, see p. 322, n. 3.

ized as the kind of 'familiarity by which one's aims are ruined?'"[1] When Hsieh heard this the perspiration poured down his back and his face flushed crimson. Whereupon Ming Tao said : " This is a case of solicitude." Now his feelings were hurt by the question of his teacher, and the manifestation of his wounded feelings in his countenance do not seem to fit in with " solicitude". What, then, did Ming Tao mean by his remark ?

Chu Hsi. Let us discuss this question now. Why did he call it " solicitude " and not " conscientiousness ? " Let each one of you give his own opinion.

Li Li Ch'êng answered : Probably he had in mind the theory of consciousness of pain.[2]

The Master did not accept this. The next day, the question being put to him again, the Master said : It was simply this : When Hsieh Hsien Tao heard what Ming Tao said he was moved, and the fact that he was so moved was itself a good thing. But you must not say that all students should desire to be moved in the same way. Moreover, the four Feelings—solicitude, conscientiousness, courtesy, and moral insight—do not all come at once. In the narrow sense solicitude is one of four, in the wide sense it includes the four. When one is moved then all follow. When he spoke of solicitude, the other three—conscientiousness, courtesy, and moral insight—were all included.

48. Chao Kung Fu asked : It is said, " Heaven enters

[1] See 學 案, pt. xiv, f. 6. Ming Tao's quotation is from the Shu Ching, pp. 348-9 ; cf. Legge's note on 玩.

[2] Cf. p. 323, n. 1.

into all things, and there is nothing excluded from its
operation, just as Love enters into all actions, without
exception." Does this not mean that in every single thing
there is Divine Law, and in every deed there is Love?

Answer. Yes, Heaven is embodied in things, and Love
is embodied in actions. Moreover, to say that Heaven
enters into things and Love into actions, means essentially
that the substance of a thing is Heaven, and the substance
of an action is Love. The construction of the sentence
arises from the necessity of expressing the idea in terms
of the higher in each case.[1]

Chih Tao asked: Is it the same meaning as in the
sentence: "They enter into all things and there is nothing
without them"?[2]

Answer. Yes.

Question. You, sir, in your *Commentary on the Yi*
explain the phrase "enter into things" by the expression
"to manage affairs".[3] What is the connexion?

Answer. The phrase "to manage affairs" has the
same meaning as "to have the management of affairs"[4]

[1] That is, 天 and 仁 must be the subject of the sentence in each case,
and therefore 體 has to be used as a verb and in a transitive sense. It is
thus equivalent to " makes itself the substance of ", or, as in the translation, " enters into," " is embodied in," " is inherent in."

[2] D.M., p. 261.   [3] Cf. *Yi Ching*, p. 408.

[4] The meaning of 事 之 幹 as it occurs in the passage in the *Yi*, to
which allusion is made, is doubtless as Legge translates it " faculty of
action ", or the gift of managing affairs. But the quotation of it here is
not because of its meaning but because of its construction. 幹 事 and
爲 事 之 幹 are parallel in construction to 體 物 and 爲 物 之 體.
It is as if in the one case the phrases were rendered " to frame affairs "
and " to be the framework of affairs ", and in the other case, " to be
embodied in things " and " to be the body of things ".

and to say " enter into things " is the same as saying " to be the substance of things ".

Kung Wen asked : What about the after-part of the passage which says : " It embraces ˙the three hundred rules of ceremony, and the three thousand rules of demeanour '.[1] There is not a single thing without Love."

Answer. " It embraces 'the three hundred rules of ceremony and the three thousand rules of demeanour' ' ", but Love must be recognized as the framework.

49. *Question.* How do you explain the statement, " To be sincere, earnest, empty of self and calm is the foundation of Love ? "

Answer. To be sincere, empty of self, and calm is the foundation of the practice of Love.

THIRTY-TWO SECTIONS FROM THE " COLLECTED WRITINGS ".

1. From the two statements, that to give birth to things is the Mind of Heaven and Earth, and that men and other creatures each receive this Mind of Heaven and Earth as their mind, it follows that to express the virtue of the mind, although the supremacy and unity of the Mind are perfectly complete, one word will nevertheless cover it, and that word is none other than " Love ". Please think over this carefully. For the virtues of the Mind of Heaven and Earth are four—the principles of Origin, Beauty, Order, and Potentiality ; and the Principle of Origin unites and controls them all. In their operation they become spring, summer, autumn, and winter ; and the vital ether of spring permeates the whole. Therefore

[1] D.M., p. 286.

in the mind of man also there are four virtues, Love, Righteousness, Reverence, and Wisdom; and all are included in Love. In their operation they become affection, respect, obligation, and discrimination ; and all are united in the solicitous mind. Therefore in discussing the Mind of Heaven and Earth, when "The Principle of Origin indicated by Ch'ien"[1] and "The Principle of Origin indicated by K'un"[2] is mentioned, the substance and operation of their four virtues are all implied, without pausing to enumerate them in detail. When, in discussing the mystery of man's mind, it is said, "Love is man's mind,"[3] the substance and operation of the four virtues are again all included, without waiting to state them in detail. For the place of Love in the Moral Order is as the life-producing Mind of Heaven and Earth present in everything. Before the movement of the Feelings its substance is there in its entirety, after the movement of the Feelings its operation is infinite, and if we can truly embody and preserve it, we have within us the spring of all goodness, the root of every virtue. This is what is taught by the school of Confucius; and for this reason we are bound to lead the student to be eager in his pursuit of Love. The statements of the Sage are : *First.* "To master self and return to right principle is Love" : [4] teaching us that if we can conquer and eliminate our selfishness and return to Divine Law, the substance of this mind[5] will be invariably present, and its operation everywhere active.

[1] See *Yi Ching*, p. 213.   [2] Ibid., p. 214.

[3] Mencius, p. 290.   [4] Analects, XII, i, 1 (p. 114).

[5] " This mind " (此 心) refers to " Love " (仁).

Second. " In private life to be sedate, in handling public business to be serious, in intercourse with all to be ingenuous " : [1] these are the means by which we may preserve this mind. *Third.* " To be filial in serving one's parents, to be fraternal in serving one's older brothers, and to extend kindness to animals " : these also are the means by which we practice this mind. *Fourth.* " To seek Love and obtain it," [2] to decline a kingdom and retire, [3] to choose death and perish by starvation : [4] these are the means by which we do not lose this mind. *Fifth.* " To sacrifice life in order to perfect Love " : [5] this means that there is something we desire more than life and something that we hate more than death, and so we can avoid injury to this mind. What mind is this ? In Heaven and Earth it is that mind to produce things which fills the universe. In man it is that gentle mind which loves men and is kind to other creatures. It includes the Four Virtues, and unites the Four Terminals.

Some one said : According to your explanation, does not Ch'êng Tzǔ's statement that affection is a Feeling and Love the Nature, and that affection must not be regarded as Love, become erroneous ?

Answer. Not so. What Ch'êng Tzǔ deprecates is applying the term Love to the outflow of affection. What I maintain is that the term Love should be explained as the principle of affection. For what are termed Feeling

[1] Analects, XIII, xiv (p. 135).   [2] Analects VII, xiv, 2 (p. 63).

[3] An allusion to T'ai Po's retirement in favour of his younger brother, the father of King Wên ; see Analects, VII, i (p. 71), and Legge's note.

[4] Cf. Analects, XVI, xii, 1 (p. 179).

[5] Analects, XV, viii (p. 161).

and the Nature, although there is a distinction between them, have nevertheless each of them their place in one organic union ; how then can they be sharply separated, and made to have no connexion with each other ? What I was just now most anxious about was to prevent the student from repeating Ch'êng Tzŭ's words and not stopping to find out his meaning, lest he should end in leaving out of account altogether the feeling of affection, and confine himself to the recognition of the love-principle. I have therefore purposely dealt with this point with a view to explaining what he has omitted. Do you regard that as differing from Ch'êng Tzŭ's doctrine ?

Some one asked : The disciples of Ch'êng Tzŭ give various explanations of Love. Some say that affection is not Love, and regard the unity of all things with myself as the substance of Love. Others say that affection is not Love, and explain the term as the mind's possession of consciousness. Do you, explaining it as you do, mean to imply that these are all wrong ?

Answer. From the statement, "The universe is one with myself," we may learn how Love includes all things within the sphere of its affection : it does not tell us what Love is in its real essence.[1] From the statement, "The mind possesses consciousness," we may learn how Love includes Wisdom ; it does not tell us from what it really derives its name.[2] If you refer to Confucius' answer

---

[1] This is the answer to what " some say " as reported in the question. It is supported by the reference to Confucius' answer to Tzŭ Kung.

[2] This is the answer to what " others say " as reported in the question. It is supported by the reference to a statement by Ch'êng Tzŭ. Cf. p. 323 and n. 1.

to Tzŭ Kung's question about conferring benefits far and wide and succouring the people, and to Ch'êng Tzŭ's statement that Love is not to be explained in terms of consciousness, you will see that it is so. How then can you regard these as explaining the word Love? Instead, with vague language about unity of the substance, you confuse and hinder people, while you give nothing that will have the effect of admonition ; such error is likely to result in regarding the object as subject. Those who lay emphasis on "Consciousness" induce in men self-display and irascibleness without any suggestion of depth ; such error is likely to result in regarding desire as principle. On the one hand there is the negation of the ego,[1] on the other the reinforcing of the passions,[2] and both are wrong. Further, the "Consciousness" theory does not accord with the picture presented by the sages of "finding pleasure in the hills"[3] and so being able to preserve Love. How then can you regard this as explaining the word Love?

Because of the importance of the subject these sayings of the Philosopher are collected and formed into a treatise on Love.[4]   (The Treatise on Love.)

2. Ch'êng Tzŭ's exposition of Love throughout is very exhaustive. To sum up the main drift of his teaching a few sentences only are necessary. For example, he says, "Love is the nature-principle of life, and affection is its

---

[1] The result of " regarding object as subject " ; 忘 = 忘 己.

[2] The result of " regarding desire as principle " ; 助 = 助 欲.

[3] Analects, VI, xxi (p. 56).

[4] Probably by one of Chu Hsi's disciples, such as Wu Pi Ta.

corresponding Feeling ; the filial and fraternal spirit is
its operation ; while altruism is that by which it is made
concrete " ; and further, " To master self and return to
right principle is Love."[1] In the first three sentences
the student may learn the terminology and meaning of
Love, and in the last sentence the method of putting forth
effort in its practice. Modern scholars do not thoroughly
search into the meaning of Ch'êng Tzǔ's exposition as
a whole. Looking solely at his distinction between the
Nature and Feeling, they declare that affection and Love
have absolutely no connexion with each other. Because
he regarded altruism as coming near to Love, they say that
he defined altruism directly and most emphatically as the
substance of Love. They do not realize that Love is the
virtue of the Nature and the root of affection. It is because
there is Love in the Nature that there can be affection
among the Feelings. (In the same way, Righteousness,
Reverence, and Wisdom are also virtues of the Nature ;
Righteousness is the root of the hatred of evil, Reverence is
the root of courtesy, and Wisdom is the root of the knowledge *of good and evil*. It is because there is Righteousness in the Nature that there can be hatred of evil among
the Feelings, it is because there is Reverence in the Nature
that there can be humility among the Feelings, it
is because there is Wisdom in the Nature that there can
be knowledge *of good and evil* among the Feelings.)
But if it is choked by the selfishness of egoism, the
mystery of its substance and operation cannot be perfected. It is only by the " mastery of self and the return

[1] Analects, XII, i, 1 (p. 114).

to right principle", by "broadness of mind and a high altruism", that this substance can be comprehensively complete, its operation brilliantly manifested, and activity and repose, the root and its fruit, be united in organic unity. This is the meaning of Ch'êng Tzŭ's statements, they do not mean that affection and Love have absolutely no connexion with each other. (This point has been dealt with in detail in previous treatises. I beg again to dispose of it in a word or two. My position is that the outflow of the Nature is Feeling, that Feeling has its root in the Nature, and that there is no such thing as Feeling without the Nature or the Nature without Feeling, each a separate entity, unaffected the one by the other. You may see here the correctness or otherwise of the two positions.) Nor do they mean that the word "altruism" refers directly to the substance of Love. (Examining closely your communication I find that you say, "If altruism be extended to the whole universe so that the egoism resulting from the distinction between subject and object is entirely obliterated, then affection must be universal." I am not sure in which of these two sentences it is that you refer to the substance of Love. If you regard the universality of affection as the substance of Love, then you fall into the error of confounding Feeling with the Nature, and with your eminently clear insight you could not do that. If you regard the "extension of altruism to the whole universe so that the egoism resulting from the distinction between subject and object is entirely obliterated" as the substance of Love, then I fear that what you call "altruism" would

be but a calm emotionless indifference. But since inanimate wood and stone cannot, even in the case of things
of the same species, have mutual affection, how can there
be such a thing as universal affection ?   But neither can
I in these two sentences discover a single word expressing
the substance of Love. We must bear in mind that Love
exists originally as a nature-principle and as the creative
mind, and finds its concrete expression only in altruism;
and not that Love comes after altruism. Therefore it is
said : " Altruism as embodied in man is Love." If you
examine this statement carefully you will see that the
word " Love " is implied in the word " man ".) From the
time of the Han dynasty, the error of defining Love as
affection was because no distinction was made between
the Nature and Feeling, and so Feeling was regarded as
the Nature. To-day, in the endeavour to correct this error,
the opposite error is incurred of making the word " Love "
so vague that there is nothing to which it can be referred,
and so the Nature and Feeling come to have no connexion
with each other. This is to go from one extreme to the
other,[1] which is simply foolish. The error leads the student
to talk of Love all day long and yet never understand its
real meaning. Moreover, the Mind of Heaven and Earth
and the virtues of the Nature and Feelings are also involved in the same obscurity. In my opinion Ch'êng Tzŭ
would never have meant anything of the kind. (Reply
to Chang Ch'in Fu's[2] essay on Love.)

[1] Lit. : " To correct a crooked thing beyond the straight position," so
that it becomes crooked in the opposite direction.

[2] Chang Ch'ih (張 栻); see p. 191, n. 3.

3. Upon a further perusal of the three points contained in another communication of yours, it seems to me that though with your excellent insight you have realized the mistakes of your first essay, still in this fresh treatment of your subject, there are a few small errors which suggest that you have not examined it with sufficient care. Respectfully, therefore, I discuss the matter once more. It has already become unnecessary to discuss Mencius' expressions, " first informed " and " first in apprehension," which Kuang Chung quotes[1] to explain Shang Ts'ai's statement that " the Mind has consciousness ".[2] And as to his talk about " knowing this " and " apprehending this ", I do not know what it is we are to know or what we are to apprehend. Indeed, seeing that he is wrong in the fundamental part of the subject it is immaterial whether we discuss it or not. On reading your treatise I find that you regard the " this " as Love ; that is, you take " knowing this " and " apprehending this " as meaning " knowing Love " and " apprehending Love ". Now Love is really the virtue of my mind ; who is it then that is to teach me to know it and apprehend it? As to the quotation from Mencius, Ch'êng Tzŭ has already explained it in detail, to the effect that " to know " is to know an event (to know that this particular action ought to be

---

[1] Hu Kuang Chung ; see p. 37, n. 2. The passage referred to is to be found in the 學 案, pt. xlii, f. 20 ; cf. also p. 323, n. 1, of this volume. For his allusions to Mencius, see Mencius, p. 246.

[2] The word " consciousness " is a compound expression consisting of the two ideographs, 知 " to know ", and 覺 " to perceive ".

thus), and "to apprehend" is to apprehend a law (to know the principle because of which this action ought to be thus). The meaning is already perfectly plain, and there is no necessity to seek for some recondite mystery in the phrase. Besides, Ch'êng Tzǔ's idea and that of Shang Ts'ai really have no connexion with each other. "Consciousness" as used by Shang Ts'ai is consciousness of cold and heat, hunger and repletion, and similar sensations, and although you extend its application to intercourse with spiritual beings, it is still the same consciousness and not a different thing ; it is simply a question of the difference in the importance of the thing to which it is applied. This, however, is the operation put forth by Wisdom alone ; but it is only the man of Love who can combine them. Therefore we may say that in the man of Love the Mind has consciousness, but we cannot say that the Mind's possession of consciousness is what we term Love. For when we say that in the man of Love the Mind has consciousness we refer to the fact that Love includes the operation of the four virtues, as though you said that the man of Love knows the objects of conscientiousness and courtesy ; while if you say that the Mind's possession of consciousness is what we term Love, then I answer that this is not that from which Love derives its name. You, now, instead of inquiring into what it derives its name from, point to what it includes as the substance of Love ; as has been said, "the man of Love is sure to possess courage," and "the man of Virtue is sure to have correct speech".[1] But how could you go

[1] Analects, XIV, v (p. 140)

on to regard courage as Love, and correct speech as Virtue ?
With reference to Po Fêng's insisting upon regarding consciousness as Love, you, honoured friend, are opposed to
it, and yet in your arguments on the degree of consciousness you scarcely avoid proving his contention for him,
a position which I would not venture to commend.   As
for Po Fêng's further statement, that what Shang Ts'ai
means is simply the possession of mental energy, and
that if we obtain this mental energy the operations of
Heaven and Earth become our own operations, the theory,
indeed, is lofty and mysterious enough, but, as he does not
know the meaning of Shang Ts'ai's terms, and as there is
no indication as to the starting point,[1] but only a sudden
reference to this mental energy, it is a case in which the
loftier the conception and the more mysterious the
language, the less foundation do we find for it when we
look into the constitution of our own personality.   As
to what he says of the operations of Heaven and Earth
becoming our own operations, I fear he has simply heard
or imagined these things, but has never attained to such
an experience.   (Reply to Chang Ch'in Fu's[2] essay on
Love.)

4. Ch'êng Tzŭ's thought for others in collating all the
passages in Confucius and Mencius which treat of Love,
with a view to a general statement on the subject, was
most opportune.   But to devote oneself exclusively to this
kind of work I fear would unavoidably produce a tendency
to indulge in hasty and short-cut methods, resulting in the

[1] That is, in obtaining the mental energy.
[2] See p. 191, n. 3.

evil of ill-digested theories, a tendency you must not fail to be on your guard against. Speaking generally, before the two Ch'êngs, scholars knew nothing of the word Love; the statements of the saints and sages concerning Love they simply construed in terms of affection. It was from the time of the two Ch'êngs that scholars began to realize that the word could not be explained simply as affection. But this idea did not escape its own attendent error. For by confining the attention to the discussion of Love there was neglect of the work of " holding fast and preserving the mind "[1] and of "nurture and maturity ",[2] so that again there was no satisfaction or pleasure in the study,[3] nor any real " mastery of self and return to right principle ".[4] Not only did this result in the " beclouding which leads to foolish simplicity ",[5] but there was a complete divorce from the word " affection ". Thus, building upon empty guesswork without any real perception of the subject, their theories became wild and grotesque with all sorts of fallacies, to the extent that it had been better to know nothing of the deeper meaning of the word Love at all, and simply interpret it as affection! I have said that if there is a genuine desire to seek Love, certainly there is no way so near of attainment as the energetic practice

[1] Mencius, p. 285.

[2] 涵 = " to nourish "; 泳 = " to swim about in water", immersed in it, and revelling in it.

[3] The proper result of the " nurture ".

[4] The proper result of the " holding fast, etc."

[5] Confucius mentions this as the result of " the love of being benevolent without the love of learning " (好 仁 不 好 學); see Analects, XVII, viii, 3 (p. 186).

of it. But to try and exhibit it without study means the anxious uncertainty of groping in the dark like a blind man, the result of which is the "beclouding of a foolish simplicity". If we are earnest and perfect our knowledge, each of these supplementing the other, we shall avoid this evil. If, again, we desire to understand the content of the term "Love", we cannot do better than follow up the word "affection". If we understand how Love comes to be affection and how the latter still cannot fill out the idea of Love, the meaning and content of the term will stand out clearly before our eyes, and there will be no need to look for it wildly, in uncertainty as to whether it is or is not a reality. (Reply to Chang Ching Fu.)[1]

5. Looking carefully at your "Preface to The Exposition of Love", I find the statement, "Though one's desire is to use one's utmost endeavour in the practice of Love, yet, through lack of clearness in the apprehension of goodness, one's faults are more than can be enumerated." This passage does not appear satisfactory. To have Love, it is true, you need to apprehend goodness clearly, but this is not the chief meaning of the word "Love". Confucius therefore always contrasted Love with Wisdom. In these later years scholars in their explanation do not differentiate it from Wisdom, so that in estimating the errors in the deeds of the minister Tzŭ Wên and of Ch'ên Wên Tzŭ [2] the representation of them is superficial and not like the

[1] Chang Ch'ih (張 栻), *style* Ching Fu ; see J. P. Bruce, *Introduction to Chu Hsi and the Sung School*, chap. iv.

[2] Analects, V, xviii, i, 2 (pp. 43, 44).

language and thought of the Sage. I fear that the teaching
of your "Preface", from beginning to end is not
altogether free from this same error. (Reply to Chang
Ching Fu.)[1]

6.   To discuss Love in terms of affection is like ascending
to the heights from the lowlands ; in this way we can
prosecute our search from that which lies close at hand,
and come very near to attainment. The modern theory,
which eliminates at once all connexion between the two
is like going a long way off to find the path which lies
near at hand. This is how it is that your mind[2] went so
far astray in your former essay, while you yourself were not
aware of your error. What you say about collating passages
in order to arrive at a statement of the doctrine of Love
also seems to me to be at fault. It is just what the
modern scholar does—disliking what is troublesome he
chooses what is easy, and avoiding the difficulties he seeks
a short cut. This custom has already increased to such
an extent that scholars everyday are taking the shortest
and therefore the most dangerous routes.[3] If they continue
to pursue this method, I fear their spirit of impatience
for results and eagerness for rapidity will grow still more,
the mind will be more urgent and more distracted, and
so they will fall into the opposite of what they seek, and
be destitute of Love.   They have not realized that in

[1] See above.

[2] 區　區 = " small " and hence " the mind " ; it is similar in its idea
to that of 寸　地.

[3] 險　薄, lit. " dangerous and shallow," and so " sparing of trouble "
as the dangerous short-cut.

Ch'êng Tzǔ's collection of sayings,[1] there is the exhortation "from the study of the lowly to understand high things",[2] so that in his case his method was perfectly complete. If we thoroughly investigate it and energetically practice it how can we fall into such error? (Reply to Chang Ching Fu.)

7. You say : " When selfishness is eliminated, there is broadness of mind and high altruism, there is living union with the whole universe, the principle of affection is received into the heart, its operation is manifested without, and in all the universe there is not a single thing which does not come within the circle of my Love.[3] This means that the principle of affection is the original possession of my nature and is not achieved by effort." (These few sentences again are not satisfactory.)[4] For when our selfishness is eliminated, the broadness of mind with its high altruism majestically penetrates in all directions, and there is nothing to hide the substance of Love. Now when the principle is not hidden there is living union with all things in the universe, and the operation of Love is universal. But what we call the principle of affection is the possession of my original Nature. All that the broadness of mind with its high altruism does is to bring it into evidence ; it is not the cause of its existence.[5] By

---

[1] See p. 361.   [2] Analects, XIV, xxxvii, 2 (p. 153).   [3] Cf. p. 367.

[4] There seems to have been a lacuna here in the original text ; hence the sentence in brackets supplied by the editor. The sentence, however, should be read as if without the brackets as part of Chu Hsi's criticism of the passage quoted.

[5] Note the difference between 在 and 有 ; 有 means " to exist " 在 means " to exist and also to be present ", i.e. in evidence.

living union it penetrates in all directions, but it is not preserved by this living union. These few sentences are somewhat inexact; I beg you, therefore, to examine into them again. The principle of affection towards men is Love. If Heaven and Earth and all things were non-existent, this principle would not be lessened thereby. From this you may gather what is the substance of Love; after which you are in a position to assert the living union with all things and its all-inclusive operation. For this principle of affection is essentially conservative,[1] and to bring in all things in the universe is to reduce it to an absurdity, as is shown in the Master's reply to Tzǔ Kung's question about "conferring benefits far and wide" and "succouring the people",[2] and in the sentence, "Do we not see in Fu the Mind of Heaven and Earth?" For in the return of the Positive Mode the Mind of Heaven and Earth is perfected and satisfied, and we need not wait to look for it elsewhere.[3] Again, take Lien Hsi's remark about the grass having the same impulse as his own:[4] if it be as is asserted in the present day, the words "the same as" are all you can retain of this remark. What then has become of the words "his own impulse"? (Reply to Chang Ch'in Fu.)[5]

[1] 約 = 儉 約, " to restrain."
[2] Analects, VI, xxviii, 1 (p. 58).
[3] Yi Ching, p. 233. " Fu " is the twenty-fourth hexagram, and symbolizes the idea of " returning ". In the preceding hexagram, the strong line—the positive mode—has reached the top; here it "returns" at the bottom of the figure.
[4] See p. 338.
[5] See p. 191, n. 3.

8. "To look upon the world as not having a single thing which is not Love ": this also is open to question. For to say, " To look upon the world as not having a single thing which is not within the sphere of my Love," is allowable ; but to say that things ARE my Love is not correct.[1] For things are things, while Love is mind : how can you say that a thing is mind ? (Reply to Chang Ch'in Fu.)

9. With reference to the meaning of the word " Love ", Mencius in his use of the word " Mind " combines the substance with its operation, and uniting the Nature and Feeling he speaks of them both as one. Ch'êng Tzǔ, in his account of the Nature makes careful distinctions ; separating the substance from its operation, he contrasts them one with the other. (Reply to Lü Po Kung.)[2]

10. As to my statement, that "Love is the love of creating in the Mind of Heaven and Earth, and that men and other creatures receive it as their mind",[3] although it was the extempore utterance of a hypothesis, I contend, nevertheless, that it exactly expresses the truth that there is no separation between Heaven and Man. The statement is somewhat subtle, but if you understand it you will see that in the midst of their all-comprehensive unity there is a natural distinction between Love and Mind, and that though there is this fine distinction, they cannot be torn apart. (Reply to Ho Shu Ching.)

[1] Cf. p. 365.
[2] Lü Tsu Ch'ien (呂 祖 謙), elder brother of Lü Tzǔ Yo, a very close friend of Chu Hsi. His style was Po Kung. See J. P. Bruce, *Introduction to Chu Hsi and the Sung School*, chap. iv.
[3] Cf. p. 351.

11. Love is all penetrating, therefore solicitude is all-penetrating : this is precisely the mysterious inseparable-ness of the substance from its operation. If Love were all-penetrating, but there were limits to the penetrating power of solicitude, then we should have the substance great and its operation small, an all-round perfection in the substance and imperfection in its operation. You may see the point in the incident in which Hsieh Tzŭ was hurt by Ch'êng Tzŭ's words and turned red in the face while the perspiration poured down him : it was what is termed "the sense of shame", but Ch'êng Tzŭ referring to it said, "This is solicitude".[1] (Reply to Ho Shu Ching.)

12. As to the exposition of Love in terms of conscious-ness, Ch'êng Tzŭ has already exposed its error ; for when you explain Love as consciousness, you have only expressed what is its operation, and even then you have not expressed it all. It is best to use the word "affection" as the most correct explanation of the operation of Love, and one which has an all-round completeness.[2] (Reply to Ho Shu Ching.)

13. *In your latest communication you say* : "The original Mind of man is invariably Love, but having become submerged in creaturely desire, it has lost this virtue. Hence we must use our most earnest endeavour, then only can we regain the Love of the original Mind." Therefore the sentence in your former letter, "Love is the fruit of earnest endeavour," as you see it now, only

---

[1] See pp. 348-9.   [2] Cf. p. 323.

expresses the second half of your present statement ; [1] while the sentence, " The Mind originally is a perfect thing," expresses only the first half of the statement. But the two sentences are not wrong, they simply lack an all-round completeness. If you say : " The Mind is that which connects the beginning with the end, while Love is the original excellence of the mind-substance ; but since this Mind, although we still possess it, has become submerged in creaturely desire, its original excellence has been lost, and can only be regained by earnest endeavour "— then you will come somewhat nearer to a true statement. The language of Mencius, it is true, is comprehensive, but man has never been without this Mind, and if perchance he comes to be destitute of Love, it is simply that the original excellence of the Mind has been lost. You must still make some distinction, however, between the words "Mind" and " Love" to be correct. I recall that the Master Li [2] said, "When Mencius said 'Love is man's Mind',[3] he did not mean that Mind is the definition of Love" : this statement has considerable force.   (Reply to Ho Shu Ching.)

14. Your statement, "Solicitude apparently does not proceed from consciousness," is very good.   But as to your further assertion, " The word ' consciousness ' is not necessarily bad," I never meant that it was : I only said that where we need to put forth our effort is not in

---

[1] The statement with which this section opens.

[2] Li Yen P'ing ; see J. P. Bruce, *Introduction to Chu Hsi and the Sung School*, chap. iv.

[3] Mencius, p. 290.

consciousness but in reverent care.   Shang Ts'ai said, "Seriousness is the method of constant watchfulness," [1] which is correct, but there may be a tendency to regard such watchfulness as in itself Love, and this would not be satisfactory.   (Reply to Yu Ch'êng Chih.)

15.   Although Mencius in his discourses on Love gave two interpretations : "solicitude," and "man's mind" ; and Ch'êng Tzŭ also used the word in both a narrow and a comprehensive sense ;   nevertheless, if in the narrow sense of solicitude you can discern man's mind, then in the comprehensive use of the word you will perceive its entire substance.   It is only because in your understanding of this point [2] you are not accurate that you fail to recognize its complete substance ; seeking to clothe your exposition in swelling words, and masking it with your own vivid imagination, you fail to realize that the bigger your language the less trenchant will your meaning be.   In the explanations given by Ch'êng Tzŭ the most apt is the simile of the seed corn ; [3] but this does not represent altruism as Love : and at the same time is particularly subtle. You now set aside all this, and insist on taking some laudatory *obiter dictum* of the *Commentary on the Yi* [4] as a direct definition of the meaning of the word, and so not only do you miss the meaning of Love, but you also wrongly interpret the " Commentary ".   (Reply to Lü Tzŭ Yo.) [5]

[1] 學 案, pt. xxiv, f. 9. For Shang Ts'ai see p. 322, n. 3, and p. 323, n.1.
[2] The point that Love is to be explained by solicitude.
[3] See p. 235.
[4] By Ch'êng I.   [5] See p. 207 and n. 3.

16. The word "Love", it is true, must not be thought of solely from the point of view of its manifested operation, but neither must we lose sight of the fact that it is a principle capable of manifested operation. Otherwise the word would have no connotation at all, and would be incapable of definition. Note, too, " the Principle of Origin, the first of all the virtues "[1] is the first step in the beginning of all things,[2] the original substance capable of manifested operation. You must not make the original substance of Love one thing and its manifested operation a different thing. (Reply to Lü Tzǔ Yo.)

17. The meaning of the word "Love" must be sought along one line of thought and on one principle of definition, then your doctrine will be in union with what has gone before. If not, it will become what we know of as everything being one soul, a hazy Buddha Mind, and the very word "Love" will have no application at all. (Reply to Lü Tzǔ Yo.)

18. *Question.* Your kind criticism and instruction with reference to my questionings I have now mastered. For in the man of Love the Mind has consciousness, but we must not call consciousness Love, because consciousness pertains to Wisdom. Law is one, its functions are diverse, and there are degrees in the feeling of affection. Now the regulation of this diversity, and of these degrees, belongs to Reverence, to make them accord with what they ought to be belongs to Righteousness. Righteousness,

[1] *Yi Ching*, p. 408.　　　　　　　[2] Ibid., p. 213.

Reverence, and Wisdom are all Love : it is Love alone that
can include these three. But in respect of whence their
names are derived each has its own province, and we must
investigate the distinctions between them ; otherwise they
will all be jumbled together, and there will be no means
of knowing which is Love, which is Righteousness, or
which is Wisdom.

Answer. Your explanation of the word Love is very
good. It is important to bring the four principles together,
and by comparison make them throw light on each other ;
then we can see the distinctions between them clearly, and
in the midst of the distinctions see the union of all
and headship of the one. This is the true presentation of
the inclusion of the four in Love. Scholars of recent
years have confined their attention to the word "Love"
and given no thought to the other three. Hence the uncertainty and mistiness of their ideas ; they start by
asserting the inclusion of the four, but do not really know
in what sense they are so included. Now that we have
you, with your depth of thought and clear discrimination,
scholars will have someone on whom they can rely. (Reply
to Lü Tzŭ Chung.)

19. In your communication you say : The similes of
"feeling the pulse"[1] and "observation of the chicken,"[2]
are certainly good, but at the very time of observation there
are numerous cross-currents in consciousness so that the
Mind is divided in its operations and a hindrance to

[1] See p. 341-2 and notes.
[2] See pp. 338-9 ; cf. n. 2 on the next page.

itself, with the result that not only can we not perceive what Love is, but the strength and rapidity of the pulse, the appearance of the phenomenon in the chicken, we have no time to properly observe. I have thought over these statements, but by feeling the pulse we observe the circulation of blood through the body,[1] and by watching young chickens we can observe the manifestation of life ; [2] therefore these two phenomena are used to teach men, just as the physicians' saying about numbness [3] and Chou Tzŭ's not removing the grass from his house are used.[4] (Reply to Lin Tsê Chih.)

20. In the study of the word " Love " you must from the one operation learn the fullness of its entire substance, and from the entire substance you must learn the reality of its single operation ; then your understanding will be living and have unity, without sluggishness or obstruction. (Reply to Wang Tzŭ Ho.)

21. You must bear in mind that the expression " Virtue of the mind " belongs to Ch'êng Tzŭ's simile of the seed-corn. The expression " The principle of affection " is exactly what is meant when we say that Love is the feeling

[1] Love (仁) permeates all things just as the blood permeates the entire body.

[2] In the young chicken the skin is so thin and transparent that you can actually see life at work, in contrast to the old bird when the skin is too thick for such observation. Similarly in spring, in all nature you can actually see life springing to birth in contrast to late autumn and winter, when life, though present, is hidden. Spring is the season that corresponds to 仁 (Love), hence the use of the young chicken as an illustration of Love.

[3] See p. 323, n. 1.　　　　　　　　　[4] See p. 338 and n. 1.

of affection before it is put forth, and that affection is the love-principle after it is put forth. You must keep your reasoning in line with this thought and not import extraneous ideas, involving the subject in confusion and indistinctness. If your understanding of Love is in accord with this, there is no objection to the assertion of union with all things in the universe ; but if you do not grasp this, and still make union with all things in the universe to be Love, you will find, on the contrary, that there is no connexion at all. (Reply to Chou Shun Pi.)

22. In your instructive communication you quote the phrases, "Fine words and insinuating appearance,"[1] and "The firm, the enduring, the simple, and the modest",[2] as indicating the method of the practice of Love which the Sage taught and which men might thus obtain for themselves. I have some doubt with reference to this, though, in my former communication, I did not touch upon it. For these two phrases exactly represent what the Sage teaches as to how men in setting to work should guard against calamity and establish their hearts. If we can abstain from "fine words and insinuating appearance", and cultivate "simplicity and modesty", the mind will not break loose from restraint, and we shall be near to Love. The phrases were not intended merely to teach us what Love is. For the most part the teaching hitherto has been a sacrifice of heart and strength in seeking to understand

[1] Confucius said, "Fine words and an insinuating appearance are seldom associated with Love " ; see Analects, I, iii (p. 3).

[2] Confucius said : " The firm, the enduring, the simple, and the modest, are near to Love ; see Analects, XIII, xxvii (p. 138).

the word "Love", with the result that the more ingenious the explanation is, the more superficial is the representation of Love. To-day, upon investigating the gracious teaching of the sages, we find that their aim was that men should practise it in their own person and act in accord with its doctrine, cultivate inward rectitude and conquer selfishness, make all forms of frivolity, meanness, self-exaltation, and contempt of others dissolve into nothingness, and that we should preserve and never lose the honest and kindly, just and upright character of our original mind. This is Love. Practice and effort in it may differ according to its degree in each man's disposition, but the important thing is energetic practice and ripe maturity. If we can really attain to this we shall know its meaning and spirit, for it is not to be known by imagination and guesswork, nor are we to wait for imagination and guesswork before we can know it. (Reply to Wu Hui Shu.)

23. From the point of view of the Nature, Love has not as yet flowed forth, but its energizing principle includes the four principles. It is quite certain that it does not refer to the same thing as the word Truth. You must discriminate more clearly between them to be accurate. (Reply to Chêng T'zŭ Shang.)[1]

24. *Question.* With reference to the sentence "Altruism as embodied in man is Love", Mr. Li in a former question regarded the word "Love" as wholly referring to mankind as a race. I said that it ought not

[1] See p. 5, n. 3.

to be so explained, but Mr. Li understood you, sir, to say that the emphasis was to be placed on the word "man". I have now received your criticism and instruction, from which it appears that this is not the case. I beg to submit my own opinion expressed to the best of my ability, and ask you to determine the matter. My view of the passage is this: The word "man" refers to this my person. It differs from the word as used in the phrase, "Love is the distinguishing characteristic of man," in the *Doctrine of the Mean*,[1] and should not be emphasized. The important word is "embodied"; for "Love is the virtue of the mind", it controls the Nature and the Feelings, and rules all actions. It is essentially the most characteristic element in my personality. Altruism is simply the principle of Love. If you speak of altruism *per se* you are speaking of a principle merely, which has no reference to myself. Therefore it must be embodied in my person. Union is then established between myself and the principle, and this is called Love. This accords with the words of Mencius, "As united with man's person it is Moral Law."[2] But as to the question how altruism is to be embodied, and how it comes to be termed Love, the answer is that it is no more than the complete elimination of selfishness until this mind is all-pervading, perfectly pure and bright, wholly characterized without and within by the altruism of Divine Law, and springing to birth again and yet again without any break. Then the life-producing impulse of Heaven and Earth will constantly abide. Therefore, in the state of stillness before

[1] D.M., p. 269.   [2] Mencius, p. 361.

manifestation, it is sparkling with intelligence and un-clouded, like the virtue of the one Yüan, the Principle of Origin, brightly shining in the " Fu in the midst of the earth ",[1] with not a single event or thing which is not wrapped up in this my principle of life. In its movement in response to affection by the external world, the " grief " is combined with "distress" like the positive ether of spring developing in the "Yü above the earth ",[2] with not a single event which is not united by this principle, and not a single thing which is not provided for by this Vital Impulse. This is how the embodiment of altruism comes to be Love. By it we can exercise sympathy, by it we can manifest affection. Although it may become Righteous-ness, or Reverence, or Wisdom, or Sincerity, wherever it is it is all-pervading. I do not know if this is correct or not.

Answer. This statement is correct. If it were not as you state it, then it would be like the Buddhist's sacrifice

[1] See the Fu hexagram ䷗ in the *Yi Ching*, p. 107. The upper half is the K'un trigram ☷ symbol of earth ; the lower half is the Chên trigram ☳ symbol of thunder or movement. The bottom line is strong and is the " returning " line which gives to the whole hexagram its name, and also its symbolic meaning of " brightness ", which develops " from day to day and month to month as the strong line makes its way " ; see Legge's note on p. 109. From this analysis of the hexagram we see that Chên, representing bright movement, is below K'un, which repre-sents earth ; hence the phrase " Fu in the midst of the earth ".

[2] The Yü hexagram is the converse of the above. It has the Chên trigram above the K'un, thus ䷏ ; see *Yi Ching*, p. 91. Thus the Yü is " above the earth ". The Chên is symbolical of thunder which begins to develop in the spring of the year.

of self to feed a tiger ; it may be altruism but it is not Love. (Reply to Ch'ên An Ch'ing.)[1]

25. *Question.* Mr. Lü[2] says with reference to Mencius' doctrine of solicitude[3] : "For if there is a real wounding of my heart, and not a mere figure of speech, I shall then recognize the universe as all of one substance with myself, the life-producing mind as all my own mind, the distress of others as my own distress. This is not achieved by calculating thought or forced effort." This use of the expressions "all of one substance with myself" and "all my own mind" means, does it not, nothing more than the assertion of the unity of Law ?

Answer. Not unity of Law only, but of Ether as well. (Reply to Ch'ên An Ch'ing.)

26. Altruism is without feeling, Love has the feeling of affection. Altruism pertains to Law, and Love pertains to personality. What is altruism but "the mastery of self and the return to right principle"[4] with the elimination of every atom of selfishness. What is Love but "attachment to parents, love of the people, and kindness to other creatures?"[5] Reasoning from this you will get the idea. (Reply to Yang Chung Ssû.)

27. *Question.* With reference to the passage beginning with the words, "The Principle of Origin, of the Four

---

[1] Ch'ên Ch'un (陳 淳), one of Chu Hsi's disciples ; see p. 195, n. 2.

[2] Probably Lü Tsu Ch'ien ; see J. P. Bruce, *Introduction to Chu Hsi and the Sung School,* chap. iv.

[3] Cf. Mencius, p. 78.   [4] Analects, XII, i, l (p. 114).

[5] Mencius, p. 352.

Attributes, corresponds to Love in the Five Cardinal Virtues," I [1] would say that taking the one virtue in the narrow sense we have the operation of Love, taking the four in a comprehensive sense, we have the substance of Love.   The operation of Love is no other than affection ; but affection is not adequate to express the substance of Love : you must include the four in your statement, then only do you get the substance of Love.

Answer.   Love as a single virtue is the very thing that includes the four.   You must not leave this and find some other Love to unite the four.[2]   (Reply to Têng Wei Lao.)

28. *Question*.   How do you explain the statement : "Love is the virtue of the mind, the principle of affection ? " [3]

Answer.   Love, as the virtue of the mind is like humidity as the virtue of water, or heat as the virtue of fire ; as the principle of affection, it is like the root of a tree or the spring from which water flows.   Make a study of it with this idea in mind.   (Reply to Tsêng Tsê Chih.)

29. Your statement that when there is the absence from the mind of selfish desire we have the complete substance of Love, is correct ; but you must remember that there is here an original Vital Impulse, presenting the phenomenon of an overflowing joy : this is necessary to

---

[1] 絅, Ch'iung, refers to the speaker.

[2] That is, the operation of Love (仁) is affection (愛), and if the substance, 仁, comprises the four, then so also does its operation, 愛. In other words, what applies to the immanent attribute applies also to its outflow, the transitive attribute.

[3] See p. 381.

complete the idea. Yen Tzŭ "did not allow his joy to be affected.[1] That is, when by his efforts he had attained to Love, there was spontaneous joy, altogether independent of poverty, or wealth, or high estate, or low estate, so that they could not affect it. In the case also of the virtuous and wise, with their joy and longevity,[2] when attainment is reached the result naturally follows. (Reply to Lin Tê Chiu.)

30. *Question.* On examining Confucius' use of the word "Love", as when he said to Yen Tzŭ it is the "mastery of self and the return to right principle",[3] it seems as if the method of Love is perfectly set forth and nothing left unstated. When we come to Mencius, although he continually refers to Love as man's Mind,[4] yet his idea is that we should infer it from the feeling of solicitude, and his tendency is to emphasize the word affection. Although his teaching is subtle and incisive, yet it is not like that of the Sage[5] in breadth and completeness, and in its quality of leading men themselves to attain to it by devoting themselves to quiet thought and energetic practice. Is not this because Mencius lived in a time of battle and bloodshed, when the need was to find some way of saving men from fire and flood, or to give medicine to men stricken down by disease?

---

[1] Yen Hui (顏 回), *style* Tzŭ Yüan (子 淵), often called Yen Yüan. This saying is part of a famous eulogy spoken by Confucius; see Analects, VI, ix (p. 52), and note.

[2] Cf. Analects, VI, xxi (p. 56).

[3] Analects, XII, i, 1–2 (p. 114); cf. note above.

[4] e.g. Mencius, p. 290.

[5] Confucius.

Answer. Ch'êng Tzŭ said : " The Principle of Origin
in the Four Attributes corresponds to Love in the Five
Cardinal Virtues. In the narrow sense it is but one, in
the comprehensive sense it includes four. As the feeling
of solicitude it is used in the narrow sense, as the mastery
of self it is used in the comprehensive sense." But it is
this one virtue which includes the four, for they are not
two things. Therefore in the *Collected Comments on
the Analects*[1] it is said, "Love is the virtue of the
mind, the principle of affection." This is excellently
expressed, and is well worth thinking over. You must not
say, however, that Mencius' statements are not equal to
those of Confucius in all-round completeness. Mencius
also speaks of Love in the comprehensive sense—
for example, in the statement "Love is man's Mind"[2]—
and Confucius speaks of it in the narrow sense—
for example, in the statement that it is to "love[3] all
men ".[4] Your statement that Mencius used the word
solicitude because of the bloodshed of his time is also
wrong. Further, you should keep in view the fact that
though Confucius did not contrast Righteousness with
Love, he constantly contrasted Wisdom with Love. (Reply
to Ou-Yang Hsi Hsün.)

31. If in the "Literary Remains" we study the discussion of the passage, "Filial piety and fraternal
submission ! Are they not the root of all benevolent

[1] A collection of comments by various writers, compiled by Chu Hsi.
[2] Mencius, p. 290.
[3] 愛 = the emotion love, or affection.
[4] Analects, XII, xxii (p. 124).

actions ? " with the sayings, "Love is the Nature, filial piety and fraternal submission are its operation", "Universal affection is Love ", and the reply to the theory that "the Mind is like a seed-corn", and then compare these three sections with the words of the former saints and sages, we shall find that there is nothing to call in question. The statement that "solicitude cannot unite the three" is strongly questioned also by our friend Ho, and he cannot come to a decision upon it ; but it is not difficult to understand. If again you carefully study the chapter in Mencius on the "commiserating mind ",[1] and, in the "Additional Remains ",[2] Ming Tao's remark on the philosopher Hsieh[3] that his memory was "the kind of familiarity by which one's aims are ruined", then it will all become clear. (Reply to someone not named.)

32. *Question.* Love is the life-producing Mind of Heaven and Earth which is received by all men as their mind. Hence its substance pervades heaven and earth and unites all things in the universe, its principle includes the Four Terminals and unifies all goodness, because it comprises all the virtues of the mind, and rules the Nature and Feeling. It is what is called the Principle of Origin of Ch'ien and K'un. Therefore, it is from this that we get our definition[4] of its name and meaning ; that is,

[1] Mencius, p. 79.

[2] The 外 書, as stated in the preface to that work, was a compilation of the Ch'êng sayings supplementary to the 遺 書.

[3] Hsieh Shang Ts'ai ; see pp. 348–9.

[4] 語 is a verb = "to define ".

from its transforming and nurturing influence, its mildness and purity, its simplicity and liberality, its repro-
ductive life and deathlessness, it is termed Love.   But
men obscure it by their selfishness, and so its life-principle
ceases, Divine Law is banished, hardening and insensibility ensue, and they become cruel.   To embody Love
men must cleanse themselves absolutely from selfish desire,
be so broad-minded that there will be nothing to obscure
the life-producing substance of heaven and earth ;   their
hearts must be true and sincere, earnest and solicitous,
lovable as the gentle spring which we would fain retain
always.   Uniting the internal and external, the great and
the minute, the end and the beginning, it is wholly Divine
Law in its pervading activity, all-encompassing, reaching
everywhere, all-uniting.   In the Ether flowing from the
one source it permeates everywhere without interruption,
and may well be regarded as the all-comprehensive perfect
substance without defect.   If there be one spot with never
so small a defect, never so minute an event that its care
cannot reach, one short moment in which there is never so
slight a separation, then this mind has become selfish.
When selfishness is in progress the life-principle ceases,
Law does not penetrate, and there is numbness and the
cutting off of affection :   in such a case, how can there be
perfection ?   Love is like our body: when the blood circulates perfectly throughout, we are absolutely free from
disease ;   but if there be one finger which the blood fails
to reach, it is dumb and destitute of Love.[1]   Yen Tzŭ
"for three months did not depart from Love";[2] after

[1] Cf. p. 323, n. 1.   [2] Analects, VI, v (p. 50).

the three months there was some slight departure, but there was an immediate return, the obstruction melted away, and once more there was no departure. It appears to me that during the three months there was the phenomenon of one "resting in Love".[1] After the three months it was attained by effort.[2] Is it so?

Answer. After attainment there would be no effort, but after a while it might be that again there was a departure. (Reply to Ch'ên An Ch'ing.)

[1] See Analects, IV, ii (p. 29).
[2] Cf. D.M., p. 277.

THE PHILOSOPHY OF
HUMAN NATURE

BOOK VII

BEING BOOK XLVIII OF
THE COMPLETE WORKS OF CHU HSI

———

LOVE AND RIGHTEOUSNESS

LOVE, RIGHTEOUSNESS, REVERENCE, AND WISDOM

LOVE, RIGHTEOUSNESS, REVERENCE, WISDOM, AND SINCERITY

———

SINCERITY

INGENUOUSNESS AND TRUTH

INGENUOUSNESS AND SYMPATHY

SEDATENESS AND SERIOUSNESS

BOOK VII

LOVE AND RIGHTEOUSNESS

(FIFTEEN SECTIONS FROM THE " CONVERSATIONS ".)

1. Chao Chih Tao asked for an explanation of Love and Righteousness from the point of view of substance and operation, motion and rest.

Answer. Love certainly is the substance, and Righteousness is the operation ; but Love and Righteousness are each of them both substance and operation in different aspects. Investigate this thoroughly yourself.

2. Love and Righteousness are reciprocally substance and operation, motion and rest. The substance of Love is essentially inert, but its operation is infinite in its pervasive activity. The operation of Righteousness is essentially active, while its substance in every case remains inflexible.[1]

3. The awful majesty of Righteousness is the conserving[2] aspect of Love.

4. When we say that Love pertains to the positive mode, and Righteousness to the negative, the term Love refers to outgoing activity, and the term Righteousness to conservation. On the other hand, Yang Tzŭ's saying, " As actuated by Love he is weak, as actuated by Righteousness

[1] Righteousness, in its operation, varies according to the innumerable varieties of phenomena to be dealt with, but, in each case, there is an inflexible principle on which the phenomenon ought to be treated.

[2] Lit. " gathering in " as in harvest. Righteousness is that element in Love which does not let itself go in wanton sentiment and weak tolerance of wrong. It gathers itself in so that it is strong and true in pure altruism.

he is strong,"[1] expresses a different idea.[2]   The fact is, you cannot say it must be either one or the other ; it depends upon the point of view.

5. The Master, replying to the statement of some difficulties by Shu Chung, said: In Love the substance is strong and its operation weak ; in Righteousness the substance is weak and its operation strong.

Kwang Ch'ing said : From the point of view of the Supreme Ultimate, Love is strong and Righteousness weak.   From the point of view of the Two Modes inherent in the individual thing, the operation of Love is weak and the operation of Righteousness strong.

Answer.   It is so too.   Love contains the idea of flowing movement and activity put forth, but its operation is tender and gentle.   Righteousness contains the idea of deliberation as to what is in accord with right, but its operation is decisive and distinct.

6.   Love and Righteousness are like the Two Modes which are two modes of the one Ether : the positive is the ether in process of expansion, and the negative is the ether after the process of contraction has set in.   Love is Righteousness just as it has come to birth, and Righteousness is Love in retrocession.   The important point is that Love cannot exhaust the whole meaning of Moral Law.   Moral Law is universally diffused in

[1] See 揚 子 法 言, pt. xii, f. 18.   Yang Tzŭ is Yang Chu (揚 朱), the egoist.   The "he" refers to the "noble man", concerning whom Yang Tzŭ has been questioned.

[2] "Weak" refers to the negative mode, and "strong" to the positive, the opposite of what is said in the preceding sentence.

all things ; Love cannot exhaust it, but it can and does
imply it in its full substantive meaning. If we know the
positive we know the negative ; if we know Love we know
Righteousness. When we know the one we know all the
rest.

7. Asked about the statement, "Righteousness is the
material of Love," the Philosopher replied : Righteousness
has the meaning, "to cut off," "to sever"—it is the quality
of decision, after which it sends forth Love in abundance.
"Not to look at anything, listen to anything, say anything,
or do anything inconsistent with right principle,"[1] is the
quality of decision. The passage, "If for one day a man
can master self and return to right principle, the whole
empire will return to Love,"[2] expresses the pervading
activity of Love.

8. *Question.* Mencius regarded solicitude as the
terminal of Love, and conscientiousness as the terminal of
Righteousness. Chou Tzŭ said : "Affection is Love, and
to do what is right is Righteousness."[3] But, from the
subjective point of view, while it is true that solicitude and
affection are the outflow of a mind actuated by Love, conscientiousness is shame at what is unrighteous ; that is, it
is a negative expression, and does not refer directly to
the terminal of Righteousness. The word "right", again,
refers to objective phenomena. What then is the actual
meaning of Righteousness as it is subjectively ?

---

[1] Analects, XII, 1, 2 (p. 114) ; cf. p. 201 of this volume.

[2] Ibid., XII, i, 1 (p. 114).

[3] Quoted from the "T'ung Shu", see 學 案, pt. ii, f. 4.

Answer. Subjective Righteousness is the determinate decision in favour of what is objectively right.

9. Righteousness is like a sharp knife severing many bonds.

10. Righteousness is like a sword held horizontally, by which every phenomenon as it presents itself is cut in two, as may be illustrated in the statements, "The noble man considers Righteousness to be essential,"[1] "He considered Righteousness to be of the highest importance,"[2] "Righteousness requires that he should not eat,"[3] "Righteousness requires that he should not ride,"[4] "When we have a fine discrimination of the rightness of things,[5] so that we enter into the inscrutable and spirit-like in them, we attain to the largest practical application of them."[6] That is, to be perfectly practised in righteousness is to perceive the practical use of things.

11. From the definition of Love as the virtue of the mind[7] it follows that Love includes the four virtues. But in the definition of Righteousness as the law of the mind the reference is to Righteousness only.

Answer. That is correct.

[1] Analects, XV, xvii (p. 163).
[2] Ibid., XVII, xxiii (p. 193).
[3] *Yi Ching*, p. 311.
[4] Ibid., p. 295.
[5] This rendering differs from Legge's, but a gloss quoted in the Imperial Commentary gives this meaning of 義. The gloss reads: 義者。事理之宜也. The context here certainly requires this meaning rather than that given by Legge.
[6] Ibid., p. 390.

[7] Cf. p. 328.

12. *Question*. The expression, "The virtue of the mind," refers comprehensively to the entire substance of all the virtues, while "The principle of affection" refers particularly to the single substance of one virtue ; and, although we use the word substance, its operation is also included. The expression, "Law of the mind," refers to subjective Righteousness, and "Oughtness of an act" to objective Righteousness ; and so the subjective and objective are united.[1]

Answer. The expression, "Law of the mind," also refers to the entire substance of Righteousness, and "Oughtness of an act" to the fact that in all the countless ramifications of phenomena which present themselves to us there is inherent in every single thing the principle on which it "ought" to be dealt with. Nor does the expression refer to external things only ; whatever it is that presents itself to us, there is some duty embedded in it ; and [the performance of] that duty is Righteousness.

The Philosopher then referred to I Ch'uan's statement, "From the point of view of the object, it is Law ; from the point of view of my conduct in relation to the object, it is Righteousness."[2]

The Philosopher further said : Righteousness is like a sharp knife, which will cut through whatever presents itself : it is not the cutting of the knife but the knife itself that is Righteousness.

13. The universe consists of one Ether which divides into the negative and positive modes, and, because it is

[1] D.M., p. 283.   [2] 粹言, pt. 1, f. 6.

by the interaction of these two modes that all things are produced, all phenomena assume the aspect of relativity. Heaven is contrasted with earth, life with death, speech with silence, activity with repose, because the source [1] from which they spring itself contains this principle of relativity. Hence of the four virtues two only are mentioned, corresponding to the Two Modes; and for the same reason we find it stated that, " In representing the Law of Heaven they used the terms ' Negative ' and ' Positive,' and in representing the Law of Man they used the terms ' Love and Righteousness '." [2]

14. With regard to the correlative terms " Negative and Positive ", " Weak and Strong ", " Love and Righteousness " : it would seem as if the order should be Righteousness and Love, because Love should correspond to the positive. If Love be not positive and strong, how could it exercise so much creative power ? Although Righteousness is strong it is self-conserving, while Love is self-imparting. This again is the negative enfolded within the positive and the positive within the negative, each containing hidden within it the root of the other. Or take the manner in which men act to-day in regard to rewards and punishments : if it is a case of reward the deed is done at once and without hesitation, but if it is a case of punishment by death there is delay, hesitation, and an unwillingness to decide. There is a case of the self-imparting of the positive mode and the retraction of the negative, of the

[1] The " source " is the Two Modes, which, as negative and positive, themselves contain the " principle of contrariety ".

[2] *Yi Ching*, p. 423.

affinity of Love and Righteousness for the positive and negative modes respectively.

15. Ch'ên Chung Wei[1] asked: Kuei Shan said, "As one in principle it is Love, as diverse in function it is Righteousness."[2] Does this mean that Love is the substance and Righteousness its operation?

Answer. Love is simply the flowing forth; Righteousness lies in its obligation to flow in a particular direction. Like water, the flowing movement of which is Love; its flow as rivers, or its collection in pools and ponds, is Righteousness. The feeling of solicitude is Love, the difference in the varying degrees of affection due to parents, to brothers, to neighbours, and to friends and acquaintances, is Righteousness. Again, respectfulness is but one, but there are many different ways of showing respect, dependent upon whether it is accorded to the sovereign, or to elders, or to sages. So also with Reverence: "The ancestral temple of the Son of Heaven embraced seven shrines, the temple of the prince of a state embraced five shrines";[3] this was Reverence, but the question whether it should be seven or five shrines belongs to Righteousness. Reverence is the grace of Law, and Righteousness is the oughtness of actions. Lü Yü Shu said: "The meaning of the dictum, "The Decree of Heaven is what we term the Nature"[4] may be expressed thus: That the nine clans

---

[1] Ch'ên Chung Wei, *style* Chêng Kuang (政 廣), was a native of Shui Yang (瑞 陽); he held important offices under the Government, but, owing to an unsuccessful accusation against Chia Ssŭ Tao, a tyrannical and traitorous Prime Minister, he retired into private life.

[2] 學 案, pt. xxv. f. 10.   [3] *Li Chi*, i, 223.   [4] D.M., p. 247.

have no regrets concerning the differing grades of mourning
clothes ; or that from the palace to the lowest grade of
lictors, there are none who venture to contend in regard to
the differing grades of ceremonial apparel, is because the
Divinely conferred Nature is so." Again, take a home
with ten families : that every father is tender to his son,
and every son filial to his father, and the neighbours all
respect them, is as it should be. The tenderness and the
filialness are Love ; that each son is affectionate to his
own father, and each father tender to his own
child is Righteousness. These things cannot be separated.
In its outflow it is Love, but in the very moment that Love
is called into movement there are present Righteousness,
Reverence, and Wisdom ; it is not that when Love comes
into operation Righteousness remains behind to be set free
after a little while. In a word, it is one principle, but with
many well-marked distinctions.

(FIVE SECTIONS FROM THE " COLLECTED WRITINGS ".)

1.   I have already said that the pervading activity and
manifested operations of the Nature as ordained by Heaven
are manifest in daily life : there is not a moment when it
is not so, there is not a thing into which they do not
enter ; and the great source, the complete substance, from
which they proceed is what we term Love. But within
this, every phenomenon has its own natural distinctive
characteristics ; for example, the four points of the compass, with the zenith and nadir, have their unchangeable
positions, from which they never err by a hair's-breadth.
This   is   what   we   term   Righteousness.   The   " Law

of man "[1] is "represented" by these two only, but these
two are inseparable. Therefore the student in seeking
Love and in perfecting Righteousness will not fail to use
both of them together. In his pursuit of Love his elimination of selfishness and return to Divine Law will be
operative in the sphere of everyday life. In perfecting
Righteousness his discrimination between the true and
false and between what is lawful and not lawful will be
applied to every thought. For there is nothing that does
not come within the scope of Divine Law and man's mind,
of substance and its operation, and which cannot be regarded as having distinctions. Mencius said to the King
of Ch'i : "By weighing we know what things are light and
what heavy. By measuring we know what things are long
and what short. The relations of all things may be thus
determined, and it is of the greatest importance to estimate
the motions of the mind. I beg your Majesty to measure
it."[2] Here indeed is the method by which to seek Love,
and the foundation of the practice of Righteousness!
Mencius truly possessed the secret of knowing the right
thing to say![3] (Reply to Chiang Yüan Shih.)

2. *Question.* Yu Tzŭ considered filial piety and
fraternal submission to be the foundation of Love.[4]
Mencius regarded serving one's parents as Love and serving
one's older brother as Righteousness.[5] What is the
explanation of this discrepancy ? Is it not to be found in

[1] Referring to the passage in the *Yi Ching* quoted in the *T'ai Chi T'u Shuo*, see J. P. Bruce, *Introduction to Chu Hsi and the Sung School*, chap. vi.
[2] Mencius, p. 20.　　[3] Ibid., pp. 65, 67.
[4] Analects, I, ii, 2 (p. 3).　　[5] Mencius, p. 332.

this : The school of Confucius in their discussion of Love included the operation in the substance, and this is what is termed Love in its comprehensive sense ; while Mencius when he used the word Love always contrasted it with its correlative Righteousness, that is, he used it in its narrow sense. In serving one's parents all that is needed is to be ruled by affection. Righteousness is the duty of affection. When we extend to our elders the affection with which we serve our parents, and so fulfil the duty of such affection, then the Law of Love is in operation.

Answer. Your explanation is correct. (Reply to Wu Po Fêng.)

3. Seeing that Love is the principle of affection, it is evident that Righteousness is the principle of obligation, because both are the original substance preceding the manifestation and affection and duty are their operation. You, however, say that Righteousness is the obligation of Law,[1] which is to make Righteousness the manifestation of the original substance, and comes near, does it not, to the error of making Love subjective and Righteousness objective (Reply to Chiang Shu Ch'üan.)

4. The practice of Righteousness is by the operation of Love, therefore the student must constantly preserve this mind ;[2] thus only will he be able thoroughly to estimate the principles of things. If not, there will be no controlling

[1] The word here translated " Law " is 理, the same as that rendered " principle " above. Note the play upon the two words 宜 and 理 in the expressions 宜 之 理 and 理 之 宜, the law or principle of obligation, and the obligation of Law or right principle.

[2] That is, Love.

faculty in the mind, and he will be unable to estimate right and wrong or to fulfil his duty in life. This is why the school of Confucius always puts the pursuit of Love first. For Love is the source of all things and the foundation of all things, and therefore the understanding and nurture of Love must be put before everything else ; then only shall we secure our starting point. (Reply to Li Yüan Han.)

5. *Question.* Yu Tzŭ considered filial piety and fraternal submission to be the root of Love.[1] Mencius distinguishes between serving one's parents and obedience to one's elder brother, regarding the one as the fruit of Love, and the other as the fruit of Righteousness.[2] Is respectful submission the determining factor in Righteousness, or the inherent rightness of things ?

Answer. If right is made the determining factor, respectful submission will be included in it. (Reply to Lin Tê Chiu.)

LOVE, RIGHTEOUSNESS, REVERENCE, AND WISDOM

(TEN SECTIONS FROM THE " CONVERSATIONS ".)

1. *Question.* How would you classify Love, Righteousness, Reverence, and Wisdom, according to their substance and operation ?

Answer. Their classification may be seen from their relation to the Two Modes ; Love and Reverence are positive, Righteousness and Wisdom are negative ; the former

[1] Analects, I, i, 2 (p. 3).   [2] Mencius, p. 189.

are operation, the latter are substance. Spring and summer are positive, autumn and winter are negative. According to this dual classification of Love and Righteousness, the originating[1] season of spring and the growing season of summer are Love, the gathering-in season of autumn and the storing season of winter are Righteousness. Described in terms of the four, spring is Love, summer is Reverence, autumn is Righteousness, and winter is Wisdom. Love and Reverence are centrifugal and give out. Righteousness is stern and incisive, Wisdom stores up, as a man stores up many things in his mind so that they are invisible, and the greater his wisdom the more deeply they are stored. This accords exactly with the passage in the *Yi*, " In representing the Law of Heaven they used the terms ' Negative ' and ' Positive ', in representing the Law of Earth they used the terms ' Weak ' and ' Strong ', in representing the Law of Man they used the terms ' Love ' and ' Righteousness '." [2] The commentators as a rule regard Love as weak and Righteousness as strong ; but this is a mistake, it is Love that is strong and Righteousness weak. For the movement of Love is outward, and so is inflexible and forceful ; Righteousness gathers in, its movement is inward, and so appears externally as weak.

2. *Question.* Love and Reverence are positive and forceful ; Righteousness and Wisdom are negative and

---

[1] 作 is equivalent to 生, "to produce." Spring is the season in which life has its beginning.

[2] *Yi Ching*, p. 423.

yielding. Righteousness is divisive, its sphere is determined, its idea is that of gathering in, and naturally is negative and yielding. But how could you describe Wisdom ?

Answer. Wisdom is still more devisive, its idea of gathering-in is still more prominent ; for example, you know a thing to be true or you know it to be false. You know it and that ends it, it has no further function, differing in this respect from the other three. Wisdom knows, and then hands on the matter to the other three, solicitude, conscientiousness, and courtesy ; so that its gathering-in quality is more keen even than that of Righteousness.

3. The inclusion of the three in Love is in this way : Righteousness, Reverence, and Wisdom all have flowing movement and therefore are gradually evolved from Love. Love and Wisdom, Origin and Potentiality, are the phenomena of the beginning and end ; and these two termini are in each case the most important of the four principles, as we see in the diagrams K'an and Chên, in which all things take their rise and find their consummation, while Kên is the connecting point between them.[1]

4. Wei Tao[2] asked: Love includes Righteousness,

---

[1] *Yi Ching*, pp. 425-6 ; see Legge's note on p. 426.

[2] Surnamed Yeh (葉), *style* Chih Tao (知 道), a native of Wên Chou (温 州). Yeh Wei Tao was a keen student of literature. After taking his degree of Chin Shih he accepted the post of teacher in a college at Ê Chou (諤 州). In response to inquiries made by the Emperor Li Tsung concerning Chu Hsi's pupils, Wei Tao was mentioned as one of the most prominent, and the title of Doctor of the Imperial Academy was conferred upon him. He was the author of several works on the Classics.

Reverence, and Wisdom ; solicitude includes conscientiousness, courtesy, and moral insight ; the Principle
of Origin includes Beauty, Utility, and Potentiality, and
spring includes summer, autumn, and winter. What I do
not understand is how, of the Five Agents, Wood includes
Fire, Metal, and Water.

Answer. Wood is the vital ether by which things have
life ; apart from this vital ether, Fire, Metal and Water
could not possibly exist ; this is how it is that Wood
includes the other three.

5. The Four Terminals are like the Four Virtues ; if
we take them individually there is a line of demarcation
between each ; if we classify them, Love and Righteousness form the main divisions. Hence it is said : " Love
is man's Mind, Righteousness is man's path."[1] In the
same way the section on Ch'ien in the "Fourth
Appendix"[2] refers to them in one place as the "Four
Virtues" ;[3] and in another place says, "The Principle
of Origin represented by Ch'ien is what gives their
beginning to all things, and secures their growth and
development. The principles of Utility and Potentiality
refer to the Nature and Feelings."[4]

6. Chêng Ch'un, speaking of the four principles of the
Nature, said that they alternately control and are sub-
sidiary to each other, but that they are united under the
headship of Love and Wisdom. In the statement,
" Respectfulness without Reverence becomes laborious

[1] Mencius, p. 290.
[2] The Fourth Appendix of the *Yi Ching*.
[3] *Yi Ching*, p. 408.
[4] Ibid., p. 415.

bustle," [1] Reverence is regarded as the controlling principle. In the statement, " The noble man in everything considers Righteousness to be essential ",[2] Righteousness is regarded as the controlling principle.   For the Four Virtues are never separated.   In contact with affairs they are severally manifested as in reciprocal relation. Let a man silently meditate upon this and he will understand it.

Answer. What you say is true.

7.   The word " Love " must be taken in conjunction with Righteousness, Reverence, and Wisdom, if we would understand its true meaning.   Love itself is the original substance of Love, Reverence is Love expressing itself in graceful form, Righteousness is Love in judgment, and Wisdom is Love discriminating.   It is like the difference between the four seasons which all proceed from the Spring. Spring is the birth of the Vital Impulse, summer is the development of the Vital Impulse, autumn is the consummation and winter the storing up of the Vital Impulse. The four are resolved into two, and the two into one, and thus all are united under one head, and gathered into one source.   Therefore it is said : " The Five Agents *resolve into the* one negative and the one positive ether ; the negative and positive ethers *resolve into the* one Supreme Ultimate." [3]

The Philosopher said further : Love is the head of the Four Principles, but Wisdom can be both beginning and

[1] Analects, VIII, ii, 1 (p. 72).

[2] Ibid., XV, xvii (p. 163).

[3] Cited from Chou Tzŭ's *T'ai Chi T'u Shuo* ; see J. P. Bruce, *Introduction to Chu Hsi and the Sung School*, chap. vii·

end, just as the Principle of Origin is the head of the Four Attributes, but has its source not in the Principle of Origin, but in the Principle of Potentiality.[1] For unless the transforming influences of the universe are gathered into unity they cannot be sent forth and diffused. In the conjunction of Love and Wisdom [3] is the very pivot of the myriad transformations. The revolutions of this principle are endless, the union is never dissolved. Therefore, if there were no Potentiality there could be no Origin.

8. Reverence is the going forth of Love, Wisdom is the storing up of Righteousness. If we extend this thought to men's natural dispositions, we shall find that the gentle and honest disposition is generally humble and courteous, while the man who knows everything is sharp and exacting.

9. The feeling of solicitude is solicitude from beginning to end ; the other three are solicitude in the beginning but end as conscientiousness, courtesy and moral insight respectively. Without solicitude these three are dead, because solicitude is the fountain-head from which the other three proceed.

10. Love and Reverence represent the idea of giving out life, Righteousness and Wisdom represent the idea of gathering in.

(THREE SECTIONS FROM THE "COLLECTED WRITINGS".)

1. Hsiao Shu, having noticed the Master's reply to Secretary Hwang's question on the classification of the

[1] As the spring grows out of winter.
[2] Love grows out of Wisdom as spring out of winter.

Four Virtues according as they are forceful or yielding,[1] said : They are described both separately and altogether. My views on them separately I have already handed to you. As to the statement of them taken together, my understanding of them is that when in operation some are active and some inactive, and from this point of view Love and Reverence are forceful, and Righteousness and Wisdom are yielding. But if we consider what really constitutes them the Four Virtues, then Love is the mind that cannot bear to see suffering, and seems to have the idea of gentleness and yielding ; while Reverence has its fixed and unchangeable grades, and seems to be negative and finely discriminating. Is there not then, in the case of these two, a yielding within their forcefulness. Righteousness again in its decisive judgment and rigid[2] sternness seems to have the idea of strong decision; Wisdom in its unimpeded comprehensive flow seems to have the idea of the positive mode and of activity. Is there not, in the case of these two, a forcefulness within their yielding ? Whence it may be seen that the negative and the positive modes are never separate. I do not know if this is correct.

Answer. I fancy that what I said at the time was that dividing them are four and uniting them are two. But expressed in your way the idea is the same ; it is the same as in the statement, " Water is negative and has its root

---

[1] See p. 398, section 2.

[2] 方 is " square ", and so " rigid ", in that it cannot be rolled along the ground as a " round " object can.

in the positive, Fire is positive and has its root in the negative."[1] (Reply to Li Hsiao Shu.)

2. The Nature is the all-comprehensive substance of the Supreme Ultimate, and in its essence is undefinable ; but within it are innumerable principles which are summed up in four leading comprehensive principles. To these, then, the names Love, Righteousness, Reverence, and Wisdom are given. The school of Confucius did not give full expression to this aspect of the question ; it was Mencius who first elaborated it, the reason being that in the time of Confucius the doctrine of the goodness of the Nature was not in question. But although Confucius did not enunciate the doctrine in detail, his statement was none the less complete. In the time of Mencius, heresies sprang up like bees in swarms, and the goodness of the Nature was repeatedly denied. Mencius was concerned lest this truth should be obscured, and considered how he might make it clear. If the all-comprehensive entire substance alone had been stated, the fear was that it would be like a steel-yard with no marks to indicate the different weights, or a foot-rule without inches, and in this way he would be unable to make the meaning clear to people generally ; he therefore found other language to express the truth, marking off its fourfold distinctions. This was the beginning of the doctrine of the Four Terminals. For even before their manifestation, the Nature, though "still and without movement",[2] is not a vague empty nothingness, but comprises an orderly framework of principles, so that when

---

[1] See 精 義, pt. i, f. 7.   [2] *Yi Ching*, p. 370.

acted upon by the external world there is an immediate
subjective response ; as when men " see a child fall into
a well "[1] there is the response of the principle of Love,
and the feeling of solicitude assumes visible form.   Or
if we appear at a temple, or before the Throne, there is
the response of the principle of Reverence, and the feeling
of respect assumes visible form.   For from within, all
principles proceed, comprehensive and complete, each one
perfectly clear and distinct, so that whatever we meet with
in our environment we are affected by it and respond to
it.   Thus the Four Terminals in their going forth have
each its different manifestation.   Mencius therefore
analysed the Nature into these four, and taught the student
to recognize that within the all-comprehensive complete
substance there is a marvellous orderliness from which
the goodness of the Nature may be known.   But before the
manifestation of the Four Terminals, the all-comprehensive complete substance is imperceptible by any of the
senses ; how then can its marvellous orderliness be
known ?   The answer is, the investigation of these principles is possible in their manifestation.   Everything that
exists has its source and root.   Although the principles
of the Nature are invisible, their manifestation in the
Terminals is fully capable of investigation.   So that from
solicitude we may surely infer the existence of Love, and
similarly we can infer Righteousness from conscientiousness, Reverence from respectfulness, and Wisdom from
moral insight.   If there were no such inward principles,
how could there be the visible terminals ?   From the visible

[1] Mencius, p. 78.

terminal we unhesitatingly infer the inward principle. Therefore Mencius said : "If we look at the Feelings which flow from the Nature, we may know that they are constituted for the practice of what is good."[1]   This is what Mencius meant in saying that the Nature is good, for we know it by tracing the Feelings back to their source. Having clearly understood the distinction between these four principles, it was necessary to understand further that, of these four, Love and Righteousness stand to one another in the position of correlatives. For Love is Love, but Reverence is the manifestation of Love ; Righteousness is Righteousness, but Wisdom is hidden Righteousness ; just as there are four seasons, but spring and summer belong to the positive mode, and autumn and winter to the negative. Hence it is said : " In representing the Law of Heaven they used the terms ' Negative ' and ' Positive ', in representing the Law of Earth they used the terms ' Weak ' and ' Strong ', and in representing the Law of Man they used the terms ' Love ' and ' Righteousness '."[2]   From this we may know that apart from the principle of duality the Law of Heaven and Earth could not be set forth ; therefore, though there are four principles, they are represented by the two.   And although Love and Righteousness thus stand to one another in the position of correlatives, and so we have the two, Love nevertheless permeates and unites all the four.   For "in the narrow sense Love is only one, but in the comprehensive sense it includes the four". Therefore Love itself is the original substance of Love,

[1] Mencius, p. 278.   [2] Yi Ching, p. 423.

Reverence is Love expressing itself in graceful form,
Righteousness is Love in judgment, and Wisdom is Love
discriminating. It is like the four seasons which, though
they differ one from another, all proceed from the spring.
Spring is the birth of spring, summer is the growth of
spring, autumn is its consummation, and winter is the
storing up of spring. From the four we arrive at two,
and from the two at the one ; thus all are united under
one head and gathered into one source. Hence it is said :
" The Five Agents *resolve into the* one negative and the
one positive ether ; the negative and positive ethers *resolve
into the* one Supreme Ultimate." [1] This assuredly is the
Law of Heaven and Earth.[2] Love includes the four principles and the place of Wisdom is at the end of the four ;
for winter is the storage season " in which all things take
their rise and find their consummation." [3] Wisdom has
the idea of storage, together with that of the end and the
beginning. Thus solicitude, conscientiousness and respectfulness, all have something to perform, while wisdom itself
does nothing ; its province is simply to distinguish
between what is true and what is false—whence we get
the expression " hidden stores ". Again, solicitude, conscientiousness, and respectfulness each have but one aspect,
while moral insight has two. Seeing that it distinguishes
what is true, it also distinguishes what is false ; and in
this we have an image of the consummation and the

[1] Quoted from Chou Tzŭ's *T'ai Chi T'u Shuo* ; see J. P. Bruce, *Introduction to Chu Hsi and the Sung School*, chap. vii.

[2] Referring to a later paragraph in the *T'ai Chi T'u Shuo* ; ibid.

[3] See p. 399.

beginning of all things. Therefore Love is the head of the four principles, while Wisdom can be both beginning and end.[1] It is like the Originating Ether which, although the premier attribute, still does not spring from the principle of Origin, but from Potentiality ; for unless the transforming influences of Heaven and Earth are gathered into unity they cannot be sent forth and diffused. This is an unmistakable principle. In the conjunction of Love and Wisdom is the very pivot of the myriad transformations. The revolutions of this principle are endless, the union is never dissolved. This it is that Ch'êng Tzŭ refers to when he speaks of Motion and Rest as alternating without an end, and of the two Modes as alternating without a beginning.[2]   (Reply to Ch'ên Ch'i Chih.)

3.   *Question.* Of the four attributes of Ch'ien, to regard Potentiality as corresponding to winter does not raise any difficulty in my mind, but of man's four virtues to regard Wisdom as corresponding to winter seems to me not clear. How can the labour of the whole year, the consummation of all things, be fully represented in winter as the clear discrimination of Wisdom ?

Answer. The ruling characteristics of Wisdom are storing up and discriminating ; it has intelligence but no activity, and this is the phenomenon of winter. (Reply to Miu Tzŭ Hui.)

[1] Cf. p. 401.
[2] 粹 言, pt. i, f. 11.

LOVE, RIGHTEOUSNESS, REVERENCE, WISDOM, AND SINCERITY

(THREE SECTIONS FROM THE "CONVERSATIONS".)

1. Someone asked.: How is it that to the four virtues of the Nature, another, Sincerity, is added, the whole number being termed the Five Nature-Principles ?

Answer. Sincerity gives reality to[1] the four, so that Love has a real existence, and Righteousness has a real existence, and Reverence and Wisdom. It is like Earth, one of the Five Agents ; if there were no Earth, there would be nothing to contain the other four.[2] Again, it is like the sphere of Earth in the Four Seasons ; it rules as sojourner for eighteen days in each of them,[3] or if you

---

[1] 誠 實 is used in a verbal sense, " to make real."

[2] Earth is the field in which Water, Fire, Metal, and Wood, have their existence, the " mother " as it were of them all—as of course is the case in the physical sphere.

[3] The Four Agents Wood, Fire, Metal, and Water, correspond respectively to the Four Seasons, Spring, Summer, Autumn, and Winter, and to the Four Virtues, Love, Reverence, Righteousness, and Wisdom. In the case both of the Virtues and of the Agents there is a fifth, viz : Earth and Sincerity. But there is no fifth season. How then is the analogy carried out ? In the case of the Virtues, Sincerity qualifies all the rest, i.e. gives *reality* to them. In the case of the Agents, similarly, Earth is regarded as the ground of existence for the rest : and of the seasons, while they are ruled respectively by Wood, Fire, Metal, and Water, Earth enters into all as the ruling Agent for the last eighteen days each season. The summer season, however, is regarded as specially related to Earth and is called its own special sphere (lit. original home. 本 宮). Thus while Earth " rules " in all seasons, the Spring, Autumn, and Winter are not its special sphere.

say that it rules absolutely in the Wu Chi days,[1] that is because its own special sphere is the summer,[2] and it is therefore more powerful in that season. The phrase in the *Yüeh Ling*, " Right in the middle is Earth," refers to this.[3]

2. *Question.* Recently, in your weighty instruction on the meaning of Love, you said : " You must neither put it in the place of, nor must you eliminate it from Righteousness, Reverence, Wisdom, and Sincerity ; then you will understand the sense in which it unites the Five Virtues." You, excellent sir, now use the tree as an illustration ; but, while the vitality resides in the root of a tree, can you, in view of the organic union prevailing throughout, say that the branches and twigs, flowers and leaves, are without this vitality ?

Answer. Certainly not. It is just like the Four Seasons. Spring corresponds to Love, and is characterized by the Vital Impulse ; in the Summer we see its persistent and permeating principle ; in the Autumn we see it perfecting the fruit ; and in winter we see its correctness and strength. In all four seasons there is no cessation of the Vital Impulse ; even though the leaves fall and are scattered, the Vital Impulse is still there. The fact is, there is but one Law in the universe, but it has various

[1] There are certain days in which each Agent is specially powerful. They are, in the case of each Agent, represented by those Celestial Stems which form the combination to which their Agent specially corresponds ; thus : Wood corresponds to 甲 乙, Fire to 丙 丁, Earth to 戊 己 [*wu chi*] Metal to 庚 辛, and Water to 壬 癸.

[2] See p. 409, n. 3.

[3] See *Li Chi*, p. 280 ; and the note on pp. 281-2.

names in accordance with its different manifestations. Each of the Four Virtues corresponds to one of the Five Agents ;[1] but Sincerity is the one which corresponds to Earth, the one by which we know that the Four Principles, Love, Righteousness, Reverence, and Wisdom, have a real existence and are not mere figments of the imagination. Again, it is like the Four Attributes of Ch'ien, of which Origin is the chief, and next to it is Potentiality as revealing the meaning of the end and beginning. Apart from the Principle of Origin there could be no birth, apart from the Principle of Potentiality there could be no end, apart from an ending there would be no means of making a beginning, and without a beginning the end could never be consummated, and so on in endless revolution. This is what is referred to in the sentence, " The sages grandly understood the connexion between the end and the beginning."[2]

3. In the "investigation of principles", the principles are to be sought for in one's own person. They are none other than Love, Righteousness, Reverence, and Wisdom. Look at all the myriad transformations and you will find nothing without these four principles. You, sir, need only to examine the common affairs of daily life, and you will find that there is nothing without them. As to Sincerity, it is so called as expressing the reality of the existence of the other four. Sincerity is reality, and reality means

[1] The numbers "four" and "five" are as in the original text. Strictly speaking, the Virtues and Agents are said to be four or five according as sincerity and earth are included or not ; but the numbers are often, as here, used loosely.

[2] See *Yi Ching*, p. 213.

that a thing IS. In terms of the substance, there really are Love, Righteousness, Reverence, and Wisdom. In terms of their operation, there really are solicitude, conscientiousness, respectfulness, and moral insight ; it cannot be that they are counterfeit. Search the universe and where can you find counterfeit Love, counterfeit Righteousness, counterfeit Reverence, or counterfeit Wisdom ? Therefore Sincerity is defined as the expression of the fact that they have a real existence and are not counterfeit.

(THREE SECTIONS FROM THE " COLLECTED WRITINGS ".)

1. The assertion of distinctions between the Five Virtues is to show that the Five Agents in the Nature have each their own individual characteristics, which must be distinguished without separating them. You must not say that prior to being affected by the external world there are no distinctions, and that subsequently there are. You will get the true idea from Ch'êng Tzŭ's section beginning "Void like the boundless desert".[1] (Reply to Lin Tê Chin.)

2. My former letter dealt with the doctrine that Love, Righteousness, Reverence, and Wisdom correspond severally to the Five Agents and the Four Seasons. This is the ancient doctrine of the early Confucianists, and is not to be regarded lightly. Although your recent letter does not go so far as to depreciate it, yet, fearing that my letter did not fully explain the most important part of this truth, I feel that I must exhaustively investigate the subject

[1] See p. 297.

for you. For in the whole universe there is but one Ether, dividing into the negative and positive modes, and so becoming two entities; the positive therefore is Love, and the negative is Righteousness. But the two modes again divide each into two. The positive mode therefore in its beginning is Wood, Spring, and Love; in its fullness it becomes Fire, Summer, and Reverence ; the negative mode in its beginning is Metal, Autumn, and Righteousness; at its extreme it becomes Water, Winter, and Wisdom. For no sooner does the solicitude of Love proceed from within than the respectfulness of Reverence manifests itself outwardly in all its fulness ; no sooner does the conscientiousness proceeding from Righteousness penetrate from without inwards, than Wisdom's moral insight in its completeness conceals itself within. Therefore, since the phenomena are of this nature, it is manifest that the comparison is not false nor the generalization exaggerated. If you quietly think it over in your own mind you will see that it is so. The same reasoning applies to the Four Ultimata. If you collectively examine all the classical passages it will be still more obvious, and you will see that it is not merely the recent hypothesis of my insignificant self. Of the Five Agents, the four have each their counterpart, but earth placed at the centre [1] is the ground of the other four agents, the ruling factor in the Four Seasons. This in man is Sincerity and has

[1] Cf. p. 409-10 and notes. In the order of etherial production, Earth comes in the centre of the Five Agents; thus: Wood, Fire, EARTH, Metal, Water. These in the same order, with the exception of Earth, correspond to the seasons, Wood to Spring, Fire to Summer, Metal to Autumn, and Water to Winter, while Earth rules in all.

the meaning of reality ; it is the ground of the Four Virtues, the ruling factor in all good. (The five notes, five colours, five flavours, five odours, five organs, and five creeping things, are all classified in the same way).[1]   For Heaven and Man are one, the subjective and objective are one Law, flowing and permeating in organic union so that there is no separating barrier.   Not to realize this means that though living in the universe we are ignorant of the law of that universe's existence ; though possessed of the form and countenance of a man, we are ignorant of the very principles which make us to be man.   This doctrine therefore very closely concerns us, its importance is even greater than that of the doctrines discussed in my former letter ; it is not merely a collection of insignificant items.   (Reply to Yüan Chi Chung.)

3.   Ch'êng Kung asked : The Book of the Analects treats chiefly of Love, while Mencius combines Love and Righteousness.   It seems to me that Confucius was speaking of the primordial Ether, while Mencius spoke of its Two Modes, and I should say that Love is the substance and Righteousness is the operation.

[1] The " five notes " which compose the Chinese musical scale are 角, 徵, 宮, 商, 羽, Chio, Ch'ih, Kung, Shang, and Yü, corresponding to the notes of the Western scale with the omission of the subdominant and leading notes.   The " five colours " are 青, 赤, 黃, 白, 黑, blue, red, yellow, white, and black   The " five flavours " are 酸, 苦, 甘, 辛, 鹹, sour, acrid, sweet, bitter, and salt.   The " five odours " are 羶, 焦, 香, 腥, 朽, rank, scorched, fragrant, frowzy, and rotten.   The " five organs " are 脾, 肺, 心, 肝, 腎, spleen, lungs, heart, liver, and kidneys.   The " five creeping things " are 鱗, 羽, 倮, 毛, 介, scaly, feathered, bare-skinned, hairy, and shell-covered. See the *Yüeh Ling*, Book IV in the *Li Chi*, *Sacred Books of the East*, vol. xxvii.

The Master said : The language of Confucius and Mencius had its similarities and dissimilarities which ought certainly to be explained. But what we need to concern ourselves about now is to understand what Love is, and what Righteousness is. When we understand these two terms, clearly distinguishing their respective meanings,[1] and so obtain the means of using our efforts in the sphere of our own duty, then we shall be in a position to discuss the similarities and differences in the language of the two sages. If we do not understand these two terms, and are negligent of our duty, of what advantage will it be to us in the affairs of life to be able to talk oracularly about the language of the sages, and how shall we expound the ethical principles embodied in these two words ? In substance the doctrine is this : Heaven, in the creation of all things, endowed each with its own Nature. But the Nature is not a material thing ; it is a principle inherent in me. Therefore that which gives to the Nature a substantive existence consists of Love, Righteousness, Reverence, Wisdom, and Sincerity—these five, and the principles of the whole universe, are included in them. Han Wên Kung [2] said that there are five principles which constitute man's Nature, and his statement was very true. But his doctrine was by later teachers of philosophy mixed with the doctrines of Buddhism and Taoism, and so the Nature came to be regarded as equivalent to Consciousness and Intelligence, differing from the original trend of the doctrine of the Nature as taught by the saints and sages.

---

[1] 義 理 here means " meaning and principles ".
[2] The Philosopher Han Yü.

Of these five, that which we term Sincerity is the principle of reality ; as in the case of Love, Righteousness, Reverence, and Wisdom, they are all real, with nothing false in them. Therefore there is no need to say anything further on the term Sincerity. But there are differences between the other four terms which must be distinguished. For Love is the principle of mild gentleness and kindly affection. Righteousness is the principle of judgment and decision ; Reverence is the principle of respectfulness and reserve ; Wisdom is the principle of discrimination between right and wrong. The possession of the whole of these four is what constitutes the original substance of the Nature. Before their going forth they are illimitable and invisible ; after their going forth into operation Love becomes solicitude, Righteousness conscientiousness, Reverence respectfulness, and Wisdom moral insight, manifesting themselves according to circumstances, each having its ramifications, but without confusion. These are what we term the Feelings. Therefore Mencius said, " Solicitude is the terminal of Love, conscientiousness is the terminal of Righteousness, respectfulness is the terminal of Reverence, and moral insight is the terminal of Wisdom." [1] When they are called terminals it is as though there were things within which are invisible, and it is only by means of threads put forth and manifested externally that we are able to trace their existence. For within the one mind the Four Virtues have each their lines of demarcation ; and their nature-principles and feelings, substance and operation, also have their respective differences. These

[1] Mencius, p. 79.

must be clearly understood, and afterwards within these four we shall recognize the larger distinction between Love and Righteousness ; just as the creations and transformations of Heaven and Earth, the course of the seasons, do not really go beyond the one negative and one positive mode. After we have clearly apprehended this, we must follow it up by understanding the term Love, which represents the Vital Impulse permeating and flowing in the midst of the four. Love itself is the original substance of Love, Righteousness is Love in judgment, Reverence is Love expressing itself in graceful form, Wisdom is Love discriminating. Just as in the case of the vital ether of spring which permeates the Four Seasons : spring is the birth of life, summer is its growth, autumn is the retraction, and winter the storing up of life. The idea, therefore, is expressed exactly in Ch'êng Tzŭ's statement : " The Principle of Origin of the Four Attributes corresponds to Love in the Five Cardinal Virtues ; in the narrow sense it is but one, in the comprehensive sense it includes the four." When Confucius spoke only of Love he was speaking of it in its comprehensive sense, and, though he spoke only of Love, the other three, Righteousness, Reverence, and Wisdom, were included in it. Mencius, in speaking of Love and Righteousness in combination, spoke in the narrow sense. But he did not import an additional concept Righteousness into the teaching of Confucius ; he simply made distinctions within the one principle. Again, the further combination of Reverence and Wisdom with these two is similar ; for Reverence is the manifestation of Love, and Wisdom is the storing up of Righteousness, but Love pervades all the four. With regard to substance and operation, there are again two ways of expressing the relation, for from the point of view of Love as subjective, and Righteousness as objective, it is said : " Love is man's mind, and Righteousness is man's path," [1] and so Love and Righteousness are regarded as reciprocally substance and operation. If we discuss it from the point of view of Love corresponding to the feeling of solicitude and Righteousness to conscientiousness, we shall with reference to the one principle, distinguish between before manifestation, when we have its substance, and after manifestation, when we have its operation. If we understand this perfectly, and see it clearly, then, whether we regard it subjectively or objectively,[2] or in any other way, everything will be clear. But we must in daily life use exact investigation, and devote time to it.

Kung [3] asked further: In the time of the Three Dynasties [4] they only spoke of the " Mean " [5] and of " Perfection ".[6] In the replies of Confucius to his questioners he discoursed on what Love is. How do you explain this ?

Answer. The expressions " Mean " and " Perfection " are to-day misunderstood as to their language and meaning, neither have I time just now to explain them in detail.

[1] Mencius, p. 290.

[2] Lit. :} " elegant as fine carving," i.e. carving on the surface, which represents the external or objective, as contrasted with " penetrating inwards ", or the subjective. " In any other way," lit. is : " perpendicularly, horizontally, right way up, or upside down."

[3] Ch'êng Kung, named at the beginning of the section ; see p. 414.

[4] Referring to the Emperors Yao, Shun, and Yü.

[5] See *Shu Ching*, p. 62.

[6] Ibid., pp. 328 ff.

But that it was not till the time of Confucius that the term " Love " was expounded is because the various sages passed on the truth from one to another, so that it was only in his time, and by gradual stages, that it could be expounded clearly. The superiority of Confucius to Yao and Shun may be seen in this among other things. (The Yü Shan Exposition.)

SINCERITY [1]

(TEN SECTIONS FROM THE "CONVERSATIONS".)

1. Ch'êng is reality and also guilelessness. From the Han dynasty downwards it was regarded solely as guilelessness. When Ch'êng Tzŭ appeared he interpreted it as reality, and the scholars who succeeded him dropped the meaning of guilelessness, forgetting that in the *Doctrine of the Mean* both meanings occur ; we must not regard Ch'êng as meaning only reality, and guilelessness as something different from Ch'êng.

2. *Question.* What is meant by saying that the Nature is Truth ? [1]

Answer. The Nature is substantive, Truth is abstract. The word " Nature " is the name of a principle, the word " Truth " is the name of a quality. The Nature is like this fan, Truth is as if to say, it is well made.

---

[1] *Ch'êng* (誠), though a different word from the fifth of the cardinal virtues, which is hsin (信), is similar in meaning, especially in its twofold interpretation of " truth " and " sincerity ". The word Ch'êng, however, is used in a more profound sense than hsin. Ch'êng is the absolute "Truth"; it is that " Sincerity " which is the very foundation of Divine Law, 天 理 之 本 然 ; see D.M., p. 277 and note.

The Philosopher said further : Wu Fêng[1] said, "Truth is the ethical principle of the Decree, the Mean is the ethical principle of the Nature, Love is the ethical principle of the Mind." This statement is excellent in its discrimination. I would, however, prefer the word "virtue" to "ethical principle" as more apt. The expression "ethical principle" does not perfectly fit the meaning.

3. The Master asked his pupils how they would distinguish between Sincerity and Seriousness.

They each quoted Ch'êng Tzŭ's statement[2] as the correct answer.

The Master said : Seriousness is the opposite of wantonness. Sincerity is the opposite of deception.

4. Sincerity is reality. Seriousness is awe.

5. Someone asked : Is Truth the substance and Love its operation ?

Answer. Law is one. As having real existence it is Truth. As to substance, it is the reality of the four principles—Love, Righteousness, Reverence, and Wisdom; as to operation, it is the reality of the four feelings—solicitude, conscientiousness, respectfulness and moral insight. Therefore it is said : "The Five Cardinal Virtues, and the hundred varieties of conduct, apart from Truth have no existence, for thus they would have no reality, and so could not even be named."

6. Some one asked : Is it possible by concentration to attain to Sincerity and Seriousness ?

[1] Hu Wu Fêng, see p. 23, n. 2.   [2] See p. 423.

Answer. Sincerity and Seriousness are not identical.
Sincerity is the principle of reality. It is to be the same
whether before men's faces or behind their backs.   In
doing a thing, to do it perfectly is Sincerity. If we do it
partially, and talk exaggeratedly about how we will do
it, while all the time we are really indifferent as to whether
we do it in this particular way or not—that is the opposite
of Sincerity. Seriousness is to be " cautious and apprehensive ".[1]

7. I Ch'uan said: "Singleness of mind is what is termed
Sincerity, wholeheartedness is what is termed Ingenuousness." I regard ingenuousness as in some respects the
operation of Sincerity ; for example, when we say we
"hate a bad smell, and love what is beautiful ",[2] and in
fact do so completely — that is Sincerity. If we do so
to the extent of only eight or nine-tenths and to the extent
of one-tenth do not, then there is an admixture of the
empty and false, and that is not Sincerity. Ingenuousness
is to be wholehearted, and to be wholehearted is the same
as what I am saying is the explanation of Sincerity ;
therefore I say, Ingenuousness is in some respects the
operation of Sincerity.

8. Singleness of Mind is what is termed Sincerity,
wholeheartedness is what is termed Ingenuousness.
Sincerity is spontaneous reality, apart from any action
accompanying it :[3] it is subjective. Ingenuousness, on

1 D.M., p. 248.
2 G.L., p. 230.
3 Lit. : " but at this point it is as yet unaccompanied by action."

the other hand, is seen in dealing with affairs and things :
it is objective.

9. *Question.* " To be devoid of anything false is the
path of Sincerity." [1] Is the way to seek Sincerity, then,
not to allow any self-deception ?

Answer. He who is devoid of anything false is a saint.
To say that the saint is devoid of anything false is all
right, but you cannot say that the saint must not allow
self-deception.

Question. Is not this just the same as is expressed in the
passage : " Sincerity is the law of Heaven, to think upon
Sincerity and so attain to it is the law of man" ? [2]

Answer. Yes, to be devoid of anything false is spontaneous Sincerity, to allow no self-deception is Sincerity
acquired by effort.

10. Wei Tao [3] asked about the passage : " To be devoid
of anything false is what is termed Sincerity ; not to allow
self-deception is a lower attainment."

Answer. It is not that Sincerity is because of the absence
of the false ; the absence of the false is Sincerity.   The
phrase, " the absence of the false," is all-comprehensive,
taking in the whole sphere of operation, leaving no room
for anything else in opposition to it.   The phrase, " not
to allow self-deception," implies two things in opposition
to each other. [4]

[1] 遺 書, pt. xxi, 下, f. 2.
[2] D.M., p. 277.
[3] See p. 399, n. 2.
[4] That is, I have to make up my mind *not* to deceive ; it is not the
natural spontaneous outcome of the perfect nature.

(Four Sections from the " Collected Writings ".)

1. *Question.* Liu Ch'i Chih asked Wên Kung[1] about the methods of Sincerity. Wên Kung replied: "We should begin by sincerity of speech." Is this not what is meant by the passage in the " Yi Ching" which speaks of " attention to speech and establishing sincerity ".[2]

Answer. It is near it. (Reply to Ch'êng Yün Fu.)

2. *Question.* A student[3] asked me the question : " In the *Literary Remains* it is said, 'Sincerity is followed by Seriousness' ; and of the time before we have reached Sincerity it is said, ' By Seriousness we can attain to Sincerity.' I suppose, then, that the answer to the question : How can I attain to Sincerity ? would be that there is no way so good as to be wholly guided by Seriousness ?" I[4] replied, "'Sincerity is the law of Heaven' ; [5] it may also be expressed as the principle of reality. The man in whom Seriousness is perfected is a sage. To rectify oneself and be inspired by a sense of awe may also be regarded as Seriousness. The learner should use his strength in both these directions."

Answer. Seriousness is apprehension, as if there were something feared. Sincerity is truth, and the utter absence of anything false. The meaning of the two words is

[1] Ssŭ-Ma Kuang, one of whose pupils was Liu An Shih (安 世), *style* Ch'i Chih ; see Giles' Biog. Dict., p. 489.

[2] *Yi Ching*, p. 410.

[3] One of Hu Chi Sui's pupils.

[4] 大 時 (Ta Shih) refers to the questioner himself, viz. : Hu Chi Sui, whose *ming* was Ta Shih ; see p. 22. n. 1.

[5] D.M., p. 277.

different.[1] The sentence, "Sincerity is followed by Seriousness," means : when the motives are sincere the heart
becomes upright. The sentence, "By Seriousness we can
attain to Sincerity," means : although the motives as yet
are not sincere, yet by constant apprehensiveness we shall
become afraid to allow self-deception, and so attain, to
Sincerity. This is what Ch'êng Tzŭ meant. 'Your
questioner had a glimmering of this idea, and was unable
to put it into words ; but your answer misses the point.
(Reply to Hu Chi Sui.)

3. *Question.* What is your opinion of Mr. Lü's[2] statement, "Truth (Ch'êng) is the reality of Law ? "

Answer. The meaning of the word "Ch'êng" is reality,
but its use in the classics differs in different places and cannot be expressed in one definition. For example, as Mr. Lü
uses it here it has the same meaning as in Chou Tzŭ's
saying, "What we speak of as Truth is the foundation of
sainthood,"[3] where the word means reality. In Chou Tzŭ's
saying, "The saint is wholly sincere (Ch'êng),"[4] the
meaning is that in this case the man really possesses this
principle ; as in the phrase in *the Doctrine of the Mean*,
"The individual possessed of the most entire Sincerity
that can exist under Heaven."[5] What Wên Kung[6] speaks
of as ch'êng is what "The Great Learning" refers to in
the phrase, "making the thoughts sincere" ;[7] that is,

[1] Hu Chi Sui makes them parallel.

[2] Probably Lü Yü Shu ; see p. 60, n. 1, but I have not been able to
find the passage quoted.

[3] See *T'ung Shu*, 大 全, pt. ii, chap. i.   [4] Ibid., chap. ii.

[5] D.M., p. 293.   [6] Referred to on p. 423.   [7] G.L., p. 230.

making the heart true and not allowing self-deception.
(Reply to an unnamed questioner.)

4. *Question.* Ch'êng Tzŭ said, "To be devoid of any
thing false is what is termed Sincerity ; not to allow self-
deception is a lower attainment. To be devoid of anything
false is the Sincerity of the saint : not to allow any self-
deception is the Sincerity of the learner."[1] What is your
opinion ?

Answer. This section of Ch'êng Tzŭ's is apparently a
definition of the meaning of the term, and not intended
to define the differing ranks of men. (Reply to Ch'êng
Yün Fu.)

INGENUOUSNESS AND TRUTH
(Twelve Sections from the "Conversations".)

1. Ingenuousness proceeds from within, Truth[2] has
reference to actions. Ingenuousness is the expression of
one's whole heart, Truth is perfect accord with one's
principles.

2. A true heart—this is the citadel[3] for the learner.

[1] 遺 書, pt. xxi, 下, f. 2.

[2] *Chung* (忠) and *hsin* (信) can neither of them be rendered consistently by one English word. The common rendering of *Chung* is
"loyalty", but it has a wider meaning than that word represents, and
in most cases the better rendering is "ingenuousness". Similarly with
hsin, its use is very varied. As has been seen already it is one of
the Five Cardinal Virtues, and as such is perhaps best rendered by the
word "sincerity". Here it is contrasted with "loyalty" or "ingenuousness", and explained as objective ; in this connexion its meaning is sometimes "faithfulness" or "fidelity", but most often "truth" or "truthfulness".

[3] 關 中 is Hsi An, and 河 內 is Honanfu, the ancient Lo Yang, both
former capitals of the Empire. The learner must have a "true heart" as
the *citadel* of his personality if he is to be successful.

He must first obtain this, then only can he succeed in the practice of Sincerity. If he has it not, to preserve the mind is the same as to lose it; how then can there be success? The saying, "He whose goodness is part of himself is a man of truth," [1] exactly expresses this thought.

3. Truth is the evidence of Ingenuousness. Ingenuousness is complete self-expression. [2] Manifested in deeds it becomes Truth, so that Ingenuousness is seen in Truth.

4. Ingenuousness and Truth are one and the same thing. But, as proceeding from the mind in complete self-expression it is Ingenuousness ; as tested by principle and found to be in accord with it, it is Truth. Ingenuousness is the root of Truth, Truth is the outcome of Ingenuousness.

5. Ingenuousness and Truth are one and the same thing but are related to each other, as the subjective and objective, as the source and issue, the root and fruit. Subjectively it is Ingenuousness, objectively it is Truth. You may describe them as one or separately; you will be equally correct.

6. *Question.* Ingenuousness is truth in the heart. In the service of a father it is called filial piety, in the treatment of friends it is called fidelity, it is only in the service

---

[1] Mencius, p. 366.

[2] Cf. section i. The expression 盡 己 means an exhaustive expression of self, either in word or deed, and may be either loyalty, or as is more often the case here, ingenuousness. It is to be " whole-selfed ", if the expression may be allowed, and is parallel to 盡 心, " whole-hearted." It is contrasted with 盡 物, which means " the exhaustive representation of fact ".

of the sovereign that it comes to be called loyalty.[1] Why
is this ?

Answer. In the case of parents, brothers or friends,
the essential principle of their duty is mutual affection ;
whereas, in the case of serving a sovereign, the place of
duty is one of great awe ; and whenever men in this
position act under constraint, it is because their action does
not proceed from sincerity of heart.[2] Therefore this virtue
is expressed by the Sage as " Serving the sovereign with
loyalty." [3]

Question. What is the difference between Ingenuousness and Sincerity ?

Answer. Ingenuousness and Sincerity are both the
principle of reality. Singleness of mind is Sincerity, and
whole-heartedness is Ingenuousness. Sincerity is the
fundamental ruling factor of the mind ; Ingenuousness
is the operation of sincerity, but this operation,
as Ingenuousness, is only subjectively manifested.

7. Someone asked : How are we to compare the complete self-expression of Ingenuousness in the learner with
the "indestructibility of perfect Sincerity" [4] in the saint ?

Answer. It is one and the same thing. But there
are differences in degrees of perfection. There is the
Ingenuousness of the ordinary man, the Ingenuousness
of the learner, the Ingenuousness of the wise man,

[1] The same word as that rendered ingenuousness.

[2] Constraint means that the Minister's obedience to the sovereign is
contrary to what he would do if his actions accorded with his own heart.
Constraint, therefore, is an evidence of insincerity. Note, in this and the
following sections the word translated " sincerity " is *ch'êng* (誠).

[3] Analects, III, xix (p. 25).   [4] D.M., p. 233.

and the Ingenuousness of the holy man. In the ordinary man, even though it is no more than unaffected simplicity [1] and honesty, it is still Ingenuousness.

Chih Ch'ing [2] said : The word "self" in the expression "self-expression" corresponds to "perfect sincerity", and "complete" to "indestructibility". "Perfect sincerity" corresponds to the expression "The Divine decree", and "indestructibility" to "how profound it is and undying ! " [3]

8. Wên Chên asked about the statement : "Complete self-expression is what is termed Ingenuousness, to be real is what is termed Truth." [4]

Answer. Ingenuousness and Truth are one principle ; as proceeding from the heart it is Ingenuousness, as established by actual fact it is Truth. Ingenuousness may be described as stating a matter to others wholly and exactly as it is perceived by oneself ; if one only states the half and is not willing to state the whole, it is disingenuousness. To say a thing is when it is, and is not when it is not, is Truth. They are one and the same principle ; as proceeding from the mind it is called Ingenuousness, as evidenced in objective fact it is Truth.

Wên Chên replied : "The outgoing of oneself in complete self-expression is Ingenuousness ; perfect correspondence with object is Truth." The outgoing in

---

[1] 朴 實 = 質 樸, "simple," "unaffected."

[2] Huang Kan (黃 幹), *style* Chih Ch'ing, a disciple of Chu Hsi ; see p. 246, n. 2.

[3] D.M., p. 285.

[4] The statement is by I Ch'uan ; see p. 430.

complete self-expression is to be whole-selfed.[1] Truth
as perfect correspondence with object may be illustrated
thus: To call an incense burner an incense burner and
a table a table is to be true, and not to contradict fact;
to call an incense burner a table and vice versa is to contradict fact and to be untrue.

9. *Question.* With regard to the statement, " Complete
self-expression is what is termed Ingenuousness, to be
real is what is termed Truth," since Truth is reality, and
you, sir, said the other day that Ingenuousness is reality
in the heart, I am puzzled to know what constitutes the
difference between them.

Answer. Ingenuousness is subjective, while Truth has
an objective reference. For example, the intention to do
a thing has to do with Ingenuousness; as objectively
accomplished it is Truth. Or when a man asks you what
is the property of fire, and you say, "It is heat"—that is
Ingenuousness. That it is really heat—is Truth. If there
is subjective reality there will be corresponding objective
reality ; if there is not subjective reality, then objectively
there will be the absence of reality ; as is expressed in
the statement, " Without sincerity there can be nothing ";[2]
if the mind itself is unreal, what can there be in the way
of real things in its manifestation ?[3]

---

[1] See p. 426, n. 2.   [2] D.M. p. 282.

[3] In his notes on the passage just quoted from the *Doctrine of the
Mean*, Legge translates a comment from the 日 講 thus: " All
that fill up the space between heaven and earth are things (物). They
end and they begin again ; they begin and proceed to an end ; every
change being accomplished by sincerity, and every phenomenon having

10. *Question.* In the statement, "The outgoing of oneself in complete self-expression is Ingenuousness," why not say, "To turn inwards and search oneself?"

Answer. To speak of turning inwards and searching oneself is to speak of what is wholly devoid of action ; how then could the writer[1] have connected this sentence with what follows? To express the mind in such a way that there is absolutely nothing left unexpressed—that is Ingenuousness, and Truth is included in it. As the common saying expresses it : "Men never say more than a third of what is in their mind"; to act thus is to lack Ingenuousness. To accord with and enter into objective facts and things without any conflicting element is what is termed Truth. Subsequently, I Ch'uan saw frequently that this statement was not clear, and therefore restated it thus : "Complete self-expression is what is termed Ingenuousness, to be real is what is termed Truth," which is satisfactory and clear.

11. *Question.* Ming Tao and I Ch'uan explained Ingenuousness and Truth as internal and external, subjective and objective. How is this?

Answer. "Complete self-expression is what is termed Ingenuousness"; Ingenuousness manifested in objective fact is Truth. To regard them as subjective and objective is right too. As proceeding from myself in complete

---

sincerity unceasingly in it. So far as the mind of man is concerned, if there be not sincerity, then every movement of it is vain and false. How can an unreal mind accomplish rea'things? Although it may do something it is simply equivalent to nothing."

[1] I Ch'uan ; see below.

self-expression it is Ingenuousness, as seen by others it is Truth.

Question. Are they not one and the same thing?

Answer. They are one principle.

Question. Why is the word " Truth " sometimes used and not " Ingenuousness " ?

Answer. Because it is used as including both the subjective and objective.

Question. Why is the word " Ingenuousness " sometimes used and not " Truth " ?

Answer. Apart from Ingenuousness there cannot be Truth. If there be Ingenuousness there must be Truth.

The Philosopher said further : It is like some affair which one has seen, and in relating it to others he only tells a third of what he saw, keeping back the rest. That is to be lacking in Truth, for how can it be said to be in accord with fact, and without any conflicting element? [1] If one asks me : " Where have you come from to-day ? " I ought to reply : " From the Ta Chung Temple." Therefore the Master Ch'êng said : " Singleness of mind is what is termed Sincerity, whole-heartedness is what is termed Ingenuousness ; as it is in the heart it is Honesty,[2] as manifested in objective fact it is Truth."

12. *Question.* In the statement, " Completeness in the representation of a thing is Truth," the expression " com-

[1] Refers back to a sentence in Section 10, p. 430. The illustration is a case of ingenuousness, but the Philosopher shows that it is also a case of truth.

[2] 中 孚 is the name of one of the hexagrams in the *Yi* (see *Yi Ching*, p. 199, and note on p. 290) ; hence the use here of these two words, 中 = " heart " and 孚 = " sincerity " or " honesty " in the older sense of the word ; cf. p. 304.

pleteness in the representation of a thing " is the same, is
it not, as " perfect correspondence with a thing " ? [1]
Answer. Yes.

(TWO SECTIONS FROM THE "COLLECTED WRITINGS".)

1. *Question.* You, sir, said that Ingenuousness and
Truth are one principle, but looking at the point of view
from which each is used they are different. As I understand it, they are one principle, but subjectively it is
called Ingenuousness, and objectively it is called Truth.
" Complete self-expression " refers to the mind, while the
word " thing " calls attention to the principle of the thing ;
therefore the mind which expresses itself completely is
ingenuous, and the principle which corresponds with the
thing is true. Although there is the difference between
the subjective and objective, the point is that both are
TRUTH [2] in myself.

Answer. " Mind " and " principle " cannot be contrasted
as subject and object. Substitute " act " for " principle "
and you will be right. " Perfect correspondence with
a thing " does not mean correspondence with the principle
of a thing, but in defining a certain thing to make your
definition perfectly correspond with the reality of that
thing. This is what is termed Truth. (Reply to
Fan Kung Shu.)

[1] Cf. section 10, p. 430. 盡 物, " completeness in the representation of a thing ", means that in the treatment of any matter, or in the
use of any thing, there is a complete expression of the principles inherent
in that matter or thing.

[2] *Ch'êng* (誠) a different word from the word (*hsin*) rendered Truth
in the rest of this section ; cf. p. 419, n. 1.

2. *Question.* In the statement, "Singleness of mind is what is termed Sincerity, and whole-heartedness is what is termed Ingenuousness," what really is the distinction meant? Again, does the statement, "Ingenuousness is the law of Heaven," mean the same thing as whole-heartedness?[1]

Answer. The sentence, "Singleness of mind is what is termed Sincerity," refers specially to the substance; the sentence, "Whole-heartedness is what is termed Ingenuousness," refers to the operation of this substance. The sentence, "Ingenuousness is the law of Heaven," is contrasted with "the extension of one's self", the quality of sympathy, and refers definitely to the meaning of the expression "whole-heartedness". (Reply to Lü Tzŭ Yo.)

INGENUOUSNESS AND SYMPATHY
(SEVEN SECTIONS FROM THE "CONVERSATIONS".)

1. Ch'êng Tzŭ said, "The saying, 'The Decree of Heaven, how profound it is and undying!'[2] corresponds to Ingenuousness; it is the principle of reality permeating all things. 'The method of Ch'ien is to change and transform, so that everything obtains its correct nature as ordained by Heaven,'[3] corresponds to sympathy; it is the principle of reality extended to the object."

Shou Yo asked: Explained in this way, is the meaning similar to that of the words "Ingenuousness" and "Sympathy" in the saying, "The doctrine of our Master to Ingenuousness and Sympathy, that is all"?[4]

[1] The statement is by Ming Tao, see 學 案, pt. xiii, p. 23; for its explanation see below, pp. 437-8.
[2] D.M., p. 285.   [3] *Yi Ching*, p. 213.   [4] Analects, IV, xv, 2 (p. 34).

Answer. There is but one Ingenuousness and Sympathy: How can there be two? Even the difference between that of the saint and of the ordinary man is not very great.

The Philosopher said further: Complete self-expression does not mean a complete expression of the Truth as it is in myself: complete self-expression IS Truth. (It is to be feared that there is a lacuna here.)[1] If there is a falling short of the whole, there is, to that extent, unreality. For example, I desire to be filial; although I am two-thirds filial, and only one-third short of the complete thing, I am still to that extent not true to my purpose. Even if I am nine-tenths filial, and no more than the trifling one-tenth short of the whole, I am still untrue to my purpose.

2. Ingenuousness is subjective, Sympathy is objective. Ingenuousness is the absence of even a hair's-breadth of self-deception; Sympathy is, "in my treatment of myself and others, to act equally, according to the nature of the case."[2]

3. In explaining Ingenuousness and Sympathy the Master pointed his two hands towards himself to represent Ingenuousness, and turned them outwards to represent Sympathy.

4. Ingenuousness is but one, but it produces hundreds and thousands of varieties of Sympathy.

---

[1] A note by the Chinese compiler.
[2] *Yi Ching*, p. 286.

5. The mind in equilibrium is Ingenuousness ; comparison with one's own mind is Sympathy.[1] This mode of expression is to be seen in the commentary on the " Chou Ritual ".[2]

6. *Question.* What do you mean when you say, " Comparison with one's own mind is Sympathy " ?

Answer. By " comparison " I mean to compare the mind of another with my own, and so put myself in their place. Love is not very different from Sympathy. Love is spontaneous, Sympathy springs from comparison and transference of one's self.

7. Liu asked for an explanation of Ingenuousness and Sympathy.

Answer. Ingenuousness is the principle of reality. Ingenuousness is the one principle, Sympathy is its innumerable functions. For example, the saying, " The Decree of Heaven, how profound it is and undying ; "[3] represents simply this one principle of reality in its all-pervading operations producing all things : the ox receives it and is an ox, the horse receives it and is a horse, grass and trees receive it and are grass and trees.

[1] There is a play on the word here. The word " ingenuousness " is composed of the two ideographs, 中 = " equilibrium " and 心 = " mind ". " Sympathy " is composed of 如 = " like " and 心 = " mind ". See next section.

[2] A work, believed to have been composed during the Chou dynasty, containing detailed descriptions of the duties of the various officers of state. See Wylie's *Notes on Chinese Literature* (1867), p. 4.

[3] D.M., p. 285.

436   PHILOSOPHY OF HUMAN NATURE

(FIVE SECTIONS FROM THE "COLLECTED WRITINGS".)

1.   Chang Wu Kou said, "Sympathy springs from Ingenuousness.   Ingenuousness induces self-reproach, and, knowing the difficulty of conquering ourselves, we realize that everywhere those who have not learned the meaning of their Nature are not so much to be blamed."   He also said, "When we know the difficulty in our own case of conquering self, we realize that all men everywhere ought to be treated with Sympathy."   According to my view Sympathy springs from Ingenuousness.   Ming Tao, Hsieh Tzŭ, Hou Tzŭ,[1] have all affirmed that, but their explanation is not the same as this.   To say, "When we know in our own case the difficulty of conquering self, we realize that all men everywhere ought to be treated with Sympathy," is to treat men according to our own selfishness, whereas the real meaning of Sympathy is not that at all. The Chêng Mêng says : "To blame ourselves as we blame others is to fulfil the Moral Law.   To love others as we love ourselves is to perfect Love.   Measure your expectations of men by the mass,[2] and you will find them easily led.[3]   This is the true identity of the external world with

[1] Hsieh Tzŭ is Hsieh Liang Tso ; see p. 322, n. 3.   Hou Tzŭ is Hou Chung Liang (侯 仲 良), *style* Shih Shêng (師 聖), a pupil of Ch'êng Ming Tao and highly esteemed by his master.

[2] That is : do not expect every man to be a sage.

[3] 大 全, Bk. v, f. 39.   In their original setting the three sentences quoted are given as the author's explanation of three sayings of Confucius, viz. " In the way of the noble man there are four things, to not one of which have I as yet attained " ; " What you do not like, when done to yourself, do not do to others " ; " The noble man governs men according to their nature, with what is proper to them, and as soon as they change

myself. Let everyone be in accord with principle and never disobey it. The words of the saints and sages have their guiding principles, and this is what is expressed as 'governing men according to their nature'." [1] Although the statement is, "Measure your expectations of men by the mass," the writer would also say, "The Moral Law is not far from men," [2] so that those who constitute the "mass" still possess this Moral Law. To take one's own inability to conquer selfishness, and use it as a reason for tolerating others and to assist them to perfect their wickedness, is for men to lead one another to become like birds and beasts ; and what more glaring instance of the very reverse of Ingenuousness and Sympathy could there be than that ? (Criticism of Chang Wu Kou's "exposition of the *Doctrine of the Mean*".)

2. *Question.* In the statement : "Sympathy is Love's bestowal, affection is the operation of Love," [3] I do not know what is the difference between "bestowal" and "operation".

Answer. What Sympathy bestows is affection ; if there were no Sympathy, the affection, even if it existed, could not reach its object. (Reply to Fan Tzŭ Shan.)

3. *Question.* Ch'êng Tzŭ considered Ingenuousness as the law of Heaven, and Sympathy as the law of Man. Does

what is wrong, he stops." It will be noted that the golden rule in the negative form as enunciated by Confucius assumes the positive form as explained by Chang Tsai.

[1] D.M., p. 258. It is probable that the quotation from the *Chêng Mêng* extends to this point, though it does not exactly correspond with the passage in the 大 全.

[2] Ibid., p. 257.   [3] See 學 案, pt. xiii, f. 23.

not this mean that Ingenuousness is the possession of the saint, and its operation one with Heaven itself, while Sympathy is the law of behaviour towards men?

Answer. One's behaviour towards oneself is not different in principle from one's behaviour to others. The distinction here made between Heaven and man means simply the difference between substance and its operation.[1] (Reply to Yen Shih Hêng.)

4. Your treatise on Sympathy is excellent, but in the *Great Learning* the phrase "measuring square"[2] always occurs after the phrase "investigation of things".[3] For principles must first of all be clear, and the heart true; then in what we desire or do not desire we shall naturally attain to what is correct. Afterwards, when we extend this to external things, in the treatment of them also we shall not fail to be correct, so that there will be no separation between the external world and myself. If otherwise, and, allowing ourselves to be ruled by selfishness and personal convenience, we seek to extend this to others, we shall fail even to establish the law of man; on the contrary, we shall drive a whole world into making itself a den of selfishness and evil-mongering. (Reply to Hwang Shang Po.)

5. *Question.* Modern scholars look upon Ingenuousness and Sympathy as simply substance and operation. The

---

[1] That is, the comparison is really between the *law* of Heaven and the *law* of Man, between which there is this relation of substance and operation, source and flow. Human desire originates in Divine Law and becomes evil in its flow. Cf. p. 395.

[2] G.L., p. 395.

[3] Ibid., p. 222.

substance is as expressed in the saying, " Perfection also
is undying " ;¹ its operation is as expressed in the saying,
" It fills the universe."² The substance is real and unchanging, its operation is broad and all-penetrating. But
substance and operation are from one source and cannot
be separated. Therefore Ch'êng Tzǔ said, " I regard the
two terms Ingenuousness and Sympathy as reciprocally
each the operation of the other." And the Master said,
"My doctrine is that of an all-pervading unity."³

Answer. This statement is very good. (Reply to Lü
Tzǔ Yo.)

SEDATENESS AND SERIOUSNESS⁴

(FIVE SECTIONS FROM THE "CONVERSATIONS".)

1. *Question.* Why are Love and Seriousness spoken
of in combination ?

Answer. From the time of Shang Ts'ai⁵ the word

¹ D.M., p. 285.   ² Mencius, p. 66.
³ Analects, IV, xv, 1 (p. 33).

⁴ Ching (敬) in its most frequent use is reverence as accorded to others.
Throughout this section, however, its special reference is, not to persons,
but to actions—expressing the spirit in which actions are done. Legge,
in such connexions, clinging to the idea of reverence, translates the word
by such expressions as " reverent attention ", " reverential carefulness ",
etc. Soothill and Ku Hung Ming for the most part break away from the
word " reverence " and adopt the renderings " serious ", " earnest ", and
in a few instances, " self-respect." All these meanings are to be found
in the word " ching " in different connexions. The prevailing meaning
here is an awe-inspired seriousness, the inward attitude which characterizes
the actions of the noble man, answering to sedateness, the external
demeanour appropriate to this inward attitude ; in one or two instances,
however, the word "earnestness" expresses the meaning better. Cf.
Suzuki's *Early Chinese Philosophy*, pp. 56–7

⁵ See p. 322, n. 3

" Seriousness " has been considered small and inadequate ;
it was therefore felt necessary to add the word " Love ".
But as a matter of fact there is no need for the word
" Love ". If a man has seriousness Love is included
in it.[1]

2. Sedateness has to do with demeanour, Earnestness
with action. When anything is to be done, to put one's
heart into it, and do it without any wavering of the mind,
this is Earnestness. Sedateness is objective manifestation,
Earnestness is subjective. From the point of view of
making oneself sincere, " Sedateness " is the more important word ; from the point of view of action,
" Earnestness " is more appropriate.

3. In the initial stage of learning, the word
" Seriousness " is more applicable ; in the final stage,
when the virtue is acquired, " Sedateness " is more natural.
Seriousness pertains to action. It is true that in the more
comprehensive sense we speak of " seriously cultivating
one's self ",[2] of "maintaining inward correctness by
seriousness " ; [3] but regarded only in the narrower sense
of the word it has to do with action, and Sedateness with
demeanour.

4. Apropos of the statement that the two words Sedateness and Seriousness stand in the same relation to one
another as Ingenuousness and Truth, someone said :
Seriousness is subjective, Sedateness is the objective manifestation.

---

[1] Love is the source of all virtues.   [2] Analects, XIV, xlv (p. 156).
[3] *Yi Ching*, p. 420.

Answer. When we speak of objective manifestation we are apt to think of it as nobler than the subjective, because it must reach to an overflowing fullness before it can be objectively manifested ; how then can the subjective be superior ? It must not be forgotten, however, that the subjective is the source.

5. *Question.* What is the difference between Sedateness and Seriousness ?

Answer. Sedateness refers to demeanour (" The virtue of the demeanour is called sedateness ".[1] "The hands were respectful in demeanour.")[2]   Seriousness refers to action. (" In handling public business be serious." [3] "In his duties his care is to be earnest.")[4]

Question. How does Earnestness refer to action ?

Answer. If, at this moment, I am doing anything, I must put my whole heart into it to be satisfactory—I am not, of course, speaking of bad things. If I am studying the "Analects" and my mind is on "Mencius", how can I understand what I read ? We shall never succeed in anything we do if while doing it the mind is on something else.

The Philosopher said further : Seriousness includes the idea of apprehension.

Again he said : When one is occupied about something, the mind is concentrated on that one thing ; when one is not occupied with anything, the mind is clear.

[1] *Shu Ching*, p. 326.
[2] *Li Chi*, vol. ii, p. 25.   " Respectful " is the same word (恭) as "sedate ".
[3] Analects, XIII, xix (p. 135) ; cf. Soothill.
[4] Ibid., XVI, x (p. 178) ; cf. Soothill.

Again he said : Sedateness is cautious, Seriousness is apprehensive, Dignity is majestic. Majesty and awe, however, are not the qualities with which we serve our parents, so that dignity in this connexion would be out of place. But in our bearing towards those below us there should be dignity, as is said in the passage, " Let him preside over them with dignity and they will revere him."[1] If dignity be lacking in the transaction of business the people will not revere him.

(THREE SECTIONS FROM THE " COLLECTED WRITINGS ".)

1. *Question*. The two words " Sedateness " and " Seriousness " occur frequently in the "Analects" and "Mencius"; for example, "The noble man is serious and free from fault, in intercourse with others he is sedate and courtly."[2] " In private life be sedate, in handling public business be serious."[3] " In his conduct of himself he was sedate, in serving his superiors he was serious " ;[4] "To urge one's sovereign to difficult achievements may be called showing respect for him. To set before him what is good and repress his perversities may be called showing earnestness in his behalf."[5] The Master I Ch'uan said: " The objective manifestation is what is termed Sedateness, and the subjective quality is what is termed Seriousness,"[6] for Sedateness and Seriousness are one principle in its objective and subjective aspects. If we explain the passages in the " Analects " and

---

[1] Analects, II, xx (p. 16).
[2] Ibid., XII, v, 4 (p. 117).
[3] Ibid., XIII, xix (p. 135).
[4] Ibid., V, xv (p. 42).
[5] Mencius, p. 168.
[6] 遺 書, pt. vi, f. 10.

"Mencius" according to this definition, it does not seem to fit. Is it not that they differ in degree?

Answer. Sedateness has to do with demeanour, and Seriousness with action. For the learner, Seriousness has more force than Sedateness, but from the point of view of the virtue attained to, Sedateness has more of repose. (Reply to Lien Sung Ch'ing.)

2. If we compare the statements of the saints and sages from early times to the Ch'êng school, all would put neatness in dress and gravity of demeanour first for one beginning his study. For this must be first attained to, and after that the mind is preserved, and lapse into depravity guarded against; as is said in the *Yi*: "Guarding against depravity, he preserves his sincerity."[1] Ch'êng Tzǔ's saying, "By control of outward conduct he nourished his heart," is just this idea. But we must not go off to an extreme and sink in the slough of externals, such as ceremonies and vestments. (Reply to Lü Po Kung.)[2]

3. *Question.* I have received your instructive communication. To maintain Seriousness involves fatigue, the physical element fails, and one cannot overcome one's languor. For example: Sometimes when I would hold my head erect, and be sedate in the use of my hands, I find myself unable, and so my hold on Seriousness is imperfect, and selfish thoughts spring up in my mind. Thus, though my desire is in every detail to act in accordance with the

[1] *Yi Ching*, p. 410.

[2] Lü Tsu Ch'ien (呂 祖 謙), Chu Hsi's friend; see J. P. Bruce, *Introduction to Chu Hsi and the Sung School*, chap. iv.

rules of ceremony, I fail from sheer lack of strength. I should like to know whether, if I were to maintain a serious mind simply, and allow some indulgence to the bodily members, there would be any injury to one's final success or not.

Answer. When there is unfailing Seriousness, the body will naturally assume a corresponding self-control, and it will not be necessary to wait while one deliberately settles oneself. The bodily posture will be easy and natural. If one requires consciously and deliberately to arrange one's posture, then, indeed, to continue in it long will be difficult and fatiguing. (Reply to Chu Fei Ch'ing.)